Lecture Notes in Computer Science 3417

Bernd Jähne Rudolf Mester
Erhardt Barth Hanno Scharr (Eds.)

Complex Motion

First International Workshop, IWCM 2004
Günzburg, Germany, October 12-14, 2004
Revised Papers

Springer

Volume Editors

Bernd Jähne
Universität Heidelberg
IWR und Institut für Umweltphysik
Im Neuenheimer Feld 368, 69210 Heidelberg, Germany
E-mail: Bernd.Jaehne@iwr.uni.heidelberg.de

Rudolf Mester
J.W. Goethe Universität
Institut für Informatik, vsi Arbeitsgruppe
Robert-Mayer-Str. 10, 60054 Frankfurt, Germany
E-mail: mester@iap.uni-frankfurt.de

Erhardt Barth
Universität Lübeck
Institut für Neuro- und Bioinformatik
Ratzeburger Allee 160, 23538 Lübeck, Germany
E-mail: barth@inb.uni-luebeck.de

Hanno Scharr
Forschungszentrum Jülich GmbH
Institut für Chemie und Dynamik der Geosphäre
Institut III: Phytosphäre, 52425 Jülich, Germany
E-mail: H.Scharr@fz-juelich.de

Library of Congress Control Number: 2006939854

CR Subject Classification (1998): I.5, I.4, I.3.5, I.2.10, I.2.6, F.2.2

LNCS Sublibrary: SL 6 – Image Processing, Computer Vision, Pattern Recognition, and Graphics

ISSN 0302-9743
ISBN-10 3-540-69864-7 Springer Berlin Heidelberg New York
ISBN-13 978-3-540-69864-7 Springer Berlin Heidelberg New York

Springer is a part of Springer Science+Business Media

springer.com

Printed in Germany

Typesetting: Camera-ready by author, data conversion by Scientific Publishing Services, Chennai, India
Printed on acid-free paper SPIN: 11976837 06/3142 5 4 3 2 1 0

Preface

The world we live in is a dynamic one: we explore it by moving through it, and many of the objects which we are interested in are also moving. Traffic, for instance, is an example of a domain where detecting and processing visual motion is of vital interest, both in a metaphoric as well as in a purely literal sense. Visual communication is another important example of an area of science which is dominated by the need to measure, understand, and represent visual motion in an efficient way.

Visual motion is a subject of research which forces the investigator to deal with complexity; complexity in the sense of facing effects of motion in a very large diversity of forms, starting from analyzing simple motion in a changing environment (illumination, shadows, ...), under adverse observation conditions, such as bad signal-to-noise ratio (low illumination, small-scale processes, low-dose x-ray, etc.), covering also multiple motions of independent objects, occlusions, and going as far as dealing with objects which are complex in themselves (articulated objects such as bodies of living beings). The spectrum of problems includes, but does not end at, objects which are not 'bodies' at all, e.g., when analyzing fluid motion, cloud motion, and so on. Analyzing the motion of a crowd in a shopping mall or in an airport is a further example that implies the need to struggle against the problems induced by complexity. We cannot be sure that the named or similar application areas already represent the high-end of complexity in motion analysis – actually, there will probably be even harder problems in the analysis of complex visual motion which we have not faced yet, or which we have not yet dared to address.

Based on the observation that the current state of the art in the field of motion analysis is in a rather advanced shape already, but also taking into account that there are so many real-life problems which have not been solved yet, a group of researchers from different German research institutions decided to initiate an international workshop to attract renowned scientists and young researchers from different areas of visual motion analysis.

Therefore, in October 2004, the 1st International Workshop on Complex Motion (IWCM 2004) was held at Schloss Günzburg, a beautiful mansion and scientific convention center administered by the University of Ulm (South Germany). The Steering Committee of IWCM 2004 aimed at inspiring and encouraging the members of the computer vision community to share experiences and exchange opinions on the contemporary development of the field. There were several invited talks given by renowned senior researchers who not only appreciated the historic development of research in visual motion, but demonstrated and discussed the current grand challenges in a vivid and stimulating way.

This workshop was particularly devoted to advancing the repertoire of methods dealing with complex visual motion and to initiating a more intensive and hopefully continuing discussion amongst leading experts in the field. The topics of presentations were optical flow, local motion estimation for image signals affected by strong disturbances, structure from motion, multicamera flow analysis, dynamic stereo, fluid motion analysis, the estimation of multiple motions, motion tracking, and many other areas where complex visual motion patterns have to be evaluated. In fact, there were several plenary discussions which covered open issues, unsolved problems, and also different opinions in a highly constructive manner and which apparently ignited many further discussions adjacent to the official workshop programme, and presumably initiated exchange and cooperation between researchers who had not been in direct contact before.

The workshop was organized by the members of the LOCOMOTOR Project (Nonlinear analysis of multidimensional signals: LOcal adaptive estimation of COmplex MOTion and ORientation patterns), which is part of the priority research program SPP 1114 "Mathematical methods for time series analysis and digital image processing" supported by the *German Research Council (DFG)*. We particularly appreciate the generous support that our workshop received from the *German Pattern Recognition Association (DAGM, Deutsche Arbeitsgemeinschaft für Mustererkennung)* and its president, Prof. Dr. Hans Burkhardt (University of Freiburg). Without this generous support this workshop would not have been possible. We also appreciate the kind support of Springer for giving us the opportunity to distribute the scientific essence of this workshop to the computer science and engineering community via a volume in the Springer LNCS series. We hope that the present compilation of research papers presented at IWCM 2004 reflects the diversity of challenges, the prosperity of the research field, and possibly also a bit of the enjoyable atmosphere we shared at Schloss Günzburg.

November 2006

Rudolf Mester
Bernd Jähne
Erhardt Barth
Hanno Scharr

Organization

Steering Committee

Rudolf Mester	Frankfurt University (Programme Chair, overall management)
Bernd Jähne	Heidelberg University (Workshop Proceedings)
Erhardt Barth	Lübeck University
Hanno Scharr	Research Center Jülich

Sponsoring Institutions

German Pattern Recognition Association (DAGM)
German Research Council (DFG)

Table of Contents

Optical Flow Estimation from Monogenic Phase

Michael Felsberg*

Linköping University, Computer Vision Laboratory,
SE-58183 Linköping, Sweden
mfe@isy.liu.se
http://www.isy.liu.se/cvl/

Abstract. The optical flow can be estimated by several different methods, some of them require multiple frames some make use of just two frames. One approach to the latter problem is optical flow from phase. However, in contrast to (horizontal) disparity from phase, this method suffers from the phase being oriented, i.e., classical quadrature filter have a predefined orientation in which the phase estimation is correct and the phase error grows with increasing deviation from the local image orientation. Using the approach of the monogenic phase instead, results in correct phase estimates for all orientations if the signal is locally 1D. This allows to estimate the optical flow with sub-pixel accuracy from a multi-resolution analysis with seven filter responses at each scale. The paper gives a short and easy to comprehend overview about the theory of the monogenic phase and the formula for the displacement estimation is derived from a series expansion of the phase. Some basic experiments are presented.

1 Introduction

The aim of this paper is not only to present just another optical flow estimation approach, but also to give a tutorial-like introduction to the topic of the monogenic signal and its phase. We try to strip off all theoretic background which is unnecessary and focus on a simple, concrete, and complete description of the framework. For a more formal treatment, we refer to the earlier publications on the monogenic framework [1,2,3].

Based on the monogenic phase, we then derive a simple formula for measuring oriented displacements between two images, which is then applied in a multi-scale approach for the estimation of the optical flow. This method is quite similar to the one presented in [4], with two differences: We do not know the direction of displacement in advance and we show the pure estimates, i.e., we do not post-process the point estimates with channel smoothing. Combining the point-wise estimator and a non-linear smoothing technique easily compensates errors in the estimates and partly the aperture effect, but it was not our aim to present a complete motion estimation system but rather the signal processing part of it.

2 Why Is Phase-Based Image Processing Preferable?

Before we start to introduce the framework of the monogenic phase, we motivate why we want to use phase-based methods at all. Basically, there are three reasons:

* This work has been supported by EC Grant IST-2003-004176 COSPAL and by EC Grant IST-2002-002013 MATRIS.

B. Jähne et al. (Eds.): IWCM 2004, LNCS 3417, pp. 1–13, 2007.

1. There is strong evidence that the human visual system makes use of local phase in V1 [5].
2. Phase-based processing is to a large extend invariant to changes of lighting conditions. The local image intensity can additionally be used to measure the reliability of measurements.
3. Perceptually, the reconstruction of an image from phase information is much better than that from amplitude information.

Reasons 2 and 3 have to be explained in some more detail. Note that we always consider a local region in the spatial-frequency domain, i.e., we look at local image regions at certain frequency ranges (or equivalently: at certain scales). Note in this context that we denote spatial frequency or wavenumber by 'frequency', not a frequency in the temporal sense.

2.1 The Image Model of Local Phase

Our image model that we apply in phase-based processing is

$$I(\mathbf{x}) = \tilde{A}(\mathbf{x}) \cos(\tilde{\varphi}(\mathbf{x})) + \bar{I} \tag{1}$$

where $\mathbf{x} = (x_1, x_2)^T$ indicates the spatial coordinate vector, $I(\mathbf{x})$ the image, $\bar{I}$ the average intensity (DC level), $\tilde{A}(\mathbf{x})$ the instantaneous amplitude (real-valued, non-negative), and $\tilde{\varphi}(\mathbf{x})$ the instantaneous phase [6]. The average intensity is irrelevant for the analysis of the image contents and in the human visual system it is largely compensated already during the image acquisition. In this model the decomposition into $\tilde{A}(\mathbf{x})$ and $\tilde{\varphi}(\mathbf{x})$ seems to be highly ambiguous. This is however not the case, since the amplitude is a non-negative real number. Hence, the zeros of $I(\mathbf{x}) - \bar{I}$ must be covered by zeros of $\cos(\tilde{\varphi}(\mathbf{x}))$. Assuming sufficiently smooth functions, the zero crossings are in direct correspondence to the full phase [7] and the instantaneous phase becomes a uniquely defined feature.

If we switch to a local region in the spatial-frequency domain, i.e., we consider an image region and a small range of frequencies, the model (1) becomes much simpler. Under the assumption of small magnitude variations of the considered frequency components in the local spectrum, the amplitude becomes approximately constant in the local region. It is therefore referred to as the local amplitude $A_{\mathbf{x}}$, where $\mathbf{x}$ now indicates the origin of the local region, i.e., all estimates with subscript $\mathbf{x}$ refer to the region with origin $\mathbf{x}$. The model (1) becomes for the local region

$$\tilde{I}(\mathbf{x} + \mathbf{y}) = A_{\mathbf{x}} \cos(\varphi_{\mathbf{x}}(\mathbf{y})), \tag{2}$$

where $\tilde{I}(\mathbf{x}+\mathbf{y})$ is the local image patch, $\mathbf{y}$ the local patch coordinate vector, and $\varphi_{\mathbf{x}}(\mathbf{y})$ is the local phase.

Assuming a small range of frequencies, the local phase cannot vary arbitrarily fast, it has a high degree of smoothness. Therefore, it can be well approximated by a first order series in $\mathbf{y} = 0$:

$$\varphi_{\mathbf{x}}(\mathbf{y}) \approx \mathbf{f}_{\mathbf{x}}^T \mathbf{y} + \varphi_{\mathbf{x}}(0) = f_{\mathbf{x}} \mathbf{n}_{\mathbf{x}}^T \mathbf{y} + \varphi_{\mathbf{x}}(0), \tag{3}$$

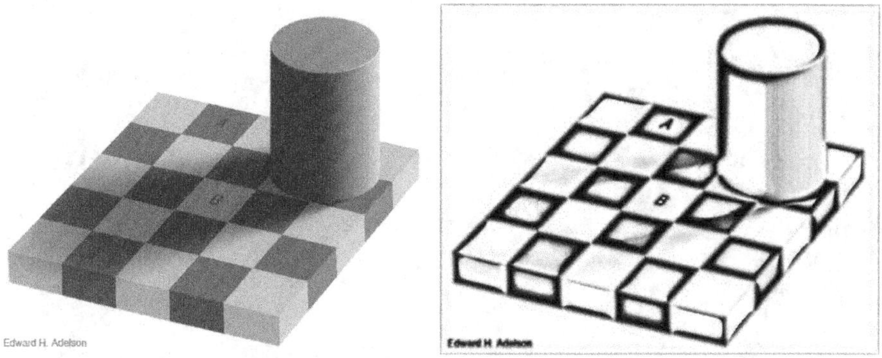

Fig. 1. The checker shadow illusion 'disillusioned'. Left: original image from *http://web.mit.edu/persci/people/adelson/checkershadow_illusion.html*. Right: reconstruction from local phase.

where $f_{\mathbf{x}}$ is the local frequency, $\mathbf{n}_{\mathbf{x}}$ is the local orientation (unit vector), and $\varphi_{\mathbf{x}}(0)$ is some phase offset. That means, our local image model directly led to the assumption of intrinsic dimensionality one [8], or simple signals [6], where $\tilde{I}(\mathbf{x}+\mathbf{y}) = \hat{I}_{\mathbf{x}}(\mathbf{n}_{\mathbf{x}}^T\mathbf{y})$ ($\hat{I}$ being a suitable 1D function).

We can group the series of the local phase (3) in two different ways:

$$\varphi_{\mathbf{x}}(\mathbf{y}) \approx f_{\mathbf{x}}(\mathbf{n}_{\mathbf{x}}^T\mathbf{y}) + \varphi_{\mathbf{x}}(0) = \bar{\varphi}_{\mathbf{x}}(\mathbf{n}_{\mathbf{x}}^T\mathbf{y}) \qquad \text{and} \tag{4}$$
$$\varphi_{\mathbf{x}}(\mathbf{y}) \approx \mathbf{n}_{\mathbf{x}}^T(\mathbf{n}_{\mathbf{x}}\mathbf{n}_{\mathbf{x}}^T\mathbf{y} f_{\mathbf{x}} + \mathbf{n}_{\mathbf{x}}\varphi_{\mathbf{x}}(0)) = \mathbf{n}_{\mathbf{x}}^T\mathbf{r}_{\mathbf{x}}(\mathbf{y}). \tag{5}$$

Whereas the former expression is a 1D function with a scalar product as an argument, the latter expression is a 2D vector field, the local phase vector $\mathbf{r}_{\mathbf{x}}$, which is projected onto the orientation vector. Although the distinction seems to be trivial, the local phase vector is simpler to estimate, because we do not need to know the local orientation in advance. We will return to this issue later.

2.2 Lighting Invariance and Perceptual Image Contents

Before we present an estimation procedure for the local phase, we continue the discussion on the reasons 2 and 3 for using phase-based methods. The decomposition of an image into local amplitude and local phase at a particular frequency range means to neglect the high frequencies, to represent the intermediate frequencies by the local phase, and to cover the lower frequencies by (more global) changes of the local amplitude. Changes of lighting conditions are then to a large extend represented by changes of the local amplitude, with the exception of moving shadow boundaries. Hence, most changes of lighting conditions are not visible in the phase representation, cf. Fig. 1.

Since the famous paper [9], it is well known that the reconstruction from the phase spectrum is much better from a perceptional point of view than the one from the magnitude spectrum. Considering the Fourier spectrum means to consider the part of the spatial-frequency domain with maximum localization in frequency and no localization in position. If we move to some point with finite localization in both spaces, the results

Fig. 2. Decomposing an image into its local phase and its local amplitude. From left to right: $\cos(\varphi_{\mathbf{x}_0})$, $A_{\mathbf{x}_0}$, $\tilde{I}(\mathbf{x}_0)$, where the intensities are adjusted to obtain similar intensity ranges. Grey means zero, white means positive values, and black means negative values. Top row: full size images. Bottom row: image detail. $\tilde{I}(\mathbf{x}_0)$ is obtained from $I(\mathbf{x}_0)$ applying the filters from [10] using scales $\{3,4,5\}$.

of the experiment from [9] still remain valid, cf. Fig. 2, although we now consider the local phase.

If the image is decomposed into its amplitude and phase information, it becomes evident that the local amplitude is basically just a measure for the confidence of the extracted phase, i.e., in technical terms it represents the signal-to-noise ratio (SNR), cf. Fig. 2, center column. The local phase represents most of the image structure, cf. Fig. 2, left column. In the areas where the amplitude is close to zero, thus meaning 'no confidence', the local phase contains mainly noise. In the regions of non-zero confidence, the cosine of the local phase results in a visual impression which comes very close to the bandpass filtered image, cf. Fig. 2, right column.

3 The Monogenic Signal: A Survey

The monogenic signal provides a framework to estimate the local phase, the local orientation, and the local amplitude of an image [3]. It can be considered as a 2D generalization of the analytic signal. Former 2D generalizations tried to estimate the local phase according to (4), which was only partly successful since the local orientation has to be known in advance to steer the filters [11,12]. In the monogenic framework, however, we

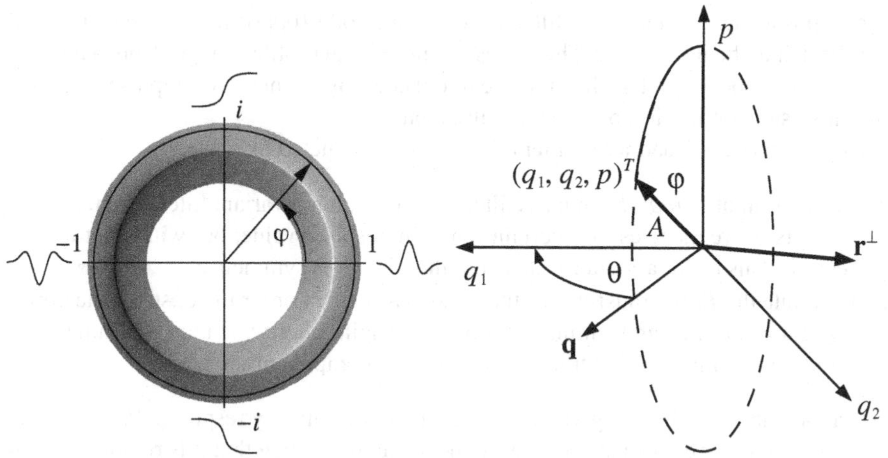

Fig. 3. Local phase models. Left: the 1D phase, the corresponding filter shapes at 1, i, -1, and $-i$, and the continuously changing signal profile (grey values in the background). Right: the local phase of the monogenic signal. The 3D vector $(q_1, q_2, p)^T$ together with the p-axis define a plane at orientation θ in which the rotation takes place. The normal of this plane multiplied by the rotation angle φ results in the rotation vector $\mathbf{r}^{\perp}$.

try to estimate the local phase vector (5) instead, where the local orientation is part of the result and need not be known in advance. The estimated vector has a natural upper bound for its error [1].

3.1 Spherical Quadrature Filter

Quadrature filters in 1D are constructed in two steps:

1. Select a suitable bandpass filter which is responsible for the localization in the time-frequency domain, i.e., it responds to signal contributions which are in a certain frequency range (the passband) and in a certain time window. This bandpass filter is an even filter, i.e., it is symmetric.
2. Compute the Hilbert transform of the bandpass filter in order to construct the corresponding odd, i.e., antisymmetric, filter which has the same magnitude spectrum.

Practical problems concerning computing the Hilbert transform are out of the scope of this paper. The quadrature filter pair is mostly applied as a complex filter to the 1D signal. The response is a complex signal, which is divided into magnitude and argument. One can easily show that the argument is an estimate for the local phase. In Fig. 3 left, the 1D phase interpretation is illustrated.

The figure is generated by projecting all possible phase-responses onto the filter. As a result we get those input signals which would generate the in-fed responses. Keeping the amplitude constant and varying the phase from 0 to 2π results in the sketched signal profiles (at 1, i, -1, and $-i$) and the continuously varying intensities in the background. With increasing phase angle, the quadrature filter turns from a purely even filter towards a purely odd filter. Continuing further than $\pi/2$ leads towards an even filter again, but with opposite sign. After π the filter becomes first odd (opposite sign) and finally it turns back into the initial filter. The corresponding signal profile changes from a positive impulse over a positive step (from inside to outside), over a negative impulse, and over a negative step, until it is a positive impulse again.

The 2D spherical quadrature filters (SQF) are constructed likewise:

1. Select a suitable *radial* bandpass filter, i.e., a rotation invariant filter. The passband consists of frequencies of a certain range in absolute value, but with arbitrary direction. This bandpass filter is an even filter, i.e., it is symmetric.
2. Compute the *Riesz* transform of the bandpass filter in order to construct the corresponding odd, i.e., antisymmetric about the origin, filter which has the same magnitude spectrum. The odd filter consists of two components.

The radial bandpass filter is given by some suitable frequency response $B_e(\rho)$, where (ρ, ϕ) are the polar coordinates of the frequency domain, such that it is rotational symmetric and therefore symmetric (even) about the origin. The corresponding antisymmetric (odd) filters are then given by

$$B_{o1}(\rho, \phi) = i \cos\phi \, B_e(\rho) \qquad \text{and} \qquad B_{o2}(\rho, \phi) = i \sin\phi \, B_e(\rho). \tag{6}$$

All together, an SQF provides three responses; the even filter response $p(\mathbf{x}) = (I * b_e)(\mathbf{x})$ and the two odd filter responses $\mathbf{q}(\mathbf{x}) = (q_1(\mathbf{x}), q_2(\mathbf{x}))^T = ((I * b_{o1})(\mathbf{x}), (I * b_{o2})(\mathbf{x}))^T$.

3.2 Extracting Local Phase

The local amplitude can be extracted likewise as in the 1D case by calculating the magnitude of the 3D vector:

$$A_{\mathbf{x}} = \sqrt{q_1(\mathbf{x})^2 + q_2(\mathbf{x})^2 + p(\mathbf{x})^2}, \tag{7}$$

cf. Fig. 4 for an example. The phase, however, cannot be extracted as the argument of a complex number, since we need two angles to describe the 3D rotation from a reference point (on the p-axis) into the SQF response. These angles are indicated in Fig. 3, and they have direct interpretations in terms of local orientation and local phase.

It has been shown in [3] that an image patch with intrinsic dimensionality one and local orientation θ (w.r.t. the horizontal axis) results in a response of the form $(q_1(\mathbf{x}), q_2(\mathbf{x}), p(\mathbf{x}))^T = (\cos\theta \, q(\mathbf{x}), \sin\theta \, q(\mathbf{x}), p(\mathbf{x}))^T$ for a suitable $q(\mathbf{x})$, i.e., according to Fig. 3, the rotation takes place in a plane which encloses angle θ with the (q_1, p)-plane. For non-zero $\mathbf{q}$ this angle can hence be estimated as

$$\theta_{\mathbf{x}} = \tan^{-1}\left(\frac{q_2(\mathbf{x})}{q_1(\mathbf{x})}\right) \in (-\pi/2; \pi/2], \tag{8}$$

where an orientation – direction ambiguity occurs, since the directional sense of a 2D signal cannot be extracted from a local signal [6], i.e., $\mathbf{q}$ and $-\mathbf{q}$ map onto the same orientation, cf. Fig. 4.

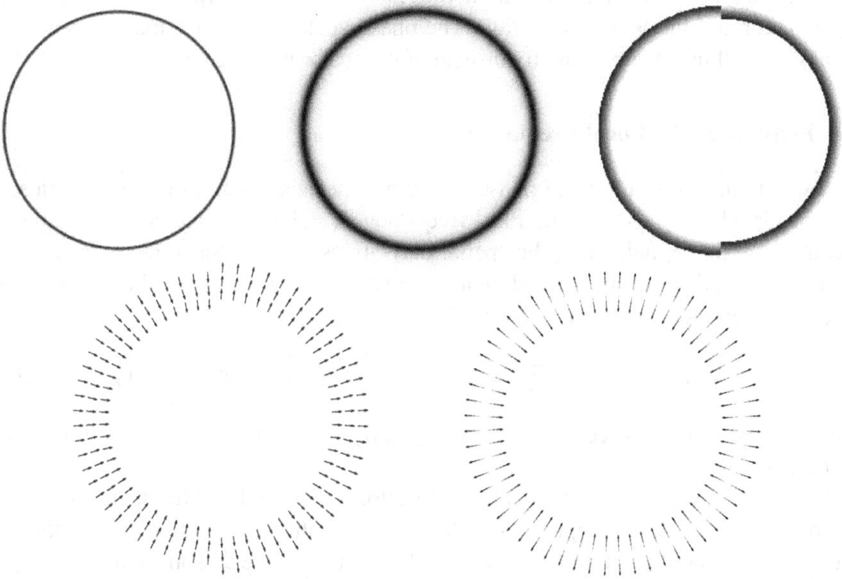

Fig. 4. Upper row from left to right: original signal, local amplitude (in both cases white means zero and black means large values), local phase according to (4) (black means negative phase, white means positive phase). Bottom row left: local orientation. Right: local phase vector. The length of the phase vector is encoded in grey values. The local orientation and phase are only displayed for sufficiently large amplitude.

A further result from [3] is the connection between Hilbert transform and Riesz transform, which practically means that a 1D projection of an SQF results in a 1D quadrature filter. Since a signal with intrinsic dimensionality of one is constant along a certain orientation, it leads to a 1D projection of the involved filter kernels. Hence, p and q from the previous paragraph can be considered as a 1D quadrature filter response and the local phase is given by $\arg(p+iq)$. However, we do not know the correct sign of q, since it depends on the directional sense of θ. The best possible solution is to project $\mathbf{q}$ onto $(\cos\theta,\,\sin\theta)$:

$$\bar{\varphi} = \arg(p + i(\cos\theta\, q_1 + \sin\theta\, q_2)) = \arg(p + i\mathrm{sign}\,(q_1)|\mathbf{q}|), \tag{9}$$

see also Fig. 4. The sign depends on q_1, because $\theta \in (-\pi/2; \pi/2]$ which corresponds to the quadrants with positive q_1, i.e., $(\cos\theta,\,\sin\theta) = \mathrm{sign}\,(q_1)\,\mathbf{q}/|\mathbf{q}|$. The derived phase estimate is actually an estimate according to (4), since $\mathbf{q}$ can be considered as a steerable filter projected onto $\mathbf{n} = (\cos\theta,\,\sin\theta)$.

In order to obtain a continuous representation of orientation and phase, both are combined in the phase vector

$$\mathbf{r} = \bar{\varphi}\,(\cos\theta,\,\sin\theta)^T = \frac{\mathbf{q}}{|\mathbf{q}|}\arg(p + i|\mathbf{q}|), \tag{10}$$

cf. Fig. 3, right, and Fig. 4. Note that the rotation vector $\mathbf{r}^{\perp}$ is perpendicular to the local phase vector and the local orientation. The phase vector $\mathbf{r}$ is an estimate according to (5) and we will use it subsequently instead of the scalar phase $\bar{\varphi}$.

3.3 Estimating the Local Frequency

As pointed out above, the local phase model was derived from a first order series expansion (3) which contained the local frequency $f_{\mathbf{x}}$. The latter can also be estimated directly from the signal, using the spatial derivatives of (10). Since the first order approximation leads to an intrinsic dimensionality of one, we only need to consider the directional derivative along $\mathbf{n_x}$ w.r.t. $\mathbf{y}$ ($\nabla = (\partial_{y_1}, \partial_{y_2})$):

$$\bar{f}_{\mathbf{x}} = (\mathbf{n}_{\mathbf{x}}^T \nabla)\varphi_{\mathbf{x}}(\mathbf{y}) \approx (\mathbf{n}_{\mathbf{x}}^T \nabla)(\mathbf{n}_{\mathbf{x}}^T \mathbf{r}_{\mathbf{x}}(\mathbf{y})) = \nabla^T \mathbf{n}_{\mathbf{x}} \mathbf{n}_{\mathbf{x}}^T \mathbf{r}_{\mathbf{x}}(\mathbf{y}) = \nabla^T \mathbf{r}_{\mathbf{x}}(\mathbf{y}), \tag{11}$$

where the last step is correct, since $\mathbf{r}_{\mathbf{x}}(\mathbf{y}) = \mathbf{n}_{\mathbf{x}}\mathbf{n}_{\mathbf{x}}^T \mathbf{y} f_{\mathbf{x}} + \mathbf{n}_{\mathbf{x}}\varphi_{\mathbf{x}}(0)$, i.e., collinear with $\mathbf{n}_{\mathbf{x}}$, cf. (5).

Hence, the divergence of the local phase vector yields the local frequency. However, we do not even need to compute these derivatives explicitly, which would by the way result in some trouble with the wraparounds [13]. Instead, we do some calculus on (10) (where we leave out some indices for convenience):

$$\begin{aligned}
\nabla^T \mathbf{r} &= \nabla^T \frac{\mathbf{q}}{|\mathbf{q}|} \arg(p + i|\mathbf{q}|) \\
&\overset{\mathbf{q}/|\mathbf{q}|=\pm\mathbf{n}}{=} \frac{\mathbf{q}^T}{|\mathbf{q}|} \nabla \arg(p + i|\mathbf{q}|) \\
&\overset{\partial \arg = \partial \tan^{-1}}{=} \frac{\mathbf{q}^T}{|\mathbf{q}|} \nabla \tan^{-1}\left(\frac{|\mathbf{q}|}{p}\right) \\
&= \frac{\mathbf{q}^T}{|\mathbf{q}|} \frac{1}{1 + \frac{|\mathbf{q}|^2}{p^2}} \frac{p\nabla|\mathbf{q}| - |\mathbf{q}|\nabla p}{p^2} \\
&= \frac{\mathbf{q}^T}{|\mathbf{q}|} \frac{1}{p^2 + |\mathbf{q}|^2} \frac{p(\nabla \mathbf{q}^T)\mathbf{q} - |\mathbf{q}|^2 \nabla p}{|\mathbf{q}|} .
\end{aligned} \tag{12}$$

Since we know that we deal with an intrinsically 1D region, $\mathbf{q}$ itself is also 1D, and we can write it as

$$\mathbf{q}(\mathbf{y}) = \mathbf{n} q(\mathbf{n}^T \mathbf{y}),$$

such that

$$\mathbf{q}^T (\nabla \mathbf{q}^T)\mathbf{q} = |q|^2 \mathbf{n}^T (\nabla \mathbf{n}^T q)\mathbf{n} = |q|^2 \mathbf{n}^T \nabla q = |\mathbf{q}|^2 \nabla^T \mathbf{q},$$

and finally

$$\nabla^T \mathbf{r} = \frac{p\nabla^T \mathbf{q} - \mathbf{q}^T \nabla p}{p^2 + |\mathbf{q}|^2} . \tag{13}$$

By this expression we can directly estimate the local frequency $\bar{f}_{\mathbf{x}}$ by a quotient consisting of the three filter responses and their four partial derivatives $\partial_1 p$, $\partial_2 p$, $\partial_1 q_1$, and $\partial_2 q_2$.

3.4 A Concrete Filter Set

Up to now, we have not specified a particular set of SQF. Suitable filter sets have to be chosen according to the application. In most cases, the radial bandpass filter B_e will be designed in the Fourier domain. The frequency responses for the corresponding two other filters are given by means of (6). The spatial derivatives of these filters are obtained by multiplying the frequency responses of the former with $i\rho\cos\phi$ resp. $i\rho\sin\phi$ according to the derivative theorem of the Fourier transform [6]. The impulse responses of all filters are computed by numerical optimization, see e.g. [6].

This optimization becomes unnecessary if the inverse Fourier transforms of all frequency responses are known. This is the case for filters based on the Poisson filter series [10] which have been used for the following experiments. Starting point are the Poisson filters and their Riesz transforms (lower case: spatial domain, upper case: frequency domain, Fourier transform according to [6]):

$$h_e(\mathbf{x};s) = \frac{s}{2\pi(s^2+|\mathbf{x}|^2)^{3/2}} \qquad H_e(\rho,\phi;s) = \exp(-\rho s) \tag{14}$$

$$h_{o1}(\mathbf{x};s) = \frac{x_1}{2\pi(s^2+|\mathbf{x}|^2)^{3/2}} \qquad H_{o1}(\rho,\phi;s) = i\cos\phi\exp(-\rho s) \tag{15}$$

$$h_{o2}(\mathbf{x};s) = \frac{x_2}{2\pi(s^2+|\mathbf{x}|^2)^{3/2}} \qquad H_{o2}(\rho,\phi;s) = i\sin\phi\exp(-\rho s). \tag{16}$$

The SQF for the Poisson filter series with zero value and zero first derivative at $\rho = 0$ is given for arbitrary scale $s > 1$ by

$$b_e(\mathbf{x};s) = h_e(\mathbf{x};s-1) - 2h_e(\mathbf{x};s) + h_e(\mathbf{x};s+1) \tag{17}$$

$$b_{o1}(\mathbf{x};s) = h_{o1}(\mathbf{x};s-1) - 2h_{o1}(\mathbf{x};s) + h_{o1}(\mathbf{x};s+1) \tag{18}$$

$$b_{o2}(\mathbf{x};s) = h_{o2}(\mathbf{x};s-1) - 2h_{o2}(\mathbf{x};s) + h_{o2}(\mathbf{x};s+1). \tag{19}$$

The derivatives of these filters are straightforward to compute in either domain.

4 Optical Flow Estimation

In this section we will propose a method for two-frame optical flow estimation. Optical flow estimation is the first step towards motion estimation. The optical flow might differ essentially from the motion field, but this aspect is out of the scope of this paper. There are several methods for optical flow estimation known from the literature, among these a phase-based method for the two-frame case, see e.g. [13]. We will adapt this approach for the monogenic framework.

4.1 Local Displacements

The main idea of flow from phase is to make a local displacement estimation by a first order series expansion of the phase, which was a popular disparity estimation technique in the 90ies [14, 15, 16]. This series has to be slightly adapted for the phase vector [4].

We start with the assumption that the new frame is obtained from the old one by a local displacement $\mathbf{d}(\mathbf{x})$:

$$I_{\text{new}}(\mathbf{x}) = I_{\text{old}}(\mathbf{x} - \mathbf{d}(\mathbf{x})). \tag{20}$$

In our local image model, this assumption maps directly to the phase vectors:

$$\mathbf{r}_{\text{new}}(\mathbf{x}) = \mathbf{r}_{\text{old}}(\mathbf{x} - \mathbf{d}(\mathbf{x})). \tag{21}$$

Assuming $|\mathbf{d}(\mathbf{x})|$ is sufficiently small, we can approximate the phase of the new frame by a first order expansion (c.f. (5)):

$$\mathbf{r}_{\text{new}}(\mathbf{x}) \approx \mathbf{r}_{\text{old}}(\mathbf{x}) - \mathbf{n}(\mathbf{x})\mathbf{n}^T(\mathbf{x})\mathbf{d}(\mathbf{x})f(\mathbf{x}). \tag{22}$$

Rearranging this equation and assuming a constant displacement in the neighborhood $\mathcal{N}$, we obtain $\mathbf{d}_{\mathcal{N}}$ from the linear system

$$\sum_{\mathbf{x}\in\mathcal{N}} \mathbf{r}_{\text{diff}}(\mathbf{x}) = \sum_{\mathbf{x}\in\mathcal{N}} [\mathbf{r}_{\text{old}}(\mathbf{x}) - \mathbf{r}_{\text{new}}(\mathbf{x})] = \sum_{\mathbf{x}\in\mathcal{N}} [\mathbf{n}(\mathbf{x})\mathbf{n}^T(\mathbf{x})f(\mathbf{x})]\mathbf{d}_{\mathcal{N}}, \tag{23}$$

where the phase vector difference is modulo π (concerning the vector magnitude). In practice, the phase vector difference is calculated from the 3D rotation which relates the two SQF responses. This can be done easiest in the algebra of quaternions, resulting in the following four components:

$$\begin{aligned} p_{\text{diff}} &= p_{\text{old}} p_{\text{new}} + \mathbf{q}_{\text{old}}^T \mathbf{q}_{\text{new}} \\ \mathbf{q}_{\text{diff}} &= p_{\text{old}} \mathbf{q}_{\text{new}} - \mathbf{q}_{\text{old}} p_{\text{new}} \\ c_{\text{diff}} &= \mathbf{q}_{\text{old}}^T \mathbf{q}_{\text{new}}^{\perp}. \end{aligned}$$

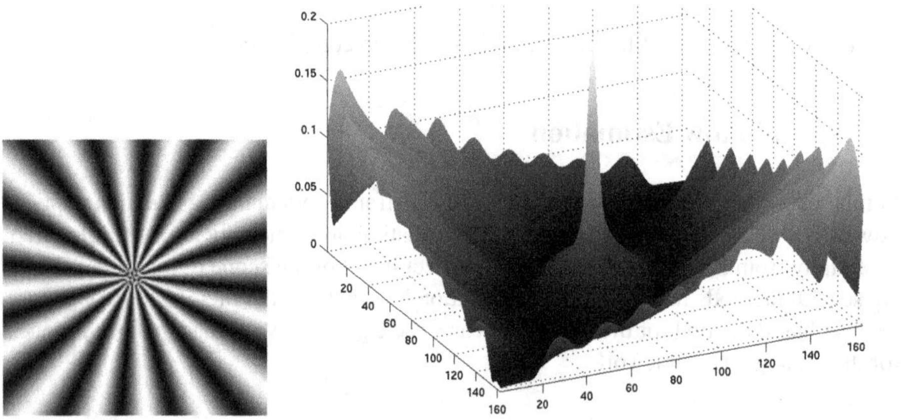

Fig. 5. Flow estimation experiment with synthetic pattern. Left: pattern (Siemens star). Right: absolute error for constant motion estimate with windowed averaging (binomial filter) in (23). The true motion vector was $(\sqrt{2}, \sqrt{3})$.

The first three components describe the local displacement, i.e., extracting the 'phase vector' from $(\mathbf{q}_{\text{diff}}^T, p_{\text{diff}})^T$ using (10) yields the phase difference for (23). Note that the amplitude of $(\mathbf{q}_{\text{diff}}^T, p_{\text{diff}})^T$ can be used as a measurement of reliability.

The fourth component is somehow special: it describes the rotation of the local orientation. This rotation angle is obtained as

$$\psi(\mathbf{x}) = \sin^{-1}\left(\frac{c_{\text{diff}}}{|\mathbf{q}_{\text{new}}||\mathbf{q}_{\text{old}}|}\right). \tag{24}$$

The two fields, i.e., the optical flow $\mathbf{i}(\mathbf{x})$ and the local rotation field $\psi(\mathbf{x})$ are not independent, but they can be used in parallel to enhance the consistency of the estimated fields, cf. also [17].

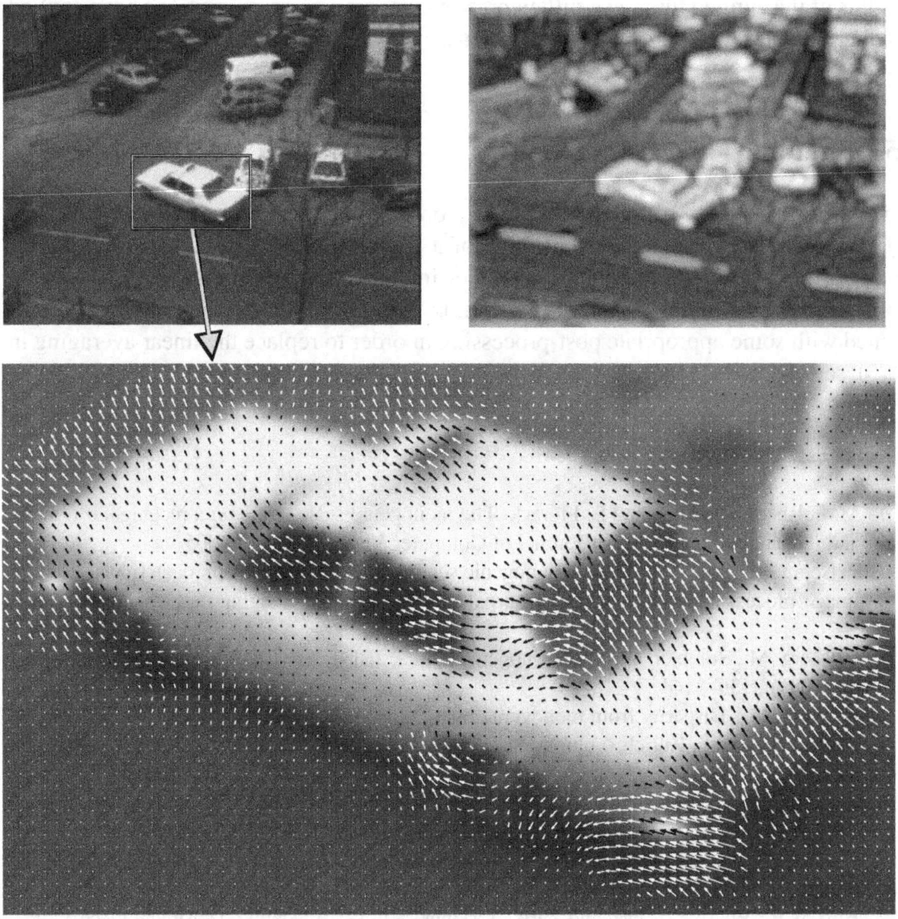

Fig. 6. Experiments on the taxi sequence. Upper left: one frame of the sequence. Upper right: confidences of the estimates in logarithmic scale (white means high confidence). Bottom: estimated flow field for a smaller region of the frame.

Note that (23) is directly related to the brightness constancy constraint equation (BCCE). If the intensity in the BCCE is replaced with the phase vector, i.e., constraining phase vector constancy, and by approximating the time derivative with a finite difference, we obtain (23).

4.2 Some Examples

There is definitely a need for detailed experiments and comparisons to other methods, but at the current state, we only present some basic experiments on synthetic data with known ground truth, see Fig. 5, and the taxi sequence, see Fig. 6. In the synthetic experiments, we have applied constant translational motion to the synthetic pattern.

For the taxi sequence, cf. Fig. 6, we have applied a single scale estimation. This was possible, since the flow field has small magnitudes (< 3), such that the convergence radius of the applied filter was sufficient. Note that no post-processing has been applied to the estimates, i.e., the only regularization is given by the applied bandpass filter (here: $s = 2$).

5 Summary and Outlook

We have presented a self-contained survey on the monogenic framework and derived optical flow estimation as an application of it. The method needs, however, further investigation concerning the quality of the estimates in comparison to other two-frame methods. For obtaining a full motion estimation system, the method has to be combined with some appropriate post-processing in order to replace the linear averaging in (23), see e.g. [18].

References

1. M. Felsberg, R. Duits, and L. Florack. The monogenic scale space on a rectangular domain and its features. International Journal of Computer Vision, 64(2–3), 2005
2. Felsberg, M., Sommer, G.: The monogenic scale-space: A unifying approach to phase-based image processing in scale-space. Journal of Mathematical Imaging and Vision **21** (2004) 5–26
3. Felsberg, M., Sommer, G.: The monogenic signal. IEEE Transactions on Signal Processing **49** (2001) 3136–3144
4. Felsberg, M.: Disparity from monogenic phase. In v. Gool, L., ed.: 24. DAGM Symposium Mustererkennung, Zürich. Volume 2449 of Lecture Notes in Computer Science., Springer, Heidelberg (2002) 248–256
5. Mechler, F., Reich, D.S., Victor, J.D.: Detection and discrimination of relative spatial phase by V1 neurons. Journal of Neuroscience **22** (2002) 6129–6157
6. Granlund, G.H., Knutsson, H.: Signal Processing for Computer Vision. Kluwer Academic Publishers, Dordrecht (1995)
7. Hurt, N.E.: Phase Retrieval and Zero Crossings. Kluwer Academic, Dordrecht (1989)
8. Krieger, G., Zetzsche, C.: Nonlinear image operators for the evaluation of local intrinsic dimensionality. IEEE Transactions on Image Processing **5** (1996) 1026–1041
9. Oppenheim, A., Lim, J.: The importance of phase in signals. Proc. of the IEEE **69** (1981) 529–541

10. Felsberg, M.: On the design of two-dimensional polar separable filters. In: 12th European Signal Processing Conference, Vienna, Austria. (2004)
11. Knutsson, H., Wilson, R., Granlund, G.H.: Anisotropic non-stationary image estimation and its applications: Part I – restoration of noisy images. IEEE Trans. on Communications **COM–31** (1983) 388–397
12. Freeman, W.T., Adelson, E.H.: The design and use of steerable filters. IEEE Transactions on Pattern Analysis and Machine Intelligence **13** (1991) 891–906
13. Jähne, B.: Digital Image Processing. Springer, Berlin (2002)
14. Fleet, D.J., Jepson, A.D., Jenkin, M.R.M.: Phase-based disparity measurement. Computer Vision, Graphics, and Image Processing. Image Understanding **53** (1991) 198–210
15. Maimone, M.W., Shafer, S.A.: Modeling foreshortening in stereo vision using local spatial frequency. In: International Robotics and Systems Conference, IEEE Computer Society Press (1995) 519–524
16. Maki, A., Uhlin, T., Eklundh, J.O.: A direct disparity estimation technique for depth segmentation. In: Proc. 5th IAPR Workshop on Machine Vision Applications. (1996) 530–533
17. Schnörr, C.: Variational methods for fluid flow estimation. In Jähne, B., Barth, E., Mester, R., Scharr, H., eds.: Complex Motion, Proceedings 1st Int. Workshop, Günzburg, Springer Verlag, Heidelberg (2007) 124–145
18. Forssén, P.E.: Multiple motion estimation using channel matrices. In Jähne, B., Barth, E., Mester, R., Scharr, H., eds.: Complex Motion, Proceedings 1st Int. Workshop, Günzburg, Springer Verlag, Heidelberg (2007) 54–65

Optimal Filters for Extended Optical Flow

Hanno Scharr*

Institute for Chemistry and Dynamics of the Geosphere, ICG III
Forschungszentrum Jülich GmbH, 52425 Jülich, Germany
H.Scharr@FZ-Juelich.de

Abstract. Estimation of optical flow and physically motivated brightness changes can be formulated as parameter estimation in linear models. Accuracy of this estimation heavily depends on the filter families used to implement the models. In this paper we focus on models whose terms are all data dependent and therefore are best estimated via total-least-squares (TLS) or similar estimators. Using three different linear models we derive *model dependent* optimality criteria based on transfer functions of filter families with given fixed size. Using a simple optimization procedure, we demonstrate typical properties of optimal filter sets for optical flow, simultaneous estimation of optical flow and diffusion, as well as optical flow and exponential decay. Exemplarily we show their performance and state some useful choices.

1 Introduction

Optical flow is very well known and has a wealth of applications, see e.g. [1, 23, 24] in this volume or [2, 8, 21] for overviews on different estimation techniques. Estimation of optical flow with physically motivated brightness changes has been introduced and applied in [6, 7]. It can be formulated generally as parameter estimation in linear models that can be written in the form $\boldsymbol{d}^T\boldsymbol{p} = 0$. There $\boldsymbol{d}$ is the so called data vector and $\boldsymbol{p}$ contains the sought for parameters. For differential optical flow techniques $\boldsymbol{d}$ is build by applying a spatio-temporal filter family to the image data and thus turning it into a vector-valued image sequence. But models exist, where some of the components of $\boldsymbol{d}$ do not depend on the data, e.g. when gray value sources are present like a laser induced heat spot in a thermal image sequence. As shown e.g. in [6] parameters corresponding to the data-dependent components have to be estimated by total-least-squares-like methods (TLS), the others by ordinary-least-squares. In the cases covered here, all components of $\boldsymbol{d}$ have to depend on the input image sequence. Consequently we use a TLS-estimator (structure tensor [9]) in all performance tests. Only for pure optical flow we also use the Combined-Local-Global (CLG) estimator from [3], in order to show the impact of optimized filters in state-of-the-art variational estimators (error reduction about a factor 0.3 to 0.5).

A demonstration of the influence of filter families is given in Fig. 1. There the initial outline of a plant leaf (Fig. 1**a**) is represented by a spline (white line). The outline is tracked through the image sequence by moving the control points of the spline according to the optical flow field. Fig. 1**b** shows the outcome using central differences

* This work has partly been funded by DFG SPP1114 (SCHA 927/1-2).

B. Jähne et al. (Eds.): IWCM 2004, LNCS 3417, pp. 14–29, 2007.

Fig. 1. Demonstration of filter accuracy by optical flow tracking. Left: first image. Middle: tracked with 3-tab derivative. Right: tracked with 5-tab optimized filter family.

to build spatio-temporal derivatives in the Structure Tensor. The motion is heavily underestimated and features many outliers. Fig. 1**c** shows the result using the identical algorithm but the 5x5x5 filters shown in Tab. 3. There are no visible deviations from the optimal tracking result.

As the outcome of the parameter estimation heavily depends on the filters used to build the data vector $\boldsymbol{d}$, a good choice of these filters is crucial for high accuracy. Consequently performance evaluations of optical flow techniques (e.g. [2, 8]) should consider the same filter choices for all techniques, but usually don't. We do a performance evaluation like this for the Structure Tensor and the CLG-estimator for several filter choices to justify this claim. The main contribution of this paper however is to show how to get good filter families, state and evaluate them for optical flow, optical flow and diffusion as well as optical flow and exponential decay.

In Sec. 3 we show how to derive an optimization scheme for filter families. This optimization uses the ideal estimation outcome for parameters in a model formulated in fourier domain, thus *model dependent filters* will be derived. The optimality criterion is based on the transfer functions of the filters in a family. Consequently we will briefly recapitulate transfer functions of symmetric and antisymmetric filters, smoothing filters, consistent derivatives and the spatial Laplacian for spatio-temporal image sequences in Sec. 2. A few examples of optimal filter families are discussed in Sec. 4.

Related work. Due to the well understood properties of derivative filters for numerics of PDE, the need for filter optimization has not been noticed for quite some time. A collection of heuristic, non-optimal filter design approaches can be found in the first sections of [11] or in [16, 17]. During the last decade many authors investigated filter optimization. Beginning with transfer functions of single filters (e.g. [13, 22]) more and more sophisticated optimization schemes have been developed (e.g. [4, 5, 12, 14, 15]). The approach presented in [5] is a special case of the one presented here, namely pure optical flow with separable weight functions in the error norm (see Sec. 3). Thus we will not compare the filters stated there to the ones given here. The optimization strategy used here was first presented in [20] and has already been applied to many different filters and filter families [11, 18]. But to the best of my knowledge there is no publication presenting a filter optimization scheme for extended motion estimation.

2 Consistent FIR-Filters

Some of the filters presented in this section are called 'derivative' or 'idenitity'. The meaning of this is that in the limit of vanishing pixel distances they become the continuous derivative or identity operator. In numerics of finite differences this property is called consistency. One can show (see e.g. [18, 19]) that it can be expressed via the coefficients of the Taylor expansion of the transfer function in the origin of the Fourier domain. E.g. for an ideal first order derivative, only the first[1] coefficient is non-zero, for a second order derivative the second and so on. A discrete operator is called consistent, if all coefficients up to the last non-zero coefficient are identical to the coefficients of the continuous operator. Thus consistency gives us a set of constraint equations we have to fulfill if we want to call an operator 'derivative' oder 'identity'. But it is only defined at the center of the Fourier domain. Thus for special applications we can drop these constraints if we know that our images do not contain data around the Fourier origin, i.e. low frequency components. But for most applications this is not the case, thus we stick with consistency.

2.1 One-Dimensional Filters

All filter families optimized in this paper are composed of 1d filters. Most of them are separable filters, only the Laplacian is more complicated. In the following we use the filter notation [2]

$$h(r) = [h_0, h_1, \ldots, h_R] := \sum_{r=0}^{R} h_r \delta(r - r_0)$$

where $h(r)$ denotes the spatial filter. We use $\hat{h}(\tilde{k})$ for its transfer function. The filters used in this paper are given next.

1D Symmetric. Symmetries in filters reduce their free parameters and thus yield more stable optimizations. For odd symmetric filters $h(r) = [h_R, \ldots, h_1, h_0, h_1, \ldots, h_R]$ the transfer function is

$$\hat{h}(\tilde{k}) = h_0 + 2\sum_{r=1}^{R} h_r \cos(\pi r \tilde{k}) \tag{1}$$

1D Antisymmetric. These filters can be used for odd order derivatives. With the filter $h(r) = [h_R, \ldots, h_1, 0, -h_1, \ldots, -h_R]$ the transfer function we get is

$$\hat{h}(\tilde{k}) = 2\mathrm{i}\sum_{r=1}^{R} h_r \sin(\pi r \tilde{k}) \tag{2}$$

1D Smoothing. The sum over all coefficients in smoothing filters must be 1. This is the constraint one can also derive for consistent identities. Thus smoothing filters are identity filters. This observation will be needed in the model for optical flow and

---

[1] We denote the DC-component as coefficient zero.

[2] Please note that a filter has to be mirrored before it is applied to the data. Thus the usual notation for a 2-tab derivative in numerics is $[-1, 1]$ in filter notation it is $[1, -1]$.

exponential decay (cmp. Eqs. 27 and 29). We use symmetric filters and directly implement the constraint. In the odd case (i.e. R is odd) we get for h_0

$$h_0 = 1 - 2\sum_{r=1}^{R} h_r \tag{3}$$

and the transfer function

$$\hat{h}(\tilde{k}) = 1 + 2\sum_{r=1}^{R} h_r(-1 + \cos(\pi r\tilde{k})) \tag{4}$$

1D First Derivative. The constraints for consistent first derivatives are

$$\sum_{r=1}^{R} h_r = 0 \quad \text{and} \quad \sum_{r=1}^{R} h_r r = 1 \tag{5}$$

We use antisymmetric filters and get

$$h_1 = \frac{1}{2} - \sum_{r=2}^{R} h_r(r) \tag{6}$$

as constraint for the odd case. The transfer function then is

$$\hat{h}(\tilde{k}) = \mathrm{i}\sin(\pi\tilde{k}) + 2\mathrm{i}\sum_{r=2}^{R} h_r(\sin(r\pi\tilde{k}) - r\sin(\pi\tilde{k})) \tag{7}$$

1D Second Derivative. Consistent second derivatives are used to build Laplacian kernels. The constraints are

$$\sum_{r=1}^{R} h_r = 0, \quad \sum_{r=1}^{R} h_r r = 0 \quad \text{and} \quad \sum_{r=1}^{R} h_r r^2 = 2 \tag{8}$$

Using symmetric filters we need two coefficients to depend on the others. We choose

$$h_0 = -2 + 2\sum_{r=2}^{R} h_r(r^2 - 1) \qquad h_1 = 1 - \sum_{r=2}^{R}(h_r r^2) \tag{9}$$

and get the transfer function

$$\hat{h}(\tilde{k}) = -2 + 2\cos(\pi\tilde{k}) + 2\sum_{r=2}^{R} h_r\left[r^2 - 1 + \cos(r\pi\tilde{k}) - r^2\cos(\pi\tilde{k})\right] \tag{10}$$

2.2 Spatio-temporal Filters

We compose spatio-temporal filters using the 1d filters above. For all filters of a filter family we use the same support, which does neither need to have the same length in each dimension nor need all lengths to be exclusively even or odd. For the motion estimation models covered here we need 3 different filter types: Identities, first order derivatives and spatial Laplacians. Most applications use them in 2, 3, and 4 dimensions, but higher dimensional filters can be constructed via the same rules.

Identities. An identity $\mathcal{I}$ is composed of 1d smoothing filters $\mathcal{I}^{(1)}$ in all dimensions

$$\mathcal{I}^{(2)} = \mathcal{I}_x^{(1)} * \mathcal{I}_t^{(1)} \tag{11}$$

$$\mathcal{I}^{(3)} = \mathcal{I}_x^{(1)} * \mathcal{I}_y^{(1)} * \mathcal{I}_t^{(1)} \tag{12}$$

where upper indices indicate the dimensionality and lower indices the applied direction.

First Order Derivatives. Gradients are calculated by first order derivatives $\mathcal{D}$. The 1d derivative filters are smoothed in all cross directions:

$$\mathcal{D}_x^{(2)} = \mathcal{D}_x^{(1)} * \mathcal{I}_t^{(1)} \qquad \mathcal{D}_t^{(2)} = \mathcal{I}_x^{(1)} * \mathcal{D}_t^{(1)} \tag{13}$$

$$\mathcal{D}_x^{(3)} = \mathcal{D}_x^{(1)} * \mathcal{I}_y^{(1)} * \mathcal{I}_t^{(1)} \quad \mathcal{D}_y^{(3)} = \mathcal{I}_x^{(1)} * \mathcal{D}_y^{(1)} * \mathcal{I}_t^{(1)} \quad \mathcal{D}_t^{(3)} = \mathcal{I}_x^{(1)} * \mathcal{I}_y^{(1)} * \mathcal{D}_t^{(1)} \tag{14}$$

Spatial Laplacians. Multidimensional spatial Laplacians $\mathcal{L}$ are sums of second derivatives $\mathcal{L}^{(1)}$ in all spatial directions. Thus they are

$$\mathcal{L}^{(2)} = OL_x^{(1)} * OI_t^{(1)} \tag{15}$$

$$\mathcal{L}^{(3)} = (OL_x^{(1)} * OI_y^{(1)} + OI_x^{(1)} * OL_y^{(1)}) * OI_t^{(1)} \tag{16}$$

As we have introduced all necessary filter transfer functions and rules to build single n-dimensional filters, we will now show how to optimize their coefficients in special filter families.

3 Filter Design as Optimization

In order to construct optimality criteria for extended optical flow estimation we use a general optimization scheme. It has been used before in [11, 18, 20], operates in the whole fourier space, and allows complex nonlinear optimizations of filter families.

We call a discrete filter family *optimal for a model* if results calculated with this filter and results calculated with the ideal operator differ as little as possible. The problems involved in finding this optimal filter family are to find a good design criterion for a given model and a well adapted optimization scheme. We use the following notions:

Objective function. The objective function is the function to minimize in order to optimize filter properties. In our case it is the difference between a reference and an ansatz function.
Reference function. This function fully fulfills the design criterion derived from a specific model and thus can be used to test other functions against. For extended motion estimation filter families are optimized. Each of these filters correspond to an ideal operator, e.g. first or second order derivatives. Thus all examples shown here use a reference function build with the transfer functions of these ideal operators (cmp. Sec. 3.2).
Ansatz function. Like the reference function consists of transfer functions of ideal operators, the ansatz function consists of transfer functions of discrete filters. It depends on the coefficients of the discrete filters in the family (cmp. Sec. 3.2).
Error functional or norm. The objective function, i.e. differences between ansatz and reference, has to be measured with an appropriate error functional. We use a weighted L_2 norm in fourier domain, where the weights model the expected energy distribution in fourier domain. Thus wave vectors with high expected amplitude have higher weights than those with low amplitudes (cmp. Sec. 3.3).
Optimization strategy. Depending on the error functional different optimization strategies have to be applied. Linear optimizations in Euklidean norm are simple to solve, but for nonlinear cases, other norms or parameter values with fixed-point accuracy more sophisticated optimization schemes have to be applied [18]. In the case presented

here, floating-point accuracy in weighted L_2 norm, an implementation using Matlabs `lsqnonlin`-function is appropriate.

We will now show how to choose ansatz and reference functions according to the models involved in extended optical flow computation. We will then have a closer look at the error norm.

3.1 Linear Models for Extended Optical Flow

The general linear model for the estimation of extended optical flow is (cmp. [6, 7])

$$\boldsymbol{d}^T \boldsymbol{p} = 0 \tag{17}$$

where $\boldsymbol{d}$ and $\boldsymbol{p}$ are the data vector and the parameter vector, respectively. Some simple models are

- **optical flow (OF):** $g_x U + g_y V + g_t = 0$

$$\boldsymbol{d} = [g_x, g_y, g_t]^T \qquad \boldsymbol{p} = [U, V, 1]^T \tag{18}$$

  where g is the image sequence and lower indices denote derivatives in these directions.
- **OF and exponential decay:** $g_x U + g_y V + g_t = \kappa g$

$$\boldsymbol{d} = [g_x, g_y, g_t, g]^T \qquad \boldsymbol{p} = [U, V, 1, -\kappa]^T \tag{19}$$

  with a decay constant κ.
- **OF and isotropic diffusion:** $g_x U + g_y V + g_t = d\triangle g$

$$\boldsymbol{d} = [g_x, g_y, g_t, \triangle g]^T \qquad \boldsymbol{p} = [U, V, 1, -d]^T \tag{20}$$

  where $\triangle g$ denotes the spatial Laplacian $(g_{xx} + g_{yy})$ and d is a diffusion constant or 'diffusivity'.

In general the parameter vector contains the sought for extended flow parameters. The data vector $\boldsymbol{d}$ is obtained by filtering the input image sequence g with a filter family.

3.2 Objective Functions for Extended OF

As Eq. 17 indicates, $\boldsymbol{p}$ is point-wise perpendicular to $\boldsymbol{d}$. Thus the correct estimation of the direction of $\boldsymbol{d}$ is of high importance, its absolute value does not matter. This observation is the key to our filter design criterion. For each wave vector $\tilde{\boldsymbol{k}}$ in fourier domain (i.e. a planar wave in spatial domain) we calculate the data vector and normalize it. This is the normalized vector of transfer functions of the applied operators, i.e. ideal operators or a discrete filter family. We will explain this in more detail for the above mentioned models.

Pure Optical Flow. For pure optical flow the data vector $\boldsymbol{d}$ is the spatio-temporal gradient.

$$\boldsymbol{d} = [g_x, g_y, g_t]^T \tag{21}$$

Using ideal derivative operators for a given planar wave

$$g(\boldsymbol{x}, \tilde{\boldsymbol{k}}) = A(\tilde{\boldsymbol{k}}) \exp(i\pi\tilde{\boldsymbol{k}}(\boldsymbol{x} - \boldsymbol{x}_0)) \tag{22}$$

Eq. 21 becomes

$$\hat{\boldsymbol{d}}(\tilde{\boldsymbol{k}}) = [i\pi\tilde{k}_x,\, i\pi\tilde{k}_y,\, i\pi\tilde{k}_t]^T\, g(\boldsymbol{x}, \tilde{\boldsymbol{k}}) \tag{23}$$

The ideal filter family consists of spatial derivatives along the coordinate axes and the vector of its transfer functions is $[i\pi\tilde{k}_x,\, i\pi\tilde{k}_y,\, i\pi\tilde{k}_t]^T$. By normalization of Eq. 23 we get the reference function

$$\frac{\hat{\boldsymbol{d}}}{|\hat{\boldsymbol{d}}|}(\tilde{\boldsymbol{k}}) = \frac{\tilde{\boldsymbol{k}}}{|\tilde{\boldsymbol{k}}|} \tag{24}$$

as $i\pi g(\boldsymbol{x}, \tilde{\boldsymbol{k}})$ cancels out. It is worth to note that the reference function Eq. 24 is independent of amplitude A and phase $\boldsymbol{x}_0$ of the data. What is more, instead of the ideal operators $i\pi\tilde{k}_{x,y,t}$ we are allowed to use regularized versions $i\pi\tilde{k}_{x,y,t}\, B(\tilde{\boldsymbol{k}})$ as long as we use the same $B(\tilde{\boldsymbol{k}})$ for all operators. This is equivalent to prefiltering the data g, but in contrast to common assumptions (cmp. e.g. [5]) this kernel does *not* need to be isotropic. In fact, when combined using different discrete derivators e.g. 2-tab and 3-tab, its anisotropy is used to compensate differences between these filters (see [19]).

Applying discrete 3d derivative filters (Eq. 14, we omit the upper index) with transfer functions $\hat{\mathcal{D}}_x(\tilde{k})$, $\hat{\mathcal{D}}_y(\tilde{k})$, and $\hat{\mathcal{D}}_t(\tilde{k})$ to the planar wave (Eq. 22) we get

$$\hat{\boldsymbol{d}}_h(\tilde{\boldsymbol{k}}) = [\hat{\mathcal{D}}_x(\tilde{k}),\, \hat{\mathcal{D}}_y(\tilde{k}),\, \hat{\mathcal{D}}_t(\tilde{k})]^T\, g(\boldsymbol{x}, \tilde{\boldsymbol{k}}) \tag{25}$$

By normalization of Eq. 25 we get

$$\frac{\hat{\boldsymbol{d}}_h}{|\hat{\boldsymbol{d}}_h|}(\tilde{\boldsymbol{k}}) = \frac{[\hat{\mathcal{D}}_x(\tilde{k}),\, \hat{\mathcal{D}}_y(\tilde{k}),\, \hat{\mathcal{D}}_t(\tilde{k})]^T}{\sqrt{|\hat{\mathcal{D}}_x(\tilde{k})|^2 + |\hat{\mathcal{D}}_y(\tilde{k})|^2 + |\hat{\mathcal{D}}_t(\tilde{k})|^2}} \tag{26}$$

and as above $i\pi g(\boldsymbol{x}, \tilde{\boldsymbol{k}})$ cancels out. The ansatz function thus is the normalized vector of filter transfer functions.

Optical Flow and Exponential Decay. Using the same approach as above we can derive reference and ansatz function for Eq. 19. We apply ideal filters to the planar wave Eq. 22 and get

$$\hat{\boldsymbol{d}}(\tilde{\boldsymbol{k}}) = [i\pi\tilde{k}_x,\, i\pi\tilde{k}_y,\, i\pi\tilde{k}_t,\, 1]^T\, g(\boldsymbol{x}, \tilde{\boldsymbol{k}}) \tag{27}$$

By normalization we get

$$\frac{\hat{\boldsymbol{d}}}{|\hat{\boldsymbol{d}}|}(\tilde{\boldsymbol{k}}) = \frac{1}{\sqrt{\pi^2\, \tilde{\boldsymbol{k}}^2 + 1}}[i\pi\tilde{k}_x, i\pi\tilde{k}_y, i\pi\tilde{k}_t, 1]^T \tag{28}$$

as $g(\boldsymbol{x}, \tilde{\boldsymbol{k}})$ cancels out. Again, the reference function is the normalized vector of ideal filter transfer functions and regularization is allowed.

Using discrete derivative filters as above (Eq. 25) and an identity filter $\mathcal{I}$ (Eq. 12), i.e. a smoothing filter when using regularized filters, we get as ansatz function

$$\frac{\hat{\boldsymbol{d}}_h}{|\hat{\boldsymbol{d}}_h|}(\tilde{\boldsymbol{k}}) = \frac{[\hat{\mathcal{D}}_x(\tilde{k}),\, \hat{\mathcal{D}}_y(\tilde{k}),\, \hat{\mathcal{D}}_t(\tilde{k}), \hat{\mathcal{I}}(\tilde{k})]^T}{\sqrt{|\mathcal{D}_x(\tilde{k})|^2 + |\hat{\mathcal{D}}_y(\tilde{k})|^2 + |\hat{\mathcal{D}}_t(\tilde{k})|^2 + |\hat{\mathcal{I}}(\tilde{k})|^2}} \tag{29}$$

Optical Flow and Isotropic Diffusion. Analoguous to the two models above, for Eq. 20 we get the reference function

$$\frac{\hat{\boldsymbol{d}}}{|\hat{\boldsymbol{d}}|}(\tilde{\boldsymbol{k}}) = \frac{1}{\sqrt{\tilde{\boldsymbol{k}}^2 + \pi^2 \tilde{\boldsymbol{k}}^4}}[i\tilde{k}_x, i\tilde{k}_y, i\tilde{k}_t, -\pi \tilde{\boldsymbol{k}}^2]^T \tag{30}$$

and the ansatz function is

$$\frac{\hat{\boldsymbol{d}}_h}{|\hat{\boldsymbol{d}}_h|}(\tilde{\boldsymbol{k}}) = \frac{[\hat{\mathcal{D}}_x(\tilde{k}), \hat{\mathcal{D}}_y(\tilde{k}), \hat{\mathcal{D}}_t(\tilde{k}), \hat{\mathcal{L}}(\tilde{k})]^T}{\sqrt{|\hat{\mathcal{D}}_x(\tilde{k})|^2 + |\hat{\mathcal{D}}_y(\tilde{k})|^2 + |\hat{\mathcal{D}}_t(\tilde{k})|^2 + |\hat{\mathcal{L}}(\tilde{k})|^2}} \tag{31}$$

where $\mathcal{D}_x$, $\mathcal{D}_y$, and $\mathcal{D}_t$ denote 3d derivatives (Eq. 14, without upper index) and $\mathcal{L}$ is a spatial Laplacian (Eq. 16).

3.3 Error Functionals

So far we have described how to construct a reference function $f_r(\tilde{\boldsymbol{k}})$ and an ansatz function $f_a(\tilde{\boldsymbol{k}}, h)$. Here $\boldsymbol{h}$ denotes all free filter coefficients of the sought for filter family. In order to minimize the difference between f_r and f_a we need to define an error functional e

$$e(\boldsymbol{h}) = \left\| w(\tilde{\boldsymbol{k}}) \left(f_r(\tilde{\boldsymbol{k}}) - f_a(\tilde{\boldsymbol{k}}, \boldsymbol{h}) \right) \right\| \tag{32}$$

It calculates the difference in a weighted norm. The weight function $w(\tilde{\boldsymbol{k}})$ allows to specify statistical importance of different wave vectors $\tilde{\boldsymbol{k}}$.

In this paper we only use the most common norm, L_2-norm (square root of the sum of squares, weighted Euklidean norm),

$$e(\boldsymbol{h}) = \sqrt{\frac{\int w^2(\tilde{k}) \left(f_r(\tilde{\boldsymbol{k}}) - f_a(\tilde{\boldsymbol{k}}, \boldsymbol{h}) \right)^2 \mathbf{d}\tilde{\boldsymbol{k}}}{\int w^2(\tilde{k}) \mathbf{d}\tilde{\boldsymbol{k}}}} \tag{33}$$

Generally optimization has to be done in the whole first Brillouin zone of the Fourier space. The dimension of this space depends on the dimension of the data, not on the dimension of the filter family vectors. Using a symmetric weight function $w(\tilde{\boldsymbol{k}})$ and symmetric filter families allows calculation on a fraction of this space. E.g. if the weight function and all filters are symmetric or antisymmetric with respect to the coordinate axes only the positive quadrant (octant etc.) has to be processed.

In all example calculations we use the weight functions

$$w(\tilde{\boldsymbol{k}}, n) = \prod_{i=1}^{D} \cos^n(\pi \tilde{k}_i/2) \qquad \text{or} \qquad w(\tilde{\boldsymbol{k}}, m, c) = \frac{1}{(|\tilde{k}| + c)^m} \tag{34}$$

The first weight function is the transfer function of a (n+1)-tab binomial filter [10], which is often used for simple preprocessing or to build a Gaussian scale space. The second corresponds to typical spectra in natural scenes and was used e.g. in [5,22]. We use the values $n = 4$, $m = 2$ and $c = 0.25$. In most cases the choice of the weight function is not critical. But for applications with distinct spectra, e.g. motion estimations where the mean velocity is known not to be zero, the expected spectrum of the image data should be used.

4 Results

We will show some results for all objective functions defined above. Despite of giving extensive tabular results of all filter coefficients, we will demonstrate filter properties and general behavior of the filter families.

4.1 Pure Optical Flow

For optical flow a gradient filter family has to be optimized according to Eqs. 24 and 26 and Eq. 32

$$\left\| w(\tilde{\boldsymbol{k}}) \left(\frac{\hat{\boldsymbol{d}}}{|\hat{\boldsymbol{d}}|}(\tilde{\boldsymbol{k}}) - \frac{\hat{\boldsymbol{d}}_h}{|\hat{\boldsymbol{d}}_h|}(\tilde{\boldsymbol{k}}) \right) \right\| \rightarrow \min \tag{35}$$

For support areas with the same length in every direction, e.g. 3×3 or $5 \times 5 \times 5$, all derivative filters and their cross smoothing kernels have exactly the same coefficients. Thus we only state a 1d derivative and a single cross-smoother per filter family (Tab. 3). We observe, that there is not much difference between the coefficients stated for 2d and 3d kernels. Consequently there is no urgent need to optimize for higher dimensions.

The influence of the weight function is considerable. The weight function Eq. 34, left, allows for better and better filters, the larger their size is (cmp. Tab. 3, top, error e). Using the weight function Eq. 34, right, results in much less improved filters (cmp. Tab. 3, bottom, error e). This is due to the fact that the largest errors are at highest frequencies and there the smoothing kernels have least influence on the errors. Consequently it is a good idea not to use highest frequency data for motion estimation if possible, e.g. by moderately presmoothing the data. Fortunately the derivatives presented here, especially the ones using weight function Eq. 34, left, already smooth the data by their inherent smoothing and cross smoothing kernels. Thus the filters derived by the cos-like weight function are good choices in general applications.

To demonstrate the accuracy achieved by these filters, we plot the maximal angular error of a few filter choices in Fig. 2. The angular errors are reduced by approximately 1 order of magnitude for 3-tab filters and 4 orders of magnitude for 5-tab filters.

For performance evaluation of optical flow techniques, the angular error measure given in [2],eq. 3.38, combined with synthetic or calibrated image sequences with ground truth has become a gold standard. For the test here we use two well known test sequences, namely 'Yosemite'[3] (without clouds) and 'Marble'[4], the Structure Tensor local TLS-estimator [9], and the 3d-filter sets from Tab. 3, top, as well as central differences ('3-tab'). Sample images from the two sequences are shown in Fig. 3. Angular errors are stated in Tab. 1. We see that errors decay with increasing filter size and fill factors become larger. Consequently usual comparative performance evaluations of OF-techniques need to consider filter families.

We also test the Combined-Local-Global (CLG) estimator first published in [3] with these filters. Here in addition to the filters from Tab. 3, top, and central differences ('3-tab'), we applied simple filter families known from numerics. A 5-tab kernel $[-1, 8, 0, -8, 1]/12$ applied in x- and y-direction and a 2-tab kernel $[1, -1]$ in t-direction (denoted

[3] http://www.cs.brown.edu/people/black/images.html

[4] http://i21www.ira.uka.de/image_sequences

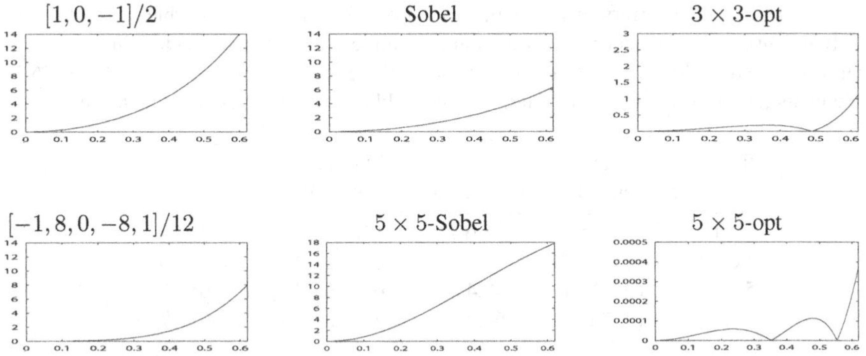

Fig. 2. Orientation estimation of a sinusoidal planar wave in 22,5°-direction, the direction of maximal error. Illustrated is the absolute value of the orientation error in degrees. Please note the different scaling. Top: 3×3 filter, bottom: 5×5 filter. 5×5-Sobel is $[-1, 8, 0, -8, 1]_x/12 * [1, 4, 6, 4, 1]_y/16$. The optimized filters are the ones from Tab. 3, top.

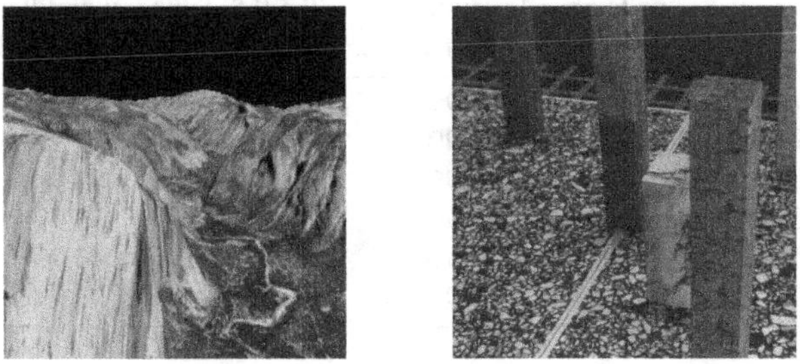

Fig. 3. Images from 'Yosemite' (left) and 'Marble' (right)

'5,5,2'). And a 7-tab kernel $[1, -9, 45, 0, -45, 9, -1]/60$ applied in x- and y-direction and a 2-tab kernel $[1, -1]$ in t-direction (denoted '7,7,2'). Results for CLG are shown in Tab. 2.

In order to demonstrate this accuracy improvement we tracked the outline of a plant leaf and visualized it by B-splines (Fig. 1). After 43 frames the non-smoothed filters show many outliers and underestimate the overall velocity. With optimized filters no observable error occurs.

4.2 Optical Flow and Exponential Decay

For optical flow and exponentially decaying brightness a gradient filter family is combined with an identity filter. We have to optimize the ansatz given by Eq. 29 via the reference Eq. 29 and the error Eq. 32

$$\left\| w(\tilde{\boldsymbol{k}}) \left(\frac{\hat{\boldsymbol{d}}}{|\hat{\boldsymbol{d}}|}(\tilde{\boldsymbol{k}}) - \frac{\hat{\boldsymbol{d}}_h}{|\hat{\boldsymbol{d}}_h|}(\tilde{\boldsymbol{k}}) \right) \right\| \to \min \tag{36}$$

Table 1. Mean angular errors of OF estimates using 'Yosemite' and 'Marble' sequences, the Structure Tensor TLS-estimator and different filter families. 3-tab denotes central differences, the other filters are the 3d-sets from Tab. 3. For 'Yosemite' the structureless, cloud free area is 26.1% of the image, in 'Marble' no ground truth velocity field is given for 12.1% of the image.

filter	Yosemite ang. error [°]	fill-factor	Marble ang. error [°]	fill-factor
3-tab	16.8 (± 25.2)	35.6%	17.7 (± 26.9)	36.0%
3x3x3	10.8 (± 24.7)	51.5%	8.6 (± 22.0)	50.4%
5x5x5	4.0 (± 11.1)	58.4%	6.9 (± 17.3)	65.3%
7x7x7	3.1 (± 7.6)	64.3%	4.3 (± 9.4)	67.4%

Table 2. Mean angular errors of OF estimates using 'Yosemite' sequence, the 2d CLG estimator and different filter families. '3-tab' denotes central differences, '5,5,2' and '7,7,2' are explained in the text, the other filters are the 3d-sets from Tab. 3. For 'Yosemite' the structureless, cloud free area is 26.1% of the image, thus 73.9% fill-factor is 100% of the available area.

filter	no temporal prefilter		(0.5,0.5) temporal prefilter	
	ang. error [°]	fill-factor	ang. error [°]	fill-factor
3-tab	6.95 (± 6.58)	73.9%	4.57 (± 3.75)	73.9%
5,5,2	8.30 (± 6.85)	73.9%	5.54 (± 4.85)	73.9%
7,7,2	8.53 (± 6.98)	73.9%	5.64 (± 4.89)	73.9%
3x3x3	3.13 (± 3.65)	73.9%	2.59 (± 2.58)	73.9%
5x5x5	2.80 (± 3.20)	73.9%	2.54 (± 2.46)	73.9%
7x7x7	2.68 (± 2.95)	73.9%	2.52 (± 2.41)	73.9%

At first glance the outcome of the filter optimization is amazing: The filter coefficients are exactly the same as the ones for pure optical flow (except for the 3×3-case where a difference is in the 3rd digit). The reason is that the smoothing kernels try to be close to the inherent smoothing in the derivative kernels. To demonstrate this we plot derivative filters $\mathcal{D}^{(1)}$ and smoothed ideal derivatives $i\pi\tilde{k}\mathcal{I}^{(1)}$ in the same diagram (Fig. 4). This property has directly been optimized in [5]. Very similar results are stated there, compare Tab. 3, bottom with Table I in that paper. For other supports this behavior is also true, but the smoothers in one direction adapt to the derivative in the same direction. Thus e.g. the derivative used for $\mathcal{D}_x^{(2)}$ affects the smoother in $\mathcal{D}_y^{(2)}$ and vice versa (cmp. Eq. 13). The identity $\mathcal{I}^{(3)}$ can be constructed using the cross smoothing kernels of the derivatives. We conclude that the optimized filters approximate ideal derivatives of regularized data.

4.3 Optical Flow and Diffusion

For optical flow and diffusion a gradient filter family is combined with a spatial Laplacian. We have to optimize the ansatz given by Eq. 31 via the reference Eq. 30 and the error functional Eq. 32

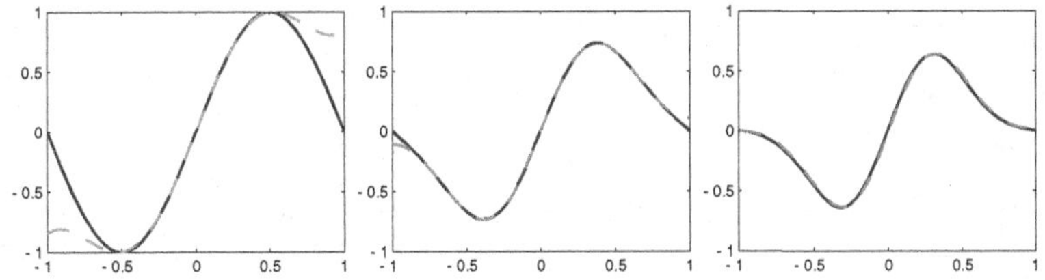

Fig. 4. Derivative filters $\mathcal{D}^{(1)}$ (solid dark line) and ideal smoothed derivatives $i\pi\tilde{k}\mathcal{I}^{(1)}$ (dashed light line). From left to right: 3×3, 5×5 and 7×7 from Tab. 3.

$$\left\| w(\tilde{\boldsymbol{k}}) \left(\frac{\hat{\boldsymbol{d}}}{|\hat{\boldsymbol{d}}|}(\tilde{\boldsymbol{k}}) - \frac{\hat{\boldsymbol{d}}_h}{|\hat{\boldsymbol{d}}_h|}(\tilde{\boldsymbol{k}}) \right) \right\| \to \min \tag{37}$$

As spatial smoothing in a Laplacian does not occur in 2d but in 3d and higher dimensions, we not only state 2d filters (Tab. 4) but also 3d filter families. The 1d filters of the $5 \times 5 \times 5$ family are shown in Fig. 5 in order to visualize symmetries. For the 2d filters we observe that spatial and temporal derivatives and smoothers no longer use the same coefficients, but the larger the filters get the less severe the differences are.

Similar to the approach in [2, 8] we also test the performance of the 3d filter sets on sinusoidal plaid test sequences. The initial image at time $t = 0$ is

$$g(x, y, 0) = \cos(kx) + \cos(ky)$$

Given a fixed velocity vector (U, V) and diffusion coefficient d (Eq. 20) for these sequences the diffusion equation can be solved in closed form. Thus we have ground truth and can calculate absolute and relative errors of the estimated parameters. In Fig. 6 relative errors of the estimated velocities U and diffusivities d (Eq. 20) are given. In Fig. 6 first and second row U is varied and $d = 0.1$, $V = 0$ are fixed. In Fig. 6 third and fourth row d is varied and $U = 0.25$pixel/frame, $V = 0.5$pixel/frame are fixed. The four curves in each plot correspond to different wave-numbers k of the sinusoidal pattern, $k \in \{0.03125, 0.0625, 0.125, 0.25\}$. Looking at the first row, we observe that the optimized filters (3x3x3 in $\mathbf{b}_1$ and 5x5x5 in $\mathbf{c}_1$) perform better than the non-optimized ones ($\mathbf{a}_1$). The error of the 5x5x5-filters in addition is nearly independent of the wave-number k (i.e. the different curves). The second row shows, that the estimation of the diffusivity does not depend on U as long as U is small enough and the 5x5x5-filters are again least dependent on k. In the third row non of the filter sets show large dependencies on the varying value of the diffusivity d when estimating U. Errors are in the same range as in the first row. In the last row we see, that no matter which filter set we use, small diffusivities are hardest to estimate, especially on large structures (solid red line, $k = 0.03125$). But only the 5x5x5-filter set keeps the systematic error in the permill range for all other cases. As an overall result we see, that only the 5x5x5-filters keep the relative estimation errors of velocities and diffusivities in the low permill range for a wide range of wave-numbers, diffusivities and velocities.

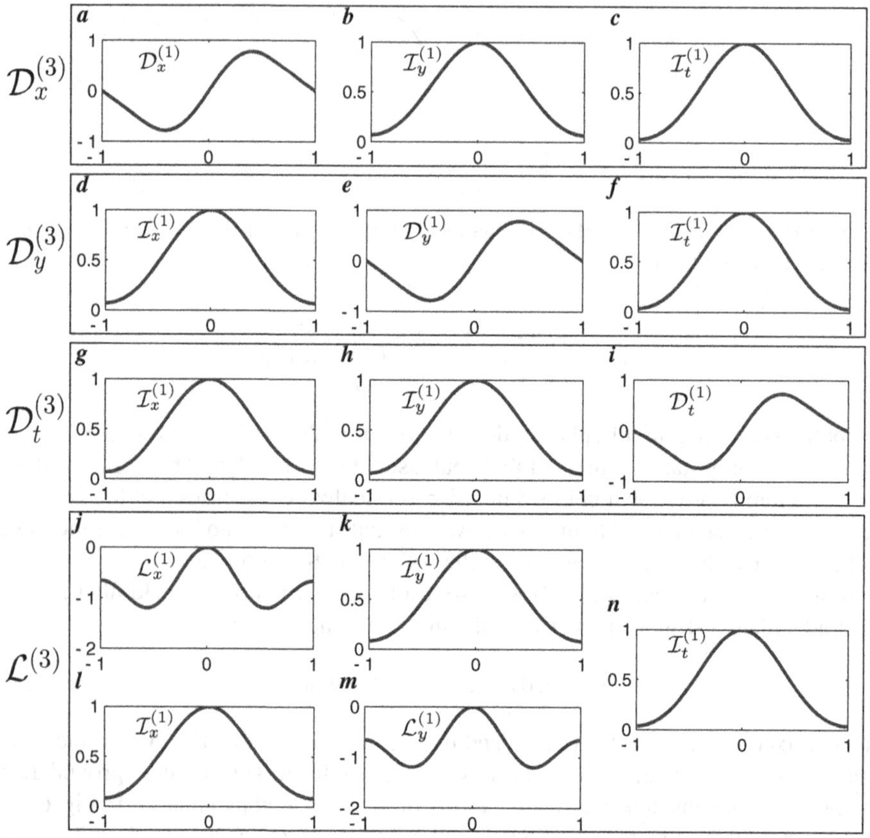

Fig. 5. Optical flow and diffusion: Transfer functions of the 1d filters composing the $5 \times 5 \times 5$ filter family stated in Tab. 5. **a – c** : $\mathcal{D}_x^{(3)}$, **d – f** : $\mathcal{D}_y^{(3)}$, **g – i**: $\mathcal{D}_t^{(3)}$, **j – n**: $\mathcal{L}^{(3)}$.

5 Summary and Conclusion

We presented filter families optimized for extended optical flow estimation. Filter optimization can be done in fourier domain and should use the whole first Brillouin zone. By analyzing the optical flow model equation, we observed that in the cases considered here only the direction of the data vector $\boldsymbol{d}$ is of importance. Consequently we derived an objective function, that optimizes the *normalized* vector of filter family transfer functions. For pure optical flow and optical flow combined with exponential brightness changes the resulting filters can be derived by a simpler optimization ([5, 22]), as long as the weight function $w(\tilde{\boldsymbol{k}})$ is separable. For other cases, e.g. the presented optical flow and diffusion or non-separable or anisotropic weight functions, the full Fourier space optimization scheme is more appropriate. All consistent first and second derivative filters found here are close to regularized versions of ideal derivators. The optimal filter families adapt all free coefficients in order to use the same 3d regularization in every filter

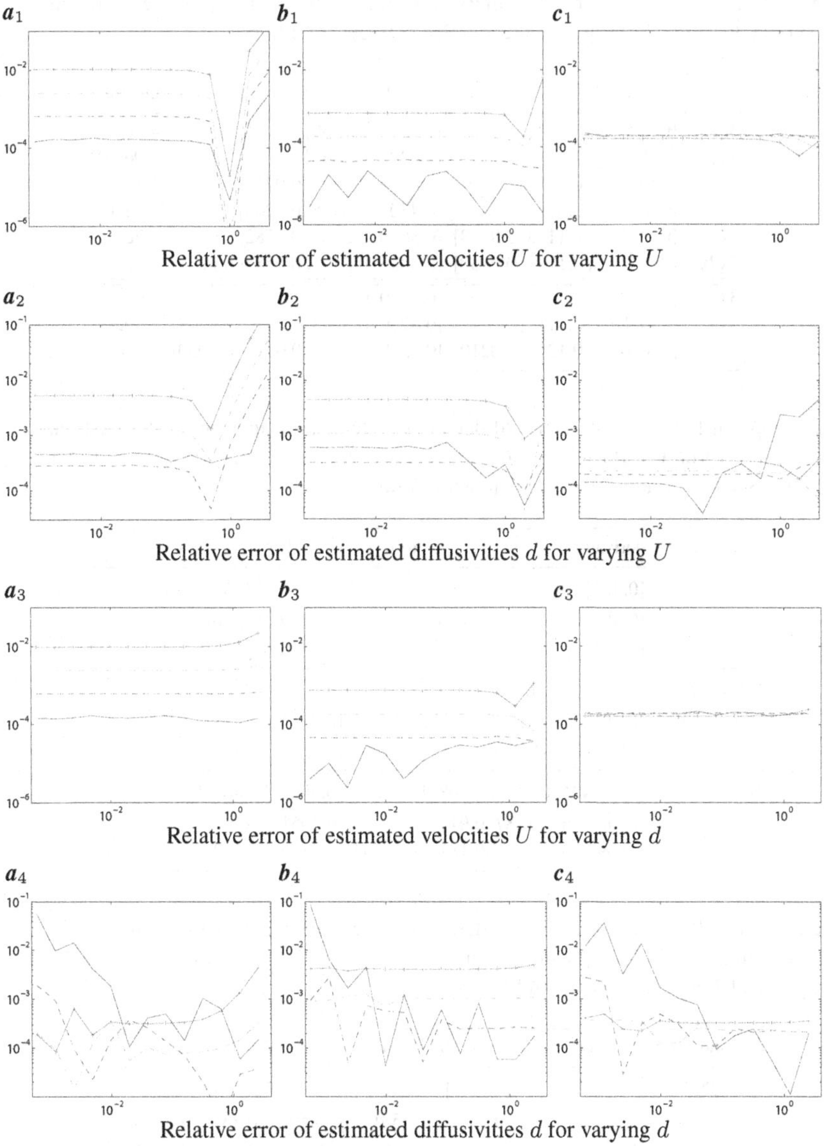

Fig. 6. Optical flow and diffusion. The solid, dashed, dashed-dotted and crossed curves correspond to wave-numbers k =0.03125, 0.0625, 0.125, 0.25, respectively, in a sinusoidal test sequence. **a** : central differences, **b** : 3x3x3-optimized filters, **c** : 5x5x5-optimized filters (see Tab. 5).

of the family. Then errors introduced by the regularization of the derivators cancel out. Non-surprisingly the optimized filters perform much better than non-optimized ones. The larger the filters get, the more accurate they are, but also the more they regularize. We showed that angular orientation errors are reduced up to 4 orders of magnitude

Table 3. Pure optical flow: Gradient filters. Top: weight function Eq. 34, left, bottom: weight function Eq. 34, right. See Eqs. 1 and 2 and Sec. 2 to get full filters.

size	derivator $\mathcal{D}^{(1)}$, h_0 to h_R	smoother $\mathcal{I}^{(1)}$, h_0 to h_R	error e
3x3	[0, 0.5]	[0.6341, 0.1830]	4.6e-9
3x3x3	[0, 0.5]	[0.6326, 0.1837]	2.9e-10
5x5	[0, 0.3339, 0.0831]	[0.4713, 0.2413, 0.0231]	3.5e-12
5x5x5	[0, 0.3327, 0.0836]	[0.4704, 0.2415, 0.0233]	2.3e-13
7x7	[0, 0.2239, 0.1188, 0.0128]	[0.3850, 0.2462, 0.0582, 0.0031]	1.2e-14
7x7x7	[0, 0.2232, 0.1190, 0.0130]	[0.3845, 0.2461, 0.0583, 0.0031]	1.7e-15
3x3	[0, 0.5]	[0.5450, 0.2275]	3.6e-7
5x5	[0, 0.2767, 0.1117]	[0.4260, 0.2493, 0.0377]	2.59e-7
7x7	[0, 0.1886, 0.1243, 0.0210]	[0.3568, 0.2440, 0.0716, 0.0060]	2.57e-7

Table 4. Optical flow and diffusion: 2d derivative filters and Laplacians optimized via Eq. 37. Weight function Eq. 34, left. Error values are $e_{3\times3} = 2.6e-7$, $e_{5\times5} = 5.4e-11$ and $e_{7\times7} = 9.4e-14$. See Eqs. 1 and 2 and Sec. 2 to get full filters.

size	filter	derivator $\mathcal{D}^{(1)}$ or $\mathcal{L}^{(1)}$, h_0 to h_R	smoother $\mathcal{I}^{(1)}$, h_0 to h_R
3x3	$\mathcal{D}_x^{(2)}$	[0, 0.5]	[0.6885, 0.1558]
	$\mathcal{D}_t^{(2)}$	[0, 0.5]	[0.7209, 0.1396]
	$\mathcal{L}^{(2)}$	[-2, 1]	[0.5546, 0.2227]
5x5	$\mathcal{D}_x^{(2)}$	[0, 0.3732, 0.0634]	[0.4714, 0.2414, 0.0229]
	$\mathcal{D}_t^{(2)}$	[0, 0.3341, 0.0829]	[0.5047, 0.2325, 0.0151]
	$\mathcal{L}^{(2)}$	[-0.7547, 0.1698, 0.2075]	[0.4717, 0.2410, 0.0232]
7x7	$\mathcal{D}_x^{(2)}$	[0, 0.2494, 0.1128, 0.0083]	[0.3856, 0.2462, 0.0579, 0.0031]
	$\mathcal{D}_t^{(2)}$	[0, 0.2246, 0.1187, 0.0127]	[0.4051, 0.2466, 0.0491, 0.0018]
	$\mathcal{L}^{(2)}$	[-0.3951, -0.0160, -0.1811, 0.0324]	[0.3856, 0.2462, 0.0579, 0.0031]

Table 5. Optical flow and diffusion: 3d derivative filters and Laplacians optimized via Eq. 37. Weight function Eq. 34, left. The error values are $e_{3\times3\times3} = 7.3e-8$ and $e_{5\times5\times5} = 4.1e-12$. See Eqs. 1 and 2 and Sec. 2 to get full filters.

nd-filter	1d-filter	$3\times3\times3$, h_0 and h_1	$5\times5\times5$, h_0 to h_2
$\mathcal{D}_x^{(3)}$	$\mathcal{D}_x^{(1)}$	[0, -0.5]	[0, -0.371, -0.0645]
	$\mathcal{I}_y^{(1)}$	[0.6893, 0.1553]	[0.5029, 0.2331, 0.0155]
	$\mathcal{I}_t^{(1)}$	[0.6683, 0.1658]	[0.4702, 0.2417, 0.0232]
$\mathcal{D}_y^{(3)}$	$\mathcal{I}_x^{(1)}$	[0.6893, 0.1553]	[0.5029, 0.2331, 0.0155]
	$\mathcal{D}_y^{(1)}$	[0, -0.5]	[0, -0.371, -0.0645]
	$\mathcal{I}_t^{(1)}$	[0.6683, 0.1658]	[0.4702, 0.2417, 0.0232]
$\mathcal{D}_t^{(3)}$	$\mathcal{I}_x^{(1)}$ and $\mathcal{I}_y^{(1)}$	[0.6902, 0.1549]	[0.5028, 0.2331, 0.0155]
	$\mathcal{D}_t^{(1)}$	[0, -0.5]	[0, -0.3327, -0.0836]
$\mathcal{L}^{(3)}$	$\mathcal{L}_x^{(1)}$ and $\mathcal{L}_y^{(1)}$	[-2, 1]	[-0.7446, 0.1631, 0.2092]
	$\mathcal{I}_x^{(1)}$ and $\mathcal{I}_y^{(1)}$	[0.4878, 0.2561]	[0.5066, 0.2300, 0.0167]
	$\mathcal{I}_t^{(1)}$	[0.5894, 0.2053]	[0.4705, 0.2413, 0.0235]

(Fig. 2), leading to severely improved accuracy in optical flow estimation (Tab. 1 and Tab. 2). Thus optimized filter families are a key ingredient for highly accurate motion and brightness estimations by extended optical flow.

References

1. H. Badino. A robust approach for ego-motion estimation using a mobile stereo platform. In this volume, 2004.
2. J.L. Barron, D.J. Fleet, and S.S. Beauchemin. Performance of optical flow techniques. *International Journal of Computer Vision*, 12(1):43–77, 1994.
3. A. Bruhn, J.Weickert, and C.Schnörr. Combining the advantages of local and global optic flow methods. *DAGM 2002, Springer*, 454–462, 2002.
4. M. Elad, P. Teo, and Y. Hel-Or. Optimal filters for gradient-based motion estimation. In *ICCV'99*, 1999.
5. H. Farid and E.P. Simoncelli. Optimally rotation-equivariant directional derivative kernels. In *7th Int'l Conf Computer Analysis of Images and Patterns*, Kiel, 1997.
6. C. Garbe. *Measuring Heat Exchange Processes at the Air-Water Interface from Thermographic Image Sequence Analysis*. PhD thesis, Univ. Heidelberg, 2001.
7. H. Haußecker and D. J. Fleet. Computing optical flow with physical models of brightness variation. *PAMI*, 23(6):661–673, June 2001.
8. H. Haußecker and H. Spies. Motion. In B. Jähne, H. Haußecker, and P. Geißler, editors, *Handbook of Computer Vision and Applications*. Academic Press, 1999.
9. B. Jähne. *Spatio-temporal image processing*, volume 751. Springer, Berlin, 1993.
10. B. Jähne. *Digital Image Processing*. Springer, 4 edition, 1997.
11. B. Jähne, H. Scharr, and S. Körkel. Principles of filter design. In *Handbook of Computer Vision and Applications*. Academic Press, 1999.
12. Behz. Kamgar-Parsi, Behr. Kamgar-Parsi, and A. Rosenfeld. Optimally isotropic laplacian operator. *IEEE Trans. Img. Proc.*, 8(10), Oct. 1999.
13. H. Knutsson and M. Andersson. Optimization of sequential filters. Technical Report LiTH-ISY-R-1797, CV Lab., Univ. Linköping, 1995.
14. H. Knutsson, M. Andersson, and J. Wiklund. Multiple space filter design. In *Proc. SSAB Symposium on Image Analysis*, Göteborg, Schweden, 1998.
15. H. Knutsson, M. Andersson, and J. Wiklund. Advanced filter design. In *Proc. SCIA*, 1999.
16. A. V. Oppenheim and R. W. Schafer. *Discrete-Time Signal Processing*. Prentice Hall, 1989.
17. J. G. Proakis and D. G. Manolakis. *Digital Signal Processing, Principles, Algorithms, and Applications*. Macmillan, 1992.
18. H. Scharr. *Optimal Operators in Digital Image Processing*. U. Heidelberg, 2000.
19. H. Scharr. Optimal filter families for extended optical flow. Report, Computational Nano-Vision Group, Santa Clara CA 95054, USA, 2002.
20. H. Scharr, S. Körkel, and B. Jähne. Numerische Isotropieoptimierung von FIR-Filtern mittels Querglättung. In *DAGM'97*, pages 367–374, 1997.
21. C. Schnörr and J. Weickert. Variational image motion computation: Theoretical framework, problems and perspectives. In *DAGM'2000*, pages 476–487, 2000.
22. E. Simoncelli. Design of multidimensional derivative kernels. In *First IEEE Int'l Conf on Image Processing*, volume I, pages 790–793, Austin, Texas, Nov. 1994.
23. A. v. d. Hengel, W. Chojnacki, and M. J. Brooks. Determining the translational speed of a camera from extended optical flow. In this volume, 2004.
24. F. Woelk and R. Koch. Robust monocular detection of independent motion by a moving observer. In this volume, 2004.

Wiener-Optimized Discrete Filters for Differential Motion Estimation

Kai Krajsek and Rudolf Mester

J. W. Goethe University, Frankfurt, Germany
{krajsek, mester}@iap.uni-frankfurt.de
http://www.cvg.physik.uni-frankfurt.de/

Abstract. Differential motion estimation is based on detecting brightness changes in local image structures. Filters approximating the local gradient are applied to the image sequence for this purpose. Whereas previous approaches focus on the reduction of the systematical approximation error of filters and motion models, the method presented in this paper is based on the statistical characteristics of the data. We developed a method for adapting separable linear shift invariant filters to image sequences or whole classes of image sequences. Therefore, it is possible to optimize the filters according to the systematical errors as well as to the statistical ones.

1 Introduction

Many methods have been developed to estimate the motion in image sequences. A class of methods delivering reliable estimates [1] are the differential based motion estimators containing a wide range of different algorithms [1, 2, 3]. All of them are based on approximation of derivatives on a discrete grid and it turns out that this approximation is an essential key point in order to achieve precise estimates [1, 4]. Many different methods have been developed in the last decade trying to reduce the systematical approximation error [5, 6, 7, 8, 9, 10]. The fact that all real world images are corrupted by noise has been neglected by these methods. In addition to these approaches we propose a prefilter adapted to the statistical characteristics of the signal and the noise contained in it. This approach was originally presented in [11] and further developed into a general framework in [12]. We tested this approach with a model autocovariance function and with real image sequences. Furthermore, we developed a method for adapting any separable linear shift invariant filter to a given image sequence or to a whole class of image sequences.

1.1 Differential Approaches to Motion Analysis

The general principle behind all differential approaches to motion estimation is that the conservation of some local image characteristics throughout its temporal evolution is reflected in terms of differential-geometric descriptors. In its simplest form the assumed conservation of brightness along the motion trajectory through space-time leads to the well-known brightness constancy constraint equation (BCCE), where $\frac{\partial s}{\partial r}$ denotes

B. Jähne et al. (Eds.): IWCM 2004, LNCS 3417, pp. 30–41, 2007.

the directional derivative in direction $\boldsymbol{r}$ and $\boldsymbol{g}$ is the gradient of the gray value signal $s(\boldsymbol{x})$:

$$\frac{\partial s}{\partial \boldsymbol{r}} = 0 \quad \Leftrightarrow \quad \boldsymbol{g}^T \boldsymbol{r} = 0. \tag{1}$$

Since $\boldsymbol{g}^T \boldsymbol{r}$ is proportional to the directional derivative of s in direction $\boldsymbol{r}$, the BCCE states that this derivative vanishes in the direction of motion. In order to cope with the *aperture problem* and to decrease the variance of the motion vector estimate, usually some kind of weighted averaging is performed in a neighborhood V, using a weight function $w(\boldsymbol{x})$ leading to the optimization problem

$$\int_V w \left|\boldsymbol{g}^T \boldsymbol{r}\right|^2 \, \mathrm{d}\boldsymbol{x} \longrightarrow \min$$

$$\Rightarrow \quad \boldsymbol{r}^T \mathbf{C}_g \boldsymbol{r} \longrightarrow \min \qquad \text{with} \quad \mathbf{C}_g := \int_V w \boldsymbol{g}\boldsymbol{g}^T \, \mathrm{d}\boldsymbol{x}$$

The solution vector $\hat{\boldsymbol{r}}$ is the eigenvector corresponding to the minimum eigenvalue of the *structure tensor* $\boldsymbol{C}_g$ (cf. [13, 14]). In order to calculate the structure tensor, the partial derivative of the signal has to be computed at least at discrete grid points. The implementation of the discrete derivative operators itself is a formidable problem, even though some early authors [2] apparently overlooked the crucial importance of this point.

1.2 Discrete Derivative Operators

Since derivatives are only defined for continuous signals, an interpolation of the discrete signal $s(\boldsymbol{x}_n), n \in \{1, 2, ..., N\}, \boldsymbol{x}_n \in \mathbb{R}^3$ to the assumed underlying continuous signal $s(\boldsymbol{x})$ has to be performed [5] where $c(\boldsymbol{x})$ denotes the continuous interpolation kernel

$$\left.\frac{\partial s(\boldsymbol{x})}{\partial \boldsymbol{r}}\right|_{\boldsymbol{x}_n} = \left.\frac{\partial}{\partial \boldsymbol{r}} \left(\sum_j s(\boldsymbol{x}_j) c(\boldsymbol{x} - \boldsymbol{x}_j) \right)\right|_{\boldsymbol{x}_n} = \left.\sum_j s(\boldsymbol{x}_j) \underbrace{\left(\frac{\partial}{\partial \boldsymbol{r}} c(\boldsymbol{x} - \boldsymbol{x}_j) \right)}_{d_{\boldsymbol{r}}(\boldsymbol{x}-\boldsymbol{x}_j)}\right|_{\boldsymbol{x}_n} . \tag{2}$$

The right hand side of equ. (2) is the convolution of the discrete signal $s(\boldsymbol{x}_n)$ with the sampled derivative of the interpolation kernel $d_{\boldsymbol{r}}(\boldsymbol{x}_n)$, the impulse response of the derivative filter

$$\frac{\partial s(\boldsymbol{x}_n)}{\partial \boldsymbol{r}} = s(\boldsymbol{x}_n) * d_{\boldsymbol{r}}(\boldsymbol{x}_n). \tag{3}$$

Since an ideal discrete derivative filter $d_{\boldsymbol{r}}(\boldsymbol{x}_n)$ has an infinite number of coefficients [15], an approximation $\hat{d}_{\boldsymbol{r}}(\boldsymbol{x}_n)$ has to be found. In an attempt to simultaneously perform the interpolation and some additional noise reduction by smoothing, often Gaussian functions are used as interpolation kernels $c(\boldsymbol{x})$ [14]. In the next section, some approaches for designing derivative kernels are presented, showing that Gaussian functions might not be the best choice for this purpose.

2 Previous Work on Filter Design

Methods for approximating derivative filters represent a well established field in digital signal processing of one-dimensional signals [15]. The derivative at a certain sample is approximated by differences of weighted neighboring sample values. The weights are chosen in such a way that the transfer function is as close as possible to the transfer function of the ideal sampled derivative. The application of these techniques for one dimensional signals to three dimensional space-time signals can be a source of highly inaccurate optical flow estimates [4]. The problem of filter design with respect to gradient based optical flow estimation was first tackled by SIMONCELLI [5]. He suggested to optimize the partial derivative filters and the interpolation kernel simultaneously. The approach of SCHARR [7] directly tries to minimizes the systematical error between the filter kernel and the ideal derivative filter mask. The approach of ELAD ET AL. [9] is based on the thesis that for optical flow estimation it is not really necessary to approximate the ideal derivative as closely as possible, but to design the filter kernel according to the final goal, i.e. for maximum accuracy of the optical flow estimates. The error between the ideal filter mask and the approximated one is the starting point for another optimization approach suggested by ROBINSON and MILANFAR [10]. The error results in a bias of the estimated direction of motion depending on the discrete derivative and interpolation kernel. The filters are optimized with respect to this bias. All recent filter design approaches try to reduce the systematical errors caused by approximating derivative filters and motion models. The fact that all real world images sequences are corrupted by noise has been neglected so far. Furthermore, the characteristics of the signal in the form of the power spectrum has only been used in order to increase the precision in certain frequency domains; however, it has not been used to adapt the filter directly to the signal. These two aspects have been considered in the framework developed in [11,12] which is the basis of the signal and noise adapted (SNA)-filter presented in this work.

3 Wiener-Filter Approach

The SNA-filter approach is motivated by the well-known fact that each signal which has a unique preference direction in space-time may be prefiltered by (almost) any transfer function $P(\boldsymbol{f})$[1] (except complete nullification of the signal) without changing the direction of the eigenvectors of $\boldsymbol{C}_g$ [11].

More general, we can exchange the directional derivative filter $d_{\boldsymbol{r}}(\boldsymbol{x}_n)$ in the BCCE by any other steerable filter $h_{\boldsymbol{r}}(\boldsymbol{x}_n)$ which only nullifies the signal when applied in the direction of motion. The shape of the frequency spectrum of an orientated signal is a plane $K_{\boldsymbol{r}}$ going through the origin of the Fourier space and its normal vector $\boldsymbol{n}$ points to the direction of motion $\boldsymbol{r}$ [14]. Thus, the transfer function $D_{\boldsymbol{r}}(\boldsymbol{f})$ has to be zero in that plane, but the shape of $D_{\boldsymbol{r}}(\boldsymbol{f})$ outside $K_{\boldsymbol{r}}$ can be chosen freely as long as it is not zero at all. If the impulse response $d_{\boldsymbol{r}}(\boldsymbol{x}_n)$ shall be real-valued, the corresponding transfer function $D_{\boldsymbol{r}}(\boldsymbol{f})$ has to be real and symmetric or imaginary and antisymmetric or a linear combination thereof. The additional degrees of freedom to design the shape outside $K_{\boldsymbol{r}}$

[1] Note that signals and operators in the Fourier domain are labeled with capital letters.

make it possible to consider both the spectral characteristics of the signal and the noise in the filter design. For deriving the optimal prefilter we model the observed image signal z in a spatio-temporal block of dimension $N \times N \times N$ by

$$z(i,j,k) = s(i,j,k) + v(i,j,k) \ .$$

Here, $v(i,j,k)$ denotes the observation (measurement) noise. For the subsequent steps, it is convenient to arrange the elements of the blocks s, v, and z in vectors $\boldsymbol{s}, \boldsymbol{v}$, and $\boldsymbol{z}$. In the following subsection, the framework developed in [11, 12] for designing such a *Wiener prefilter* is presented.

3.1 The Canonical Basis

The first step is to change into the canonical basis, the coordinate frame of vectors $\boldsymbol{y}$ which are obtained from vectors $\boldsymbol{s}$ by a rotation $\boldsymbol{A}$ according to

$$\boldsymbol{y} = \boldsymbol{A}\boldsymbol{s}, \quad |\boldsymbol{y}| = |\boldsymbol{s}|$$

such that the covariance matrix $\boldsymbol{C}_y \equiv \mathsf{Cov}[\boldsymbol{y}]$ is diagonal. It is well known that this rotation is performed by the *principal component analysis (PCA)* or *Karhunen-Loève transform (KLT)*. In this new coordinate frame, we have

$$\boldsymbol{C}_y \overset{def}{=} \mathsf{Cov}[\boldsymbol{y}] = \mathsf{diag}\left\{\sigma_{yi}^2\right\} \tag{4}$$

The row vectors of the orthonormal (i.e. rotation) matrix $\boldsymbol{A}$ are given by the unit norm eigenvectors of the covariance matrix $\boldsymbol{C}_s \equiv \mathsf{Cov}[\boldsymbol{s}]$, i.e. $\boldsymbol{A}$ is the solution to the eigensystem problem

$$\boldsymbol{A}\mathsf{Cov}[\boldsymbol{s}]\,\boldsymbol{A}^T = \mathsf{diag}\left\{\sigma_i^2\right\} \quad | \ \boldsymbol{A}\boldsymbol{A}^T = \boldsymbol{I}$$

In the new coordinate frame, we have

$$\text{signal vector (unobservable):} \quad \boldsymbol{y} = \boldsymbol{A}\boldsymbol{s} \tag{5}$$

$$\text{noise vector (unobservable):} \quad \boldsymbol{u} = \boldsymbol{A}\boldsymbol{v} \tag{6}$$

$$\text{observed vector:} \quad \boldsymbol{w} = \boldsymbol{y} + \boldsymbol{u} = \boldsymbol{A}\boldsymbol{z} \tag{7}$$

Since the original noise covariance matrix was a scaled unit matrix, and since $\mathbf{A}$ is a rotation, the covariance matrix of the noise vector $\boldsymbol{u}$ contained in $\boldsymbol{w}$ remains simple:

$$\boldsymbol{C}_u \overset{def}{=} \mathsf{Cov}[\boldsymbol{u}] = \sigma_v^2 \boldsymbol{I} \tag{8}$$

Estimating the value of $\boldsymbol{y}$ means now to minimize the loss function

$$J(\hat{\boldsymbol{y}}) = (\hat{\boldsymbol{y}} - \mathsf{E}[\boldsymbol{y}])^T \mathbf{C}_y^{-1} (\hat{\boldsymbol{y}} - \mathsf{E}[\boldsymbol{y}]) + (\hat{\boldsymbol{y}} - \boldsymbol{w})^T \mathbf{C}_u^{-1} (\hat{\boldsymbol{y}} - \boldsymbol{w})$$

The *minimum mean squared error (MMSE)* estimate of $\boldsymbol{y}$ is then given by

$$\hat{\boldsymbol{y}} = \left(\boldsymbol{C}_y^{-1} + \boldsymbol{C}_u^{-1}\right)^{-1} \left(\boldsymbol{C}_y^{-1}\mathsf{E}[\boldsymbol{y}] + \boldsymbol{C}_u^{-1}\boldsymbol{w}\right) \tag{9}$$

It is relatively simple to compute (and to interpret!) this estimate in the canonical coordinate frame. For the white noise case, also denoted as *independent identically distributed (i.i.d.)* noise, the covariance matrix $\boldsymbol{C}_v$ of the noise term remains proportional to a unity matrix under any arbitrary rotation of the coordinate frame. With the specific covariance matrices which we have here (see equ. (4) and equ. (8)), we obtain:

$$\hat{\boldsymbol{y}} = \mathsf{diag}\left\{\frac{\sigma_{yi}^2}{\sigma_v^2 + \sigma_{yi}^2}\right\} \boldsymbol{w} \tag{10}$$

Since σ_{yi}^2 is the power of the signal and σ_v^2 the power of the noise in the regarded 'spectral component', this result is also according to our intuitive expectation. Using equ. (7) together with equ. (10) we obtain:

$$\hat{\boldsymbol{s}} = \boldsymbol{A}^{-1}\hat{\boldsymbol{y}} = \boldsymbol{A}^{-1}\mathsf{diag}\left\{\frac{\sigma_{yi}^2}{\sigma_v^2 + \sigma_{yi}^2}\right\} \boldsymbol{w} = \boldsymbol{A}^T\mathsf{diag}\left\{\frac{\sigma_{yi}^2}{\sigma_v^2 + \sigma_{yi}^2}\right\} \boldsymbol{A}\boldsymbol{z} \tag{11}$$

This means that for obtaining a MMSE estimate of the signal, the observed signal vector $\boldsymbol{z}$ has to be transformed (rotated) into the canonical coordinate frame, the canonical coordinates have to be attenuated according to the fraction $\sigma_{yi}^2/(\sigma_v^2 + \sigma_{yi}^2)$ and finally rotated back into the original coordinate frame.

3.2 The Optimized Filter

In the preceding section we have shown how to obtain a MMSE estimate of the signal. Since we are dealing with linear shift invariant operators we can optimize our filter in one step. Starting point for the filter design is a filter already optimized for the noise free case denoted as $\boldsymbol{h}$:

$$\boldsymbol{h}^T\hat{\boldsymbol{s}} = \boldsymbol{h}^T \underbrace{\boldsymbol{A}^T\mathsf{diag}\left\{\frac{\sigma_{yi}^2}{\sigma_v^2 + \sigma_{yi}^2}\right\} \boldsymbol{A}}_{\boldsymbol{R}}\, \boldsymbol{z} = (\boldsymbol{R}\boldsymbol{h})^T \boldsymbol{z} \tag{12}$$

In the last equation we used the symmetry property of the matrix $\boldsymbol{R}$. In [12] it has been proven that $\boldsymbol{R}\boldsymbol{h}$ is the best approximation of $\boldsymbol{h}$ for the given signal $\boldsymbol{z}$. In the following sections we will denote filters optimized according to equation (12) as signal and noise adaptive filters or SNA-filters.

4 Covariance Structure

We developed a model auto-covariance function in order to investigate the influence of the covariance on the adapted filter masks. Let us assume that the image signals we are dealing with are generated by shifting a given two dimensional image with constant speed (v_x, v_y) in an certain direction. Obviously, the resulting three-dimensional auto-covariance function $\varphi_{ss}(x, y, t)$ is then

$$\varphi_{ss}(x, y, t) = \tilde{\varphi}_{ss}(x - v_x t,\;\; y - v_y t).$$

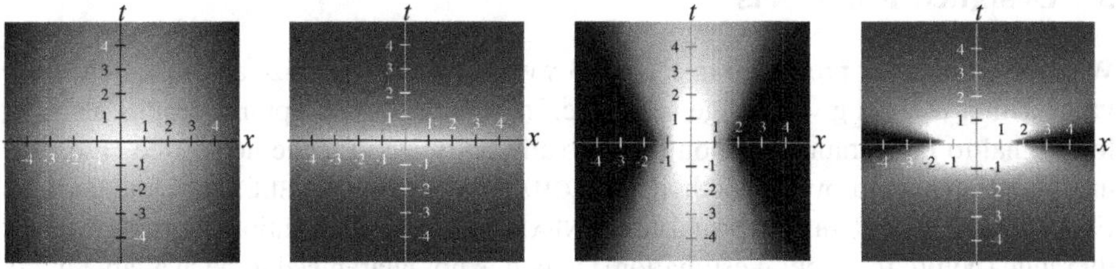

(a) (b) (c) (d)

Fig. 4.1. Examples of spatio-temporal autocovariance functions. (a) High spatial correlation, small motion vectors ($\Rightarrow$ high temporal correlation); (b) high spatial correlation, large motion vectors ($\Rightarrow$ small temporal correlation); (c) small spatial correlation, small motion vectors ($\Rightarrow$ high temporal correlation); (d) small spatial correlation, large motion vectors ($\Rightarrow$ small temporal correlation).

If the motion vector (v_x, v_y) itself is generated by a random process, there is a distribution for the new position $(x(t), y(t))$ at time instant t. The overall 3D auto-covariance results from a convolution of the *purely spatial* auto-covariance function $\tilde{\varphi}_{ss}(x, y)$ with the *position distribution function* $\zeta(x, y, t)$. In order to be able to describe the structure of the resulting spatio-temporal auto-covariance process analytically, we assume here that both $\tilde{\varphi}_{ss}(x, y)$ as well as $\zeta(x, y, t)$ are sufficiently well described by Gaussian functions.

$$\tilde{\varphi}_{ss}(x, y) = \frac{1}{2\pi\sigma_r^2} \exp\left(-\frac{x^2 + y^2}{2\sigma_r^2}\right)$$

$$\zeta(x, y, t) = \frac{1}{2\pi\eta^2 t} \exp\left(-\frac{x^2 + y^2}{2\eta^2 t}\right) \delta(t)$$

Convolving $\varphi_{ss}(x, y)$ with $\zeta(x, y, t)$ leads to

$$\varphi_{ss}(x, y, t) = \frac{1}{2\pi(\sigma_r^2 + \eta^2 t)} \exp\left(-\frac{x^2 + y^2}{2(\sigma_r^2 + \eta^2 t)}\right) \tag{13}$$

This formula looks complicated, but it can be described as follows:

- The 3D auto-covariance function has a global maximum at $(x, y, t) = (0, 0, 0)$;
- in the plane $t = 0$ we find the original purely spatial auto-covariance function $\varphi_{ss}(x, y)$;
- cross-sections of $\varphi_{ss}(x, y, t)$ in constant-time planes $\{x, y = \text{arbitrary}, t = \text{const}\}$ show an increasing spread in the x, y directions with increasing absolute value of t;

Figure 4 illustrates the effects of varying σ_r (spatial width of the auto-covariance function for $t = 0$) and η (temporal 'diffusion rate', proportional to the length of the expected motion vector per time step).

5 Designed Filter Sets

With the framework presented in section 3 we are able to optimize any linear shift invariant filter $\boldsymbol{h}$ for a given image sequence. In order to obtain optimal results also for low signal to noise ratios, $\boldsymbol{h}$ should be already optimized for the noise free case. We use filters optimized by the methods of SCHARR and SIMONCELLI. The methods of ELAD ET AL. and ROBINSON and MILANFAR use prior information about the velocity range (before the motion estimation!) which is not guaranteed to be available in all applications. If this information is available it should be used to adapt the filter to it. However, our approach is already adapted to the motion range reflected in the covariance function of the image sequence which can easily be estimated. In the following, we demonstrate the adaptive behavior of our filters to different covariance structures. The images are assumed to be corrupted with i.i.d noise. The covariance matrices for each filter mask are computed from the sampled model auto-covariance function or the auto-covariance function measured from the whole space time volume of the corresponding image sequence. The following figures show slices of derivative operators. For the signal to noise ratio S/N, we assume 10 dB as well as no additional noise. In order to demonstrate the significant influence of the covariance structure on the SNA-filter we start with the simple 1d 3-tap filter $(\frac{1}{2}, 0, -\frac{1}{2})$.

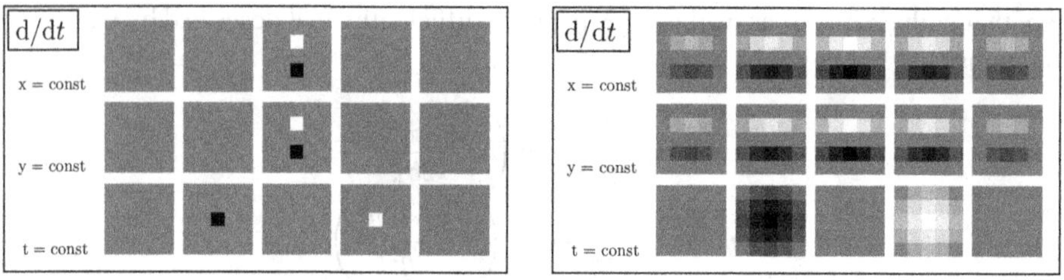

Fig. 5.1. 3-tap derivative SNA-filter based on $(\frac{1}{2}, 0, -\frac{1}{2})$ in t direction for small correlation in space and time (left) and for small correlation in time and large correlation in space (right). In each frame slices through filter masks are shown for x=constant (upper row), y=constant (middle row) and t=constant (lower row).

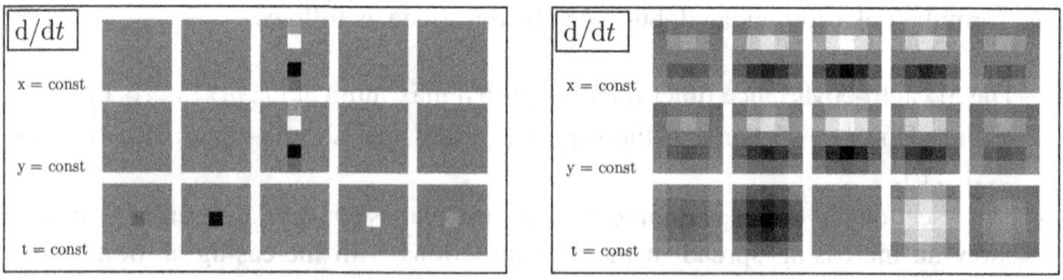

Fig. 5.2. 3-tap derivative SNA-filter based on $(\frac{1}{2}, 0, -\frac{1}{2})$ in t direction for large correlation in time and small correlation in space (left) and for large correlation in space and time (right). In each frame slices through filter masks are shown for x=constant (upper row), y=constant (middle row) and t=constant (lower row).

The filter (fig. 5.1, left) designed for small correlations in spatial as well as in temporal direction is not influenced by the optimization procedure. For higher correlation in spatial (fig. 5.1, right) or temporal (fig. 5.2, left) direction the filter is extended in the corresponding direction. The size of the filter is adaptively adjusted to the corresponding characteristics of the signal expressed by the covariance function. The SNA filter is not only adapted to the temporal, like the filter of ELAD's approach, but also towards the spatial characteristics of the signal.

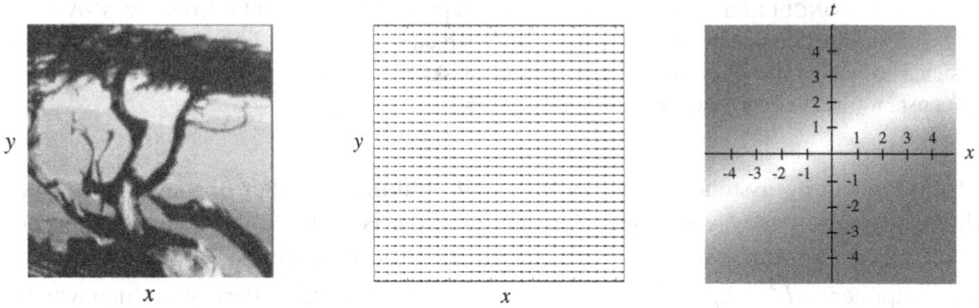

Fig. 5.3. Translating tree: Left: One frame of the image sequence. Middle: Motion field. Right: Slide through the corresponding auto-covariance function showing a clear structure in direction of motion $\boldsymbol{r}$.

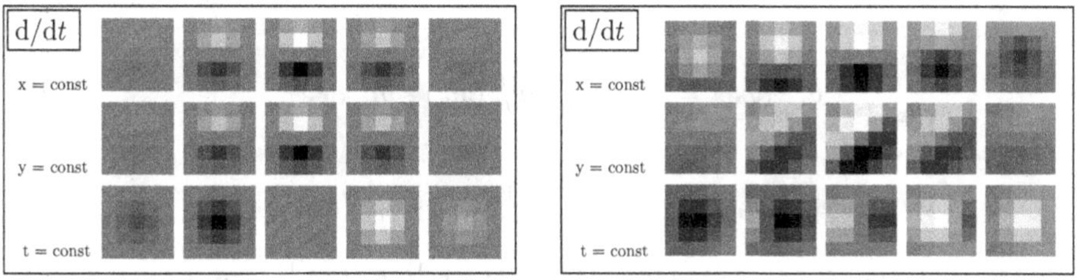

Fig. 5.4. SIMONCELLI derivative filter (left) and SIMONCELLI derivative SNA-filter (right) in t direction according to the covariance structure of the translating tree sequence and a signal to noise ratio S/N of 10 dB. The filter masks are shown for t=constant (upper row), y=constant (middle row) and t=constant (lower row).

Now we will have a look on the influence of measured auto-covariance function on SNA-filters. In fig. 5.4 the original SIMONCELLI filter (left) and the SNA SIMONCELLI filter (right) optimized for the translating tree sequence (fig. 5.3, left) for S/N=10 dB, are depicted. The structure of the auto-covariance function (shown in fig. 5.3, right) with the maximum being aligned with the direction of motion, is reflected in the filter masks. The partial derivative operator does not point along the corresponding principal axes any more but are adjusted towards the mean direction of motion of the space time volume. In fact this arises from the fact that the process which generates the signal and which we assume to be isotropic has not been approbate sampled. Nonetheless, we could segment the image sequence in regions where the direction

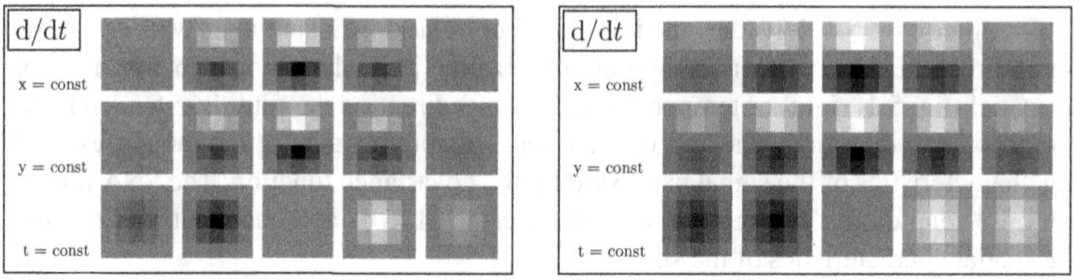

Fig. 5.5. SIMONCELLI derivative filter (left) and separable SIMONCELLI derivative SNA-filter (right) in t direction according to the covariance structure of the translating tree sequence and a signal to noise ratio S/N of 10dB. The filter masks are shown for x=constant (upper row), y=constant (middle row) and t=constant (lower row).

of motion can be assumed to be constant and optimize the filter to these regions individually. Another way to cope with this problem is to force the adapted filters to point along the principal axis which can be achieved by individually optimizing the 1d components $d_i^{(1)}(\boldsymbol{x}_n), b_i^{(1)}(\boldsymbol{x}_n)\ i \in \{x, y, t\}$ of a separable derivative filter where $d_i^{(1)}, i \in \{x, y, t\}$ denotes the 1d derivative kernels and $b_i^{(1)}$ the 1d smoothing kernels. The 3d filter masks are then constructed by smoothing the derivative kernel in all cross directions

$$d_x^{(3)}(\boldsymbol{x}_n) = d_x^{(1)}(\boldsymbol{x}_n) * b_y^{(1)}(\boldsymbol{x}_n) * b_t^{(1)}(\boldsymbol{x}_n) \tag{14}$$

$$d_y^{(3)}(\boldsymbol{x}_n) = b_x^{(1)}(\boldsymbol{x}_n) * d_y^{(1)}(\boldsymbol{x}_n) * b_t^{(1)}(\boldsymbol{x}_n) \tag{15}$$

$$d_t^{(3)}(\boldsymbol{x}_n) = b_x^{(1)}(\boldsymbol{x}_n) * b_y^{(1)}(\boldsymbol{x}_n) * d_t^{(1)}(\boldsymbol{x}_n). \tag{16}$$

Let us consider the derivative in t direction and let $\boldsymbol{b}_x^{(1)}, \boldsymbol{b}_y^{(1)}, \boldsymbol{d}_t^{(1)}$ be vectors representing the derivative and smoothing masks, respectively. Instead of optimizing the filter $\boldsymbol{d}_t^{(3)}$, representing a $N \times N \times N$ partial derivative filter mask in t direction, we optimize the 1d derivative masks $\boldsymbol{d}_t^{(1)}$ along the t axes and the smoothing kernels $\boldsymbol{b}_x^{(1)}, \boldsymbol{b}_y^{(1)}$ applied in all cross directions. The response of $\boldsymbol{d}_t^{(1)}$ to the signal $\boldsymbol{z} = \boldsymbol{s} + \boldsymbol{v}$

$$\boldsymbol{d}_t^{(1)T} \boldsymbol{z} = \boldsymbol{d}_t^{(1)T} \boldsymbol{s} + \boldsymbol{d}_t^{(1)T} \boldsymbol{v} \tag{17}$$

is again the sum of a signal term $\tilde{\boldsymbol{s}} = \boldsymbol{d}_t^{(1)T} \boldsymbol{s}$ and a noise term $\tilde{\boldsymbol{v}} = \boldsymbol{d}_t^{(1)T} \boldsymbol{v}$ such that we can again adapt the next filter with respect to the covariance structure of the filtered signal. Since the application of the 1d filter in direction t induces only correlation in t direction the noise term for the cross directions could be assumed again as i.i.d. noise. The results of this procedure delivers SNA-filters without pointing in the average direction of motion as shown in fig. 5.5 for the SIMONCELLI derivative filter in t direction. The separable SNA-filter behaves equivalently to the non-separable ones for different correlation models as shown in fig. 5.6 and fig. 5.7.

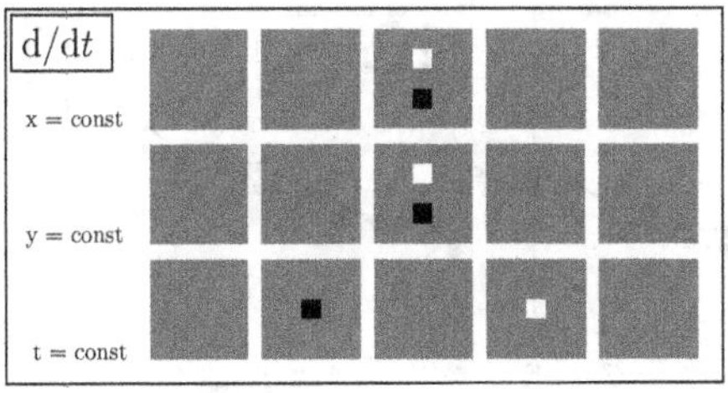

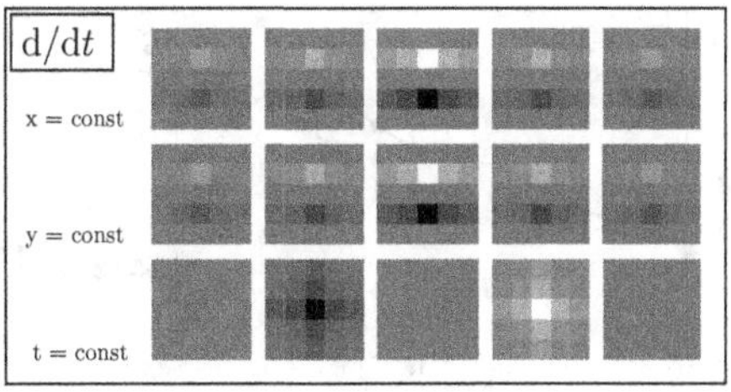

Fig. 5.6. 3-tap derivative separable SNA-filter based on $(\frac{1}{2}, 0, -\frac{1}{2})$ in t direction for small correlation in space and time (left) and for small correlation in time and large correlation in space (right). In each frame the filter masks are shown for x=constant (upper row), y=constant (middle row) and t=constant (lower row).

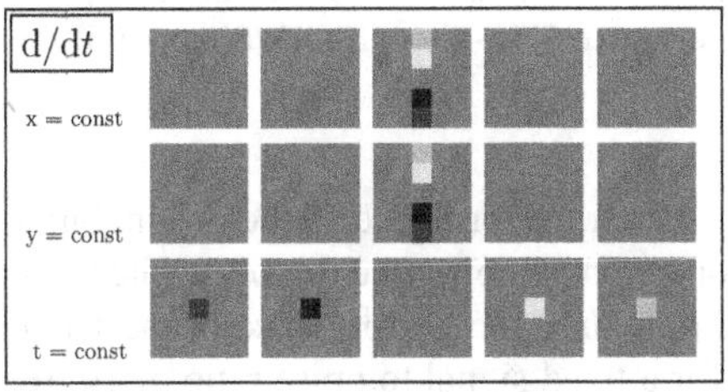

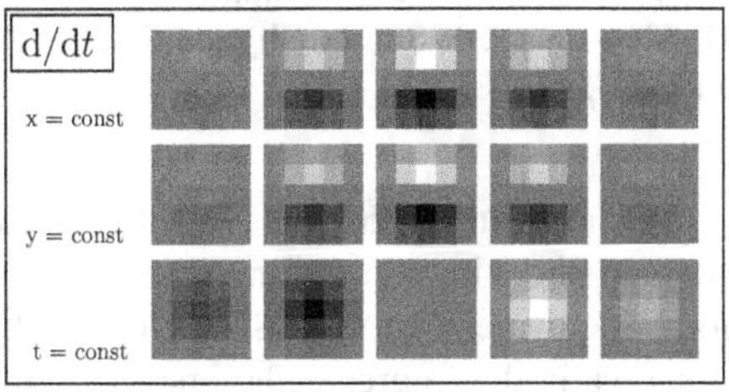

Fig. 5.7. 3-tap derivative separable SNA-filter based on $(\frac{1}{2}, 0, -\frac{1}{2})$ in t direction for large correlation in time and small correlation in space (left) and for large correlation in time and space (right). In each frame the filter masks are shown for x=constant (upper row), y=constant (middle row) and t=constant (lower row).

6 Experimental Results

In this section, we present examples showing the performance of our optimization method. For the test we use two image sequences, together with the true optical flow denoted as Yosemite (without clouds) and translating tree[2]. The optical flow is estimated with the tensor based method described in section 1.1. For all experiments an average volume of size $20 \times 20 \times 5$ and filters of size $5 \times 5 \times 5$ are applied. For the weighting function $w(\boldsymbol{x})$ we choose a Gaussian function with standard deviation of 6 in spatial and 2 in temporal direction. For performance evaluation the average angular error (AAE) [1] is computed. In order to achieve a fair comparison between the different filters but also between different signals to noise ratios S/N we computed all AAEs for the same density determined by applying the *total coherence measure* and the *spatial coherence measure* [14]. We optimized the SCHARR and the SIMONCELLI filter for every individual signal to noise ratio S/N in a range from 20 dB to 10 dB (for i. i. d. noise). To each image sequence we applied the original SIMONCELLI or SCHARR filter and the SNA-filter for the actual signal to noise ratio and the SNA-filter for 10dB.

[2] The translating tree sequence has been taken from Barron's web-site and the Yosemite sequence from *http://www.cs.brown.edu/people/black/images.html*

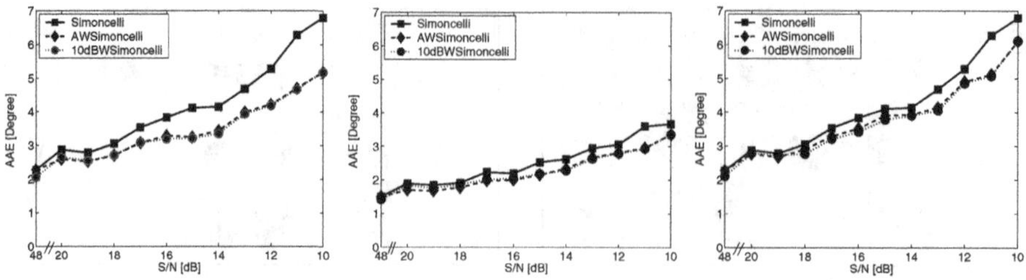

Fig. 6.1. Left and middle: average angular error (AAE) computed for the Yosemite sequence for a density of (left and right: 90% and middle: 60%) with the SNA-filter for different signal to noise ratios (10dB-20dB), 48dB denotes the images sequence without additional noise, only quantization noise. Applied filters: Original SIMONCELLI filter, SIMONCELLI SNA-filter (AWSimoncelli) and SIMONCELLI SNA-filter (10dBWSimoncelli) for a fixed $S/N = 10$dB; right: same sequence as in the left and middle figure but original SIMONCELLI filter, SIMONCELLI separable SNA-filter (AWSimoncelli) and SIMONCELLI separable SNA-filter (10dBWSimoncelli) for a fixed $S/N = 10$dB.

As shown in fig. 6.1 the SNA-filters yield a better performance as the original non adapted filters in case the image sequence is corrupted by noise (the SCHARR filter performs equivalently to the SIMONCELLI filter, thus only the performance of the latter is shown in the figures). The optimized filter for a fixed signal to noise ratio of 10 dB performs equivalently as the SNA-filter optimized for the actual S/N ratio. For lower densities (60%) as shown in (fig. 6.1, middle) the gain of performance decreases. The confidence measures firstly sort out those regions for which the estimation is, even in the case of no additional noise (48dB), hard to estimate. These are regions where the aperture problem persists (sorted out by the spatial coherence measure) despite the averaging and in those regions with nearly no structure (sorted out by the total coherence measure). The separable SNA-filter (fig. 6.1, right) increases also the performance, but less then the non-separable one.

7 Summary and Conclusion

We presented filters (SNA-filters) optimized according to the characteristics of signal and noise. The SNA-filter design is completely automatic without the need of any assumption on the flow field characteristics as opposed to previous approaches [9, 10]. All information necessary for the filter design can be obtained from measurable data. Furthermore, our filter adapts to the characteristics in spatial and temporal direction based on the covariance structure of the image sequence. We showed considerable improvement when applying these filters in combination with the local total least square estimator (structure tensor approach). Designing the filter according to the covariance of the whole image can lead to filter aligned to the average direction of motion. Nonetheless, the filter could be individually adapted to regions where constant motion can be assumed. To design filters for whole image sequences or even whole classes of filters we developed a separable SNA derivative filter which is adapted along the principal axis and thus by construction points only along the principle axis. Also this type of filters increases the precision of the motion estimation.

Acknowledgement. This work was funded by DFG SPP 1114.

References

1. Barron, J.L., Fleet, D.J., Beauchemin, S.S.: Performance of optical flow techniques. Int. Journal of Computer Vision **12** (1994) 43–77
2. Horn, B., Schunck, B.: Determining optical flow. Artificial Intelligence **17** (1981) 185–204
3. Lucas, B., Kanade, T.: An iterative image registration technique with an application to stereo vision. In: Proc. Seventh International Joint Conference on Artificial Intelligence, Vancouver, Canada (August 1981) 674–679
4. Simoncelli, E.P.: Distributed Analysis and Representation of Visual Motion. PhD thesis, Massachusetts Institut of Technology, USA (1993)
5. Simoncelli, E.P.: Design of multi-dimensional derivative filters. In: Intern. Conf. on Image Processing, Austin TX (1994)
6. Knutsson, H., Andersson, M.: Optimization of sequential filters. Technical Report LiTH-ISY-R-1797, Computer Vision Laboratory, Linköping University, S-581 83 Linköping, Sweden (1995)
7. Scharr, H., Körkel, S., Jähne, B.: Numerische Isotropieoptimierung von FIR-Filtern mittels Querglättung. In: Mustererkennung 1997 (Proc. DAGM 1997), Springer Verlag (1997)
8. Knutsson, H., Andersson, M.: Multiple space filter design. In: Proc. SSAB Swedish Symposium on Image Analysis, Göteborg, Sweden (1998)
9. Elad, M., Teo, P., Hel-Or, Y.: Optimal filters for gradient-based motion estimation. In: Proc. Intern. Conf. on Computer Vision (ICCV'99). (1999)
10. Robinson, D., Milanfar, P.: Fundamental performance limits in image registration. IEEE Transactions on Image Processing **13** (2004)
11. Mester, R.: A new view at differential and tensor-based motion estimation schemes. In Michaelis, B., ed.: Pattern Recognition 2003. Lecture Notes in Computer Science, Magdeburg, Germany, Springer Verlag (2003)
12. Mühlich, M., Mester, R.: A statistical unification of image interpolation, error concealment, and source-adapted filter design. In: Proc. Sixth IEEE Southwest Symposium on Image Analysis and Interpretation, Lake Tahoe, NV/U.S.A. (2004)
13. Bigün, J., Granlund, G.H.: Optimal orientation detection of linear symmetry. In: First International Conference on Computer Vision, ICCV, Washington, DC., IEEE Computer Society Press (1987) 433–438
14. Haussecker, H., Spies, H.: Motion. In Handbook of Computer Vision and Applications (1999) 310–396
15. Jähne, B., Scharr, H., Körkel, S.: Principles of filter design. In Handbook of Computer Vision and Applications (1999) 125–153

Boundary Characterization Within the Wedge-Channel Representation

Ullrich Köthe

Cognitive Systems Group, University of Hamburg
koethe@informatik.uni-hamburg.de

Abstract. Junctions play an important role in motion analysis. Approaches based on the structure tensor have become the standard for junction detection. However, the structure tensor is not able to classify junctions into different types (L, T, Y, X etc.). We propose to solve this problem by the wedge channel representation. It is based on the same computational steps as used for the (anisotropic) structure tensor, but stores results into channel vectors rather than tensors. Due to one-sided channel smoothing, these channel vectors not only represent edge orientation (as existing channel approaches do) but edge direction. Thus junctions cannot only be detected, but also fully characterized.

1 Introduction

Feature-based algorithms constitute a large method class for various aspects of image analysis, including object recognition, motion estimation, stereo matching and shape from motion/stereo. The correct detection and characterization of image features such as edges and corners is crucial for these methods to produce accurate results or to succeed at all. In this paper we are interested in generic feature detection methods, i.e. methods that are not bound to a specific application and do not require prior (global) knowledge about the expected objects as provided by geometric shape models, eigenfaces and so on. Under the generic paradigm, features are detected in a bottom-up fashion, and the amount of information extracted from the original image data – without the help of the high-level system – should be maximized. Note that we do not question the usefulness of top-down image analysis. Our goal is rather the independent optimization of bottom-up processing so that the high-level system can start from intermediate data of the best possible quality.

In the context of motion analysis, corners and junctions are of utmost importance because they often arise from 3D features (object corners) that are stable under perspective projection and motion, or indicate important projection phenomena such as occlusion. Accurate junction characterization improves the robustness of feature tracking and correspondence estimation and aids in the correct interpretation of the measured flow fields. Over the years, the ability of local bottom-up operators to extract high-quality junction information has steadily improved. One early approach is to apply an edge operator to the image and then detect corners and junctions as edge crossings in the resulting symbolic edge representation. However, this method is problematic because edge models break down near junctions, and the propagation of these errors leads to inaccurate, missed or hallucinated junctions which have to be repaired by high-level assumptions or heuristics.

B. Jähne et al. (Eds.): IWCM 2004, LNCS 3417, pp. 42–53, 2007.

The introduction of the structure tensor [1, 5, 6] extended the boundary model to include 2-dimensional features explicitly by integrating gradient information over a neighborhood. Recently, it was observed that the accuracy of the structure tensor can be improved by moving from linear to anisotropic integration [9], e.g. with an hourglass filter [7]: When the filter only smoothes along edges, nearby structures do not interfere with each other except at junctions where it is desired. Thus, the anisotropic structure tensor has effectively a higher resolution. However, it does not solve another problem: second order 2×2 tensors can only represent a single independent orientation (the other one is always at $90°$ of the first). Information at which angles the edges meet at a junction is therefore unavailable. One can distinguish intrinsically 1- and 2-dimensional locations, but classification of different junction types is impossible.

Independently of these "mainstream" methods a number of dedicated junction characterization algorithms have been proposed, see [8, 12] for surveys. They build upon one-sided filters that determine whether there is an edge in a particular sector of the neighborhood of the given point. The complete junction characteristic can than be interpolated from the responses of a family of filters covering the entire neighborhood. However, these methods are problematic on two reasons: First, they use complicated filters that cannot be applied at fine scales due to aliasing in the sampled filter coefficients. Systematic investigations of their robustness don't seem to exist. Second, a difficult integration problem is posed when unrelated approaches are used for edge detection and junction characterization: The results don't fit exactly together, and inconsistencies in the integrated boundary representation are unavoidable.

In this paper, we propose a junction characterization method that directly generalizes the established structure tensor framework by means of the channel representation. The channel representation [2, 4, 10] is a carefully designed method for the discretization of continuous quantities (orientation in our case) with the goal that important properties of the original data distribution (e.g. the mean and mode) can be recovered accurately from the channel weights. We keep the idea of anisotropic integration of the gradient map, but instead of collecting the integrated data into a tensor, we store them in orientation channels. Depending on the number of channels, we can determine several independent orientations as long as they do not fall into a single or adjacent channels. Unlike previous work with orientation channels, we use one sided channel smoothing filters, so that we can keep track from which *direction* an edge enters the junction. A similar idea with slightly different filters was also proposed in [11]. This new *wedge channel representation* extends existing work by allowing us to precisely determine the degree of a junction, and distinguish various junction types even if they have the same degree (e.g. T and Y-junctions for degree 3).

2 Boundary Characterization with the Structure Tensor

Given an image $f(x, y)$, the structure tensor is based on the gradient of f, which is usually calculated by means of Gaussian derivative filters:

$$f_x = g_{x,\sigma} \star f, \qquad f_y = g_{y,\sigma} \star f \tag{1}$$

Fig. 1. From left to right: Original image; gradient squared magnitude; trace of structure tensor; small eigenvalue of structure tensor; eigenvector orientations

where $\star$ denotes convolution, and $g_{x,\sigma}, g_{y,\sigma}$ are the derivatives in x- and y-direction of a Gaussian with standard deviation σ:

$$g_\sigma(x,y) = \frac{1}{2\pi\sigma^2} e^{-\frac{x^2+y^2}{2\sigma^2}} \tag{2}$$

The gradient tensor $\mathbf{Q}$ is obtained by calculating, at each point of the image, the Cartesian product of the gradient vector $(f_x, f_y)^T$ with itself.

$$\mathbf{Q} = \begin{pmatrix} f_x^2 & f_x f_y \\ f_x f_y & f_y^2 \end{pmatrix} \tag{3}$$

Spatial averaging of the entries of this tensor, usually with a Gaussian filter, then leads to the structure tensor [1,5,6]:

$$\mathbf{S}_{ij} = g_{\sigma'} \star \mathbf{Q}_{ij} \qquad (i,j \in \{1,2\}) \tag{4}$$

The trace of the structure tensor (which is identical to the spatial average of the gradient squared magnitude) serves as a boundary indicator, whereas the gradient itself is only an edge indicator and gives no response at some junction types. Spatial maxima of the small eigenvalue of the structure tensor indicate junctions (see fig. 1). However, when two edges run close to each other, linear integration smears these edges into each other. This is desirable for edges that cross at a junction, but at other locations, e.g. when the edges run in parallel, it is not. The problem can be solved by replacing linear smoothing with an anisotropic filter such as the hourglass proposed in [7]. The hourglass kernel is defined as a polar separable function, where the radial part is a Gaussian, but the angular part modulates the Gaussian so that it becomes zero perpendicular to the local edge direction ϕ:

$$h_{\sigma',\rho}(r,\psi,\phi) = \begin{cases} \frac{1}{N} & \text{if } r = 0 \\ \frac{1}{N} e^{-\frac{r^2}{2\sigma'^2}} e^{-\frac{\tan(\psi-\phi)^2}{2\rho^2}} & \text{otherwise} \end{cases} \tag{5}$$

where ρ determines the strength of orientedness (the hourglass opening angle), and N is a normalization constant that makes the kernel integrate to unity, see fig. 2 left. At every point in the image, this kernel is rotated according to the local edge orientation defined by $\phi(x,y)$, so that smoothing only occurs along the edge. The anisotropic structure tensor $\mathbf{T}$ is obtained by applying the hourglass to the gradient tensor $\mathbf{Q}$:

$$\mathbf{T}_{ij}(x,y) = \sum_{x',y'} h_{\sigma',\rho}(r,\psi,\phi(x',y'))\, \mathbf{Q}_{ij}(x',y') \tag{6}$$

$$\text{with } r = \sqrt{(x-x')^2 + (y-y')^2} \text{ and } \psi = \tan^{-1}\left(\frac{y-y'}{x-x'}\right)$$

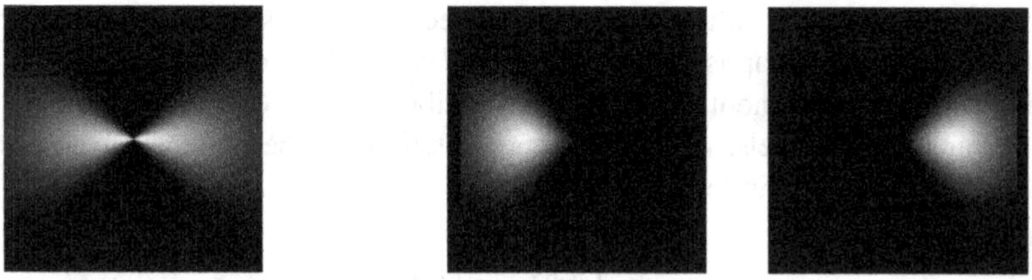

Fig. 2. Left: Hourglass like filter according to (5), with $\rho = 0.4$ and $\phi = 0$; Right: Hourglass filter multiplied with r^2 and split into two halves h_- and h_+

Fig. 3. From left to right: Original image; gradient squared magnitude; trace of structure tensor; trace of anisotropic structure tensor

and $\phi(x', y')$ is the edge direction at the point (x', y'). At junctions, this tensor equals the linear structure tensor, but it removes the undesired behavior at other locations, see fig. 3. With $\rho = 0.4$, the hourglass has an opening angle of about $22.5°$ and can be applied at small scales σ' without significant angular aliasing.

While the tensors $\mathbf{S}$ and $\mathbf{T}$ are good junction detectors, they cannot be used for junction characterization. The information obtained from the eigenvectors only describes the orientation of isolated edges correctly. At corners and junctions one eigenvector typically points into the most salient region, and the other is at $90°$ of the first, fig. 1 right. This is a fundamental limitation of second order tensors. More detailed orientation information is in principle available in the anisotropic integration framework, because the exact edge orientation $\phi(x', y')$ is fed into the hourglass filter. This information is lost when the gradient tensors are added to form the structure tensor. Therefore, we keep the idea of hourglass filtering, but change how the collected data are represented afterwards: we replace the tensor by a *channel representation*.

3 The Channel Representation

The channel representation was developed by [2,4,10] as a tool for estimating the local distribution of certain measurements. It can be considered as a generalization of histograms. Like the latter, a channel representation consists of bins (here called channels, hence the name) whose weights encode the probability, confidence or frequency of a specific range of the measured quantity. But unlike histograms, where bins are separate, i.e. are only influenced by values that fall in between each bin's borders, channels *overlap*. The amount of overlap is determined by the channel encoding function Θ which can be understood as a smoothing filter that distributes every exact measurement over a certain range of channels. A channel representation can be obtained from either a continuous function or a finite set of samples:

$$c_k = \int \Theta(t-k) f(t)\, dt \tag{7}$$

$$c_k = \sum_i \Theta(t_i - k) f_i \tag{8}$$

where c_k is the weight of channel k, $f(t)$ is a continuous weighting function for value t, whereas f_i is the discrete weight of the ith sample taken at point t_i. The definitions can be generalized to multiple dimensions in the obvious way.

An example for the continuous variety of the channel representation is the image itself. Here, $f(\mathbf{t})$ is the analog image that would be produced by an ideal pinhole camera, and c_{ij} is the discrete image we observe. The channel encoding function Θ is in this case formed by the combined effect of camera point spread function, defocus blur, and sensor response. In this paper we will be interested in discrete channel representations of local orientation: At every pixel, we store a 1D channel vector that encodes the orientation and strength of edges in a window around the pixel (more details below).

A representative value of the measured quantity can be reconstructed (decoded) from the channel representation in several ways. A global estimate is given by the mean over all channels. However, this is often not a very useful data description, as it smears all information together, regardless of whether the mean is *typical* or remote from any actual measurement. This is similar to linear smoothing of a checker board image, whose average intensity is gray, although gray did never occur in the original. More typical representatives can be obtained by switching to *robust* channel decoding [2]. This is best achieved by looking at the *mode* (the global maximum) or the set of all maxima of the channel histogram. These values are always near measurements that frequently occurred and thus tell more about what actually happened in a given set of samples.

Robust decoding requires an error norm that determines how many neighboring channels are considered in the estimation of each maximum. This can be understood as the reconstruction of a continuous weighting function from the discrete channel weights by means of a convolution with a continuous decoding function Ψ, followed by an analytic calculation of the global or local maxima of the reconstructed function. The functions Θ and Ψ must fulfill several criteria. Most importantly, it is required that both the global and robust reconstruction methods exactly reproduce the value t of a single encoded measurement. Second, the encoding function should be a partitioning of unity, i.e. the sum of a set of Θ-functions placed at the channel centers should be identically one in the entire domain of possible t-values. Likewise, the function Ψ should integrate to unity (this requirement was not posed in [2]). These two requirements ensure that the total confidence (weight) is preserved under channel encoding and decoding. Finally, both Θ and Ψ should be simple functions with small support so that computations can be efficiently executed.

In this paper we follow the *spline* channel model proposed by [2]. In this model Θ is the second order B-spline:

$$\Theta(t) = b_2(t) = \begin{cases} \frac{3}{4} - t^2 & |t| < \frac{1}{2} \\ \frac{1}{2}(\frac{3}{2} - |t|)^2 & \frac{1}{2} \leq |t| < \frac{3}{2} \\ 0 & \text{otherwise} \end{cases} \tag{9}$$

Robust decoding consists of a sequence of two filters. First, a first order recursive filter is applied with the transfer function

$$R(u) = \frac{4}{3 + \cos(u)} \tag{10}$$

where u is the frequency coordinate. Since the orientation domain is cyclic, the filter response should be computed in the Fourier domain to avoid border errors. Recursive filtering is followed by a convolution with Ψ defined by

$$\Psi(t) = \begin{cases} \frac{23}{48} - \frac{1}{4}t^2 & |t| < \frac{1}{2} \\ \frac{5-2|t|}{12}\, b_2(|t| - 1) + \frac{1}{2}\, b_2(t) & \frac{1}{2} \leq |t| < \frac{5}{2} \\ 0 & \text{otherwise} \end{cases} \tag{11}$$

The local maxima of the resulting continuous function are the robust estimates of the dominant orientations. Due to our normalization requirement for Ψ this differs slightly from [2], but it gives the same maxima. In practice, the convolution with Ψ needs not be executed, because the local maxima can be found directly by solving a quadratic equation in each channel interval, and the height of each maximum is given by a cubic function. Using these definitions, we achieve a reasonable channel overlap while computations remain relatively simple.

Encoding and decoding alone would not make the channel representation a worthwhile concept. Its real significance stems from the fact that we can perform linear or anisotropic *channel smoothing* before decoding. If one channel histogram is attached to every pixel, channel smothing is done by interpreting corresponding channel values c_k across all pixels as one image that can be smoothed independently of all other channels. Channel smoothing has an important advantage over direct smoothing of the original measurements: Only values close to the channel center are coded in every channel image. Therefore, only values that likely result from the same distribution are averaged. Consider again the checker board, this time with added noise. Then linear averaging would still give us a useless gray, whereas in a channel representation noisy black and white samples would be averaged separately, resulting in two representative averages for black and white. Channel smoothing can be performed both in a linear and an anisotropic way [3].

4 Channel Coding of the Gradient Orientation

In every pixel we have a gradient squared magnitude $m(x, y) = |\nabla f(x, y)|^2$ and an edge direction $\phi(x, y)$ perpendicular to the gradient. The magnitude is interpreted as

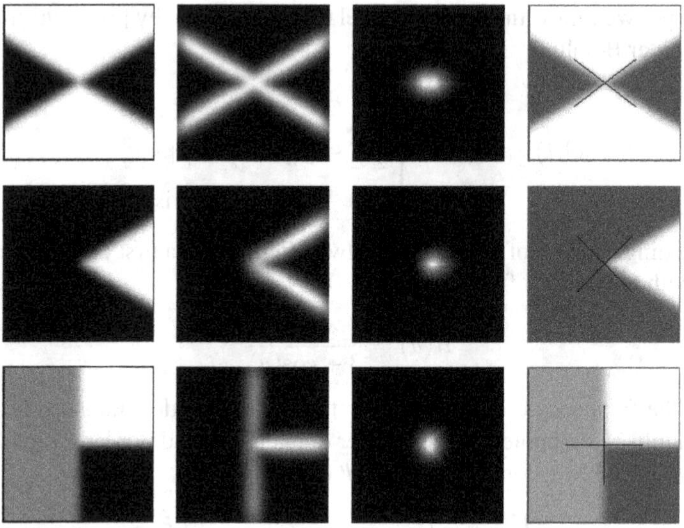

Fig. 4. From left to right: Original image; total channel weight; small eigenvalue of auxiliary tensor (14); edge orientation (all images with anisotropic channel smoothing)

the confidence of the direction measurement. The angle must first be transformed to the channel domain by a linear mapping. When n channels are available, the mapping is

$$t(\phi) = n\frac{\phi}{\phi_{\max}} \qquad \phi(t) = \phi_{\max}\frac{t}{n} \tag{12}$$

where $\phi_{\max} = \pi$ or $\phi_{\max} = 2\pi$ depending on whether we work with orientation or direction. In this paper, we use orientation and choose $n = 8$, resulting in a channel spacing of 22.5°. A single gradient measurement is encoded into channel c_k as

$$c_k(x, y) = m(x, y)\ \Theta\big(\Delta(t(\phi(x, y)), k)\big) \tag{13}$$

Since the angular domain is periodic, the difference between t and the channel center k must be taken modulo n: $\Delta(t, k) = \min(|t - k|, |t - k + n|, |t - k - n|)$ (note that the channel index equals the channel center here).

When channel encoding is followed by linear channel smoothing, the result is similar to the linearly integrated structure tensor: The sum of all channel weights at a given pixel is the local boundary strength analogous to the tensor trace. In order to distinguish 1D and 2D locations it is beneficial to transform the channel weights into an auxiliary tensor according to:

$$\mathbf{A} = \begin{pmatrix} \sum_k c_k \cos^2(\phi_k) & \sum_k c_k \cos(\phi_k)\sin(\phi_k) \\ \sum_k c_k \cos(\phi_k)\sin(\phi_k) & \sum_k c_k \sin^2(\phi_k) \end{pmatrix} \tag{14}$$

where $\phi_k = k\,\phi_{\max}/n$ is the center angle of channel k. As usual, the tensor's small eigenvalue is large at corners and junctions. At spatial maxima of the junction strength, we can now do something that was not possible with the structure tensor: we can recover the orientation of the edges that contributed to the junction response by computing (with the function Ψ) at which angles the confidence becomes maximal (however, maxima with confidence below a certain threshold should be dropped as insignificant).

Like the structure tensor, channel encoding can be improved by switching to anisotropic channel smoothing. Here we have two possibilities. First we can apply the standard procedure: We define an anisotropic smoothing filter and apply it in every channel so that the main filter orientation equals the center angle ϕ_k of the channel [3]. However, since the center angle is only an approximation of the encoded edge orientation, smoothing occurs not always exactly along the edge. Therefore, we prefer a different approach here: Since we encoded only a single gradient before channel smoothing, the exact edge orientation is still known. We can thus apply the filter at exactly the correct angle. This brings us back to the hourglass formula (6). But instead of tensor entries, we now propagate magnitude/orientation pairs according to (13):

$$c_k(x,y) = \sum_{x', y'} h_{\sigma',\rho}(r, \psi, \phi(x',y'))\, m(x',y')\, \Theta\big(\Delta(t(\phi(x',y')), k)\big) \qquad (15)$$

(r, ψ, ϕ are as in (6)). Since we can apply this formula with an arbitrary number of channels, we have control over the angular resolution of our junction characterization. However, at small scales, channel spacing and hourglass opening angle should not drop below $22.5°$ in order to avoid angular aliasing. Fig. 4 shows the results of these computations for a number of example configurations.

5 Wedge Channel Coding

Fig. 4 also reveals a principal problem with the approach sketched so far: Since forward and backward propagation of edge information is performed in the same way, the information wether an edge entered the junction from left or right, from top or bottom, is lost. Consequently, we are unable to distinguish a corner (degree 2) from a T-junction (degree 3) or a saddle point (degree 4), because the channel representations have only two maxima in all cases.

We solve this problem by breaking the symmetry of forward and backward propagation. It turns out that a slightly modified hourglass kernel is ideal for this purpose. First, we multiply the hourglass with r^2 (the squared distance from he filter center). This is useful because gradients near a junction center do not contain valid orientation information and their exclusion leads to more accurate orientation estimates. Second, we split the kernel along the axis perpendicular to the edge into two halves (fig. 2 right). This does not introduce a discontinuity because the kernel is zero along this axis. Finally, we double the number of channels, and the first half of the channel vector receives edge contributions coming from angles between 0 and π, whereas the second half takes the contributions from π to 2π. In the kernel, the rule is reversed: we call h_+ the kernel that distributes information downwards (into the first half of the channel vector), and h_- the

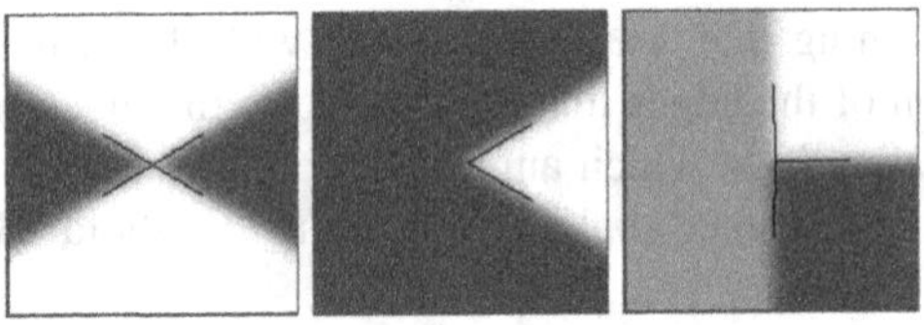

Fig. 5. Edge direction for the same images as in fig. 4, calculated from the wedge channel representation

kernel that distributes upwards (into the second half). The channel smoothing formula (15) must be split accordingly:

$$c_{k<n}(x,y) = \sum_{x'} \sum_{y'>0} h_+(r, \psi, \phi(x',y'))\, m(x',y')\, \Theta\big(\Delta(t(\phi(x',y')), k)\big) \tag{16}$$

$$c_{k\geq n}(x,y) = \sum_{x'} \sum_{y'<0} h_-(r, \psi, \phi(x',y'))\, m(x',y')\, \Theta\big(\Delta(t(\phi(x',y') + \pi), k)\big) \tag{17}$$

Note that ϕ is still taken modulo π (i.e. is the edge orientation), but we use twice as many channels as before ($0 \leq k < 2n$) and set $\phi_{\text{max}} = 2\pi$. The other algorithm steps are mostly uneffected by this change: The boundary strength can still be calculated as the sum of the channel weights, edges and corners can be distinguished by the small eigenvalue of the auxiliary tensor (14), and the orientation of the confidence maxima indicates the direction of the contributing edges. But the number of these maxima is now a true estimate of the junctions' degree. Corners have 2 maxima, whereas saddles have 4. It is even possible to distinguish different kinds of degree 3 junctions: a T-junction has two opposing maxima, but a Y-junction hasn't. A possible check for this classification is as follows: first calculate the number of maxima from the 2π channel representation. Then create an auxiliary channel vector ranging from 0 to π whose weights are the sum of the weights of opposite channel pairs from the original channels, and determine the number of its maxima. If this number is lower, one or more edges did not end at the junction, but crossed it.

Fig. 5 show some results obtained with the wedge channel representation. The discrepancy between the recovered orientations and the ground truth is below 1°. To obtain such a high accuracy, the hourglass kernel must be large enough: When the gradient image has scale σ_g (as determined by the combined effect of the camera point spread function and the gradient filter), the scale of the hourglass should be $2\sigma_g ... 3\sigma_g$, depending on the junction configuration (T-junctions seem to require scales near $3\sigma_g$). On the other hand, smaller kernels may be necessary in order to prevent neighboring junctions from interfering. Then the method still works, albeit with reduced accuracy. Finally, it should be noted that there is no need to compute the rather expensive wedge channel representation at every point. It suffices to first detect corners and junctions using the eigenvalues of the anisotropic structure tensor, and perform the more expensive analysis only there. The high similarity between the kernels involved ensures that results remain consistent.

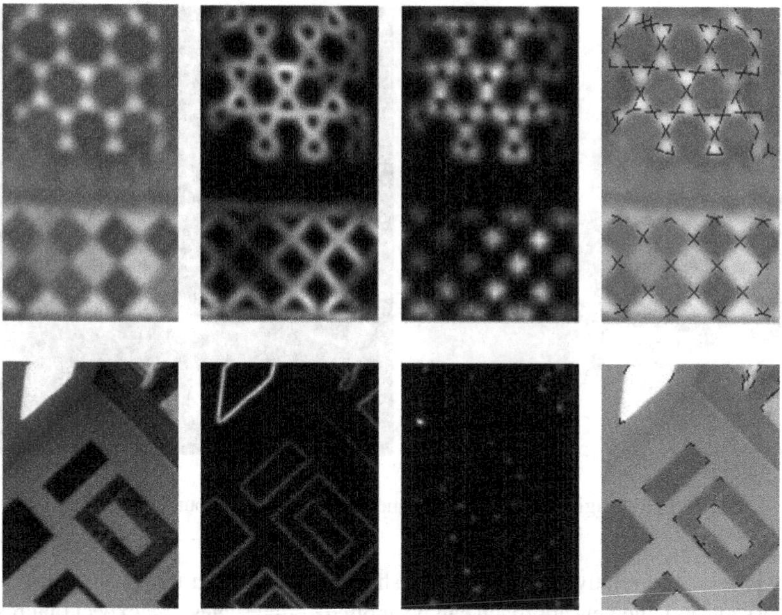

Fig. 6. From left to right: Original; boundary strength (total wedge channel weight); junction strength (small eigenvalue of auxiliary tensor); edge directions around the detected junctions: lines of length 3 pixels were drawn into the directions found

6 Results and Conclusions

We applied the wedge channel method to a number of real images (figs. 6 and 7). It can be seen that most corners are found correctly by the wedge channel representation, with few false positives. In a few cases, junctions give rise to a multi-modal response. The main advantage over the traditional structure tensor approach is the ability to perform detailed junction characterization. The estimated directions of the edges starting at each junctions have been marked. They are correct in most cases, although sometimes one edge is missing, or there is an extra response. Geometric accuracy is not always satisfying and needs further investigation. It should be noted, however, that the first and third images shown are not as easy to analyse as it may look at first sight: The tiled wall has very low resolution (diameter of the smallest tiles is 3 pixels), and the blocks image is relatively noisy.

Nevertheless, I believe that the wedge channel representation has a great potential because it directly generalizes well established edge and junction detection methods. It performs essentially the same computational steps as used in the anisotropic structure tensor calculations, only the final result is stored in a different way in order to keep as much information as possible: Depending on the number of channels, several independent edge directions can be recovered from the channels representation, in contrast to only one from a tensor. In contrast to existing orientation channel work, the wedge channel representation measures edge direction, so that the correct junction degree can be estimated. This is not possible with orientation channels, let alone the structure

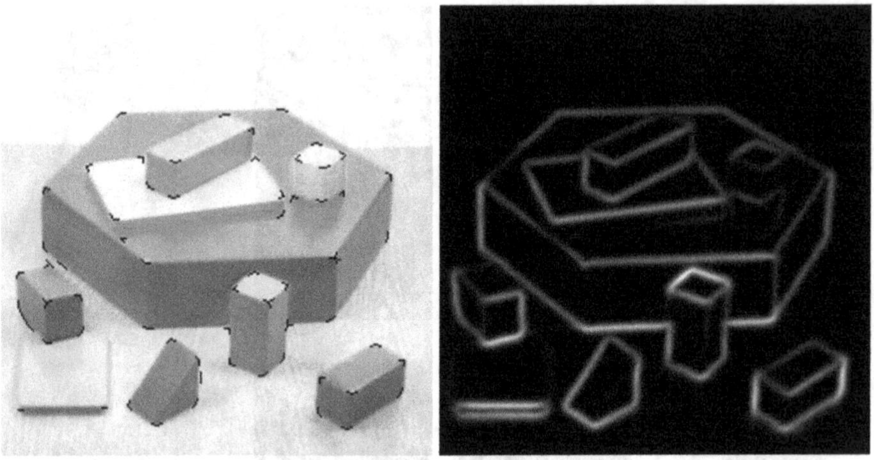

Fig. 7. Left: Original with junctions and edge directions; boundary strength

tensor. Due to the relatively simple filter shapes (Gaussian gradient and anisotropic hourglass masks), the new approach can be applied at fine scales. We expect that results can be further improved when the various parts of the algorithm are tuned to optimally fit together.

References

1. J. Bigün, G. Granlund: *Optimal Orientation Detection of Linear Symmetry*, in: ICCV 87, Proc. 1st Intl. Conf. on Computer Vision, pp. 433-438, 1987
2. M. Felsberg, P.-E. Forssen, H. Scharr: *Efficient Robust Smoothing of Low-Level Signal Features*, Linköping University, Computer Vision Laboratory, Technical Report LiTH-ISY-R-2619, 2004
3. M. Felsberg, G. Granlund: *Unisotropic Channel Filtering*, in: Proc. 13th Scandinavian Conf. on Image Analysis, pp. 755-762, Springer LNCS 2749, 2003
4. G. Granlund: *An Associative Perception-Action Structure Using a Localized Space Invariant Information Representation*, in: Proc. Intl. Workshop on Algebraic Frames for the Perception-Action Cycle, Springer LNCS, 2000
5. W. Förstner: *A Feature Based Correspondence Algorithm for Image Matching*, Intl. Arch. of Photogrammetry and Remote Sensing, vol. 26, pp. 150-166, 1986
6. C.G. Harris, M.J. Stevens: *A Combined Corner and Edge Detector*, Proc. of 4th Alvey Vision Conference, 1988
7. U. Köthe: *Edge and Junction Detection with an Improved Structure Tensor*, in: Michaelis et al. (Eds.): Pattern Recognition, Proc. 25th DAGM Symposium, Springer, 2003
8. M. Michaelis: *Low Level Image Processing Using Steerable Filters*, PhD Thesis, GSF-BEricht 30/95, Christian-ALbrechts-Universität Kiel, 1995
9. H.-H. Nagel, A. Gehrke: *Spatiotemporal Adaptive Estimation and Segmentation of OF-fields*, in: ECCV 98, Proc. 5th European Conf. on Computer Vision, vol. II, LNCS 1407, pp. 86-102, Springer, 1998

10. H.P. Snippe, J.J. Koenderink: *Discrimination Thresholds for Channel-Coded Systems*, Biological Cybernetics, vol. 66, pp. 543-551, 1992
11. H. Spies, B. Johansson: *Directional Channel Representation for Multiple Line-Endings and Intensity Levels*, in: ICIP 03, Proc. IEEE Intl. Conf. on Image Processing, 2003
12. W. Yu: *Local Orientation Analysis in Images and Image Sequences Using Sterrable Filters*, PhD Thesis, Bericht Nr. 2012, Christian-ALbrechts-Universität Kiel, 2000

Multiple Motion Estimation Using Channel Matrices

Per-Erik Forssén[1] and Hagen Spies[2]

[1] Computer Vision Laboratory, Department of Electrical Engineering
Linköping University, SE-581 83 Linköping, Sweden
[2] R&D ContextVision AB, Storgatan 24
SE-582 23 Linköping, Sweden

Abstract. The motion field from image sequences of a dynamic 3D scene is in general piecewise continuous. Since two neighbouring regions may have completely different motions, motion estimation at the discontinuities is problematic. In particular spatial averaging of motion vectors is inappropriate at such positions. We avoid this problem by channel encoding brightness change constraint equations (BCCE) for each spatial position into a channel matrix. By spatial averaging of this channel representation and subsequently decoding we are able to estimate all significantly different motions occurring at the discontinuity, as well as their covariances. This paper extends and improves this multiple motion estimation scheme by locally selecting the appropriate scale for the spatial averaging.

1 Introduction

The motion field from image sequences of a dynamic 3D scene is in general piecewise continuous. Since two neighbouring regions may have completely different motions, motion estimation at the discontinuities is problematic. In particular this means that linear estimation of motion parameters in regions containing a boundary is inappropriate. Furthermore, effects such as shadows and transparency can result in there actually being several valid motions at a single image location [1].

The problem of smoothing across edges can be solved to some extent by doing motion estimation in a small neighbourhood, and then applying edge preserving filtering, or robust estimation techniques to the resultant motion field. This will reduce noise, and eliminate outliers in the initial measurements, but the required size of the local region will vary considerably due to the *aperture problem* (the motion in an intrinsic-1D neighbourhood is ambiguous, see e.g. [1, 2]). Furthermore we will still run into problems if the local region contains several valid motions, as in the case of transparency and thin elongated objects such as tree branches.

In order to make the initial linear estimation region even smaller, one could instead replace the initial motion estimation step with a *motion constraint* estimation step. A popular motion constraint is the brightness change constraint equation (BCCE), which relates spatial and temporal derivatives (f_x, f_y, f_t) of the signal f, with the local image plane motion $\begin{bmatrix} u & v \end{bmatrix}^T$

$$u f_x(x, y) + v f_y(x, y) + f_t(x, y) = 0 \,. \quad (1)$$

B. Jähne et al. (Eds.): IWCM 2004, LNCS 3417, pp. 54–65, 2007.

The BCC-equation is based on the assumption of constant intensity, and can be derived from a first order Taylor expansion of a signal undergoing an infinitesimal translation. Since (1) is valid also in regions where the aperture problem is present, it can be correctly estimated using much smaller spatial windows. By clustering BCCEs in the u–v plane within a local region we can then estimate several local image plane motions. Examples of this approach are e.g. [1, 3], where the EM algorithm has been used to do the clustering.

The BCCE is actually an incorrect motion model in a number of situations: 1) if the illumination changes, 2) at the occlusion boundary when the background is non-constant, 3) if two motions are present, as is the case at e.g. moving shadow boundaries and reflections.

We have previously [4] developed a clustering technique which can automatically reject most of the incorrect motion constraints, and estimate several solutions to a system of constraints in a local neighbourhood, by encoding motion constraint estimates in *channel matrices*, performing spatial averaging of the matrix elements, and then decoding. Averaging the channel matrices adds the assumption that the motion is locally constant.

There have been several other attempts to determine multiple motions, e.g. [5, 6, 7, 8]. For a discussion of the Fourier properties of multiple motions see [9]. Often some type of filter bank is used where the filter outputs are either combined into a multiple motion likelihood function or used as separate constraints in an over-determined system of equations. In the presented approach we use simple derivative filters to yield the constraint equation that is input into our estimation scheme.

1.1 Organisation of Paper

This paper is organised as follows: In section 2, we describe the channel representation of motion constraints, and conversion to and from it. In section 3, we describe how the channel representation can be used to estimate optical flow, and demonstrate the behaviour of the algorithm using the well known "Hamburg taxi", and a synthetic sequence. In section 4 we introduce an algorithm which locally adapts the size of the region in which motion is estimated, and in section 5 we compare this method to least-squares optical flow using the "flower garden" sequence.

2 Channel Representation

Channel representation [10, 11, 12] is a technique to represent single or multiple statements with associated confidences in a uniform manner. Channel representation has applications in learning, clustering and edge-preserving filtering [10].

In the channel representation, a measurement u, and its confidence r are represented as a vector $\boldsymbol{\Phi}$ of K channel values Φ_k. The channel values are computed by passing the measurement u through a set of shifted *kernel functions* $g(u-k)$, and weighting the result with the confidence[1] r, i.e. $\Phi_k(u,r) = rg(u-k)$. Averaging in the channel representation followed by a *local decoding* is a way to estimate the modes of the PDF $p(u)$ [10].

[1] If no confidence is available, we simply set $r = 1$.

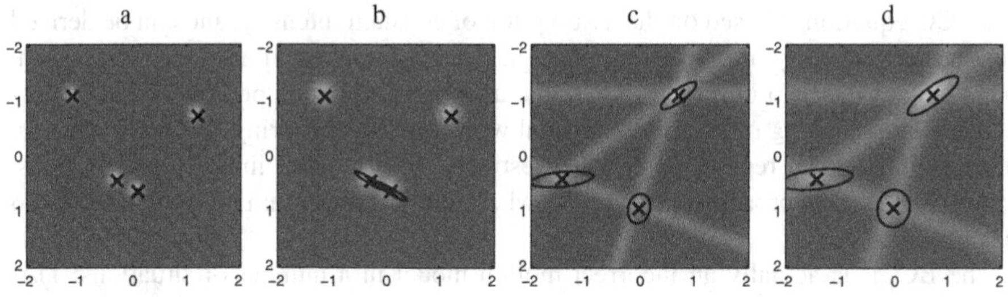

Fig. 1. Example of channel histograms with sampling distance $\Delta u = 0.1$. a) and b) Encoding of points with $\sigma = \Delta u$ and $\sigma = 1.5\Delta u$, c) and d) Encoding of lines with $\sigma = \Delta u$ and $\sigma = 1.5\Delta u$. Decoded mode locations are visualised as crosses, and the covariances as ellipses.

Common kernel choices are $\cos^2$, B-spline, and Gaussian kernels. In this paper we will use Gaussians, since decoding of a Gaussian channel vector allows recovery of both mode location and standard deviation.

2.1 Encoding of Points

When encoding a point $\begin{bmatrix} u & v \end{bmatrix}^T$ the channel value Φ_{kl} at each grid point $\begin{bmatrix} k & l \end{bmatrix}^T$ is obtained by application of a Gaussian kernel function:

$$\Phi_{kl}(u, v, r) = rg(d, \sigma) = re^{-0.5(d/\sigma)^2} \quad \text{for} \quad d^2 = (u-k)^2 + (v-l)^2 \qquad (2)$$

We only discuss the fully isotropic kernel here. Such an encoding of 2D variables is realised more efficiently as the outer product of the 1D channel vectors for the two components, u and v.

For several points the combined channel representation is simply given by the averaged channel matrix. An example with four thus encoded points is given in figure 1a and 1b for different kernel widths σ. Observe that there is an interference between two points if they are too close to each other. The number of channels, their distance and the standard deviation of the used kernel thus limits how many points we can represent simultaneously.

2.2 Encoding of Lines

Often an image measurement does not give the exact location of the parameter we want to estimate, but only determines that it lies somewhere in a one-dimensional subspace. We assume that such a linear constraint is given either in standard, or in normalised form:

$$a\,x + b\,y + c = 0 \quad \text{or} \quad x\cos\phi + y\sin\phi - \rho = 0\,, \qquad (3)$$

with $[\cos\phi,\ \sin\phi,\ -\rho] = \frac{1}{\sqrt{a^2+b^2}}\begin{bmatrix} a & b & c \end{bmatrix}$. All points (x, y) which satisfy (3) lie on the line. The distance of a specific grid point (k, l) to the line is then given by $d = |k\cos\phi + l\sin\phi - \rho|$. Channel values are again obtained by applying the Gaussian kernel to the distance:

$$\Phi_{k,l}(\rho, \phi, r) = rg(d, \sigma) = re^{-0.5(d/\sigma)^2} \quad \text{for} \quad d^2 = k\cos\phi + l\sin\phi - \rho\,. \qquad (4)$$

Each channel value encodes the likelihood that the motion has the value of the corresponding grid point. An example with four thus encoded lines is given in figure 1c and 1d for different σ.

2.3 Point Decoding

In the decoding step we want to extract the position of local peaks in the channel matrix. First we determine local maxima with grid point accuracy at (k, l). Then we model the channel values in a small neighbourhood (e.g. 3×3 or 5×5) around the local maximum using a 2D Gaussian with centre position $\mathbf{s}$, amplitude r and covariance matrix $\mathbf{C}$:

$$g(\mathbf{p} - \mathbf{s}, r, \mathbf{C}) = r \exp\left(-0.5(\mathbf{p} - \mathbf{s})^T \mathbf{C}^{-1} (\mathbf{p} - \mathbf{s})\right) \tag{5}$$

where $\mathbf{p} = \begin{bmatrix} x \; y \end{bmatrix}^T$ denotes local grid point coordinates. We can express the covariance matrix and its inverse explicitly as:

$$\mathbf{C} = \begin{bmatrix} \sigma_x^2 & \sigma_{xy} \\ \sigma_{xy} & \sigma_y^2 \end{bmatrix} \quad \text{and} \quad \mathbf{C}^{-1} = \frac{1}{\sigma_x^2 \sigma_y^2 - \sigma_{xy}^2} \begin{bmatrix} \sigma_y^2 & -\sigma_{xy} \\ -\sigma_{xy} & \sigma_x^2 \end{bmatrix} . \tag{6}$$

For each point in the decoding neighbourhood we thus obtain one constraint $\Phi_\mathbf{p} = g(\mathbf{p} - \mathbf{s})$. After taking the logarithm this constraint becomes:

$$\ln g(\mathbf{p} - \mathbf{s}) = \ln r - \frac{(x - s_x)^2 \sigma_y^2 - 2(x - s_x)(y - s_y)\sigma_{xy} + (y - s_y)^2 \sigma_x^2}{2(\sigma_2^2 \sigma_y^2 - \sigma_{xy}^2)} . \tag{7}$$

This can be written as the scalar product between a known vector $\mathbf{a}$ and an unknown parameter vector $\mathbf{m}$ with:

$$\mathbf{a} = 0.5 \begin{bmatrix} 1 \; 2x \; 2y \; -x^2 \; -y^2 \; -2xy \end{bmatrix}^T , \tag{8}$$

$$\mathbf{m} = \frac{1}{\sigma_x^2 \sigma_y^2 - \sigma_{xy}^2} \begin{bmatrix} 2 \ln r(\sigma_x^2 \sigma_y^2 - \sigma_{xy}^2) - s_x^2 \sigma_y^2 + 2 s_x s_y \sigma_{xy} - s_y^2 \sigma_x^2 \\ s_x \sigma_y^2 - s_y \sigma_{xy} \\ s_y \sigma_x^2 - s_x \sigma_{xy} \\ \sigma_y^2 \\ \sigma_x^2 \\ -\sigma_{xy} \end{bmatrix} \tag{9}$$

Stacking the constraints for each pixel on top of each other we obtain a least-squares system: $\mathbf{A}\mathbf{m} = \ln \boldsymbol{\Phi}$. The solution is obtained using the pseudo-inverse:

$$\mathbf{m} = (\mathbf{A}^T \mathbf{A})^{-1} \mathbf{A}^T \ln \boldsymbol{\Phi} . \tag{10}$$

We recognise the inverse covariance as:

$$\tilde{\mathbf{C}}^{-1} = \begin{bmatrix} m_4 & m_6 \\ m_6 & m_5 \end{bmatrix} \quad \text{thus} \quad \tilde{\mathbf{C}} = \frac{1}{m_4 m_5 - m_6^2} \begin{bmatrix} m_5 & -m_6 \\ -m_6 & m_4 \end{bmatrix} . \tag{11}$$

From (9) we find the position and peak amplitude to be given by:

$$\begin{bmatrix} \tilde{s}_x \; \tilde{s}_y \end{bmatrix}^T = \tilde{\mathbf{C}} \begin{bmatrix} m_2 \; m_3 \end{bmatrix}^T ; \; \tilde{r} = \exp(0.5(m_1 + m_4 s_x^2 + m_5 s_y^2 + 2 m_6 s_x s_y)) . \tag{12}$$

The final solution is obtained by adding the centre grid point offset $\begin{bmatrix}\tilde{u} \; \tilde{v}\end{bmatrix} = \begin{bmatrix}k \; l\end{bmatrix} + \begin{bmatrix}\tilde{s}_x \; \tilde{s}_y\end{bmatrix}$.

The expectation of the estimated covariance matrix is the sum of the noise covariance $\tilde{\mathbf{C}}_n$ and that of the encoding kernel $\mathbf{C}_b = \mathrm{diag}(\sigma^2, \sigma^2)$. Hence we can compute the covariance matrix of our estimated result to be: $\tilde{\mathbf{C}}_n = \tilde{\mathbf{C}} - \mathbf{C}_b$. Also note that the estimated amplitude $\tilde{r}$ encodes the peak likelihood and thus directly serves as a certainty measure.

In order to determine to what extent the aperture problem persists for the considered solution we can define the quotient of the eigenvalues of the covariance matrix as a simple measure. Let $\lambda_1 \geq \lambda_2$ be the eigenvalues of $\tilde{\mathbf{C}}$, then we define:

$$r_a = \lambda_2 / \lambda_1 . \tag{13}$$

To summarise: for each local peak in the channel matrix, the decoding extracts the mode location $(\tilde{u}, \tilde{v})$, the amplitude $\tilde{r}$, the covariance $\tilde{\mathbf{C}}$, and an aperture measure r_a.

2.4 Multiple Decodings

The above described decoding scheme tends to give several similar solutions if the local channel matrix structure is elongated, i.e. if r_a from (13) is small. Thus we also do a postprocessing which removes multiple solutions. As a first step, we disregard solutions with a Mahalanobis distance larger than 1 from the initial grid point, i.e.

$$\begin{bmatrix}\tilde{s}_x \; \tilde{s}_y\end{bmatrix} \tilde{\mathbf{C}}^{-1} \begin{bmatrix}\tilde{s}_x \; \tilde{s}_y\end{bmatrix}^T < 1 . \tag{14}$$

Additionally, we check if multiple solutions are within each other's Mahalanobis distance, and if so, we keep the one which has the largest aperture measure r_a.

The thus estimated peak locations and associated covariance matrices are shown in figure 1. For isolated points the covariance vanishes, i.e. we have perfect reconstruction. Increasing the kernel size σ leads to stronger interference as can be seen in figure 1b. However the elongated shape of the covariance matrix correctly captures this interference. For linear constraints we find that the intersections are correctly found, see figure 1c. Observe that the angle between the lines determines the covariance in the reconstructed point, for 90° we should have an isotropic covariance. However for small values of σ we find a slight anisotropy caused by quantisation effects. For larger σ (figure 1d) this effect disappears.

2.5 Line Decoding

In cases where the point decoding fails, i.e. when the decoded covariance matrix has a zero, or negative determinant, we revert to decoding a line instead. We do this by constraining the inverse covariance matrix to be singular. The singularity is enforced by eigenvalue decomposition on $\tilde{\mathbf{C}}^{-1}$, and setting the smallest eigenvalue to zero.

$$\begin{bmatrix} m_4 & m_6 \\ m_6 & m_5 \end{bmatrix} = \lambda_1 \mathbf{e}_1 \mathbf{e}_1^T + \lambda_2 \mathbf{e}_2 \mathbf{e}_2^T \;\Rightarrow\; \tilde{\mathbf{C}}^{-1} = \lambda_1 \mathbf{e}_1 \mathbf{e}_1^T = \begin{bmatrix} \tau_x^2 & \tau_x \tau_y \\ \tau_x \tau_y & \tau_y^2 \end{bmatrix} . \tag{15}$$

For a singular matrix the peak position $\begin{bmatrix}\tilde{s}_x & \tilde{s}_y\end{bmatrix}^T$ is not well defined. Instead we compute the minimum norm solution, cf. (12), of $\tilde{\mathbf{C}}^{-1}\begin{bmatrix}\tilde{s}_x & \tilde{s}_y\end{bmatrix}^T = \begin{bmatrix}m_2 & m_3\end{bmatrix}^T$:

$$\begin{bmatrix}\tilde{s}_x \\ \tilde{s}_y\end{bmatrix} = \frac{(\tau_x m_2 + \tau_y m_3)}{\tau_x^2 + \tau_y^2}\begin{bmatrix}\tau_x \\ \tau_y\end{bmatrix} . \tag{16}$$

Finally, the covariance is approximated by:

$$\tilde{\mathbf{C}} = 1/\lambda_1(\mathbf{e}_1\mathbf{e}_1^T + 10\,000\mathbf{e}_2\mathbf{e}_2^T) . \tag{17}$$

Note that the factor 10 000 is quite arbitrary. It is just a convenient approximation of the infinity, such that the accuracy of the orientation of $\tilde{\mathbf{C}}$ is retained.

3 Optical Flow

We now apply the presented framework to the computation of image motion. From the assumption of conserved intensity the standard optical flow constraint equation is obtained as:

$$uf_x(x,y) + vf_y(x,y) + f_t(x,y) = 0 . \tag{18}$$

Here f_x, f_y, and f_t denote the signal derivatives along space and time dimensions, and $[u,v]^T$ the motion. As there is only one equation with two unknowns, the solution is constrained to lie on a line in the parameter space. This inherent ambiguity is often referred to as the aperture problem. We encode this linear constraint as described in section 2.2, and obtain a blurred line constraint at each spatial position.

To obtain a unique solution some form of spatio-temporal smoothness is usually required. Here we simply assume the motion in each layer to be constant in a spatial neighbourhood. The channel matrix for such a neighbourhood is then obtained by averaging the individual matrices. Instead of a standard average it is desirable to give more weight to the central pixel. This is readily achieved by the use of an averaging filter $g(x,y)$ such as a Gaussian or binomial. Furthermore we might want to utilise a certainty $w(x,y)$ at each pixel. The gradient magnitude is a possible choice. In any way this certainty will be zero outside the image thus reducing border effects. The integrated channel matrix is given by a normalised average:

$$\Phi'_{kl} = \frac{g * (w \cdot \Phi_{kl})}{g * w} \tag{19}$$

where $*$ denotes convolution. We use the well known "Hamburg taxi" sequence (figure 2) to demonstrate the algorithm. Two thus computed channel matrices are shown in figure 2b and 2c for the locations indicated in figure 2a. Note that the averaged channel matrix corresponds to a sampled likelihood function with:

$$p(u,v|f) \simeq \sum_{x,y} g(x,y)w(x,y)\exp\left(-\frac{(u\,f_x + v\,f_y + f_t)^2}{2\sigma^2(f_x^2 + f_y^2)}\right) . \tag{20}$$

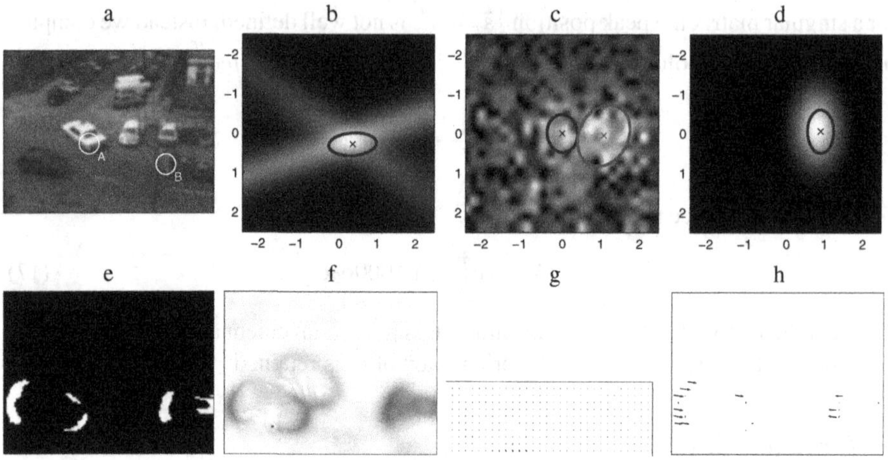

Fig. 2. Optical flow example. a) frame 25 with marked positions A and B. b) and c) show channel matrices at positions A and B respectively. d) gives the LS likelihood (21) at point B. e) shows the pixels where more than one solution is obtained, f) shows the confidence in the first estimate and g) and h) show the first and second solutions as vector plots.

(All derivatives above have an implicit spatial coordinate argument.) This can easily be derived from (3) and (4). Compare this likelihood to the standard least-squares likelihood function [13]:

$$p(u, v|f) \simeq \exp\left(\frac{-1}{2\sigma^2}\sum_{x,y} g(x,y)w(x,y)(u\,f_x + v\,f_y + f_t)^2\right). \tag{21}$$

These two likelihoods are illustrated in figure 2c and 2d for an area where a moving car is occluded by a tree. We observe that (20) clearly distinguishes the two motions while (21) averages them. The summation in (20) can be thought of as a voting mechanism which makes the approach very robust to outliers, similar to a generalised Hough transform. Note that when there is only one solution and no outliers the expectation values of (20) and (21) coincide.

Points where more than one solution is obtained are indicated in figure 2e. The outlines of two cars are clearly visible. There are no multiple motions around the bright car as its slow movement can not be separated from that of the background in this case ($\sigma = 0.2\Delta u$). The certainty of the dominant estimate is shown in figure 2f, this also drops slightly around the brighter car. Finally we show the first and second estimated motion in figure 2g and 2h respectively. Around the cars their movements are captured in the less dominant second solution.

It is possible to extract multiple motions at motion discontinuities. This is illustrated on a synthetic sequence where all four quadrants move in different directions, an example frame is given in figure 3a. The number of solutions is shown in figure 3b; At the centre we get up to four estimates and at the other discontinuities we obtain two solutions. The vector plot (figure 3c) illustrates that the motions are correctly estimated.

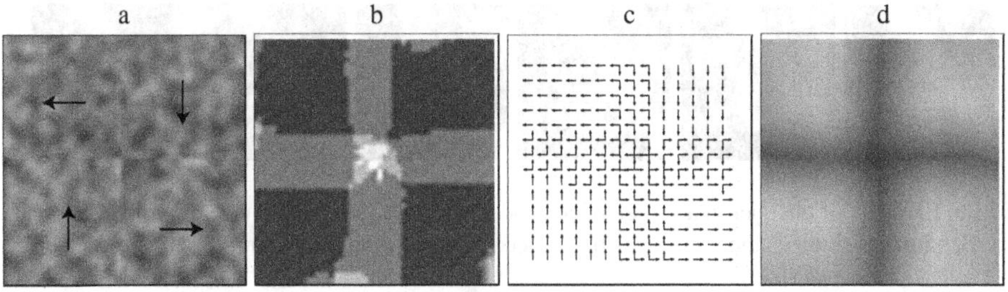

Fig. 3. Multiple motions at discontinuities. a) example image, b) number of solutions (range [0 4]), c) vector plot and d) confidence (peak amplitude) in the first estimate.

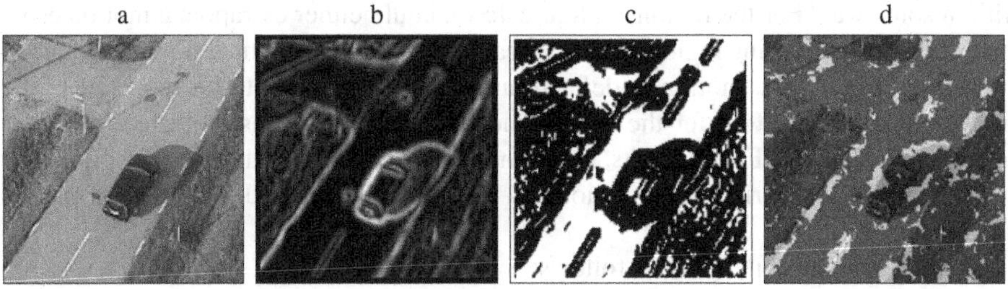

Fig. 4. Helicopter sequence. Left to right: input frame, Gradient magnitude, Thresholded gradient magnitude, thresholded r_a map (overlaid on image).

The amplitude of the dominant peak drops near the discontinuities as the energy is distributed to several peaks, see 3d.

4 Scale Selection for Optical Flow Estimation

The "Hamburg taxi" sequence is quite convenient in the sense that it does not contain elongated structures, and thus no serious aperture problems exist. In general however we may need to integrate information over quite a large region in order to get rid of aperture problems. If a local region doesn't suffer from aperture problems, however it is not desirable to use a too large estimation region. In fact, increasing the estimation region reduces the spatial localisation accuracy of the estimated motion. This is known as *the uncertainty principle* [2]. In order to keep the spatial localisation accuracy, and at the same time adapt the size of the estimation region, we compute a low-pass pyramid for each channel.

Figure 4a shows a frame from a more difficult sequence. In this sequence, the car is moving forward, and the camera is translating upwards and to the left, to compensate for the car motion. Figure 4b shows the gradient magnitude $f_m = \sqrt{f_x^2 + f_y^2}$, and figure 4c indicates regions where the magnitude is so small ($f_m < 0.005$) that the BCCE constraints are unreliable due to low SNR. For such regions, we don't provide any constraint at all, instead we set the channel matrix to all zeros. Figure 4d indicates regions where an optical flow estimation according to section 3 (using a 21-tap binomial

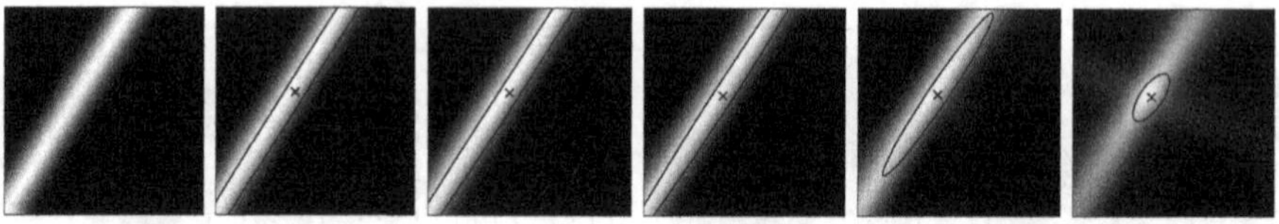

Fig. 5. Example of channel matrix behaviour under blurring. Left: initial constraint line. Second to sixth images show channel matrices from successive scales in the pyramid.

filter to average the channel matrices) resulted in a dominant motion with a very low aperture measure ($r_a < 0.01$).

Both types of problem regions (those indicated in figure 4c and 4d) have to be dealt with in some way. For the regions in figure 4c we could either extrapolate motion estimates from neighbouring regions, as is typically done in dense optical flow techniques, or we could leave the motion undefined, and leave it to a yet-to-be-specified post-processing algorithm to infer the correct motion. For the regions indicated in figure 4d we have valid BCCE constraints, but we have failed to resolve the aperture problem, and thus need to perform the estimation in a larger neighbourhood. This is the topic of this section.

First we generate a pyramid as follows:

1. Encode the BCCE constraints as channel matrices in each pixel.
2. Perform an initial spatial average, e.g. with a 15-tap binomial filter.
3. Average again using a 4-tap binomial filter.
4. Subsample to obtain the next coarser scale in the pyramid.
5. Repeat 3 and 4 until sufficiently many scales are obtained.

Figure 5 demonstrates how channel matrices at a motion discontinuity behave under blurring. Here we can see how the aperture problem is dealt with at increasingly coarser scales. The first three scales all produce very elongated solutions, indicating aperture problem or near aperture problem uncertainty. the dominant modes at the fourth and fifth scales however have more concentrated covariance matrices, and are thus good descriptions of the motion in the region. This example motivates the following scale selection algorithm:

1. Decode at finest scale
2. For all decodings with an aperture measure below a given threshold:
3. Replace with decoding at coarser scale if within Mahalanobis distance, and better wrt. aperture measure.
4. Go back to 2.

This algorithm is demonstrated in figure 6. Here we can see that initial estimates made in a relatively small region (15-tap binomial) can be improved by replacing estimates with low aperture measures. However, the method fails on very elongated structures, such as e.g. the road line at the bottom of the image. The reason for this is that the number of votes for the same motion constraint is so high, that the estimates at the end of the line fails to change the shape of the covariance matrix significantly. This clearly indicates that a better aperture measure would be desirable.

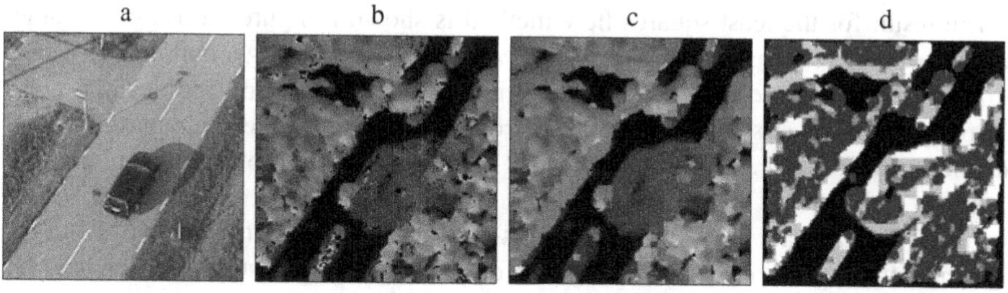

Fig. 6. Estimated motion. a) Central input frame b) Magnitude of motion estimate at scale 1 c) Magnitude of motion estimate after integrating scales 1–5. d) Chosen scale (brighter means higher scale, black means no estimate).

Fig. 7. Comparison with linear optical flow on the "flower garden" sequence. a) centre input frame (No. 5), b) magnitude of estimated motion, c) magnitude overlaid on input frame, d) result from least-squares method.

5 Experiments

We now demonstrate the difference in behaviour between the described algorithm and the least-squares optical flow algorithm of Lucas and Kanade [14]. We compute optical flow by solving a system of BCCEs in each local neighbourhood:

$$\mathbf{W}\underbrace{\begin{bmatrix} | & | \\ f_x & f_y \\ | & | \end{bmatrix}}_{\mathbf{A}}\begin{bmatrix} u \\ v \end{bmatrix} = \mathbf{W}\underbrace{\begin{bmatrix} | \\ f_t \\ | \end{bmatrix}}_{\mathbf{b}} \quad \Rightarrow \quad \begin{bmatrix} u \\ v \end{bmatrix} = (\mathbf{A}^T\mathbf{W}\mathbf{A})^{-1}\mathbf{A}^T\mathbf{W}\mathbf{b}\,. \tag{22}$$

Here $\mathbf{W}$ is a diagonal matrix containing the spatial weights in the neighbourhood.

Figure 7 shows a comparison of the channel matrix method and the least-squares flow method (22). Figure 7a shows the centre input frame, and in 7b we have depicted the magnitude (mainly contains the horizontal component) of the estimated motion field using the channel matrix method. We used 3×3 Sobel derivative filters, but blurred the input frames using a 9-tap binomial to increase the spatial support of the derivatives. We have used a channel representation with 25×25 channels with $\Delta u = 0.35$, and $\sigma = 1.3\Delta u$. The initial smoothing was done using a 61-tap binomial filter, and the rest of the pyramid was built using 4-tap filters. The motion magnitude is overlaid on the central input frame in figure 7c, to illustrate the localisation of the result. As can be seen, the localisation of the tree edges are quite good when there is structure behind the tree. Higher up, however we see that the motion of the tree spills over onto the background as well.

The result for the least-squares flow method is shown in figure 7d using the same derivative filter responses as input. Again we used a spatial neighbourhood of a 61-tap binomial filter to solve for (u, v). As can be seen, the edges are significantly more blurred, and the least-squares flow gives erroneous motions at the same places as the channel matrix, (see e.g. the bright patches at the bottom right of the image, and on the upper right part of the tree trunk). This indicates that these errors are due to erroneous BCCEs, and not to the motion estimation step. By using better derivative filters, e.g. Sharr filters [15], or by switching to a different motion constraint estimation we should thus be able to improve the results.

6 Concluding Remarks

We have presented a framework for encoding local motion constraints in a representation where averaging yields robust estimation. We wish to emphasise that the main purpose of this paper was to demonstrate the framework, and not to suggest a final motion estimation method. The channel representation framework allows the BCCE constraint to be replaced, e.g. by a phase based [16], or 3D-orientation constraint. Furthermore, we can easily combine both measurements that yield motion constraints and full motion estimates (as obtained from e.g. feature matching methods) by encoding them using the line encoding and the point encoding respectively.

For integration of estimates at different scales, the results are somewhat disappointing, since only minor improvements compared to the single scale method are obtained. Better results could probably be obtained by instead letting the covariance of the initial estimates guide the shape of the estimation region at coarser scales.

Acknowledgements

The work presented in this paper was supported by sixth framework programme COSPAL (COgnitive Systems using Perception–Action Learning), and Swedish foundation for strategic research project VISCOS (Vision in Cognitive Systems).

References

1. Jepson, A., Black, M.: Mixture models for optical flow. Technical Report RBCV-TR-93-44, Res. in Biol. and Comp. Vision, Dept. of Comp. Sci., Univ. of Toronto (1993)
2. Granlund, G.H., Knutsson, H.: Signal Processing for Computer Vision. Kluwer Academic Publishers (1995) ISBN 0-7923-9530-1.
3. Ayer, S., Sawhney, H.S.: Layered representation of motion video using robust maximum-likelihood estimation of mixture models and MDL encoding. In: Proceedings of the fifth International Conference on Computer Vision. (1995)
4. Spies, H., Forssén, P.E.: Two-dimensional channel representation for multiple velocities. In: Proceedings of the 13th Scandinavian Conference on Image Analysis. LNCS 2749, Gothenburg, Sweden (2003) 356–362
5. Shizawa, M., Mase, K.: Simultaneous multiple optical flow estimation. In: ICPR, Atlantic City, NJ, USA (1990) 274–278

6. Nestares, O., Navarro, R.: Probabilistic estimation of optical flow in multiple band-pass directional channels. Image and Vision Comp. **19** (2001) 339–351
7. Mota, C., Stuke, I., Barth, E.: Analytic solutions for multiple motions. In: ICIP. Volume 2., Thessaloniki, Greece (2001) 917–920
8. Andersson, K., Knutsson, H.: Multiple hierarchical motion estimation. In: SPPRA, Crete, Greece (2002) 80–85
9. Beauchemin, S.S., Barron, J.L.: On the fourier properties of discontinuous motion. Journal of Mathematical Imaging and Vision **13** (2000) 155–172
10. Forssén, P.E.: Low and Medium Level Vision using Channel Representations. PhD thesis, Linköping University, Sweden, SE-581 83 Linköping, Sweden (2004) Dissertation No. 858, ISBN 91-7373-876-X.
11. Granlund, G.H.: An associative perception-action structure using a localized space variant information representation. In: Proceedings of Algebraic Frames for the Perception-Action Cycle (AFPAC), Kiel, Germany (2000)
12. Nordberg, K., Granlund, G., Knutsson, H.: Representation and Learning of Invariance. In: Proceedings of IEEE International Conference on Image Processing, Austin, Texas, IEEE (1994) Also as Technical Report LiTH-ISY-R-1552.
13. Weiss, Y., Fleet, D.: Velocity likelihoods in biological and machine vision. In Rao, R. P. N., Olshausen, B. A., Lewicki, M. S., eds.: Probabilistic Models of the Brain: Perception and Neural Function. MIT Press (2001) 81–100
14. Lucas, B., Kanade, T.: An iterative image registration technique with an application to stereo vision. In: DARPA Image Understanding Workshop. (1981) 121–130
15. Weickert, J., Scharr, H.: A scheme for coherence-enhancing diffusion filtering with optimized rotation invariance. J. Visual Communication and Image Representation **13** (2002) 103–118
16. Felsberg, M.: Optical flow estimation from monogenic phase. In: IWCM04, Reisensburg, Germany (2004)

Divide-and-Conquer Strategies for Estimating Multiple Transparent Motions

Cicero Mota[1], Ingo Stuke[2], Til Aach[2], and Erhardt Barth[1]

[1] Institute for Neuro- and Bioinformatics, University of Luebeck, Germany
{mota,barth}@inb.uni-luebeck.de
[2] Institute for Signal Processing, University of Luebeck, Germany
{aach,stuke}@isip.uni-luebeck.de

Abstract. Transparent motions are additive or multiplicative superpositions of moving patterns and occur due to reflections, semi-transparencies, and partial occlusions. The estimation of transparent motions remained a challenging nonlinear problem. We here first linearize the problem in a way which makes it accessible to the known methods used for the estimation of single motions, such as structure tensor, regularization, block matching, Fourier methods, etc. We present the results for two motion layers but there is no limit to the number of layers. Finally, we present a way to categorize different transparent-motion patterns based on the rank of a generalized structure tensor.

1 Introduction

Motion estimation is a core problem in computer vision - see for example [1, 2, 3] in this volume. Most motion models used in standard applications are still rather simple and thus fail with more complex motion patterns. As a particular class of complex motion patterns, the multiple transparent motions treated here are additive or multiplicative superpositions of single moving patterns and occur due to reflections, semi-transparencies, and partial occlusions.

An algorithm for the estimation of two transparent motions was first proposed by Shizawa and Mase [4]. A layered representation of image sequences was presented in [5] and approaches based on nulling filters and velocity-tuned mechanisms have been proposed in [6, 7]. A phase-based solution for the estimation of two transparent overlaid motions and the separation of the image layers was proposed by Vernon [8], and a solution for the separation of the image layers by using the constrained least-squares method was proposed in [9]. However, the estimation of transparent motions and the separation of the corresponding layers remained a challenging nonlinear problem [10]. Here we show how this problem can be naturally split into a linear and a nonlinear part. The linear part is then accessible to known methods used for the estimation of single motions, such as methods based on the structure tensor, regularization, block matching, Fourier analysis, etc. This becomes very useful since, in our approach, the nonlinear part has a closed-form solution. For simplicity, we restrict ourselves to the case of only two transparent motions at a given location in the image. This is certainly the most likely case in applications but, theoretically, our solutions are not limited by the number of transparent layers. In fact, our results are presented such that the generalization to

B. Jähne et al. (Eds.): IWCM 2004, LNCS 3417, pp. 66–77, 2007.

more than two layers is straightforward and the principle of how to generalize has been presented before [11, 12, 13, 14]. Moreover, our approach provides confidence measures that allow for the categorization of different motion patterns and for the automatic detection of the number of moving layers. A related problem is the estimation of multiple global motions - see [15, 16] in this volume.

This paper is organized as follows. Section 2 introduces a differential constraint equation for transparent motions. The problem is then split into a linear and a nonlinear part. Two different algorithms to solve the linear part are presented and the nonlinear part is solved analytically. Section 3 introduces a Fourier domain constraint for transparent motions. The goal is to estimate the phase shifts corresponding to the motion vectors. The problem is, again, solved by splitting into linear and nonlinear parts. We show how to use the estimated phase shifts for separation of the image layers. Finally, the Fourier constraint is transformed back to the space domain to obtain a block matching constraint. Experimental results are presented for synthetic and real image sequences.

2 Differential Methods

Differential methods are based on the well-known constant brightness constraint equation [17], i.e., the motion field $\mathbf{u} = (u_x, u_y)^T$ of an image sequence $g(\mathbf{x}, t)$ is constrained by

$$u_x g_x + u_y g_y + g_t = 0 \tag{1}$$

where $g_r = \partial g / \partial r$, $r \in \{x, y, t\}$. We write the above equation in short form as $\alpha(\mathbf{u}) g(\mathbf{x}, t) = 0$, where $\alpha(\mathbf{u}) = u_x \partial/\partial x + u_y \partial/\partial y + \partial/\partial t$. Next, a similar constraint will be derived for an additive model of transparent motions.

Constraint Equation for Transparent Motions. We consider an additive superposition of two image sequences (layers) $f(\mathbf{x}, t) = g_1(\mathbf{x}, t) + g_2(\mathbf{x}, t)$. If the motion fields are sufficiently smooth to be considered 'locally constant', the layers can be modeled as $g_1(\mathbf{x}, t) = \varphi_1(\mathbf{x} - t\mathbf{u})$ and $g_2(\mathbf{x}, t) = \varphi_2(\mathbf{x} - t\mathbf{v})$ with constant motion fields $\mathbf{u}$ and $\mathbf{v}$ respectively. In this case, the operators $\alpha(\mathbf{u}) and\ \alpha(\mathbf{v})$ commute and we obtain the following constraint equation for the motion vectors [4]:

$$\alpha(\mathbf{u}) \alpha(\mathbf{v}) f(\mathbf{x}, t) = 0. \tag{2}$$

Since this transparent-motion constraint is nonlinear, the estimation of the motion vectors by the direct use of Equation (2) leads to non-convex problems. We overcome this difficulty by splitting the solution into a linear and a nonlinear part. By expanding Equation (2), we obtain

$$c_{xx} f_{xx} + c_{yy} f_{yy} + f_{tt} + c_{xy} f_{xy} + c_{xt} f_{xt} + c_{yt} f_{yt} = 0 \tag{3}$$

where $f_{rs} = \partial^2 f / \partial r \partial s$, $r, s \in \{x, y, t\}$; and

$$\begin{aligned} c_{xx} &= u_x v_x & c_{xt} &= u_x + v_x & c_{xy} &= u_x v_y + u_y v_x \\ c_{yy} &= u_y v_y & c_{yt} &= u_y + v_y \end{aligned} \tag{4}$$

are the so-called *mixed motion parameters.* In case of a multiplicative superposition $f(\mathbf{x},t) = g_1(\mathbf{x},t)g_2(\mathbf{x},t)$, the constraint is the same except for $f_{rs} = f\frac{\partial^2 f}{\partial r \partial s} - \frac{\partial f}{\partial r}\frac{\partial f}{\partial s}$ [18]. The introduction of the mixed motion parameters splits, in a natural way, the problem of transparent motion estimation in two parts: a linear part where we solve for the parameters c_{rs}, $r, s \in \{x, y, t\}$; and a nonlinear part where we solve Equation (4) for the motion vectors. Since Equation (3) is linear we can use different methods for the estimation of the mixed motion parameters. We will describe some of these methods in Section 2.1.

2.1 Linear Part: Estimation of the Mixed Motion Parameters

The Structure Tensor. Let time be parameterized such that Equation (1) reads

$$\tilde{u}_x g_x + \tilde{u}_y g_y + u_t g_t = 0 \tag{5}$$

with a unity parameter vector $\mathbf{u}_\mathrm{e} = (\tilde{u}_x, \tilde{u}_y, u_t)^T$. If the variables g_x, g_y, g_t are independent with equal variances and $\mathbf{u}_\mathrm{e}$ is constant, the best fit $\hat{\mathbf{u}}_\mathrm{e}$, in a *least-squares* sense, is the minimizer of the functional

$$E(\mathbf{u}_\mathrm{e}) = \int |\mathbf{u}_\mathrm{e} \cdot \nabla g(\mathbf{x}, t)|^2 \omega(\mathbf{x}, t)\, \mathrm{d}\Omega, \tag{6}$$

where Ω is a neighborhood of the point of interest and $\omega(\mathbf{x}, t)$ is an weighting function. Therefore, $\hat{\mathbf{u}}_\mathrm{e}$ is the minimal eigenvector of the *structure tensor* [19]

$$\mathbf{J}_1 = \int \nabla g(\mathbf{x}, t) \otimes \nabla g(\mathbf{x}, t)\, \omega(\mathbf{x}, t)\, \mathrm{d}\Omega. \tag{7}$$

The motion vector is then recovered from $\hat{\mathbf{u}}_\mathrm{e}/\hat{u}_t$.

For the mixed motion parameters, we proceed in analogy and look for a unity minimizer $\mathbf{c}_\mathrm{e} = (c_{xx}, c_{yy}, c_{tt}, c_{xy}, c_{xt}, c_{yt})^T$ of the functional

$$E(\mathbf{c}_\mathrm{e}) = \int |\mathbf{c}_\mathrm{e} \cdot \mathbf{f}_{(2)}(\mathbf{x}, t)|^2 \omega(\mathbf{x}, t)\, \mathrm{d}\Omega, \tag{8}$$

where $\mathbf{f}_{(2)} = (f_{xx}, f_{yy}, f_{tt}, f_{xy}, f_{xt}, f_{yt})^T$. Note that c_{tt} replaces 1 as the coefficient of f_{tt} in Equation (3). Again, the optimal estimator $\hat{\mathbf{c}}_\mathrm{e}$ is the minimal eigenvector of

$$\mathbf{J}_2 = \int \mathbf{f}_{(2)}(\mathbf{x}, t) \otimes \mathbf{f}_{(2)}(\mathbf{x}, t)\, \omega(\mathbf{x}, t)\, \mathrm{d}\Omega \tag{9}$$

and the mixed motion parameters are recovered from $\hat{\mathbf{c}}_\mathrm{e}/\hat{c}_{tt}$ [11].

Confidence Measures. Clearly the estimator $\hat{\mathbf{c}}_\mathrm{e}$ ($\hat{\mathbf{u}}_\mathrm{e}$) is reliable only if the minimal eigenvalue of $\mathbf{J}_2$ (or $\mathbf{J}_1$) is small compared to the others (ideally, exactly one eigenvalue should be zero). Therefore, confidence for the quality of the estimation can be derived from the eigenvalues of $\mathbf{J}_N$, $N = 1, 2$. however, it is useful to know the confidence before the estimation is performed. Let H_N, K_N, S_N represent the trace, the determinant, and the sum of the central minors of $\mathbf{J}_N$ respectively. These numbers scale as $K^{1/m} \leq (S/m)^{1/(m-1)} \leq H/m$ (with $m = (N+1)(N+2)/2$). In the ideal (noise free) case of only one zero eigenvalue, we have $K = 0$, $S \neq 0$ and in practice the above scaling relation can be used to define confidence measures [11].

Table 1. Different motion patterns (first column) and the ranks of the generalized structure tensors for 1 and 2 motions respectively (columns 2 and 3). Bars indicate motions of 1D (straight) patterns and filled circles motions of 2D patterns - see text for further details. The shown correspondences between the different motion patterns and the ranks of the two tensors can be used to identify the different motion patterns. In general, the rank of $\boldsymbol{J}_N$, $N = 1, 2, ...$ induces a natural order of complexity for patterns consisting of N additive layers [12].

Moving Pattern	rank $\boldsymbol{J}_1$	rank $\boldsymbol{J}_2$
$\circ$	0	0
$\vert$	1	1
$\vert + \vert$	2	2
$\bullet$	2	3
$\bullet + \vert$	3	4
$\bullet + \bullet$	3	5
others	3	6

Local Categorization of the Moving Patterns. Besides allowing for motion estimation, the structure tensor allows for a local categorization of the moving pattern φ : rank $\boldsymbol{J}_1 = 0$ corresponds to regions with constant intensity ($\circ$) and any motion vector is admissible in this region; rank $\boldsymbol{J}_1 = 1$ corresponds to the motion of a straight pattern ($|$), in this case admissible motion vectors are constrained by a line; other moving patterns ($\bullet$) correspond to the rank $\boldsymbol{J}_1 = 2$; and non-coherent motion like noise, appearing and disappearing objects, etc. correspond to rank $\boldsymbol{J}_1 = 3$. Remarkably, in the case of transparent motions, the categorization of the moving patterns is again accessible through the rank $\boldsymbol{J}_2$. Table 1 summarizes these correspondences. For further details see [12].

Regularization. Here we show how to apply a Horn-Schunck-type regularization method for the estimation of the mixed motion parameters. To emphasize the dependency on $\mathbf{c}$, we rewrite Equation (3) as $\mathbf{c} \cdot \mathbf{f}_{(2)\mathrm{r}} + f_{tt} = 0$, where $\mathbf{f}_{(2)\mathrm{r}} = (f_{xx}, f_{yy}, f_{xy}, f_{xt}, f_{yt})^T$. At a given time, we then look for a field $\mathbf{c} = (c_{xx}, c_{yy}, c_{xy}, c_{xt}, c_{yt})^T$ that minimizes the functional

$$\int \frac{1}{\lambda^2} |\mathbf{c} \cdot \mathbf{f}_{(2)\mathrm{r}} + f_{tt}|^2 + |\nabla \mathbf{c}|^2 \, \mathrm{d}\Omega \;, \tag{10}$$

where $\lambda = \lambda(\mathbf{x})$. The Euler-Lagrange equation is

$$(\mathbf{c} \cdot \mathbf{f}_{(2)\mathrm{r}} + f_{tt})\mathbf{f}_{(2)\mathrm{r}} = \lambda^2 \Delta \mathbf{c} \tag{11}$$

Using the approximation $h^2 \Delta \mathbf{c} \approx \check{\mathbf{c}} - \mathbf{c}$, where h is a normalization constant assimilated by λ, and solving for $\mathbf{c}$, we obtain a Gauss-Seidel iteration step defined by

$$\mathbf{c}^{k+1} = \check{\mathbf{c}}^k - \frac{\check{\mathbf{c}}^k \cdot \mathbf{f}_{(2)\mathrm{r}} + f_{tt}}{\lambda^2 + |\mathbf{f}_{(2)\mathrm{r}}|^2} \mathbf{f}_{(2)\mathrm{r}} . \tag{12}$$

This iteration step defined by (12) can be implemented either directly as in [20], by simple methods like *successive over-relaxation* or by more sophisticated methods like *multi-grid relaxation*. Next, we show how to solve for the motion vectors $\mathbf{u}$ and $\mathbf{v}$ given $\mathbf{c}$.

2.2 Nonlinear Part: Solving for the Motion Vectors

The key to our solution is the interpretation of the motion vectors as complex numbers [11], i.e., $u = u_x + \mathrm{j}u_y$, and $v = v_x + \mathrm{j}v_y$ and the observation that

$$uv = c_{xx} - c_{yy} + \mathrm{j}c_{xy} = A_0, \quad u + v = c_{xt} + \mathrm{j}c_{yt} = A_1. \tag{13}$$

In the above equations, the last equalities are just the definitions of A_0 and A_1. Hence, the motion vectors can be recovered as the roots of the complex polynomial

$$Q_2(z) = (z-u)(z-v) = z^2 - A_1 z + A_0 \tag{14}$$

since the coefficients of $Q_2(z)$ depend only on the mixed motion parameters. However, Equation (4) is a over-determined system of equations for the motion vectors. Consequently, not all possible values for the mixed motion parameters vector $\mathbf{c}$ correspond to motion vectors. To better understand this issue, we consider Equations (2) and (3) in the Fourier domain where they become

$$(u_x\xi_x + u_y\xi_y + \xi_t)(v_x\xi_x + v_y\xi_y + \xi_t)\mathbf{F}(\xi_x, \xi_y, \xi_t) = 0 \tag{15}$$

and

$$(c_{xx}\xi_x^2 + c_{yy}\xi_y^2 + c_{tt}\xi_t^2 + c_{xy}\xi_x\xi_y + c_{xt}\xi_x\xi_t + c_{yt}\xi_y\xi_t)\mathbf{F}(\xi_x, \xi_y, \xi_t) = 0 \tag{16}$$

respectively. $\mathbf{F}(\xi_x, \xi_y, \xi_t)$ represents the Fourier transform of $\mathbf{f}(x, y, t)$. Therefore, fitting the motion vectors $\mathbf{u}, \mathbf{v}$ to Equation (2) is equivalent to fitting two planes to the support of $\mathbf{F}(\xi_x, \xi_y, \xi_t)$ while fitting a parameter vector $\mathbf{c}$ to Equation (3) is equivalent to fitting a quadric to the support of $\mathbf{F}(\xi_x, \xi_y, \xi_t)$. Such a quadric represents two planes if and only if its associated matrix has exactly two nonzero eigenvalues of opposite signs. Therefore, we conclude that a vector $\mathbf{c}$ of mixed motion parameters corresponds to two motion vectors if and only if

$$\begin{vmatrix} c_{xx} & \frac{c_{xy}}{2} & \frac{c_{xt}}{2} \\ \frac{c_{xy}}{2} & c_{yy} & \frac{c_{yt}}{2} \\ \frac{c_{xt}}{2} & \frac{c_{yt}}{2} & c_{tt} \end{vmatrix} = 0 \text{ and } \begin{vmatrix} c_{xx} & \frac{c_{xy}}{2} \\ \frac{c_{xy}}{2} & c_{yy} \end{vmatrix} + \begin{vmatrix} c_{xx} & \frac{c_{xt}}{2} \\ \frac{c_{xt}}{2} & c_{tt} \end{vmatrix} + \begin{vmatrix} c_{yy} & \frac{c_{yt}}{2} \\ \frac{c_{yt}}{2} & c_{tt} \end{vmatrix} < 0. \tag{17}$$

The role of the above conditions is to exclude the case when Equation (3) is valid but the Fourier transform of the motion signal is not restricted to two planes.

2.3 Experimental Results

Figure 1 shows results for a synthetic image sequence with transparent motions. The algorithm first determines one motion using $\mathbf{J}_1$ if the confidence for one motion is high. If the confidence test fails ($H_1 > \epsilon_0$, $K_1^{2/3} > \epsilon_1 S_1$), two motions are estimated by using $\mathbf{J}_2$. If confidence for two motions fails ($K_2^{5/6} > \epsilon_2 S_2$) no motion is estimated (although this procedure could be extended for an arbitrary number of motions). The values $\epsilon_0 = 0.001$, $\epsilon_1 = 0.2$, $\epsilon_2 = 0.3$ were used for the confidence parameters. We used $[1, 0, -1]^T[1, 1, 1]$ as first order derivative filter, an integration window of $5 \times 5 \times 5$

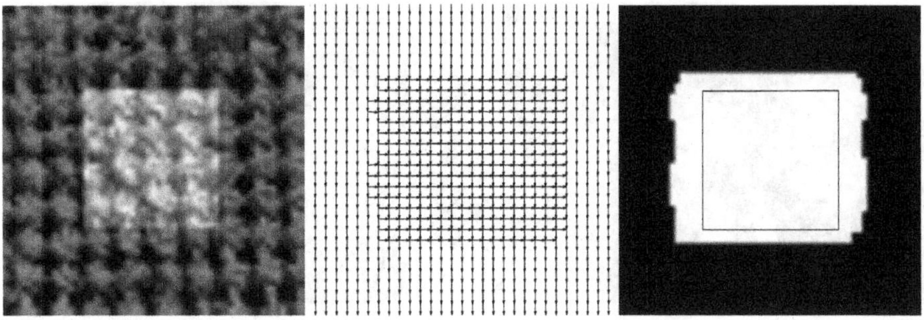

(a) (b) (c)

Fig. 1. Results for synthetic data: (a) the central frame of a synthetic input sequence to which dynamic noise with an SNR of 35 dB was added; (b) the estimated motion fields; (c) the segmentation defined by confidence for one (black) and two (white) motions. The background moved down and the foreground square to the right, the superposition of the two was additive. The means/standard-deviations for the components of the estimated motion fields are $(0.0002/0.0029, 1.0001/0.0043)$ and $(1.0021/0.0134, 0.0003/0.0129)$.

pixels and a weight function of $\omega = 1$. Second-order derivatives were obtained by applying the first order filter two times. Figure 2 shows results for more realistic image sequences. The Gauss-Seidel iteration (Equation 12) was applied to estimate the motion fields for both sequences. Gaussian derivatives with $\sigma = 1$ and a kernel size of 7 pixels were used for first order derivatives. Again, second order derivatives were obtained by applying the first-order filter twice. The parameter $\lambda = 1$ and 200 iterations were used. Even better results could be obtained with optimized filters - see [21] in this volume.

3 Extensions

3.1 Phase-Based Approach

Frequency-domain based approaches to transparent motions are based on the observation that motion induces a phase shift [8, 14, 22]. For transparent motions, the multiple phase shifts lead to the following equations.

The Constraint Equations

$$F_{t_k}(\omega) = \phi_1^k G_1(\omega) + \phi_2^k G_2(\omega), \qquad k = 0, \ldots \tag{18}$$

To obtain the phase shifts from these constraints, we first simplify notation by setting $\Phi_k = (\phi_1^k, \phi_2^k)$ and $\mathbf{G} = (G_1, G_2)$. We then obtain the following expressions:

$$F_{t_k} = \Phi_k \cdot \mathbf{G}, \qquad k = 0, \ldots \tag{19}$$

Our goal now is to obtain the phase-components vector $\Phi_1 = (\phi_1, \phi_2)$ by cancellation of the unknown Fourier-transforms vector $\mathbf{G}$ of the image layers in the system above. First, we define the polynomial

$$p(z) = (z - \phi_1)(z - \phi_2) = z^2 + a_1 z + a_2 \tag{20}$$

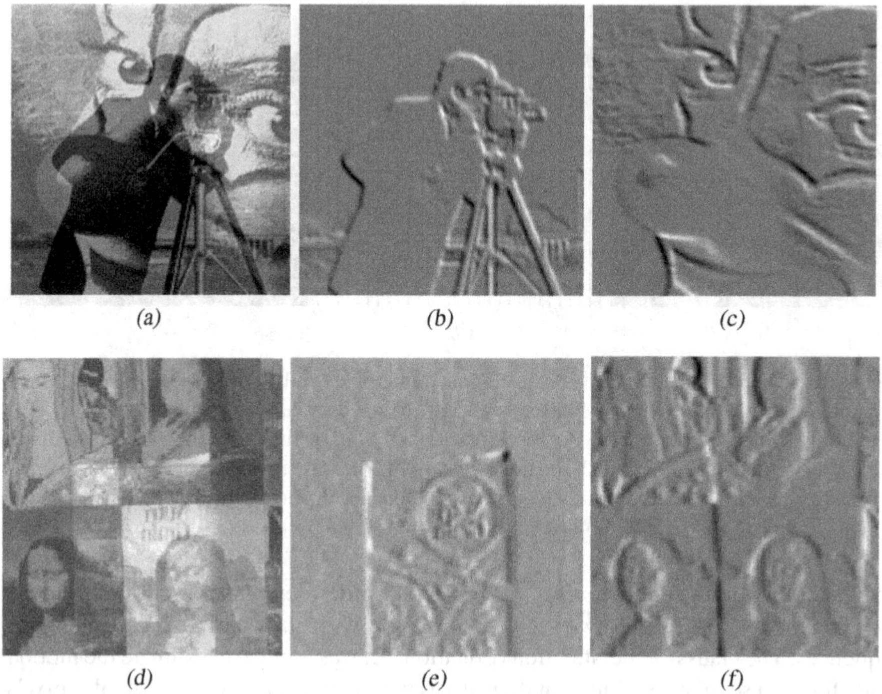

Fig. 2. Results for natural images with synthetic, additive motions (up and to the right): (a) the central frame of the input sequence; (b) the result of applying $\alpha(\hat{\mathbf{u}})$ to (a); (c) the result of applying $\alpha(\hat{\mathbf{v}})$ to (a). The errors/standard-deviations of the estimated motion components are $(0.9956/0.0106, -0.0032/0.0101)$ and $(-0.0101/0.0129, 0.9868/0.0144)$. Results for a real sequence: panels (d), (e) and (f) correspond to (a), (b), and (c) above. In this movie, the Mona-Lisa painting moves to the right and a right-moving box is transparently over-imposed due to reflections. The quality of the motion estimation is here demonstrated by showing how well the motion layers are separated.

with unknown coefficients $a_1 = -(\phi_1 + \phi_2)$, $a_2 = \phi_1\phi_2$. Now the phase terms ϕ_1, ϕ_2 are the roots of $p(z)$, i.e., $p(\phi_n) = 0$, for $n = 1, 2$. Second, we observe that

$$F_{t_{m+2}} + a_1 F_{t_{m+1}} + a_2 F_{t_m} = (\Phi_{m+2} + a_1\Phi_{m+1} + a_2\Phi_m) \cdot \mathbf{G} \tag{21}$$

$$= (\phi_1^m p(\phi_1), \phi_2^m p(\phi_2)) \cdot \mathbf{G} = 0 \tag{22}$$

and

$$F_{t_{m+2}} = -a_2 F_{t_m} - a_1 F_{t_{m+1}} \qquad m = 0, \ldots \tag{23}$$

Solving for the Phase Shifts. To solve for the phase shifts we apply again the strategy of splitting the problem into linear and nonlinear parts. First, we solve Equations (23) for a_1, a_2 (linear part). Second, we obtain the unknown phase changes ϕ_1, ϕ_2 as the roots of $p(z)$ (nonlinear problem).

Since we have two unknowns, we need at least two equations for solving for a_1, a_2. Therefore we consider the first two Equations of (23), i.e.

$$\begin{pmatrix} F_{t_2} \\ F_{t_3} \end{pmatrix} = -\begin{pmatrix} F_{t_0} & F_{t_1} \\ F_{t_1} & F_{t_2} \end{pmatrix} \begin{pmatrix} a_2 \\ a_1 \end{pmatrix}. \tag{24}$$

Clearly, we can obtain a_1, a_2 only if the matrix in the above equation is nonsingular. Nevertheless, in case of a singular but nonzero matrix, we can still obtain the phase shifts. To understand why, we will discuss all the cases in which $\mathbf{A}$ is singular. First note that the matrix $\mathbf{A}$ nicely factors as

$$\boldsymbol{A} = \begin{pmatrix} F_{t_0} & F_{t_1} \\ F_{t_1} & F_{t_2} \end{pmatrix} = \boldsymbol{B} \begin{pmatrix} G_1 & 0 \\ 0 & G_2 \end{pmatrix} \boldsymbol{B}^T \tag{25}$$

where

$$\boldsymbol{B} = \begin{pmatrix} 1 & 1 \\ \phi_1 & \phi_2 \end{pmatrix}. \tag{26}$$

Therefore,

$$\det \mathbf{A} = G_1 G_2 (\phi_1 - \phi_2)^2. \tag{27}$$

It follows that there are only two non-exclusive situations where the matrix $\boldsymbol{A}$ can become singular: (i) the Fourier transform of at least one layer vanishes at the frequency ω, and (ii) the phase shifts are equal. Therefore, we have

1. rank $\boldsymbol{A}$ = 1: the possible cases are $G_1 = 0,\ G_2 \neq 0;\ G_1 \neq 0,\ G_2 = 0$ or $\phi_1 = \phi_2,\ G_1 + G_2 \neq 0$ and we can compute the double phase or one of the two distinct phases from
$$F_{t_1} = F_{t_0}\phi. \tag{28}$$
2. rank $\mathbf{A}$ = 0: in this case $G_1 = G_2 = 0$ or $\phi_1 = \phi_2,\ G_1 + G_2 = 0$ and all equations in (18) degenerate to
$$F_{t_k} = 0, \quad k = 0, \ldots \tag{29}$$

Finally, Equation (27) implies that rank $\boldsymbol{A} \leq 1$ everywhere if and only $\phi_1 = \phi_2$ everywhere, i.e., the image sequence does not have any transparent layers.

3.2 Layer Separation

Once the phase shifts are known, it is possible to obtain the transparent layers as follows:

$$\begin{pmatrix} F_{t_0} \\ F_{t_1} \end{pmatrix} = \begin{pmatrix} 1 & 1 \\ \phi_1 & \phi_2 \end{pmatrix} \begin{pmatrix} G_1 \\ G_2 \end{pmatrix}. \tag{30}$$

Note, however, that the separation is not possible at all frequencies. The problematic frequencies are those where two or more phase values are identical because the rank of the matrix $\mathbf{B}$ is then reduced. This is an important observation because it defines the support where multiple phases can occur by the following equation:

$$\phi_1 = \phi_2 \iff e^{j(\mathbf{u}-\mathbf{v})\cdot\omega\Delta t} = 1 \iff (\mathbf{u}-\mathbf{v})\cdot\omega = 2k\pi, \qquad k = 0, \ldots \tag{31}$$

On the above defined lines, the Fourier transforms at the transparent layers cannot be separated. A possible solution would be to interpolate the values on these lines from the neighboring frequency values of the separated layers.

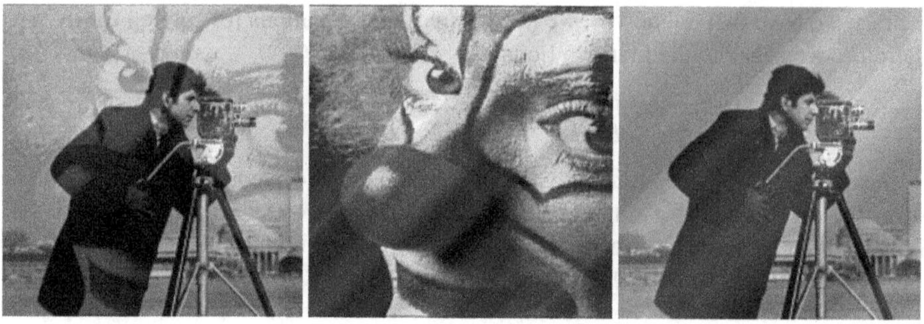

(a) (b) (c)

Fig. 3. Results of layer separation. Shown are in (a) the same input as in Figure 2a, and in (b) and (c) the separated layers. The errors due to the still incomplete interpolation of missing frequencies are seen as oriented patterns.

3.3 Block Matching

The Block Matching Constraint. By transforming Equation (23) back to the space domain, we obtain the following block matching constraint equation for transparent motions [13]

$$e(f, \boldsymbol{x}, \mathbf{u}, \mathbf{v}) = f_0(\mathbf{x} - \mathbf{u} - \mathbf{v}) - f_1(\mathbf{x} - \mathbf{u}) - f_1(\mathbf{x} - \mathbf{v}) + f_2(\mathbf{x}) = 0. \tag{32}$$

From this constraint a number of different algorithms for the estimation of multiple motions can be derived. We here present a hierarchical algorithm which is based on a combination of statistical model discrimination and hierarchical decision making. First, a single-motion model is fitted to the sequence by exhaustive search. If the fit is poor, the single-motion hypothesis is rejected and the algorithm tries to fit two transparent motions. If the confidence for two motions is low, no motion is estimated.

The Stochastic Image Sequence Model. Apart from distortions and occlusions, the block matching constraint may differ from zero due to noise. Therefore additional information about the distribution of the noise can help to determine whether or not the difference between the best block matching fit and the true motion can be explained by the noise model. Different motion types lead to different noise distributions of the error signals. This can be used to select the most likely motion model.

We model the observed image intensity at each spatial location and time step as

$$f_k(\boldsymbol{x}) = \bar{f}_k(\boldsymbol{x}) + \epsilon_k(\boldsymbol{x}), \quad \epsilon_k(\boldsymbol{x}) \sim \mathcal{N}(0, \sigma^2), \quad k = 0, 1, \ldots \tag{33}$$

Therefore, from Equation (32) and the noise model, we have

$$e(f, \mathbf{x}, \mathbf{u}, \mathbf{v}) = e(\bar{f}, \mathbf{x}, \mathbf{u}, \mathbf{v}) + \varepsilon(\mathbf{x}), \tag{34}$$

where $\varepsilon(\boldsymbol{x}) = \epsilon_0(\mathbf{x} - \mathbf{u} - \mathbf{v}) - \epsilon_1(\mathbf{x} - \mathbf{u}) - \epsilon_1(\mathbf{x} - \mathbf{v}) - \epsilon_2(\boldsymbol{x})$. Hence, in case of a perfect match of the transparent motion model, the motion-compensated residual can be modeled as

$$e(f, \mathbf{x}, \mathbf{u}, \mathbf{v}) = \varepsilon(\boldsymbol{x}) \sim \mathcal{N}(0, 4\sigma^2). \tag{35}$$

Fig. 4. Block matching results. Shown are in (a) the central frame of the same input sequence as in 1a, and in (b) the estimated motion fields. The area corresponding to the transparent object has been depicted in (b) for better visualization.

Consequently, the sum of squared differences over the block (denoted BM_2) obeys the χ^2 distribution with $|\Omega|$ degrees of freedom, i.e.,

$$\mathrm{BM}_2(\mathbf{x},\mathbf{u},\mathbf{v}) = \frac{1}{4\sigma^2}\sum_{\mathbf{y}\in\Omega} e(f,\mathbf{y},\mathbf{u},\mathbf{v})^2 \;\sim\; \chi^2(|\Omega|), \tag{36}$$

where Ω is the set of pixels in the block under consideration and $|\Omega|$ is the number of elements in Ω. A block matching algorithm can be obtained by minimization of the above expression.

If there is only one motion inside Ω, i.e. $f_1(\boldsymbol{x}) = f_0(\boldsymbol{x}-\boldsymbol{v})$, the value of

$$\mathrm{BM}_1(\boldsymbol{v}) = \frac{1}{|\Omega|}\sum_{\boldsymbol{x}\in\Omega}(f_1(\boldsymbol{x}) - f_0(\boldsymbol{x}-\boldsymbol{v}))^2 \tag{37}$$

will be small for the correct motion vector $\boldsymbol{v}$. If Ω includes two motions, the value BM_1 will be significantly different from zero for any single vector $\mathbf{v}$, because one vector cannot compensate for two motions.

Motion-Model Discrimination. There are several possibilities to find the most likely motion model. To save computation time, we opt for a significance test which allows for a hierarchical estimation of the motion vectors. If we allow a percentage α of misclassifications, we can derive a threshold T_N for BM_N, $N = 1, 2$ as follows [23]: let the null-hypothesis H_0 mean that the model of N transparent motions is correct. T_N is then determined by

$$\mathrm{prob}(\mathrm{BM}_N > T_N | H_0) = \alpha. \tag{38}$$

H_0 is rejected if $BM_N > T_N$. The threshold can be obtained from tables of the χ^2 distribution.

3.4 Experimental Results

Figure 3 shows the separation of a synthetic additive overlaid image sequence. The missing phase shifts were interpolated by averaging the neighboring values. The interpolation errors are visible as oriented structures. A better interpolation method could help to reduce the errors. Figure 4 shows the results of motion estimation by block matching with a 5×5 window. Full search has been performed to find the best match according to the confidence test described by Equation (38).

4 Discussion

We have shown how to split the problem of estimating multiple transparent motions into a linear and a nonlinear part. This strategy has allowed us to extend classical but powerful algorithms for the estimation of motion to cases where standard single-motion models would fail. We have thereby reduced the difficulties in estimating multiple transparent motions to well-known difficulties in the standard, single-motion case: noisy images, aperture problem, occlusion, etc. The algorithms have been presented for two transparent motions, but are not limited to only two motions since extensions to more motions are straightforward.

The methods presented for solving the linear part of the problem have particular trade-offs. The structure-tensor method is fast and accurate but usually does not produce dense flows; the phase-based method suffers from windowing and fast Fourier transform artifacts; the regularization approach yields dense flow fields but is slow; and, finally, the block matching algorithm is very robust to noise but rather slow and does normally not yield sub-pixel accuracy.

The method proposed for solving the nonlinear part is the key which makes the overall approach so useful and lets us conclude that the difficulties in the estimation of transparent motion are, in essence, the same as for the estimation of single motions.

Acknowledgment. We gratefully acknowledge support from the *Deutsche Forschungsgemeinschaft* received under Ba 1176/7-2.

References

1. Badino, H.: A robust approach for ego-motion estimation using a mobile stereo platform. In Jähne, B., Barth, E., Mester, R., Scharr, H., eds.: Complex Motion, Proceedings 1st Int. Workshop, Günzburg, Oct. 12–14. LNCS (2004)
2. Sühling, M., Arigovindan, M., Jansen, C., Hunziker, P., Unser, M.: Myocardial motion and strain rate analysis from ultrasound sequences. In Jähne, B., Barth, E., Mester, R., Scharr, H., eds.: Complex Motion, Proceedings 1st Int. Workshop, Günzburg, Oct. 12–14. LNCS (2004)
3. Sigal, L., Zhu, Y., Comaniciu, D., Black, M.: Graphical object models for detection and tracking. In Jähne, B., Barth, E., Mester, R., Scharr, H., eds.: Complex Motion, Proceedings 1st Int. Workshop, Günzburg, Oct. 12–14. LNCS (2004)
4. Shizawa, M., Mase, K.: Simultaneous multiple optical flow estimation. In: IEEE Conf. Computer Vision and Pattern Recognition. Volume I., Atlantic City, NJ, IEEE Computer Press (1990) 274–8
5. Wang, J.Y.A., Adelson, E.H.: Representing moving images with layers. IEEE Transactions on Image Processing **3** (1994) 625–38
6. Darrell, T., Simoncelli, E.: Separation of transparent motion into layers using velocity-tuned mechanisms. Technical Report 244, MIT Media Laboratory (1993)

7. Darrell, T., Simoncelli, E.: Nulling filters and the separation of transparent motions. In: IEEE Conf. Computer Vision and Pattern Recognition, New York, IEEE Computer Press (1993) 738–9
8. Vernon, D.: Decoupling Fourier components of dynamic image sequences: a theory of signal separation, image segmentation and optical flow estimation. In Burkhardt, H., Neumann, B., eds.: Computer Vision - ECCV'98. Volume 1407/II of LNCS., Springer Verlag (1998) 68–85
9. Szeliski, R., Avidan, S., Anandan, P.: Layer extraction from multiple images containing reflections and transparency. In: IEEE Conf. Computer Vision and Pattern Recognition. Volume 1., Hilton Head Island (2000) 246–253
10. Anandan, P.: Motion estimation and optical flow computation: a personalized view. Complex Motion, 1st Int. Workshop, Günzburg, Oct. 12–14 (2004) Invited talk.
11. Mota, C., Stuke, I., Barth, E.: Analytic solutions for multiple motions. In: Proc. IEEE Int. Conf. Image Processing. Volume II., Thessaloniki, Greece, IEEE Signal Processing Soc. (2001) 917–20
12. Mota, C., Dorr, M., Stuke, I., Barth, E.: Categorization of transparent-motion patterns using the projective plane. International Journal of Computer & Information Science **5** (2004) 129–140
13. Stuke, I., Aach, T., Barth, E., Mota, C.: Multiple-motion estimation by block-matching using markov random fields. International Journal of Computer & Information Science **5** (2004) 141–152
14. Stuke, I., Aach, T., Mota, C., Barth, E.: Estimation of multiple motions: regularization and performance evaluation. In Vasudev, B., Hsing, T.R., Tescher, A.G., Ebrahimi, T., eds.: Image and Video Communications and Processing 2003. Volume 5022 of Proceedings of SPIE. (2003) 75–86
15. Cremers, D.: Bayesian approaches to motion-based image and video segmentation. In Jähne, B., Barth, E., Mester, R., Scharr, H., eds.: Complex Motion, Proceedings 1st Int. Workshop, Günzburg, Oct. 12–14. LNCS (2004)
16. Nordberg, K., Vikstén, F.: Representation of motion fields and their boundaries. In Jähne, B., Barth, E., Mester, R., Scharr, H., eds.: Complex Motion, Proceedings 1st Int. Workshop, Günzburg, Oct. 12–14. LNCS (2004)
17. Horn, B., Schunck, B.: Determining optical flow. Artificial Intelligence **17** (1981) 185–203
18. Langley, K., Fleet, D.J.: A logarithmic transformation applied to multiplicative transparencies and motion discontinuities. Opthalmology Physiology and Optics **14** (1994) 441
19. Haußecker, H., Spies, H.: Motion. In Jähne, B., Haußecker, H., Geißler, P., eds.: Handbook of Computer Vision and Applications. Volume 2. Academic Press (1999) 309–96
20. Stuke, I., Aach, T., Mota, C., Barth, E.: Linear and regularized solutions for multiple motion. In: Proc. IEEE Int. Conf. Acoustics, Speech and Signal Processing. Volume III., Hong Kong, IEEE Signal Processing Soc. (2003) 157–60
21. Scharr, H.: Optimal filters for extended optical flow. In Jähne, B., Barth, E., Mester, R., Scharr, H., eds.: Complex Motion, Proceedings 1st Int. Workshop, Günzburg, Oct. 12–14. LNCS (2004)
22. Fleet, D.J., Jepson, A.D.: Computation of component image velocity from local phase information. International Journal of Computer Vision **5** (1990) 77–104
23. Aach, T., Kaup, A.: Bayesian algorithms for adaptive change detection in image sequences using Markov random fields. Signal Processing: Image Communication **7** (1995) 147–160

Towards a Multi-camera Generalization of Brightness Constancy

Hanno Scharr*

Institute for Chemistry and Dynamics of the Geosphere, ICG III
Forschungszentrum Jülich GmbH, 52425 Jülich, Germany
H.Scharr@FZ-Juelich.de

Abstract. Standard optical flow methods for motion or disparity estimation use a brightness constancy constraint equation (BCCE). This BCCE either handles a moving camera imaging a non-moving scene or a fixed camera imaging a moving scene. In this paper a BCCE is developed that can handle instantaneous motion of the camera on a 2D plane normal to the viewing direction and motion of the imaged scene. From the thus acquired up to 5 dimensional data set 3D object motion, 3D surface element position, and -normals can be estimated simultaneously. Experiments using 1d or 2d camera grids and a weighted total least squares (TLS) estimation scheme demonstrate performance in terms of systematic error and noise stability, and show technical implications.

1 Introduction

Motion estimation as well as disparity estimation are standard tasks for optical flow algorithms as well known from early publications (e.g. [18, 25] and many more). This paper aims to combine both scene flow [36] (i.e. 3D optical flow estimated from 2D sequences), disparity and surface normal estimation within a single optical-flow-like estimation step. As the developed model has the same form as usual brightness change constraint equations (BCCE) no special estimation framework has to be established. We use the so called Structure Tensor method [3, 17, 20] but other methods can be applied as well (e.g. the ones in [1, 16]).

In state of the art optical flow algorithms for motion estimation an image sequence of a single fixed camera is interpreted as data in a 3D x-y-t-space. In this space a BCCE defines a linear model for the changes of gray values due to local object motion and other parameters of e.g. illumination changes or physical processes (compare e.g. [15]). The result of the calculation then is a displacement vector field, i.e. local object motion and quantities of brightness change if an appropriate model is used. Using a moving camera looking at a fixed scene identical algorithms can be used to determine object depth, known as structure from camera motion (e.g. [23]).

The basic idea for the new estimation technique presented here is to interpret the camera position $\boldsymbol{s} = (s_x, s_y)$ as new dimension(s), see Fig. 1. Hence all image sequences acquired by a multi-camera setup (or a pseudo multi-camera setup as in our

* This work has partly been funded by DFG SPP1114 (SCHA 927/1-2).

B. Jähne et al. (Eds.): IWCM 2004, LNCS 3417, pp. 78–90, 2007.

target application mentioned below) are combined to sample a 4D-Volume in x-y-s_x-t-space using a 1d camera grid. If a 2D camera grid is used (as e.g. in [26]) we get a 5D-Volume in x-y-s_x-s_y-t-space.

In [6] a 2D-manifold is constructed combining all 1D trajectories of a surface point acquired by multiple cameras. This comes very close to the idea presented here. The advantage of our approach is that it is an extension of usual optical flow and consequently can easily be combined with other methods and extensions stated in the related work section.

In our target application plant growth shall be studied using a single camera on a linear XY-moving stage. From other plant growth studies (e.g. [31]) we know that plant motion can be measured by optical flow using a frame rate of less than one image per minute. Thus if image sequence acquisition with the moving stage is done within a few seconds our scene can be interpreted to be fixed for this time interval. Then the acquired image sequence samples a 4d-volume in x-y-s_x-s_y-space at a fixed point in time. In the remainder of this paper we treat our single camera on moving stage setup as a (pseudo) multi-camera setup acquiring at a single point in time.

Related Work. There is rich literature on optical flow estimation techniques (see the overviews [1, 16]) and many extensions have been developed. There are extensions towards affine motion estimation [9, 10], scene flow [36] and physically motivated brightness changes [7,13,15]. Robust estimations [4,12], variational approaches [5,18,38,39], coarse-to-fine schemes [2], regularization schemes [22,33], special filters [8,11,21] and coupled denoising methods [34] have been studied. There already exist frameworks for simultaneous motion and stereo analysis (e.g. [6, 35, 37]). But to the best of my knowledge neither a BCCE-like model using a 2d camera grid nor a model for simultaneous estimation of disparity, surface normals, and 3d optical flow has been presented so far. Preliminary results have been published in [29, 30].

Paper Organization. We start by deriving the new model in 5D (Sec. 2) followed by a compact revision of the Structure Tensor TLS estimator (Sec. 3). An experimental validation of four special cases of the novel model within this estimation framework is presented in Sec. 4. Finally we conclude with summary and outlook in Sec. 5.

2 Derivation of the New BCCE

In this section the novel BCCE shall be developed, given a 3D object/motion model, a camera model and a brightness change model.

2.1 Object, Camera and Brightness Models

As object/motion model we use a surface element at world coordinate position (X_0, Y_0, Z_0) with X- and Y-slopes Z_x and Z_y moving with velocity (U_x, U_y, U_z):

$$\begin{pmatrix} X \\ Y \\ Z \end{pmatrix} (t) = \begin{pmatrix} X_0 + U_x t \\ Y_0 + U_y t \\ Z_0 + U_z t + Z_x \Delta X + Z_y \Delta Y \end{pmatrix} \tag{1}$$

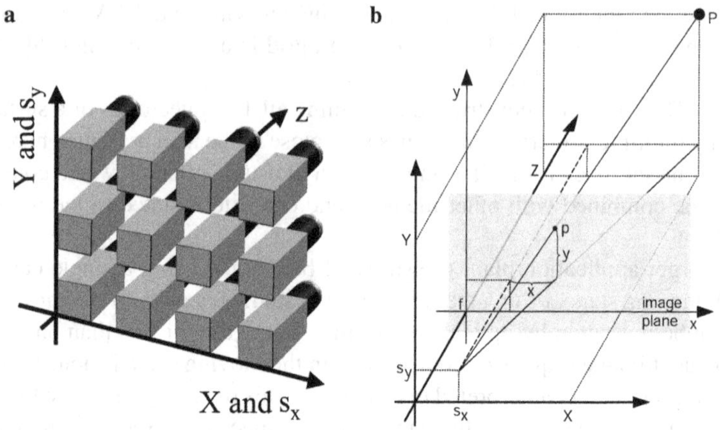

Fig. 1. a A camera grid **b** Projection of a point P by a pinhole camera

where $\triangle X$ and $\triangle Y$ are arbitrary steps in X- and Y-direction, respectively[1]. Given the slopes Z_x and Z_y the surface normal is $(-Z_x, -Z_y, 1)$.

As camera model we use a pinhole camera at world coordinate position $(s_x, s_y, 0)$, looking into Z-direction (cmp. Fig. 1**b**

$$\begin{pmatrix} x \\ y \end{pmatrix} = \frac{f}{Z} \begin{pmatrix} X - s_x \\ Y - s_y \end{pmatrix} \tag{2}$$

Varying s_x and s_y at constant time t, e.g. by using a camera grid (see Fig. 1**a**), is called instantaneous translation. More general instantaneous motion models can be found e.g. in [19, 24], including camera rotation, Z-translation and changing focal length.

We sample (s_x, s_y)-space using several cameras each of which acquires an image sequence. We combine all of these sequences into one 5d data set sampling the continuous intensity function $I(x, y, s_x, s_y, t)$. We will now formulate the brightness model in this 5d space. We assume that the acquired brightness of a surface element is constant under camera translation, meaning we are looking at a Lambertian surface. In addition this brightness shall be constant in time, i.e. we need temporally constant illumination[2]. Consequently in our 5d space there is a 3d manifold in which I does not change, thus the total differential $\mathrm{d}I = 0$ in this manifold. The brightness model therefore is

$$\mathrm{d}I = I_x \mathrm{d}x + I_y \mathrm{d}y + I_{s_x} \mathrm{d}s_x + I_{s_y} \mathrm{d}s_y + I_t \mathrm{d}t = 0 \tag{3}$$

We use the notation $I_* = \frac{\partial I}{\partial *}$ for spatio-temporal derivatives of the image intensities I.

---

[1] These steps are taken implicitly when implementing intensity derivatives at a fixed (x, y)-image position via convolution kernels, thus we do not add them to the X and Y component.

[2] This assumption can easily be relaxed using the approach shown in [15].

2.2 Combination of the 3 Models into a Single BCCE

In order to derive a single linear equation from the above models, we first apply the pinhole camera (Eq. 2) to the moving surface element (Eq. 1) and get

$$\begin{pmatrix} x \\ y \end{pmatrix}(s_x, s_y, t) = \frac{f}{Z_0 + U_z t + Z_x \Delta X + Z_y \Delta Y} \begin{pmatrix} X_0 + U_x t - s_x \\ Y_0 + U_y t - s_y \end{pmatrix} \tag{4}$$

Consequently we can calculate the differentials $\mathrm{d}x$ and $\mathrm{d}y$:

$$\begin{pmatrix} \mathrm{d}x \\ \mathrm{d}y \end{pmatrix} = \frac{f}{Z_0 + U_z t + Z_x \Delta X + Z_y \Delta Y} \begin{pmatrix} (U_x - U_z \frac{x}{f})\mathrm{d}t - \mathrm{d}s_x \\ (U_y - U_z \frac{y}{f})\mathrm{d}t - \mathrm{d}s_y \end{pmatrix} \tag{5}$$

This equation is nonlinear in U_z. We linearize it via the assumption that U_z is small compared to the overall depth $Z_0 >> U_z t$ and omit $U_z t$ in the denominator. Using the following notation for image-based expressions

$$\begin{array}{rlll} \text{3d optical flow} & u_x = \frac{f}{Z_0} U_x & u_y = \frac{f}{Z_0} U_y & u_z = -\frac{1}{Z_0} U_x \\ \text{disparity and slopes} & v = -\frac{f}{Z_0} & z_x = \frac{Z_x}{Z_0} & z_y = \frac{Z_y}{Z_0} \\ \text{local pixel coordinates} & x = x_0 + \Delta x & y = y_0 + \Delta y & \\ \text{where } & \Delta x = \frac{f}{Z_0} \Delta X & \Delta y = \frac{f}{Z_0} \Delta Y & \end{array} \tag{6}$$

we can further approximate

$$\frac{-f}{Z_0 + Z_x \Delta X + Z_y \Delta Y} \approx \frac{-f}{Z_0}(1 - z_x \Delta X - z_y \Delta Y) = v + z_x \Delta x + z_y \Delta x \tag{7}$$

Plugging Eqs. 5–7 into the brightness model Eq. 3 yields the sought for BCCE

$$\begin{aligned} 0 = {} & I_x(v\mathrm{d}s_x + (u_x + x_0 u_z)\mathrm{d}t) + I_x \Delta x(z_x \mathrm{d}s_x + u_z \mathrm{d}t) + I_x \Delta y z_y \mathrm{d}s_x + I_{s_x} \mathrm{d}s_x \\ & + I_y(v\mathrm{d}s_y + (u_y + y_0 u_z)\mathrm{d}t) + I_y \Delta y(z_y \mathrm{d}s_y + u_z \mathrm{d}t) + I_y \Delta x z_x \mathrm{d}s_y + I_{s_y} \mathrm{d}s_y \\ & + I_t \mathrm{d}t \end{aligned} \tag{8}$$

We decompose (and rearrange) this equation into data vector d and parameter vector p:

$$\begin{aligned} \boldsymbol{d} = {} & (I_x, I_y, I_x \Delta x, I_x \Delta, I_y \Delta y, I_y \Delta x, I_{s_x}, I_{s_y}, I_t)^T \\ \boldsymbol{p} = {} & ((v\mathrm{d}s_x + (u_x + x_0 u_z)\mathrm{d}t), (v\mathrm{d}s_y + (u_y + y_0 u_z)\mathrm{d}t), (z_x \mathrm{d}s_x + u_z \mathrm{d}t), \\ & z_y \mathrm{d}s_x, (z_y \mathrm{d}s_y + u_z \mathrm{d}t), z_x \mathrm{d}s_y, \mathrm{d}s_x, \mathrm{d}s_y, \mathrm{d}t)^T \end{aligned} \tag{9}$$

and get the model equation $\boldsymbol{d}^T \boldsymbol{p} = 0$ (cmp. Eq. 10). This linear BCCE can be used for combined estimation of 3d optical flow (or scene flow) disparity and normal of the imaged surface element. In order to investigate the different terms and properties of this model, we will look at several special cases in the experiments Sec. 4. But first let us briefly review total least squares parameter estimation.

3 Revision of the Structure Tensor

In this total least squares parameter estimation method a model with linear parameters p_j has to be given in the form

$$\boldsymbol{d}^{\mathrm{T}} \boldsymbol{p} = 0 \tag{10}$$

with data depending vector $\boldsymbol{d}$ and parameter vector $\boldsymbol{p}$. Eq. 10 is one equation for several parameters (the components of the parameter vector) and thus under-determined. In our case we have one equation for each 4d or 5d pixel. Thus we add the assumption, that within a small neighborhood Ω of pixels i all equations are approximately solved by the same set of parameters $\boldsymbol{p}$. Eq. 10 therefore becomes

$$\boldsymbol{d}_i^{\mathrm{T}}\boldsymbol{p} = e_i \text{ for all pixels } i \text{ in } \Omega \tag{11}$$

with errors e_i which have to be minimized by the sought for solution $\tilde{\boldsymbol{p}}$.

Using a matrix D composed of the vectors $\boldsymbol{d}_i$ via $\mathbf{D}_{ij} = (\boldsymbol{d}_i)_j$ Eq. 11 becomes $\mathbf{D}\boldsymbol{p} = \boldsymbol{e}$. We minimize $\boldsymbol{e}$ using a weighted 2-norm

$$||\boldsymbol{e}|| = ||\mathbf{D}\boldsymbol{p}|| = \boldsymbol{p}^{\mathrm{T}}\mathbf{D}^{\mathrm{T}}\mathbf{W}\mathbf{D}\boldsymbol{p} =: \boldsymbol{p}^{\mathrm{T}}\mathbf{J}\boldsymbol{p} \stackrel{!}{=} \min \tag{12}$$

where $\mathbf{W}$ is a diagonal matrix containing the weights. In our case Gaussian weights are used (see Sec. 4). It multiplies each equation i in Eq. 11 by a weight w_i. The matrix $\mathbf{J} = \mathbf{D}^{\mathrm{T}}\mathbf{W}\mathbf{D}$ is the so called Structure Tensor. The error $\boldsymbol{e}$ is minimized by introducing the assumption $|\tilde{\boldsymbol{p}}| = 1$ in order to suppress the trivial solution $\tilde{\boldsymbol{p}} = \mathbf{0}$. Doing so the space of solutions $\tilde{\boldsymbol{p}}$ is spanned by the eigenvector(s) to the smallest eigenvalue(s) of $\mathbf{J}$. We call this space the null-space of $\mathbf{J}$ as the smallest eigenvalue(s) are 0 if the model is fulfilled perfectly, i.e. $\boldsymbol{e} = \mathbf{0}$. Usually the model is not fulfilled perfectly and the rank of $\mathbf{J}$ has to be determined somehow. In this paper we assume eigenvalues below a given threshold to be zero, but more sophisticated methods exist, e.g. [14].

Suppose there is enough variation in the data. Then in the case of standard optical flow the null-space of $\mathbf{J}$ is 1D as only data changes with respect to time are regarded [15]. In our case changes with respect to camera position (1d or 2d camera grid) and time are considered. Each of these add a dimension to the null-space, consequently it is up to 3d using the novel BCCE. Therefore we need linear combinations of up to 3 eigenvectors to solve for the parameters.

If there is not enough structure in the data the so called aperture problem occurs. Then not all parameters can be estimated. This is also known as normal flow case. We refer to the full flow case only as the handling of other cases can be deduced from literature (e.g. [32]).

4 Experiments

We want to analyze the properties of this novel model. In order to isolate special behaviour, we simplify the model equation to special cases. We use

- a 1d camera grid, no z-motion, and fronto-parallel surfaces (no normals estimated) to determine how many cameras are needed for high accuracy results (Sec. 4.1),
- a 1d camera grid with z-motion, but still fronto-parallel surfaces to demonstrate the effect of the linearization via $U_z << Z_0$ (Sec. 4.2),
- a 2d camera grid without any motion and still fronto-parallel surfaces in order to show how to estimate parameters that multiply occur in the BCCE (Sec. 4.3),
- a 2d camera grid without motion but with estimation of the normals which yield better depth estimates due to the better fitting surface model (Sec. 4.4).

The performance of the full model is still under investigation and thus unfortunately is reserved for the outlook. The first two models are investigated using a synthetic sinusoidal pattern fitting the model perfectly. For stability tests we add Gaussian noise to these sequences. The latter two models are applied to a ray-traced cube sequence.

4.1 1d Camera Grid, No z-Motion, No Normals

This model has first been introduced in [30] where a more detailed analysis can be found. We get it from Eq. 9 by setting $u_z = 0$, $z_x = 0$, $z_y = 0$, and $\mathrm{d}s_y = 0$

$$\begin{aligned} \boldsymbol{d} &= (I_x, I_y, I_{s_x}, I_t)^T \\ \boldsymbol{p} &= ((v\mathrm{d}s_x + u_x\mathrm{d}t), u_y\mathrm{d}t, \mathrm{d}s_x, \mathrm{d}t)^T \end{aligned} \tag{13}$$

The null-space of the Structure Tensor is 2d for this BCCE. We solve for v via the linear combination of the eigenvectors spanning this null-space such that the fourth entry is zero (i.e. $\mathrm{d}t = 0$ and $v = p_1/p_3$). The linear combination with vanishing third entry ($\mathrm{d}s_x = 0$) then yields $u_x = p_1/p_4$ and $u_y = p_2/p_4$.

We use 2, 3, and 5 cameras in our 1d grid. We then compute the data vector from the acquired data via optimized derivative kernels [28]:

- For 2 cameras we use separable $3 \times 3 \times 2 \times 3$-filters with x-,y-,and t-derivative $[0.5, 0, -0.5]$ and s-derivative $[1, -1]$ convolved by cross smoothing kernels in all other directions. The smoothing kernels are $[3, 10, 3]/16$ in x-, y-, and t-direction, and $[1, 1]$ in s-direction.
- For 3 cameras we use $[0.5, 0, -0.5]$ as derivative and $[3, 10, 3]/16$ as cross-smoothing.
- For 5 cameras we use a derivative kernel $[0.0838, 0.3324, 0, -0.3324, -0.0838]$ and smooth by $[0.0234, 0.2416, 0.4700, 0.24156, 0.0234]$.

The local neighborhood Ω (eq. 11) and weights W (eq. 12) are implemented by binomial filters B with variances $\sigma^2 = 2$ in x- and y-direction, $\sigma^2 = 0$ in s- and $\sigma^2 = 1$ in t-direction. These sizes have influence on the noise stability. It rises with increasing binomial filter size. As this effect is well known and identical for all camera configurations, we do not illustrate it here. For synthetic data with $I \in \{-1, 1\}$ an eigenvalue of the Structure Tensor below $\tau = 0.0012$ was considered to be zero.

In order to quantify the accuracy of the algorithm we measure velocity and disparity of a translating sinusoidal "wave"-pattern $I(x, y, s_x, t) = \cos(k_x(x - vs_x - u_xt)) * \cos(k_y(y - u_yt))$ with varying wave numbers k_x, k_y. To those sequences, normal distributed noise with a standard deviation up to $\sigma_n = 0.025$ is added. We calculated the velocity u_x and disparity v for an imaginary set of cameras.

Fig. 2 shows the relative error of the calculated velocity u_x and disparity v for different wavelengths. The run of the curves agrees well with the comparable calculations for conventional optical flow [28]. Larger optimized gradient filters have smaller angular errors[3]. Therefore the relative errors of disparity v for 3 cameras are significantly

[3] Please note, that d has to be normal to p in Eq. 13 and therefore directional errors in the gradient yield systematic errors in p.

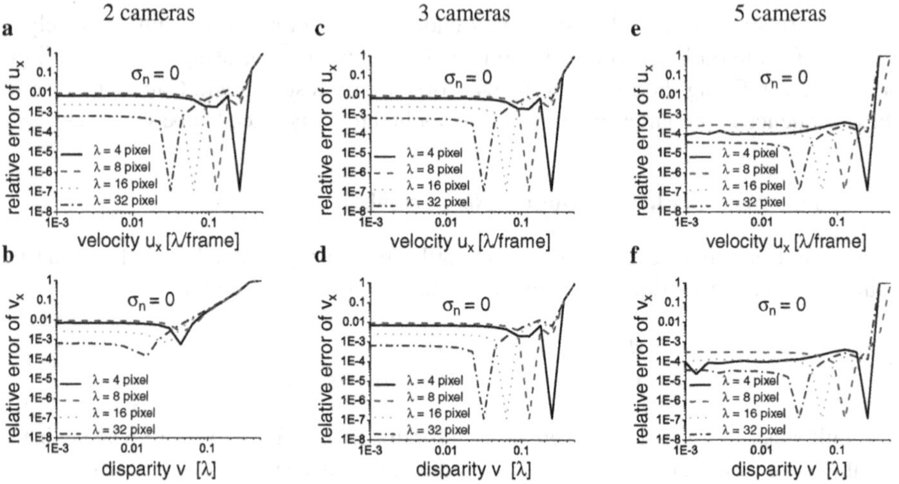

Fig. 2. Relative errors of the estimated velocity u_x and disparity v for 2 (**a**,**b**), 3 (**c**,**d**) and 5 cameras (**e**,**f**) (noise variance $\sigma_n = 0$, wavelength λ)

smaller than for the 2 camera setup. The errors of velocity u_x are nearly identical. For 5 cameras the errors of u_x and v decrease about 1.5 orders of magnitude.

For noisy data (Fig. 3) the relative error rises. Again it is stable within a percent region for 2 and 3 cameras and within a per mill region for 5 cameras when $u_x > 0.01\lambda$ or $v > 0.01\lambda$.

As the performance of the method is clearly best when using 5 cameras, we use 5 or 5×5 cameras in the remainder of the paper.

4.2 1d Camera Grid with z-Motion, No Normals

This model has first been introduced in [29] where a more detailed analysis can be found. We get it from Eq. 9 by setting $z_x = 0$, $z_y = 0$, and $\mathrm{d}s_y = 0$

$$\begin{aligned} \boldsymbol{d} &= (I_x, I_y, I_x \triangle x + I_y \triangle y, I_{s_x}, I_t)^T \\ \boldsymbol{p} &= ((v\mathrm{d}s_x + (u_x + x_0 u_z)\mathrm{d}t), (u_y + y_0 u_z)\mathrm{d}t, u_z \mathrm{d}t, \mathrm{d}s_x, \mathrm{d}t)^T \end{aligned} \tag{14}$$

The null-space of the Structure Tensor is 2d for this BCCE. We solve for the parameters using the eigenvectors spanning this space, as above. Knowing $\boldsymbol{u}$ and v we recover 3D motion and depth in world coordinates using Eq. 6.

Expression $(I_x \triangle x + I_y \triangle y) u_z$ occurring in the model $\boldsymbol{d}^T \boldsymbol{p} = 0$ is well known from affine motion models e.g. [9, 10]). There it is used for divergence estimation.

We implement the derivatives via the 5-tab filters described above (Sec. 4.1) . The local neighborhood Ω (Eq. 11) and weights W (Eq. 12) were implemented by Gaussian filters B with standard deviations $\sigma = 6$ in x- and y-direction, $\sigma = 0$ in s- and $\sigma = 1$ in t-direction. These filters B have 25 pixel length for x- and y-direction, 5 pixel length for t-direction and no filter is applied in s-direction. All other parameters are as above.

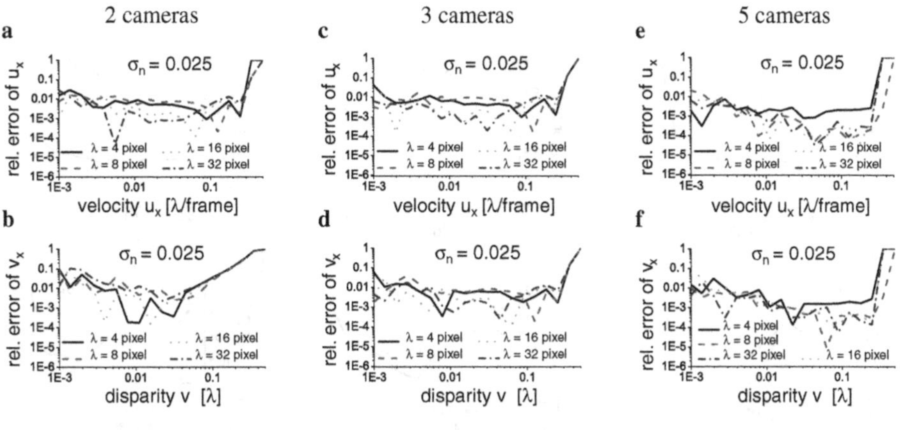

Fig. 3. Relative errors of the estimated velocity u_x and disparity v_x for 2 (**a**,**b**), 3 (**c**,**d**) and 5 cameras (**e**,**f**) (noise variance $\sigma_n = 0.025$, wavelength λ)

In order to quantify the accuracy of the used algorithm we measure velocity and disparity of a translating fronto-parallel sinusoidal "wave" pattern

$$\begin{aligned} I(x, y, s_x, t) &= \cos(K_X X) * \cos(K_Y Y) \\ X &= \tfrac{x}{f}(Z_0 + U_Z t) - U_X t + s_x \\ Y &= \tfrac{y}{f}(Z_0 + U_Z t) - U_Y t \end{aligned} \tag{15}$$

with wave numbers K_X and K_Y in world coordinates. Compare Sec. 2 for further notation. In our tests we choose $f = 10$, $Z(t_0) = 100$ at the estimation point of time t_0, $U_X = 0$, $U_Y = 0$, $U_Z = 0$ when not varied (all in arbitrary units). Wave numbers k_x and k_y in image coordinates are $k_x = K_X Z_0 + U_Z t/f$ and $k_y = K_Y Z_0 + U_Z t/f$. They are chosen to be $k_x = k_y = 2\pi/\lambda$ with $\lambda \in \{4, 8, 16, 32\}$ pixel at t_0. We calculated the 3D velocity $\boldsymbol{U}$ and depth Z for an imaginary set of five cameras. To those sequences either no noise or Gaussian noise with a standard deviation $\sigma_n = 0.025$ (i.e. 2.5%) is added.

Fig. 4**a** shows the relative error of the calculated X-velocity U_X for different wavelengths without noise. This illustrates the systematic error due to numerical and filter inaccuracies. For U_Y results are identical. The run of the curves agrees well with comparable calculations for conventional optical flow [28]. The error stays below 0.03% for displacements U_X below 4. Then smallest wavelengths produce severe errors as we come close to (inestimable) displacements near $0.5\,\lambda$. If we eliminate these wavelengths by smoothing larger displacements can be estimated accurately. Fig. 4**c** shows the relative error of the calculated Z-velocity U_Z for no noise added. Thus the systematic error stays below 0.3% for $U_Z < 0.1$ and below 3% for $U_Z < 1$. We interpret the increasing error with increasing U_Z as the error introduced due to the linearization assumption $U_Z << Z_0$. Fig. 4**e** shows the relative error of the calculated depth Z for varying disparity[4]. As calculations are similar to those for U_X and U_Y error curves are very similar, too.

[4] This can be either due to varying depth or varying baseline width.

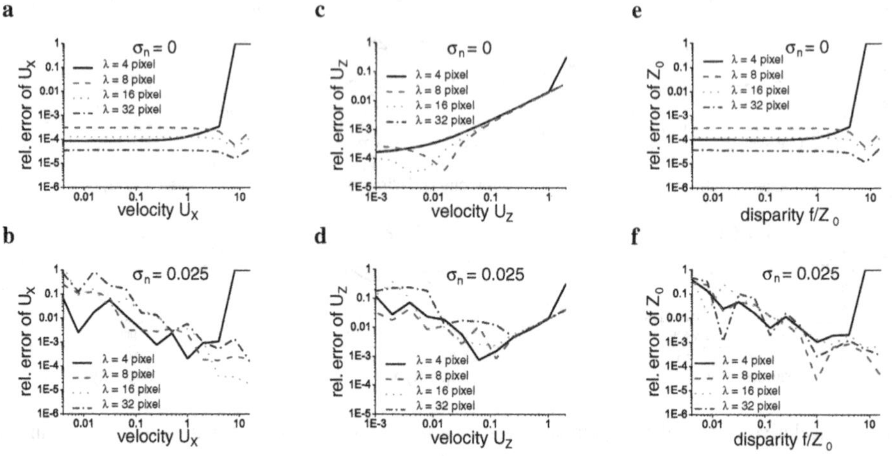

Fig. 4. Relative errors of the estimated velocity components U_X, U_Z and depth Z, calculated from synthetic data (Eq. 15) for different noises and wavelengths. Depth error is plotted for varying disparities f/Z_0.

Figs. 4**b,d,f** show the relative errors for 2.5% noise. This is realistic for CCD cameras used in our botanical experiments. The relative errors rise severely for small values of U_X, U_Z or f/Z_0 but stay between 0.1% and 1% for wide ranges of U_X, U_Z or V_X. As we calculate U_X and U_Y via the optical flow components u_x and u_y that are affected by errors in u_z, there is an error propagation from U_Z to U_X and U_Y. In our target application usually U_Z is very small thus the absolute error propagated to U_X and U_Y is small, too.

4.3 2d Camera Grid Without Any Motion, No Normals

This model is new. We get it from Eq. 9 by setting $z_x = 0$, $z_y = 0$, and $\mathrm{d}t = 0$

$$\begin{aligned} \boldsymbol{d} &= (I_x, I_y, I_{s_x}, I_{s_y})^T \\ \boldsymbol{p} &= (v\mathrm{d}s_x, v\mathrm{d}s_y, \mathrm{d}s_x, \mathrm{d}s_y)^T \end{aligned} \tag{16}$$

As this is the first time that a parameter occurs twice in the model, let us for a moment introduce "independent" disparities v_x and v_y via

$$\boldsymbol{p} = (v_x\mathrm{d}s_x, v_y\mathrm{d}s_y, \mathrm{d}s_x, \mathrm{d}s_y)^T \tag{17}$$

Again we have a 2d null-space in the Structure Tensor and thus have two eigenvectors spanning that space. If we choose a linear combination of the two such that the third entry $\mathrm{d}s_x$ is zero, we get $v_y = p_2/p_4$. Similarly we can calculate $v_x = p_1/p_3$ by setting $\mathrm{d}s_y = 0$. These disparities are the ones we would get, if we had a 1d camera grid, only. In the 2d case the two disparity estimates are not independent in general. But we can estimate their covariance matrix (e.g. via [27]) and rotate the coordinate system such that this matrix becomes diagonal[5] (cmp. Fig. 5**a**). In this coordinate system we

[5] If we used an ordinary least squares estimation scheme, this step could be done within the pseudo-inverse using the Gauss-Markov theorem.

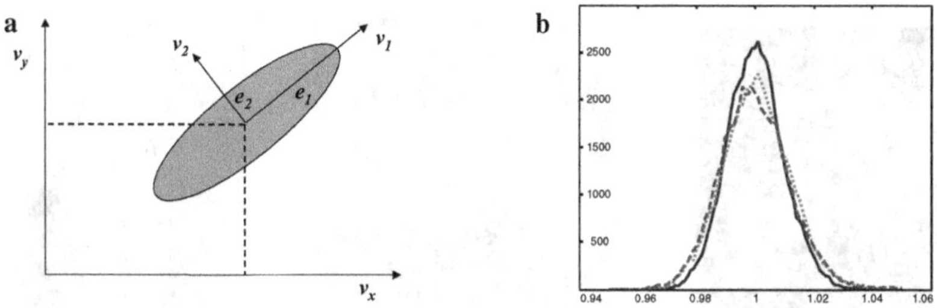

Fig. 5. Estimation of multiply occurring parameter: **a** rotation of coordinate system by error covariance, **b** accuracy gain by combination of the estimates, see text for details

can independently estimate disparities v_1 and v_2 and then combine them into a single estimate by treating them as independent measurements

$$v = \frac{\frac{v_1}{e_1} + \frac{v_2}{e_2}}{\frac{1}{e_1} + \frac{1}{e_2}} \tag{18}$$

This approach has two benefits. First, the apperture problem is solved automatically, as this only means that the error of one estimate becomes infinity and the estimate is neglected. Second, the estimation accuracy slightly improves due to two estimates instead of one. This is demonstrated in Fig. 5**b**. It shows histograms of disparities v_x, v_y and v estimated from a synthetic, sinusoidal test pattern with 10% Gaussian noise added (true value $v = 1$). Although there is no apperture problem and the same data has been used for all 3 estimates, the histogram of v (solid line) has less variance than the other two curves.

4.4 2d Camera Grid Without Motion But With Normals

This model is new. We get it from Eq. 9 by setting $\mathrm{d}t = 0$

$$\begin{aligned} \boldsymbol{d} &= (I_x, I_y, I_x\triangle x, I_x\triangle, I_y\triangle y, I_y\triangle x, I_{s_x}, I_{s_y})^T \\ \boldsymbol{p} &= (v\mathrm{d}s_x, v\mathrm{d}s_y, z_x\mathrm{d}s_x, z_y\mathrm{d}s_x, z_y\mathrm{d}s_y, z_x\mathrm{d}s_y, \mathrm{d}s_x, \mathrm{d}s_y)^T \end{aligned} \tag{19}$$

Again we have a 2d null-space in the Structure Tensor and the parameters v, z_x and z_y occur twice in the equations. Thus we estimate them using their covariance matrices as above in Sec. 4.3. This model again shows two advantages above the model from Sec. 4.3. First of course it yields the normals of the surface in addition to its depth (see Fig. 7). Second, the accuracy of depth estimation increases due to less systematic errors. This can be seen from Fig. 6, where synthetic images of a cube have been used for 3d-reconstruction of that cube. Fig. 6**b** shows the reconstruction using the model from Sec. 4.3 (Eq. 16). Especially in the steeper, left part of the cube the surface is less flat than in the reconstruction in Fig. 6**c**, where the model from Eq. 19 was applied. Please note, that all parameter settings and the input data are identical.

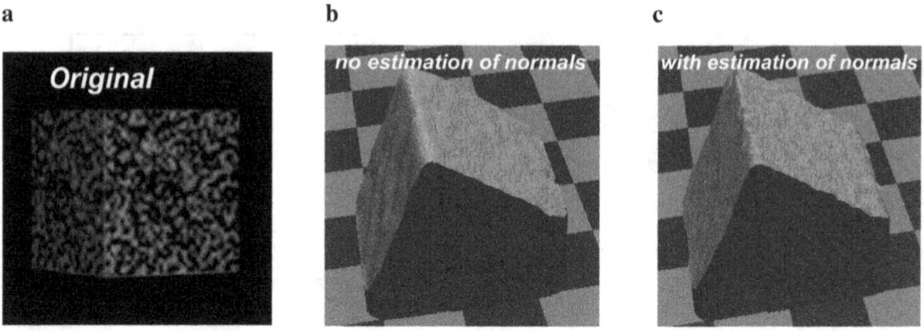

Fig. 6. Cube experiment: **a** one image of the input data, **b** reconstructed surface without normals in the model, **c** reconstructed surface with normals in the model

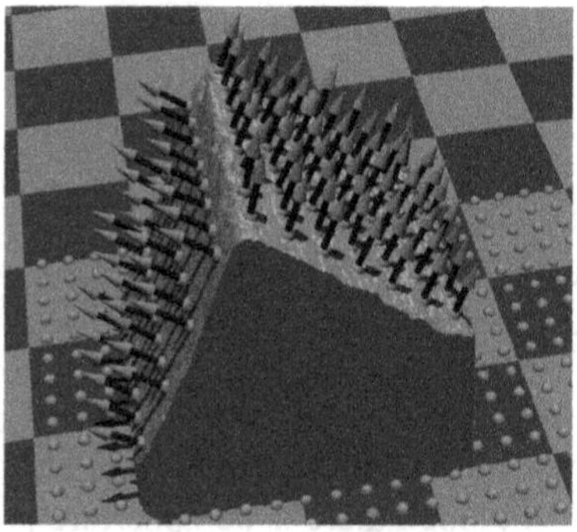

Fig. 7. Cube experiment: reconstructed surface with estimated normals as vectors

5 Summary and Outlook

We have introduced a novel model for simultaneous estimation of scene flow, disparity and surface normals in multi-camera sequences. We demonstrated its use within the Structure Tensor estimation framework but due to its BCCE-like form other optical flow methods as robust estimations, variational approaches, coarse-to-fine schemes or special regularizations may be applied as well. This will provide additional benefit e.g. higher robustness and/or faster performance. Using the Structure Tensor we have investigated special cases of this model. Especially we demonstrated that

- 5 cameras per grid dimension and optimized filters allow for low systematic errors,
- noise stability is as expected for a local TLS-estimator,
- Z-velocity shows increasing errors with increasing value due to linearization,
- using 2d camera grids results in models with multiply occurring parameters, that need a special estimation treatment,
- surface normals can be estimated within this framework reducing systematic errors.

In future work, we will investigate the full model, not only special cases. Further we will investigate additional constraints e.g. enforcing that slopes of the estimated depth field and the estimated slopes agree.

References

1. J.L. Barron, D.J. Fleet, and S.S. Beauchemin. Performance of optical flow techniques. In *IJCV*, pages 43–77, 1994. 12(1).
2. J.R. Bergen, P.J. Burt, R. Hingorani, and S. Peleg. A three-frame algorithm for estimating two-component image motion. *IEEE Transactions on Pattern Analysis and Machine Intelligence*, 14(9):886–895, 1992.
3. J. Bigün and G. H. Granlund. Optimal orientation detection of linear symmetry. In *ICCV*, pages 433–438, 1987.
4. M. Black, D. Fleet, and Y. Yacoob. Robustly estimating changes in image appearence. *CVIU*, 7(1):8–31, 2000.
5. A. Bruhn, J.Weickert, and C.Schnörr. Combining the advantages of local and global optic flow methods. In *Proc. DAGM 2002, Lecture Notes in Computer Science, Vol.2449, Springer, Berlin*, pages 454–462, Zürich, Schweiz, 2002.
6. R. Carceroni and K. Kutulakos. Multi-view 3d shape and motion recovery on the spatio-temporal curve manifold. In *ICCV (1)*, pages 520–527, 1999.
7. T. S. Jr. Denney and J. L. Prince. Optimal brightness functions for optical flow estimation of deformable motion. *IEEE Trans. Im. Proc.*, 3(2):178–191, 1994.
8. H. Farid and E. P. Simoncelli. Optimally rotation-equivariant directional derivative kernels. In *7th Int'l Conf Computer Analysis of Images and Patterns*, Kiel, 1997.
9. G. Farnebäck. Fast and accurate motion est. using orient. tensors and param. motion models. In *ICPR*, pages 135–139, 2000.
10. D. Fleet. *Measurement of Image Velocity*. Kluwer, 1992.
11. D.J. Fleet and K. Langley. Recursive filters for optical flow. *IEEE Transactions on Pattern Analysis and Machine Intelligence*, 17(1), 1995. pp. 61-67.
12. C. Garbe. *Measuring Heat Exchange Processes at the Air-Water Interface from Thermographic Image Sequence Analysis*. PhD thesis, Heidelberg University, 2001.
13. S. Gupta and J. Prince. On variable brightness optical flow for tagged mri. In *Information Processing in Medical Imaging*, pages 323 – 334, 1995.
14. W. Haerdle, S. Sperlich, and V. Spokoiny. Structural tests in additive regression. *J. Amer.Stat. Acc*, 96(456):1333–1347, 2001.
15. H. Haußecker and D.J. Fleet. Computing optical flow with physical models of brightness variation. *PAMI*, 23(6):661–673, June 2001.
16. H. Haußecker and H. Spies. Motion. In B. Jähne, H. Haußecker, and P. Geißler, editors, *Handbook of Computer Vision and Applications*. Academic Press, 1999.
17. H. Haußecker, H. Spies, and B. Jähne. Tensor-based image sequence processing techniques for the study of dynamical processes. In *Proc. Int. Symp. On Real-Time Imaging and Dynamic Analysis*, volume 32(5), pages 704–711, Japan, 1998.
18. B.K. Horn and B.G. Schunk. Determining optical flow. In *Art. Int.*, volume 17, pages 185–204, 1981.
19. M. Irani. Multi-frame optical flow estimation using subspace constraints. In *IEEE International Conference on Computer Vision (ICCV)*, Corfu, 1999.
20. B. Jähne. *Spatio-temporal image processing*, volume 751. Springer, Berlin, 1993.
21. B. Jähne, H. Scharr, and S. Körkel. Principles of filter design. In *Handbook of Computer Vision and Applications*. Academic Press, 1999.

22. T. Koivunen and A. Nieminen. Motion field restoration using vectormedian filtering on high definition television sequences. In *Proc. Vis. Comm. and Im. Proc.'90*, volume 1360, pages 736 – 742, 1990.
23. L.H.Matthies, R.Szeliski, and T.Kanade. Kalman filter-based algorithms for estimating depth from image sequences. *IJCV*, 3:209–236, 1989.
24. H.C. Longuet-Higgins and K. Prazdny. The interpretation of a moving retinal image. *Proceedings of The Royal Society of London B, 208*, pages 385–397, 1980.
25. B. Lucas and T. Kanade. An iterative image registration technique with an application to stereo vision. In *DARPA Im. Underst. Workshop*, pages 121–130, 1981.
26. Y. Nakamura, T. Matsuura, K. Satoh, and Y. Ohta. Occlusion detectable stereo–occlusion patterns in camera matrix. In *CVPR*, pages 371–378, 1996.
27. O. Nestares, D.J. Fleet, and D.J. Heeger. Likelihood functions and confidence bounds for total-least-squares problems. In *IEEE Conference on Computer Vision and Pattern Recognition*, pages 523–530, Hilton Head, South Carolina, Vol. I, 2000.
28. H. Scharr. *Optimal Operators in Digital Image Processing*. PhD thesis, University of Heidelberg, Germany, 2000.
29. H. Scharr and R. Küsters. A linear model for simultaneous estimation of 3d motion and depth. In *IEEE Workshop on Motion and Video Computing*, Orlando, Florida, USA, December 5-6 2002.
30. H. Scharr and R. Küsters. Simultaneous estimation of motion and disparity: Comparison of 2-, 3- and 5-camera setups. In *2nd IASTED International Conference Visualization, Imaging and Image Processing (VIIP 2002)*, Malaga, Spain, September 9-12 2002.
31. U. Schurr, A. Walter, S. Wilms, H. Spies, N. Kirchgessner, H. Scharr, and R. Küsters. Dynamics of leaf and root growth. In *12th Int. Con. on Photosynthesis, PS 2001*, 2001.
32. H. Spies and B. Jähne. A general framework for image sequence processing. In *Fachtagung Informationstechnik*, pages 125–132, Universität Magdeburg, 2001.
33. H. Spies, N. Kirchgeßner, H. Scharr, and B. Jähne. Dense structure estimation via regularised optical flow. In *VMV 2000*, pages 57–64, Saarbrücken, Germany, 2000.
34. H. Spies and H. Scharr. Accurate optical flow in noisy image sequences. In *ICCV'01*, pages 587–592, Vancuver, Canada, 2001.
35. R. Szeliski. A multi-view approach to motion and stereo. In *CVPR*, 1999.
36. S. Vedula, S. Baker, P. Rander, R. Collins, and T. Kanade. Threedimensional scene flow. In *ICCV 1999*, pages 722–729, 1999.
37. S. Vedula, S. Baker, S. Seitz, R. Collins, and T. Kanade. Shape and motion carving in 6d. In *CVPR 2000*, pages 592–598, 2000.
38. J. Weickert. Applications of nonlinear diffusion in image processing and computer vision. *Acta Math.Univ.Comenianae, Proc. of Algo. 2000*, LXX(1):33 – 50, 2001.
39. J. Weickert and C. Schnörr. Variational optic flow computation with a spatio-temporal smoothness constraint. Technical Report 15/2000, Comp. Vis., Graphics, and Patt. Recogn. Group, Dept. of Math. and Comp. Sci., Univ. Mannheim, Germany, July 2000.

Complex Motion in Environmental Physics and Live Sciences

Bernd Jähne

Research Group Image Processing, Interdisciplinary Center for Scientific Computing
and
Institute for Environmental Physics, University of Heidelberg, Germany
Bernd.Jaehne@iwr.uni-heidelberg.de

Abstract. Image sequence processing techniques are an essential tool for the experimental investigation of dynamical processes such as exchange, growth, and transport processes. These processes constitute much more complex motions than normally encountered in computer vision. In this paper, optical flow based motion analysis is extended into a generalized framework to estimate the motion field and the parameters of dynamic processes simultaneously. Examples from environmental physics and live sciences illustrate how this framework helps to tackles some key scientific questions that could not be solved without taking and analyzing image sequences.

1 Introduction

In computer vision motion fields are mostly used to explore 3-D space and dynamic scenes. Thus one of the most important tasks is the reconstruction of 3-D structure and 3-D motion fields ("structure from motion"). Mostly only opaque rigid objects are studied and the requirements for absolute accuracy are not that stringent because the estimates of the velocity field are integrated into an action-perception cycle. As long as this cycle converges, the accuracy is sufficient.

For scientific applications, the focus shifts from motion fields to the processes that cause change and motion in image sequences. Thus the most important task here is not the determination of motion field itself but the estimation of parameters of dynamic processes and the distinction between different models. These processes, such as chemical reactions, dispersion or growth processes, also change the objects and thus also their intensities in image sequences. Thus both motion and dynamical processes do change intensities and it is no longer possible to estimate the motion field or the parameters of dynamic processes separately. Consequently, it is required to extend motion analysis into a more general approach that allows for a simultaneous estimation of the parameters of dynamic processes and the motion field.

Such kind of problems occur also in computer vision, when the motion field has to be estimated in a scene with changing illumination or when other types of complex motion occur as discussed in this volume. Therefore it can be expected that the analysis of complex motion in computer vision will benefit from the application to scientific problems.

B. Jähne et al. (Eds.): IWCM 2004, LNCS 3417, pp. 91–103, 2007.

Fig. 1. Image sequence with a traffic scene as a space-time image. On the right side of the cube a yt slice marked by the vertical white line in the xy image is shown, while the top face shows an xt slice marked by the horizontal line (after [1]).

This paper consists of two main parts. In the first and major part (Sec. 2), a framework for the simultaneous estimation of parameters of dynamic processes and the motion field is presented and illustrated with examples from environmental physics and live sciences. In the second part (Sec. 3), some practical issues concerning the existence of a solution and its accuracy are discussed, such as rank-deficit tensors (generalized aperture problems), biased estimates, optimal filtering, the use of energy tensors instead of the structure tensor, and global regularization.

2 A Framework for the Estimation of Dynamic Processes

2.1 Local Optimization of Motion Estimation

In this section, well-known low-level motion estimators are represented in a generalized optimization approach that is suitable to be extended to the estimation of additional parameters. We start from the basic fact that motion appears as oriented structures in space-time images (Fig. 1). In the direction of motion the gray values do not change. Therefore the scalar product of a vector $\boldsymbol{p} = [u, v, 1]$ in the direction of motion is perpendicular to the spatiotemporal gradient $\boldsymbol{\nabla}_{xt}g$ is zero.

In order to find this direction and thus the velocity field $\boldsymbol{u}(\boldsymbol{x}, t)$, the following error functional can be minimized [1]:

$$e(\boldsymbol{x}, \boldsymbol{p}) = \int w(\boldsymbol{x}' - \boldsymbol{x}, t' - t) \left\| \boldsymbol{\nabla}_{xt}g^T \boldsymbol{p} \right\| \mathrm{d}^N x' \mathrm{d}t' \rightarrow \min \tag{1}$$

The spatiotemporal window function $w(\boldsymbol{x}' - \boldsymbol{x}, t' - t)$ determines the area in space and time over which the averaging takes place. For the sake of a compact notation, windowed integrals as in Eq. 1 are abbreviated by

$$\int w(\boldsymbol{x}' - \boldsymbol{x}, t' - t) \left\| \ldots \right\| \mathrm{d}^N x' \mathrm{d}t' = \overline{\left\| \ldots \right\|} \tag{2}$$

Then Eq. 1 reduces to

$$e(\boldsymbol{x}, \boldsymbol{p}) = \overline{\left\| \boldsymbol{\nabla}_{xt} g^T \boldsymbol{p} \right\|} \rightarrow \min. \tag{3}$$

Mostly an L_2-norm (least squares) is used. Then in Eq. 3 the data term contained in the spatiotemporal gradient and the parameters to be estimated can be separated yielding

$$e_2(\boldsymbol{x}, \boldsymbol{p}) = \boldsymbol{p}^T \boldsymbol{J} \boldsymbol{p} \quad \text{with} \quad \boldsymbol{J} = \overline{\boldsymbol{\nabla}_{xt} g \boldsymbol{\nabla}_{xt} g^T}. \tag{4}$$

The symmetric tensor $\boldsymbol{J}$ is known as the structure tensor and has the components

$$\boldsymbol{J}_{pq}(\boldsymbol{x}, t) = w(\boldsymbol{x}, t) * (g_p(\boldsymbol{x}, t)\, g_q(\boldsymbol{x}, t)) \quad \text{with} \quad p, q \in \{\boldsymbol{x}, t\}. \tag{5}$$

In this equation, the integral over the window function (see Eq. 2) is written as a convolution operation and the indices mark first-order derivatives.

The estimation of motion therefore reduces to an eigenvalue analysis of the tensor $\boldsymbol{J}$ and the eigenvector to the smallest eigenvalue is the parameter vector $\boldsymbol{p}$ that solves the optimization problem Eq. 3 [2]. This eigenvector is oriented into the direction of motion. (The eigenvalue solution is equivalent to a rotation of the coordinate system to principle axes.) In the ideal case of a constant motion in a noise-free image sequence, the smallest eigenvalue is zero, because the gray values do not change at all in this direction.

The computation of the structure tensor is straightforward. It can be performed as a cascade of linear convolution and (nonlinear) point operations as $\mathcal{B}(\mathcal{D}_p \cdot \mathcal{D}_q)$, where $\mathcal{B}$ and $\mathcal{D}$ are a smoothing filter of the shape of the window function and a derivative filter into the directions p and q.

For the further discussion it is important to note that the approach formulated here incorporates the standard idea of the preservation of optical flow. This can be seen immediately if the spatiotemporal gradient is split up into the spatial and temporal part and the vector $\boldsymbol{p}$ is written out. Then Eq. 3 becomes

$$e(\boldsymbol{x}, \boldsymbol{u}) = \overline{\left\| \frac{\partial g}{\partial t} + \boldsymbol{u} \boldsymbol{\nabla} g \right\|} \rightarrow \min. \tag{6}$$

2.2 Extension to Dynamic Processes

The extension of Eqs. 3 and 6 for other processes that change gray values is straightforward. The term in the norm contains an equation for conservation of gray vales:

$$\frac{\partial g}{\partial t} + \boldsymbol{u} \boldsymbol{\nabla} g = 0. \tag{7}$$

When there is only motion, temporal changes can only be caused by moving spatial gradients. Other terms that change gray values just add additional terms.

The most important processes encountered in scientific applications are briefly discussed here.

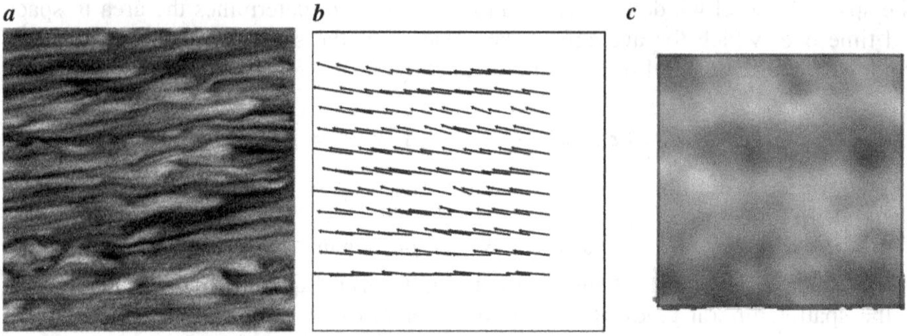

Fig. 2. Analysis of infrared image sequences of the water surface in the Heidelberg Aeolotron cooled by evaporation of water from the surface: **a** example image with a sector of about $0.3 \times 0.3\,\mathrm{m}^2$ (the temperature is proportional to the brightness of the image), **b** computed flow field, and **b** map of the computed heat flux density at the surface (source term according to Eq. 8)

2.3 Source Terms

A source term directly results in a temporal change of the gray values:

$$\frac{\partial g}{\partial t} + \boldsymbol{u}\boldsymbol{\nabla} g = s. \tag{8}$$

This equation can be reduced to

$$\boldsymbol{d}^T \boldsymbol{p} = 0. \tag{9}$$

using 4-element data and parameter vectors

$$\boldsymbol{d} = [g_x, g_y, g_t, -1]^T, \quad \boldsymbol{p} = [u, v, 1, s]^T. \tag{10}$$

The data vector contains elements that can be computed from the image sequence and results in an extended 4×4 structure tensor

$$\boldsymbol{J} = \overline{\boldsymbol{d}\,\boldsymbol{d}^T} = \begin{pmatrix} \overline{g_x^2} & \overline{g_x g_y} & \overline{g_x g_t} & -\overline{g_x} \\ \overline{g_x g_y} & \overline{g_y^2} & \overline{g_y g_t} & -\overline{g_y} \\ \overline{g_x g_t} & \overline{g_y g_t} & \overline{g_t^2} & -\overline{g_t} \\ -\overline{g_x} & -\overline{g_y} & -\overline{g_t} & 1 \end{pmatrix} \tag{11}$$

as in Eq. 4. Therefore a (total) least squares solution is again given by the eigenvector to the smallest eigenvalue of $\boldsymbol{J}$ in Eq. 11.

We encountered this type of extension, when analyzing infrared image sequences taken from water surfaces. A heat flux density at the surface directly causes a temporal change of the temperature at the water surface. The heat flux density can be negative, when the surface is cooled, e. g., by emission of radiation or by evaporation of water. An image from an infrared image sequence taken under this condition, is shown in Fig. 2a. Using Eq. 8, both maps of the flow field (Fig. 2b) and of the heat flux density (Fig. 2c) could be computed [3].

2.4 Relaxation Processes

A first order relaxation process, such as a first-order chemical reaction (we assume that the gray value in an image is proportional to the concentration of a chemical species), causes a temporal decay of the concentration proportional to the rate constant λ and the concentration g:

$$\frac{\partial g}{\partial t} + \boldsymbol{u}\boldsymbol{\nabla} g = -\lambda g \quad \text{and} \quad \boldsymbol{d} = [g_x, g_y, g_t, g]^T, \quad \boldsymbol{p} = [u, v, 1, \lambda]^T. \tag{12}$$

An ansatz of this form constitutes also an elegant solution for motion estimation with changing illumination using a multiplicative illumination model. Here λ has the meaning of a temporal rate of change of the illumination [4].

This extension was used for the determination of life times of tropospheric pollutants such as nitrous oxides from spectroscopic satellite image sequences (Sec. 3.1) and the determination of three velocity components of flow close to a free interface by a special illumination technique in a flow seeded with small particles and an absorbing dye [5]. The basic trick with this technique is that the illumination intensity is decreasing with the distance from the surface due to the absorption of light by the dye. Then the brightness of a small particle depends on its distance to the surface according to

$$g(t) = g_0 \exp\left(-\frac{z(t)}{z_*}\right), \tag{13}$$

where z_* is the penetration depth of the illumination. If a particle moves perpendicular to the surface, the intensity change is proportional to the vertical velocity:

$$\frac{\mathrm{d}g}{\mathrm{d}t} = -\frac{g_0}{z_*}\exp\left(-\frac{z}{z_*}\right)\frac{\partial z}{\partial t} = -\frac{w}{z_*}g. \tag{14}$$

This yields

$$g_t + ug_x + vg_y + w\frac{g}{z_*} = 0 \quad \text{and} \quad \boldsymbol{d} = [g_x, g_y, g_t, g/z_*]^T, \quad \boldsymbol{p} = [u, v, 1, w]^T. \tag{15}$$

2.5 Diffusion Processes

A diffusion process causes the concentration to spread out according to the instationary diffusion equation [6]. With such an additional term

$$\frac{\partial g}{\partial t} + \boldsymbol{u}\boldsymbol{\nabla} g = D\Delta g. \quad \text{and} \quad \boldsymbol{d} = [g_x, g_y, g_t, g_{xx} + g_{yy}]^T, \quad \boldsymbol{p} = [u, v, 1, -D]^T \tag{16}$$

the flow field $\boldsymbol{u}$ and the diffusion coefficient D can be estimated simultaneously. This extension is useful for flow analysis with concentration fields, where the diffusion of the visualized dye cannot be neglected. This is the case, e. g., with microfluidics [7]. Recently, this approach has been extended to handle Taylor dispersion [8].

2.6 Forces and Acceleration

Forces $\boldsymbol{F}$ applied to moving objects cause an acceleration $\boldsymbol{a} = [a, b]^T$ of the motion according to the law of Newton, $\boldsymbol{F} = m\boldsymbol{a}$. A direct estimation of acceleration is possible if not a constant but an accelerated velocity field is modeled according to

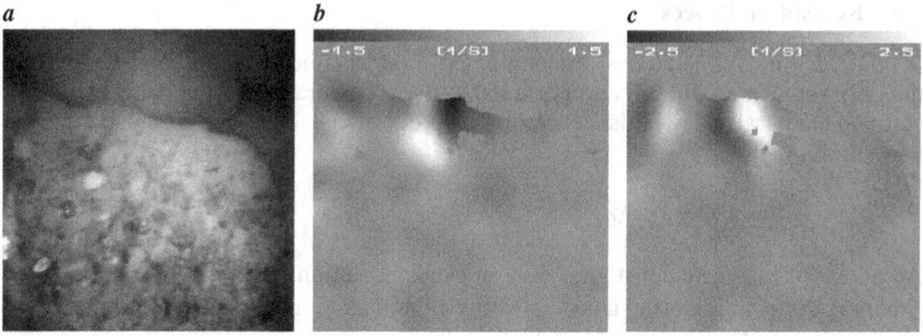

Fig. 3. Example for the study of flow in sediments. **a** One of the images of the flow of sand particles in the sediment observed with an embedded endoscope. **b** Divergence and **c** rotation of the vector field; the scale is included at the top of each image.

$$\frac{\partial g}{\partial t} + (\boldsymbol{u} + \boldsymbol{a}t')\boldsymbol{\nabla} g = 0 \quad \text{and} \quad \boldsymbol{d} = [g_x, g_y, g_t, g_x t', g_y t']^T, \quad \boldsymbol{p} = [u, v, 1, a, b]^T, \tag{17}$$

where a and b are the x and y components of the acceleration vector, respectively, and t' is a local time coordinate, which is zero in the center of the temporal window function, see Eq. 1.

2.7 Higher-Order Motion Fields

In a similar but more complex way as in Sec. 2.6, spatially changing motion fields can be modeled directly. Then the constant velocity in Eq. 7 must be replaced by a spatially changing velocity field. A motion field with first-order spatial changes that causes deformation and rotation of objects is described by the matrix

$$\boldsymbol{u} = \begin{bmatrix} a_{11} & a_{12} \\ a_{21} & a_{22} \end{bmatrix} \boldsymbol{x}' = \boldsymbol{A}\boldsymbol{x}' \tag{18}$$

and results in

$$\frac{\partial g}{\partial t} + (\boldsymbol{u} + \boldsymbol{A}\boldsymbol{x}')\boldsymbol{\nabla} g = 0 \quad \text{and} \tag{19}$$

$$\boldsymbol{d} = [g_x, g_y, g_t, g_x x', g_x y', g_y x', g_y y']^T, \quad \boldsymbol{p} = [u, v, 1, a_{11}, a_{12}, a_{21}, a_{22}]^T,$$

where x' and y' are local coordinates, which are zero in the center of the local integration window function w, see Eq. 1. The matrix $\boldsymbol{A}$ contains all possible elementary 2-D deformations: rotation, dilation, stretching, and shear [9].

If not all four degrees of freedom are possible for a certain process, deformations can be restricted. An interesting example of this kind is a homogeneous growth process, e. g., when a plant part is known to grow homogeneously in all directions. Then the matrix $\boldsymbol{A}$ reduces to a scalar growth parameter r and Eq. 19 reduces to

$$\frac{\partial g}{\partial t} + (\boldsymbol{u} + r\boldsymbol{x}')\boldsymbol{\nabla} g = 0 \quad \text{and} \quad \boldsymbol{d} = [g_x, g_y, g_t, g_x x' + g_y y']^T, \quad \boldsymbol{p} = [u, v, 1, r]^T \tag{20}$$

The direct estimation of the velocity field and the growth rate is shown in Fig. 4 [10].

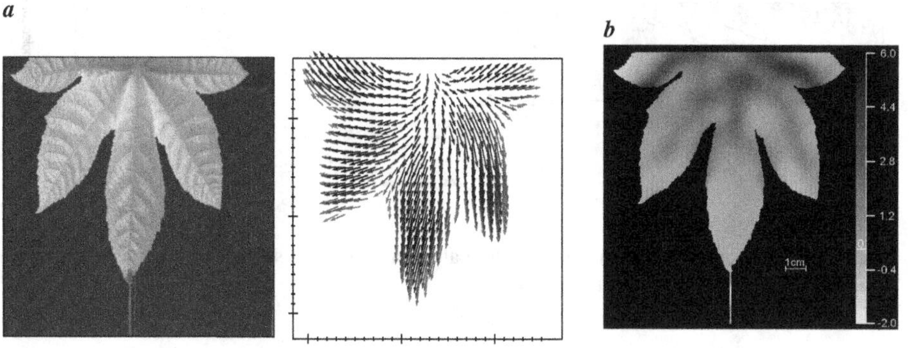

Fig. 4. **a** Leaf of a castor-oil plant and flow field due to growth; **b** growth rate (divergence of the motion field); the scale for the divergence ranges from -2.0 to 6.0 permille/min

2.8 Generalization

The essential point with all these extensions is that all parameters to be estimated appear as linear factors with terms that can be estimated from the data. Therefore the processes can be combined and it is possible to collect all parameters to be estimated in a parameter vector $\boldsymbol{p}$ and all data terms in a data vector $\boldsymbol{d}$. Therefore it is obvious that this approach can be extended to any type of dynamic processes that can be described by partial differential equations that are *linear* in the parameters to be estimated. Only processes with nonlinear parameters cannot be handled by this approach.

However, other generalizations are possible. One is the use of multi-component images. If the parameter of the dynamic process are the same in all components, the structure tensor can simply be averaged over all components. It might be appropriate to apply a weighting, if the different components have different uncertainties. If two components differ in a parameter, a joint estimate is still possible. An important application are transport processes that involve two species with different diffusion coefficients D_1 and D_2. The two species are convected by the same velocity field but the diffusion process is different. Therefore, two continuity equations are used

$$\frac{\partial g}{\partial t} + \boldsymbol{u}\boldsymbol{\nabla} g = D_1 \Delta g. \quad \text{and} \quad \frac{\partial h}{\partial t} + \boldsymbol{u}\boldsymbol{\nabla} h = D_2 \Delta h. \tag{21}$$

with two data vectors

$$\boldsymbol{d}_1 = [g_x, g_y, g_t, g_{xx} + g_{yy}, 0]^T, \quad \boldsymbol{d}_2 = [h_x, h_y, h_t, 0, h_{xx} + h_{yy}]^T,$$

but only one parameter vector

$$\boldsymbol{p} = [u, v, 1, -D_1, -D_2]^T,$$

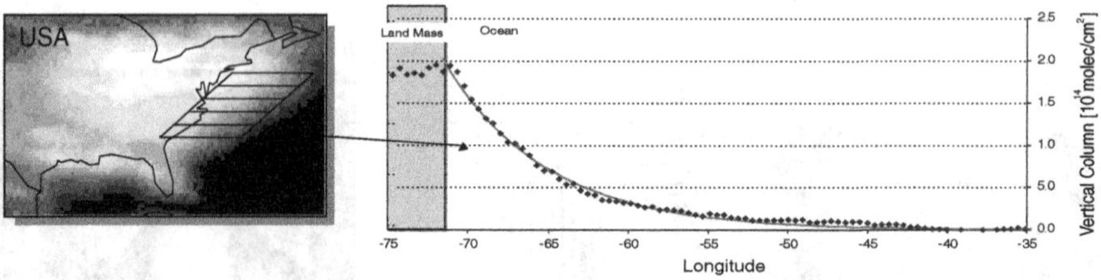

Fig. 5. Example for the stationary decay curve along a latitudinal section through a NO_2 plume at the eastern shore of the US (after [21])

and the structure tensor $\boldsymbol{J} = \overline{\boldsymbol{d}_1 \boldsymbol{d}_1^T} + \overline{\boldsymbol{d}_2 \boldsymbol{d}_2^T}$ is

$$\boldsymbol{J} = \begin{pmatrix} \overline{g_x^2} + \overline{h_x^2} & \overline{g_x g_y} + \overline{h_x h_y} & \overline{g_x g_t} + \overline{h_x h_t} & \overline{g_x(g_{xx}+g_{yy})} & \overline{h_x(h_{xx}+h_{yy})} \\ \overline{g_x g_y} + \overline{h_x h_y} & \overline{g_y^2} + \overline{h_y^2} & \overline{g_y g_t} + \overline{h_y h_t} & \overline{g_y(g_{xx}+g_{yy})} & \overline{h_y(h_{xx}+h_{yy})} \\ \overline{g_x g_t} + \overline{h_x h_t} & \overline{g_y g_t} + \overline{h_y h_t} & \overline{g_t^2} + \overline{h_t^2} & \overline{g_t(g_{xx}+g_{yy})} & \overline{h_t(h_{xx}+h_{yy})} \\ \overline{g_x(g_{xx}+g_{yy})} & \overline{g_y(g_{xx}+g_{yy})} & \overline{g_t(g_{xx}+g_{yy})} & \overline{(g_{xx}+g_{yy})^2} & 0 \\ \overline{h_x(h_{xx}+h_{yy})} & \overline{h_y(h_{xx}+h_{yy})} & \overline{h_t(h_{xx}+h_{yy})} & 0 & \overline{(h_{xx}+h_{yy})^2} \end{pmatrix}. \quad (22)$$

In this way, the estimation of the motion field utilizes data from both components, whereas the estimation of the individual diffusion coefficients is influenced only by the corresponding data.

3 Practical Issues

3.1 Rank-Deficit Generalized Structure Tensors

When the model describes the underlying dynamic process observed by an image sequence, the structure tensor has just one small eigenvalue in the ideal case, i. e., its rank is one lower than its dimension. If this is the case, all parameters can be estimated. In most cases, however, the rank will be lower.

This is already the case when just the motion field is estimated. At a straight edge, e.;g., the rank of the structure tensor is 1 and only the velocity component perpendicular to the edge can be determined ("aperture problem"). With higher-dimensional generalized structure tensors, it can be expected, that rank-deficit tensors appear even more often.

This is illustrated with an interesting example, where the combination of motion and a first-order chemical reaction results in a stationary gray value pattern. We assume a constant motion in x direction and a first-order decay rate λ. Then according to Eq. 12, a stationary profile occurs when

$$u \frac{\partial g}{\partial x} = -\lambda g \quad \text{or} \quad g = g_0 \exp[-(\lambda/u)x]. \quad (23)$$

Such stationary profiles are indeed observed in satellite image sequences of tropospheric NO_2 concentration when plumes generated at the east coast of the USA are transported to the North Atlantic Ocean by westerly winds. Over the ocean there are no sources and the NO_2 concentrations decay exponentially due to the combined action of transport and a first-order decay process.

On the other side, it is often possible to estimate parameters of dynamic processes even when it is impossible to estimate the full motion field. A simple example of this kind is the estimation of a homogeneous growth rate. The growth rate can be determined, even if only one component of the motion field can be computed. Just consider a spatial pattern that shows spatial variation only in one direction (linear symmetry). Then only the velocity component in the direction of the variations can be estimated, but not the perpendicular component. Because the growth rate is homogeneous, it can still be estimated.

3.2 Unbiased Estimation

The eigenvalue analysis gives only unbiased results if the error of all elements of the data vector are equal. While this is at least approximatively true for the estimation of the motion fields, it is no longer true if other terms with higher derivatives or terms without errors are contained in the data vector. Then it is required to apply equilibration techniques that scale the individual elements in the data vector so that all elements have equal errors. Alternatively, mixed ordinary least squares (OLS) and total least squares (TLS) techniques can be used [11].

3.3 Optimal Filtering

From the discussion in Secs. 2.1 and 2.2 it appears that good filters for motion estimation require perfect derivative operators. Fortunately, this is not true. A more closer look reveals that a surprisingly general class of filters can be used for the estimation of motion.

Because moving objects appear as oriented structures in image sequences, any operation on the gray values of image sequences that does not change the orientation of spatiotemporal patterns still will give the same velocity field. Therefore any common linear prefiltering of the image sequence with a mask $b(\boldsymbol{x}, t)$ does not change the estimated parameters. A common filter applied to all terms (including the original gray value) results only in a common factor that does not change the direction of the data vector.

This basic fact has far-reaching consequences for motion estimation. It means that any set of filters with transfer functions of the form

$$d(\boldsymbol{k}) = \mathrm{i}k_p B(\boldsymbol{k}), \tag{24}$$

provides suitable filter set. The index p refers to any of the directions x, y, and t. The set of filters in Eq. 24 thus includes the common prefiltering. There is no restriction to the common filter $B(\boldsymbol{k})$. As long as it is a smoothing filter, the derivative filters remain derivative filters. They are just replaced by regularized filter kernels. The common filter can have, however, any transfer function. Then they are no longer necessarily derivative filters. It is interesting to note that the same conclusion can be reached by a completely different train of thoughts as discussed in [12].

The wide degree of freedom for filters opens innovative ways to optimize classes of filters given the frequency distribution of noise and signals in the image sequence. It is not surprising that standard derivative filters show considerable errors in the estimation of the direction of the gradient. According to Sec. 2.1, unbiased motion estimates, however, require unbiased estimates of the direction of the gradient. The Sobel filter,

Fig. 6. Ring test pattern, the maximum wave number at the edges of the pattern is 0.5, i. e, the sampling is just 2 samples per wavelength

for example, shows deviations in the direction of the gradient up to 5° [9]. A filter with the same shape as the Sobel filter

$$\boldsymbol{D}_{x,\mathrm{opt}} = \boldsymbol{D}_x * \boldsymbol{B}_y * \boldsymbol{B}_t, \quad \boldsymbol{D}_x = \frac{1}{2}\,[1, 0, -1]\,, \quad \boldsymbol{B}_{y,t} = [p/2, 1-p, p/2]^T \tag{25}$$

shows a maximum error in the direction of the gradient of only 0.4^o with $p = 6/16$ (Sobel: $p = 1/4$) [13, 14] under the assumption of isotropic Gaussian noise in the image sequence.

While the optimization of first-order filters *alone* is a quite easy task, it is much more difficult to optimize family of filters that include first-order and second-order filters, as they are used for the joint estimation of flow and diffusion (Sec. 2.5) and zero-order (mean) and first-order filters, as they are required for relaxation processes (Sec. 2.4). Suitable optimizations are discussed in [15].

3.4 Energy Tensor

Recently, a phase invariant extension of the structure tensor was proposed [16], named the *energy tensor*. The energy tensor is defined as

$$\boldsymbol{E} = \boldsymbol{\nabla}_{xt} g \, \boldsymbol{\nabla}_{xt} g^T - g\,\boldsymbol{H} g = \begin{bmatrix} g_x^2 - g g_{xx} & g_x g_y - g g_{xy} & g_x g_t - g g_{xt} \\ g_x g_y - g g_{xy} & g_y^2 - g g_{yy} & g_y g_t - g g_{yt} \\ g_x g_t - g g_{xt} & g_y g_t - g g_{yt} & g_t^2 - g g_{tt} \end{bmatrix}, \tag{26}$$

where $\boldsymbol{H}$ is the Hesse matrix. The energy tensor can be computed accurately, using the filter optimization techniques described in Sec. 3.3 if the second-order derivative filters are computed by consecutive application of first-order filters.

a *b*

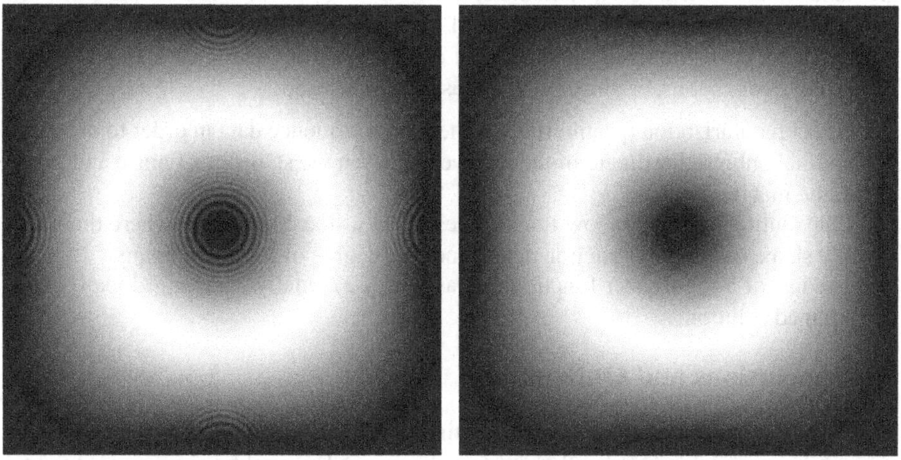

Fig. 7. Computation of **a** the trace of the structure tensor (averaged magnitude of the gradient) and **b** the trace of the energy tensor (amplitude of gradient)

It is important to note that the energy tensor requires *no* averaging. Firstly, this constitutes a significant saving in number of computing operations. Secondly, the energy tensor gives better results. This can be demonstrated by computing the structure tensor and energy tensor of the ring test pattern in Fig. 6. While the averaging of the structure tensor is not sufficient at large wavelength (small wave numbers) close to the center of the ring pattern, this effect does not show up with the energy tensor (Fig. 7). It is, however, not yet clear, whether the energy tensor can be extended in such a general way as this is the case with the structure tensor to the estimation of parameters of dynamic processes.

3.5 Generalized Regularization

Because of the sparse local information contained in image sequences, regularization approaches are required to compute dense motion fields. For the estimation of the parameters of dynamic processes, regularization becomes even more important, because more parameters have to be estimated from the same amount of data. Since the early work of [17] about global regularization, significant progress has been made. In a recent paper, [18] showed the equivalence between variational approaches and anisotropic diffusion and developed a design principle for rotationally invariant anisotropic regularizers.

It is straightforward to extend these concepts to the joint estimation of motion fields and parameters of dynamic processes because the form of the equations remains the same, only the number of parameters to be estimated has increased according to the model for the dynamic process.

In general, a spatiotemporal regularizer that constrains the parameter field is given by

$$\overline{\|\boldsymbol{d}^T\boldsymbol{p}\|} + R(\boldsymbol{\nabla}_{xt}p_k) \rightarrow \min, \tag{27}$$

where $R(\boldsymbol{\nabla}p_k)$ is a generally nonlinear function of the spatiotemporal gradient of all elements of the parameter vector. Using a regularizer that is simply a sum of squared gradients of all elements of the parameter vector $\alpha^2 \sum_k |\nabla_{xt} p_k|^2$ is a simple extension of the homogenous global regularizer used by [17]. There are three ways to vary and thus optimize the estimate of parameters of dynamic models and in each step homogeneous, inhomogeneous, or anisotropic diffusion can be used:

- Direct regularization (prefiltering) of the image sequence data in order to obtain an optimal unbiased estimate of the data vector given the statistics of noise and signal in the image sequence.
- Convolution by the window function results in a 'local' solution, where the width and shape of window function determines the degree of local averaging.
- The use of a regularizer functional R as in Eq. 27 finally leads to 'globally' constrained solution.

4 Conclusions and Outlook

Although a general framework for the estimation of dynamic processes from image sequences is available and has helped to solve some key problems in environmental physics and live sciences, there are still many open research problems. Among them are:

More efficient algorithms. More efficient algorithms are required for a more widespread application.

Sparse temporal sampling. As with all optical-flow based techniques, the techniques described in this paper require temporally densely sampled image sequences. In many practical applications this requirement cannot be met. Therefore, it is required to develop suitable multigrid and/or multiscale techniques.

Spherical quadrature filters. The relation between classical optical-flow based and quadrature-filter based techniques [19] and the recent extension to spherical quadrature filters [20] is not fully understood and requires further attention.

Nonlinear dynamic models. The most challenging problem, however, is the extension of the techniques described in this paper to nonlinear dynamic models.

Acknowledgments

First of all, I would like to thank all members of research unit FOR 240 "Image Sequence Analysis to Investigate Dynamic Processes", who with their enthusiasm and dedication for interdisciplinary research made it possible that this research unit was successful. Financial support for this research unit, the priority programs SPP 1117 "Mathematical methods for time series analysis and digital image processing" (LOCOMOTOR subproject) and SPP 1147 "Imaging Measuring Techniques for Flow Analysis" by the German Science Foundation (DFG) is gratefully acknowledged. Sediment transport (Fig. 3) was studied in a project funded by the German Federal Waterways Engineering and Research Institute (BAW), Karlsruhe.

References

1. Jähne, B.: Spatio-temporal Image Processing. Volume 751 of Lecture Notes in Computer Science. Springer, Berlin (1993)
2. Bigün, J., Granlund, G.H.: Optimal orientation detection of linear symmetry. In: Proc. ICCV'87, Washington, DC, IEEE Computer Society (1987) 433–438

3. Garbe, C.S., Spies, H., Jähne, B.: Estimation of surface flow and net heat flux from infrared image sequences. J. Mathematical Imaging and Vision **19** (2003) 159–174
4. Haussecker, H.W., Fleet, D.J.: Computing optical flow with physical models of brightness variation. IEEE Trans. PAMI **23** (2001) 661–673
5. Jehle, M., Jähne, B.: A novel method for spatiotemporal analysis of flows within the water-side viscous boundary layer. In Grant, I., ed.: 12th International Symposium Flow Visualization, Göttingen, 10–14 September 2006, Edinburgh, UK, Optimage Ltd (2006) ISBN 0-9533991-8-4.
6. Crank, J.: The Mathematics of Diffusion. 2 edn. Oxford University Press, New York (1975)
7. Garbe, C., Roetmann, K., Jähne, B.: An optical flow based technique for the non-invasive measurement of microfluidic flows. In Grant, I., ed.: 12th International Symposium Flow Visualization, Göttingen, 10–14 September 2006, Edinburgh, UK, Optimage Ltd (2006) ISBN 0-9533991-8-4.
8. Garbe, C.: Measuring and Modeling Fluid Dynamic Processes using Digital Image Sequence Analysis. Habilition thesis, Univ. Heidelberg (2007)
9. Jähne, B.: Digital Image Processing. 6 edn. Springer, Berlin (2005)
10. Schmundt, D., Stitt, M., Jähne, B., Schurr, U.: Quantitative analysis of the local rates of growth of dicot leaves at a high temporal and spatial resolution, using image sequence analysis. The Plant J. **16** (1998) 505–514
11. Garbe, C.S., Spies, H., Jähne, B.: Mixed ols-tls for the estimation of dynamic processes with a linear source term. In Gool, L.V., ed.: Pattern Recognition, Proc. 24th DAGM Symposium Zurich. Volume 2449 of Lecture Notes in Computer Science., Berlin, Springer (2002) 463–471
12. Mester, R.: The generalization, optimization, and information-theoretic justification of filter-based and autocovariance-based motion estimation. In: Proc. Intern. Conf. Image Processing (ICIP'03), Barcelona. (2003)
13. Scharr, H., Körgel, S., Jähne, B.: Numerische isotropieoptimierung von fir-filtern mittels querglättung. In Paulus, E., Wahl, F.M., eds.: Mustererkennung 1997 19. DAGM Symposium Braunschweig. Informatik aktuell, Berlin, Springer (1997) 367–374
14. Scharr, H.: Optimale Operatoren in der Digitalen Bildverarbeitung. Diss., Univ. Heidelberg (2000) 10.05.2000.
15. Scharr, H.: Optimal filters for extended optical flow. (this volume)
16. Felsberg, M., Granlund, G.H.: POI detection using channel clustering and the 2d energy tensor. In: Pattern Recognition, 26th DAGM Symposium. Volume 3175 of Lecture Notes in Computer Science., Berlin, Springer (2002) 103–110
17. Horn, B.K.P., Schunck, B.G.: Determining optical flow. Artificial Intelligence **17** (1981) 185–203
18. Schnörr, C., Weickert, J.: Variational image motion computation: theoretical framework, problems and perspectives. In Sommer, G., Krüger, N., Perwasser, C., eds.: Mustererkennung 2000. Informatik Aktuell, Berlin, Springer (2000) 476–487
19. Granlund, G.H., Knutsson, H.: Signal Processing for Computer Vision. Kluwer, Dordrecht (1995)
20. Felsberg, M.: Disparity from monogenic phase. In van Gool, L., ed.: Pattern Recognition, 24th DAGM Symposium. Volume 2449 of Lecture Notes in Computer Science., Berlin, Springer (2002) 248–256
21. Wenig, M.: Satellite Measurement of Long-Term Tropospheric Trace Gas Distributions and Source Strengths - Algorithm Development and Data Analysis. PhD thesis, Univ. Heidelberg (2001)

Bayesian Approaches to Motion-Based Image and Video Segmentation

Daniel Cremers*

Department of Computer Science
University of California, Los Angeles, USA
http://www.cs.ucla.edu/~cremers

Abstract. We present a variational approach for segmenting the image plane into regions of piecewise parametric motion given two or more frames from an image sequence. Our model is based on a conditional probability for the spatio-temporal image gradient, given a particular velocity model, and on a geometric prior on the estimated motion field favoring motion boundaries of minimal length.

We cast the problem of motion segmentation as one of Bayesian inference, we derive a cost functional which depends on parametric motion models for each of a set of domains and on the boundary separating them. The resulting functional can be interpreted as an extension of the Mumford-Shah functional from intensity segmentation to motion segmentation. In contrast to most alternative approaches, the problems of segmentation and motion estimation are jointly solved by continuous minimization of a *single* functional. Minimization results in an eigenvalue problem for the motion parameters and in a gradient descent evolution for the motion boundary. The evolution of the motion boundaries is implemented by a multiphase level set formulation which allows for the segmentation of an arbitrary number of multiply connected moving objects.

We further extend this approach to the segmentation of space-time volumes of coherent motion from video sequences. To this end, motion boundaries are represented by a set of surfaces in space-time. An implementation by a higher-dimensional multiphase level set model allows the evolving surfaces to undergo topological changes. In contrast to an iterative segmentation of consecutive frame pairs, a constraint on the area of these surfaces leads to an additional temporal regularization of the computed motion boundaries.

Numerical results demonstrate the capacity of our approach to segment objects based exclusively on their relative motion.

1 Introduction

The segmentation of images into meaningful areas can be driven by various low-level grouping criteria, such as edge information, color information or texture information. In the present work, we address the question of how to exploit motion information for the purpose of segmentation.

While traditionally researchers have suggested to first estimate a motion field and to subsequently segment the scene based on this motion field [35], the problem of motion

* Present Affiliation: Department of Computer Science, University of Bonn, Germany.

B. Jähne et al. (Eds.): IWCM 2004, LNCS 3417, pp. 104–123, 2007.

segmentation can be viewed as a chicken and egg problem: Reliable motion estimation algorithms generally require a region of support (ideally given by a segmentation of the moving object), while the computation of a segmentation assumes knowledge of the motion.

Many researchers have addressed this coupling of segmentation and motion estimation. Some have proposed to model motion discontinuities implicitly by non-quadratic robust estimators [2, 4, 21, 22, 25, 36]. Others tackled the problem of segmenting motion by treating the problems of motion estimation in disjoint sets and optimization of the motion boundaries separately [5, 14, 27, 29, 30]. Some approaches are based on Markov Random Field (MRF) formulations and optimization schemes such as stochastic relaxation by Gibbs sampling [20], split-and-merge techniques [15], deterministic relaxation [3], graph cuts [31] or expectation maximization (EM) (cf. [18, 37]). As pointed out in [37], exact solutions to the EM algorithm are computationally expensive and therefore suboptimal approximations are employed. An elegant method to directly compute both the segmentation and the motion models was recently proposed in [34], yet this approach differs from the above approaches in that it does not allow to impose smoothness of the estimated motion boundaries.

In the present paper, we propose a framework which allows to jointly solve the problems of segmentation and motion estimation by minimizing a single functional. We formulate the problem of motion segmentation in the framework of Bayesian inference. Related Bayesian formulations have been proposed in the discrete MRF framework (cf. [3]). Our formulation differs from the above approach in that it is continuous, uses a contour representation of the motion discontinuity set, can be optimized by a simple and fast gradient descent minimization and is based on a different (normalized) likelihood in the data term. The proposed functional can be interpreted as an extension of the Mumford-Shah model [24] from the case of gray value segmentation to the case of motion segmentation. Minimization leads to an eigenvalue problem for the motion parameters associated with each region, and to a gradient descent evolution for the boundary separating the regions.

This joint minimization of a *single* functional with respect to motion parameters and motion boundaries generates a pde-based solution to the above chicken and egg problem. The resulting boundary evolution can be interpreted in the way that neighboring regions compete for the boundary in terms of their motion energy. In analogy to the corresponding gray value model, which has been termed *Region Competition* [39], we therefore refer to this process as *Motion Competition*.

We propose a multiphase level set implementation of the motion competition functional, which is based on the corresponding gray value model of Chan and Vese [7]. The level set formulation permits the segmentation of several (possibly multiply connected) objects, based on their relative motion.

In order to impose temporal regularity of the estimated motion segmentation, we generalize the motion boundaries from contours in 2D to surfaces in 3D (space and time). An analogous level set implementation allows to compute several multiply-connected motion phases representing moving objects or regions over time. The present paper integrates and extends results presented in [8–12].

The paper is organized as follows. In Section 2, we formulate motion estimation as a problem of Bayesian inference. In Section 3, we consistently derive a variational framework for motion segmentation. In Section 6, we introduce a level set implementation of the proposed functional. In Section 7, we present an extension to space-time motion segmentation of videos. Numerical results for simulated ground truth data and real-world sequences are given in Section 8.

2 From Motion Estimation to Motion Segmentation

2.1 Motion Estimation as Bayesian Inference

Let $\Omega \subset \mathbb{R}^2$ denote the image plane and let $f : \Omega \times \mathbb{R} \to \mathbb{R}$ be a gray value image sequence. Denote the spatio-temporal image gradient of $f(x,t)$ by

$$\nabla_3 f = \left(\frac{\partial f}{\partial x_1}, \frac{\partial f}{\partial x_2}, \frac{\partial f}{\partial t} \right)^t . \tag{1}$$

Let

$$v : \Omega \to \mathbb{R}^3, \qquad v(x) = (u(x), w(x), 1)^t, \tag{2}$$

be the velocity vector at a point x in homogeneous coordinates.[1]

With these definitions, the problem of motion estimation now consists in maximizing the conditional probability

$$\mathcal{P}(v \,|\, \nabla_3 f) = \frac{\mathcal{P}(\nabla_3 f \,|\, v)\ \mathcal{P}(v)}{\mathcal{P}(\nabla_3 f)}, \tag{3}$$

with respect to the motion field v. For a related Bayesian formulation of motion segmentation in the discrete case, we refer to [3].

2.2 A Normalized Velocity Likelihood

In the following, we will assume t hat the intensity of a moving point remains constant throughout time. Expressed in differential form, this gives a relation between the spatio-temporal image gradient and the homogeneous velocity vector, known as *optic flow constraint*:

$$\frac{df}{dt} = \frac{\partial f}{\partial t} + \frac{\partial f}{\partial x_1}\frac{dx_1}{dt} + \frac{\partial f}{\partial x_2}\frac{dx_2}{dt} = v^t\,\nabla_3 f = 0. \tag{4}$$

The optic flow constraint has been extensively exploited in the motion estimation community. Following the seminal work of Horn and Schunck [16], researchers commonly estimate motion fields by minimizing functionals which integrate this constraint in a least-squares manner (while imposing a smoothness constraint on the velocity field). In this work, we propose an alternative geometric approach to interpret the optic flow constraint. As we will argue in the following, the resulting likelihood is more appropriate in the context of motion segmentation.

[1] For the moment, we are only concerned with two consecutive frames from a sequence. Therefore we will drop the time coordinate in the notation of the velocity field.

Except for locations where the spatio-temporal gradient vanishes, the constraint (4) states that the homogeneous velocity vector must be orthogonal to the spatio-temporal image gradient. Therefore we propose to use a measure of this orthogonality as a conditional probability on the spatio-temporal image gradient. Let α be the angle between the two vectors then:

$$\mathcal{P}\Big(\nabla_3 f(x) | v(x)\Big) \propto e^{-\cos^2(\alpha)} = \exp\left(-\frac{(v(x)^t \nabla_3 f(x))^2}{|v(x)|^2 |\nabla_3 f(x)|^2}\right). \qquad (5)$$

By construction, this probability is independent of the length of the two vectors and monotonically increases the more orthogonal the two vectors. A normalization with respect to the length of the velocity vector only has been proposed in the context of motion estimation [1]. For derivations of alternative likelihood functions from generative models of the image formation process and associated noise models, we refer to [13,26,38].

2.3 A Geometric Prior on the Velocity Field

We discretize the velocity field v by a set of disjoint regions $\Omega_i \subset \Omega$ with constant velocity v_i:

$$v(x) = \{v_i, \text{ if } x \in \Omega_i\} \qquad (6)$$

An extension to piecewise parametric motion is presented in Section 4. We now assume the prior probability on the velocity field to only depend on the length $|C|$ of the boundary C separating these regions:

$$\mathcal{P}(v) \propto \exp\Big(-\nu\,|C|\Big) \qquad (7)$$

In particular, this means that we do not make any prior assumptions on the velocity vectors v_i. Such a prior would necessarily introduce a bias favoring certain velocities. Priors on the length of separating boundaries are common in the context of variational segmentation (cf. [6,19,24]). For alternative more object-specific priors in the context of motion segmentation, we refer to [10]. As we shall see in the next section, the choice of velocity representation in (6) combined with the prior in (7) will transform the motion estimation framework into one of motion segmentation.

3 A Variational Framework for Motion Segmentation

With the above assumptions, we can use the framework of Bayesian inference to derive a variational method for motion segmentation. The first term in the numerator of equation (3) can be written as:

$$\mathcal{P}(\nabla_3 f \,|\, v) = \prod_{x \in \Omega} \mathcal{P}(\nabla_3 f(x) \,|\, v(x))^h = \prod_{i=1}^{n} \prod_{x \in \Omega_i} \mathcal{P}(\nabla_3 f(x) \,|\, v_i)^h, \qquad (8)$$

where $h = dx$ denotes the grid size of the discretization of Ω.[2] The first step is based on the assumptions that gradient measurements are spatially independent and that the

[2] The introduction of the grid size h ensures the correct continuum limit.

velocity affects the spatio-temporal gradient only locally.[3] And the second step is based on the discretization of the velocity field given in (6).

With the prior probability (7), maximizing the conditional probability (3) with respect to the velocity field v therefore amounts to

$$\max_{v} \mathcal{P}(v \mid \nabla_3 f) = \max_{v_i, C} \left\{ e^{-\nu |C|} \prod_{i=1}^{n} \prod_{x \in \Omega_i} \mathcal{P}(\nabla_3 f(x) \mid v_i)^h \right\}. \tag{9}$$

Equivalently one can minimize the negative logarithm of this expression, which is given by the energy functional:

$$E(C, \{v_i\}) = -\sum_{i=1}^{n} \int_{\Omega_i} \log\left(\mathcal{P}(\nabla_3 f(x) \mid v_i)\right) dx \; + \nu |C|. \tag{10}$$

With the conditional probability (5) on the spatio-temporal gradient, this gives:

$$\boxed{E(C, \{v_i\}) = \sum_{i=1}^{n} \int_{\Omega_i} \frac{(v_i^t \nabla_3 f(x))^2}{|v_i|^2 \, |\nabla_3 f(x)|^2} \, dx \; + \nu |C|.} \tag{11}$$

Let us make the following remarks about this functional:

- The functional (11) can be considered an extension of the piecewise constant Mumford-Shah functional [24] from the case of gray value segmentation to the case of motion segmentation. Rather than having a constant f_i modeling the intensity of each region Ω_i, we now have a velocity vector v_i modeling the motion in each region Ω_i.
- Gradient descent minimization with respect to the boundary C and the set of motion vectors $\{v_i\}$, jointly solves the problems of segmentation and motion estimation. In our view, this aspect is crucial, since these two problems are tightly coupled. Many alternative approaches to motion segmentation tend to instead treat the two problems separately by first (globally) estimating the motion and then trying to segment the estimated motion into a set of meaningful regions.
- The integrand in the data term differs from the one commonly used in the optic flow community for motion estimation: Rather than minimizing the deviation from the optic flow constraint in a least-squares manner, as done e.g. in the seminal work of Horn and Schunck [16], measure (5) introduces an additional normalization with respect to the length of the two vectors. In Section 5.3, we will argue that these normalization are essential in the case of motion *segmentation*, where differently moving regions are compared.

[3] Both of these assumptions are known to be inaccurate. More elaborate modeling of spatial correlations might lead to improved segmentation schemes.

- The functional (11) contains one free parameter ν, which determines the relative weight of the length constraint. Larger values of ν will induce a segmentation of the image motion on a coarser scale. As argued by Morel and Solimini [23], such a scale parameter is fundamental to all segmentation approaches.

4 Piecewise Parametric Motion Segmentation

Minimizing functional (11) generates a segmentation of the image plane into domains of piecewise constant motion. In order to cope with more complex motion regions, one can extend this approach to piecewise parametric motion. An extension of the geometric reasoning of Section 2.2 to parametric motion models is as follows.

The velocity on the domain Ω_i is allowed to vary according to a model of the form:

$$v_i(x) = M(x)\, p_i, \tag{12}$$

where M is a matrix depending only on space and time and p_i is the parameter vector associated with each region. A particular model which allows for expansion, contraction, rotation and shearing is the case of *affine motion* given by the matrix

$$M(x) = \begin{pmatrix} x_1 & x_2 & 1 & 0 & 0 & 0 & 0 \\ 0 & 0 & 0 & x_1 & x_2 & 1 & 0 \\ 0 & 0 & 0 & 0 & 0 & 0 & 1 \end{pmatrix}, \tag{13}$$

and a parameter vector $p_i = (a_i, b_i, c_i, d_i, e_i, f_i, 1)$ for each region Ω_i.

Inserting model (12) into the optic flow constraint (4) gives a relation which – again interpreted geometrically – states that the the vector $M^t \nabla_3 f$ must either vanish or be orthogonal to the vector p_i. We therefore model the conditional probability that the point $x \in \Omega$ belongs to the domain Ω_i by a quantity which only depends on the angle between p_i and $M^t \nabla_3 f$:

$$P(\nabla_3 f \,|\, p_i) \propto \exp\left(- \frac{(p_i^t\, M^t \nabla_3 f)^2}{|p_i|^2\, |M^t \nabla_3 f|^2} \right). \tag{14}$$

The corresponding generalization of functional (11) from piecewise constant to piecewise parametric motion segmentation is given by:

$$E(C, \{p_i\}) = \sum_i \int_{\Omega_i} \frac{|p_i^t M^t \nabla_3 f|^2}{|p_i|^2 |M^t \nabla_3 f|^2}\, dx \; + \; \nu\, |C|. \tag{15}$$

5 Energy Minimization

The functional (15) is of the form

$$E(C, \{p_i\}) = \sum_{i=1}^{n} \int_{\Omega_i} \frac{p_i^t\, T(x)\, p_i}{|p_i|^2}\, dx \; + \nu\, |C|, \tag{16}$$

where, for notational simplification, we have introduced the matrix

$$T(x) = \frac{\nabla_3 f \; M^t \; M \; \nabla_3 f^t}{|M^t \, \nabla_3 f|^2}. \tag{17}$$

This functional is minimized by alternating the two fractional steps of optimizing with respect to the motion parameters $\{p_i\}$ for fixed boundary C, and iterating the gradient descent with respect to C for fixed parameters $\{p_i\}$.

5.1 An Eigenvalue Problem for the Motion Parameters

The functional (16) can be further simplified:

$$E(C, \{p_i\}) = \sum_{i=1}^{n} \frac{p_i^t \, T_i \, p_i}{|p_i|^2} \, dx \; + \nu \, |C|, \quad \text{where } T_i = \int_{\Omega_i} T(x) \, dx, \tag{18}$$

with T given in (17). For fixed boundary C, i.e. fixed regions Ω_i, minimizing this functional with respect to the motion parameters $\{p_i\}$ results in a set of eigenvalue problems of the form:

$$p_i = \arg\min_p \frac{p^t \, T_i \, p}{p^t p}. \tag{19}$$

The parametric motion model p_i for each region Ω_i is therefore given by the eigenvector corresponding to the smallest eigenvalue of the matrix T_i defined above. It is normalized, such that the third component is 1. Similar eigenvalue problems arise in motion estimation due to normalization with respect to the velocity magnitude (cf. [1, 18]).

5.2 Motion Competition

Conversely, for fixed motion models p_i, a gradient descent on the energy (16) for the boundary C results in the evolution equation:

$$\frac{\partial C}{\partial t} = -\frac{\partial E}{\partial C} = (e_j - e_k) \, n \; - \; \nu \frac{d|C|}{dC}, \tag{20}$$

where the indices 'j' and 'k' refer to the regions adjoining the contour, n denotes the normal vector on the boundary pointing into region Ω_j, and

$$e_i = \frac{p_i^t \, T \, p_i}{p_i^t p_i} = \frac{p_i^t \, \nabla_3 f \, M^t \, M \, \nabla_3 f^t \, p_i}{|p_i|^2 \, |M^t \, \nabla_3 f|^2} \tag{21}$$

is an energy density.

Note that we have neglected in the evolution equation (20) higher-order terms which account for the dependence of the motion parameters p_i on the regions Ω_i. An Eulerian accurate shape optimization scheme as presented for example in [17] is the focus of ongoing research.

The two terms in the contour evolution (20) have the following intuitive interpretation:

- The first term is proportional to the difference of the energy densities e_i in the regions adjoining the boundary: The neighboring regions compete for the boundary in terms of their motion energy density, thereby maximizing the motion homogeneity. For this reason we refer to this process as *Motion Competition*.
- The second term minimizes the length $\mathcal{L}$ of the separating motion boundary.

5.3 Effect of the Normalization

In Section 2.2 we argued that the proposed likelihood (5) (in contrast to the commonly used least-squares formulation) does not introduce a bias with respect to the magnitude of the velocity or the image gradient.[4] As a direct consequence, the respective contour evolutions differ, as we will detail for the case of piecewise constant motion.

The proposed motion likelihood (5) results in a contour evolution of the form (20) with energy densities

$$e_i = \frac{v_i^t \, \nabla_3 f \, \nabla_3 f^t \, v_i}{|v_i|^2 \, |\nabla_3 f|^2} \tag{22}$$

This means that the term driving the contour evolution does not depend on the magnitude of the spatio-temporal gradient and it does not depend on the magnitude of the respective velocity models.

In contrast, a Horn-and-Schunck type likelihood [16] would induce contour driving terms which do not include the normalizing terms in the denominator:

$$e_i = v_i^t \, \nabla_3 f \, \nabla_3 f^t \, v_i. \tag{23}$$

This lack of normalization has two effects on the boundary evolution and resulting segmentation: Firstly the motion boundary will propagate much faster in areas of high gradient. Secondly the evolution direction and speed will be affected by the magnitude of velocities: regions with larger velocity will exert a stronger pull on the motion boundary.

6 A Multiphase Level Set Implementation

A few years after its introduction in [28], the level set based evolution of contours was adopted as a framework for image segmentation (cf. [6, 7, 19]). In contrast to explicit boundaries, the level set representation does not depend on a particular choice of parameterization. During the evolution of the boundary one avoids the issues of control point regridding. Moreover, the topology of the evolving interface is not constrained. This permits splitting and merging of the contour during evolution and therefore makes level set representations well suited for the segmentation of several objects or multiply connected objects.

Based on a corresponding gray value model of Chan and Vese [7], we will first present a two-phase level set model for the motion competition functional (16) with a single level set function ϕ. This model is subsequently extended to a multi-phase model on the basis of a vector-valued level set function.

[4] In particular, the functionals (11) and (16) are invariant to global scale transformations of the intensity: $f \rightarrow \gamma f$.

6.1 The Two-Phase Model

In this subsection, we restrict the class of permissible motion segmentations to two-phase solutions, i.e. to segmentations of the image plane for which each point can be ascribed to one of two velocity models p_1 and p_2. The general case of several velocity models $\{p_i\}_{i=1,\dots,n}$ will be treated in the next subsection.

Let the boundary C in the functional (16) be represented as the zero level set of a function $\phi : \Omega \to \mathbb{R}$:

$$C = \{x \in \Omega \mid \phi(x) = 0\}. \tag{24}$$

With the Heaviside step function

$$H(\phi) = \begin{cases} 1 \text{ if } \phi \geq 0 \\ 0 \text{ if } \phi < 0 \end{cases}, \tag{25}$$

the energy (16) can be embedded by the following *two-phase functional*:

$$E(p_1, p_2, \phi) = \int_\Omega \frac{p_1^t T p_1}{|p_1|^2} H(\phi)\, dx + \int_\Omega \frac{p_2^t T p_2}{|p_2|^2} \Big(1 - H(\phi)\Big)\, dx \\ + \nu \int_\Omega \big|\nabla H(\phi)\big|\, dx. \tag{26}$$

The first two terms in (26) enforce a homogeneity of the estimated motion in the two phases, while the last term enforces a minimal length of the region boundary given by the zero level set of ϕ.

The two-phase functional (26) is simultaneously minimized with respect to the velocity models p_1 and p_2, and with respect to the embedding level set function ϕ defining the motion boundaries. To this end, we alternate the two fractional steps:

(a) Updating the Motion Models.
For fixed ϕ, minimization of the functional (26) with respect to the motion vectors p_1 and p_2 results in the eigenvalue problem:

$$p_i = \arg\min_v \frac{v^t\, T_i\, v}{v^t v}, \tag{27}$$

for the matrices

$$T_1 = \int_\Omega T(x)\, H(\phi)\, dx \quad \text{and} \quad T_2 = \int_\Omega T(x)\, \big(1 - H(\phi)\big)\, dx. \tag{28}$$

The solution of (27) is given by the eigenvectors corresponding to the smallest eigenvalues of T_1 and T_2.

(b) Evolution of the Level Set Function.
Conversely, for fixed motion vectors, the gradient descent on the functional (26) for the level set function ϕ is given by:

$$\frac{\partial \phi}{\partial t} = \delta(\phi) \left[\nu \,\text{div}\left(\frac{\nabla \phi}{|\nabla \phi|} \right) + e_2 - e_1 \right], \tag{29}$$

with the energy densities e_i given in (21). As suggested in [7], we implement the Delta function $\delta(\phi) = \frac{d}{d\phi}H(\phi)$ by a smooth approximation of finite width σ:

$$\delta_\sigma(s) = \frac{1}{\pi}\frac{\sigma}{\sigma^2 + s^2}. \tag{30}$$

Thereby the update of ϕ is not restricted to the areas of zero-crossing, but rather spread out over a band of width σ around it. Depending on the size of σ, this permits to detect interior motion boundaries.

6.2 The General Multiphase Model

Compared to the explicit contour representation, the above level set representation permits to segment several, possibly multiply connected, moving regions. Yet, the representation of the motion boundary with a *single* level set function ϕ permits to model motion fields with only two phases (i.e. it permits only two different velocity models). Moreover, one cannot represent certain geometrical features of the boundary, such as triple junctions, by the zero level set of a single function ϕ. There are various ways to overcome these limitations by using multiple level set functions.

An elegant solution to model multiple phases was proposed by Chan and Vese in [7]. Rather than representing each phase by a separate level set function, they introduce a more compact representation of up to n phases which needs only $m = \log_2(n)$ level set functions.[5] Moreover, by definition, the suggested approach generates a partition of the image plane and therefore does not suffer from overlap or vacuum formation, a difficulty which commonly arises when modeling each region by its own level set function. We will therefore adopt this representation of Chan and Vese to implement multiple motion phases, as detailed in the following.

Consider a set of m level set functions $\phi_i : \Omega \to \mathbb{R}$, let

$$\Phi = (\phi_1, \ldots, \phi_m) \tag{31}$$

be a vector level set function and let $H(\Phi) = (H(\phi_1), \ldots, H(\phi_m))$ be the associated vector Heaviside function. This function maps each point $x \in \Omega$ to a binary vector and therefore permits to encode a set of $n = 2^m$ phases Ω_i defined by:

$$R = \{x \in \Omega \mid H\big(\Phi(x)\big) = \text{constant}\}. \tag{32}$$

In analogy to the corresponding level set formulation of the Mumford-Shah functional [7], we propose to replace the two-phase functional (26) by the *multiphase functional*:

$$\boxed{E(\{p_i\}, \Phi) = \sum_{i=1}^{n} \int_\Omega \frac{p_i^t T p_i}{|p_i|^2} \chi_i(\Phi)\, dx \; + \; \nu \sum_{i=1}^{n} \int_\Omega \big|\nabla H(\phi_i)\big|\, dx,} \tag{33}$$

where χ_i denotes the indicator function for the region Ω_i. Note, that for $n = 2$, this is equivalent to the two-phase model introduced in (26).

For further details regarding the minimization of this multiphase model, we refer to [8].

[5] During the optimization certain phases may disappear such that the final segmentation may consist of less than n phases.

6.3 Redistancing

During their evolution, the level set functions generally grow to very large positive or negative values in the respective areas of the input image corresponding to a particular motion hypothesis. Indeed, there is nothing in the level set formulation of Chan and Vese [7] which prevents the level set functions from growing indefinitely. In numerical implementations, we found that a very steep slope of the level set functions can even inhibit the flexibility of the boundary to displace. In order to reproject the evolving level set function to the space of distance functions, we intermittently iterate several steps of the redistancing equation [32]:

$$\frac{\partial \phi}{\partial t} = \text{sign}(\hat{\phi})\;(1 - |\nabla \phi|)\,, \tag{34}$$

where $\hat{\phi}$ denotes the level set function before redistancing. This transformation does not affect the motion boundaries given by the zero-crossing of ϕ. It merely enforces the gradient to be of magnitude 1.

7 Motion-Based Space-Time Segmentation of Videos

The above framework allows to segment images into regions of parametric motion based on two consecutive frames from an image sequence. Given an entire video sequence, one can apply the proposed method iteratively to consecutive frame pairs – see [9] for details. In practical applications, the inferred contour tends to jitter over time.

Rather than processing the sequence frame by frame, one can impose temporal regularity of the inferred segmentation by casting the motion segmentation problem as one of identifying volumes $D_i \subset \Omega \times [0, \tau]$ of coherent motion in space-time, where τ denotes the length of the sequence. Rather than minimizing (16) with respect to a boundary C, one minimizes by the functional

$$E(S, \{p_i\}) = \sum_{i=1}^{n} \int_{D_i} \frac{p_i^t\, T(x,t)\, p_i}{|p_i|^2}\, dx\, dt \;+ \nu\, |S|, \tag{35}$$

with respect to a surface $S \subset \Omega \times [0, \tau]$ separating the phases D_i. The constraint on the area $|S|$ of the surface imposes regularity of the segmentation both in space and in time.

The parametric representation of velocity fields (12) can be directly extended into the temporal domain, thereby allowing to consider the case of *accelerated motion* with

$$M(x,t) = \begin{pmatrix} 1\,0\,t\,0\,0 \\ 0\,1\,0\,t\,0 \\ 0\,0\,0\,0\,1 \end{pmatrix}, \tag{36}$$

and $p_i = (u, w, a_u, a_w, 1)$ modeling an accelerated motion in each domain. Combinations of models of spatial and temporal variation are conceivable to capture accelerated rotations and other kinds of motion.

For the extension of the multiphase framework of Section 6.2 to propagate motion surfaces in space-time, the reader is referred to [11].

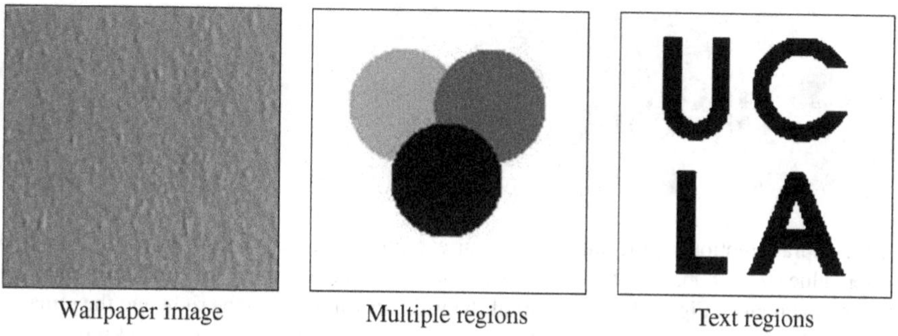

Fig. 1. Data for ground truth experiments. Specific image regions of the wallpaper shot (left) are artificially translated to generate input data.

8 Numerical Results

In the following, we will present numerical results demonstrating various properties of the proposed framework for motion segmentation.

For all experiments we determined the spatio-temporal image gradient from two consecutive images and specified a particular initialization of the boundary (or surface in the case of space-time segmentation). We subsequently minimized the functionals (33) or (35) by alternating the three fractional steps of:

- updating the motion models for all phases by solving the corresponding eigenvalue problem (27),
- evolving the level set functions by iterating the appropriate gradient descent pdes – e.g. equation (29) in the two-phase case,
- and redistancing the level set functions according to (34).

For all experiments, we show the evolving motion boundaries (and in some cases also the corresponding motion estimates) superimposed onto one of the frames. It should be noted that all results are obtained *exclusively* on the basis of the motion information.

8.1 Accurate Motion Segmentation Without Features

In order to verify the spatial precision of the motion competition approach, we performed a number of ground truth experiments in the following way. We took a snapshot of homogeneously structured wallpaper. We artificially translated certain image regions according to specific motion models. The input image and the respective image regions are highlighted (in various shades of gray) in Figure 1.

In the first example, we show that one can generate spatially accurate segmentation results exploiting only motion information, even for image sequences that exhibit little intensity variation or salient features. Figure 2 shows the contour evolution generated by minimizing functional (11). The input data consists of two wall paper images with the text region (Figure 1, right side) moving to the right and the remainder of the

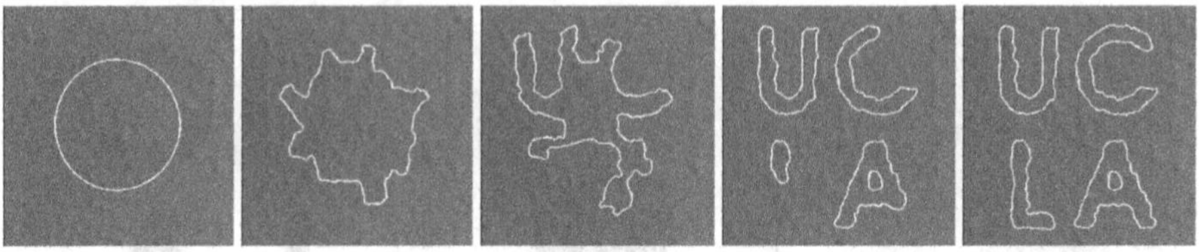

Fig. 2. Accurate motion segmentation. Contour evolution obtained with functional (26) and parameter values $\nu = 0.06, \sigma = 1$, superimposed on one of the two input frames. The input images show the text region (Figure 1, right side) of the wallpaper moving to the right and the remainder moving to the left. The motion competition framework generates highly accurate segmentations, even if the input images exhibit little in terms of salient features. Due to the region-based formulation, the initial contour does not need to be close to the final segmentation. We found that alternative initializations generate essentially identical segmentation results. The contour evolution took approximately 10 seconds in Matlab.

image plane moving to the left. Even for human observers the differently moving regions are difficult to detect – similar to a camouflaged lizard moving on a similarly-textured ground. The gradient descent evolution superimposed on one of the two frames gradually separates the two motion regions without requiring salient features such as edges or corner points.

8.2 Segmenting Several Motion Phases

In this experiment, we demonstrate an application of the multi-phase model (33) to the segmentation of up to four different regions based on their motion information. The input data consists of two images showing the wallpaper from Figure 1, left side, with three regions (shown in Figure 1, right side) moving away from the center. The upper two regions move by a factor 1.4 faster than the lower region.

Figure 3 shows several steps in the minimization of the functional (33) for two level set functions. Superimposed onto the ground truth region information are the evolution of the zero level sets of the two embedding functions ϕ_1 (black contour) and ϕ_2 (white contour), and the estimated piecewise constant motion field indicated by the black arrows.

Note that the two contours represent a set of four different phases:

$$\Omega_1 = \{x \in \Omega \mid \phi_1 \geq 0, \phi_2 \geq 0\}, \;\; \Omega_2 = \{x \in \Omega \mid \phi_1 \geq 0, \phi_2 < 0\},$$
$$\Omega_3 = \{x \in \Omega \mid \phi_1 < 0, \phi_2 \geq 0\}, \; \Omega_4 = \{x \in \Omega \mid \phi_1 < 0, \phi_2 < 0\}.$$

Upon convergence, these four phases clearly separate the three moving regions and the static background. The resulting final segmentation of the image, which is not explicitly shown here, is essentially identical to the ground truth region information. Note that the segmentation is obtained purely on the basis of the *motion information*: In the input images, the different regions cannot be distinguished from the background on the basis of their *appearance*.

8.3 Intensity Segmentation Versus Motion Segmentation

All image segmentation models are based on a number of more or less explicitly stated assumptions about the properties which define the objects of interest. The motion competition model is based on the assumption that objects are defined in terms of homogeneously moving regions. It extends the Mumford-Shah functional of piecewise constant intensity to a model of piecewise parametric motion.

In this example, we will show that despite this formal similarity the segmentations generated by the motion competition framework are very different from those of its gray value analog. The task is to segment a real-world traffic scene showing two moving cars on a differently moving background. We used two consecutive images from a sequence recorded by D. Koller and H.-H. Nagel (KOGS/IAKS, University of Karlsruhe).[6] The sequence shows several cars moving in the same direction, filmed by a static camera. In order to increase the complexity of the sequence, we artificially induced a background motion by selecting a subarea of the original sequence and shifting one of the two frames, thereby simulating the case of a moving camera.

Figure 4, top, shows the boundary evolution obtained by minimizing the two-phase model of Chan and Vese [7] for the first of the two frames. The segmentation process progressively separates bright and dark areas of the image plane. Yet, since the objects of interest are not well-defined in terms of homogeneous gray value, the final segmentation inevitably fails to capture them. The dark car in the lower left is associated with the darker parts of the street, whereas the car in the upper right is split into its brighter and darker parts.

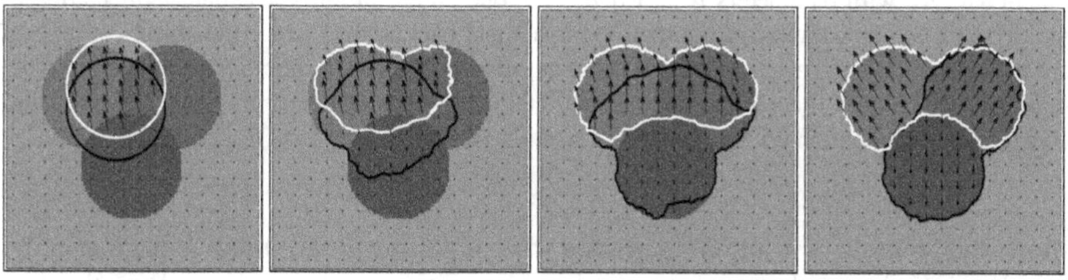

Fig. 3. Segmenting multiple moving regions. The two input images show the wallpaper of Figure 1, left side, with three circular regions moving away from the center. The magnitude of the velocity of the upper two regions is 1.4 times larger than that of the bottom region. Superimposed on the true region information are the evolving zero level sets of ϕ_1 (black contour) and ϕ_2 (white contour), which define four different phases. The simultaneously evolving piecewise constant motion field is represented by the black arrows. Both the phase boundaries and the motion field are obtained by minimizing the multiphase model (33) with parameters $\nu = 0.05, \sigma = 2$ with respect to the level set functions and the motion vectors. In the final solution, the two boundaries clearly separate four phases corresponding to the three moving regions and the static background.

In this example, the cars and the street are moving according to different motion models. The motion competition framework exploits this property. Figure 4, bottom,

[6] `http://i21www.ira.uka.de/image_sequences/`

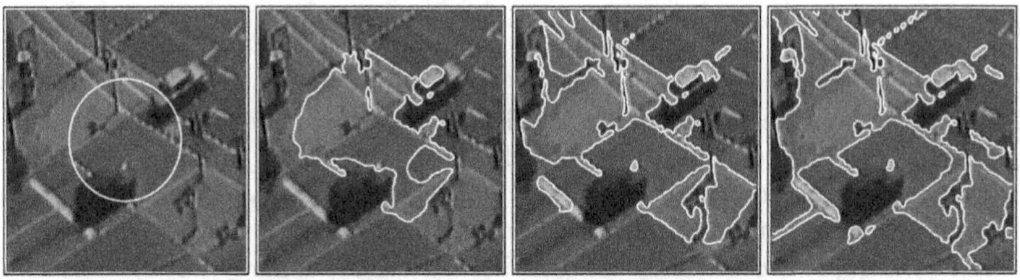

Intensity segmentation for the first of two frames.

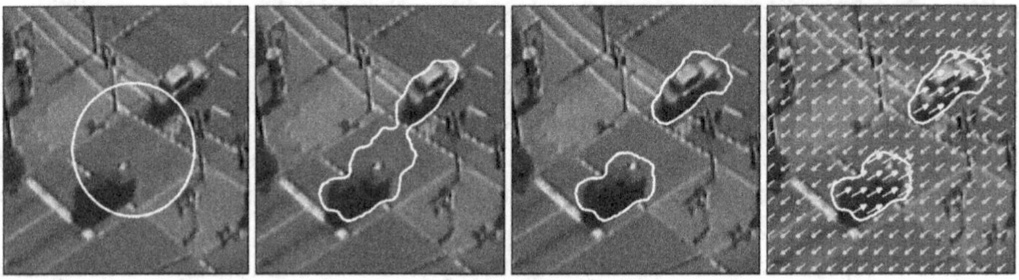

Motion segmentation generated from both frames.

Fig. 4. Intensity segmentation versus motion segmentation. Two consecutive input frames show two cars moving to the top right, and the background moving to the bottom left. **Top row:** Segmentation of the first frame from a traffic scene according to the two-phase level set model of the piecewise constant Mumford-Shah functional, as introduced by Chan and Vese [7]. The assumption of homogeneous intensity is clearly not appropriate to segment the objects of interest. **Bottom:** Motion segmentation of the same traffic scene. By minimizing the motion competition functional (26) with parameters $\nu = 1.5, \sigma = 5$, one obtains a fairly accurate segmentation of the two cars and an estimate of the motion of cars and background. Since the objects of interest are better defined in terms of homogeneous motion than in terms of homogeneous intensity, the segmentation is more successful than the one obtained by the analogous gray value model. Until convergence, the contour evolution took 41 seconds in Matlab on a 2.4 GHz computer.

show the contour evolution generated by minimizing the motion segmentation functional (26) and the corresponding motion estimates superimposed on the first frame.

The contour evolution generated by motion competition is fundamentally different from the one generated by its gray value analog. The energy minimization simultaneously generates a fairly accurate segmentation of the two cars and an estimate of the motion of cars and background. Minor discrepancies of the final segmentation may be due to several factors, in particular the weak gray value structure of the street, which prevents reliable motion estimation, and the reflections on the cars which violate the Lambertian assumption.

8.4 Segmentation by Piecewise Affine Motion

The functional (16) allows to segment piecewise affine motion fields. In particular, this class of motion models includes rotation and expansion/contraction. Figure 5 shows

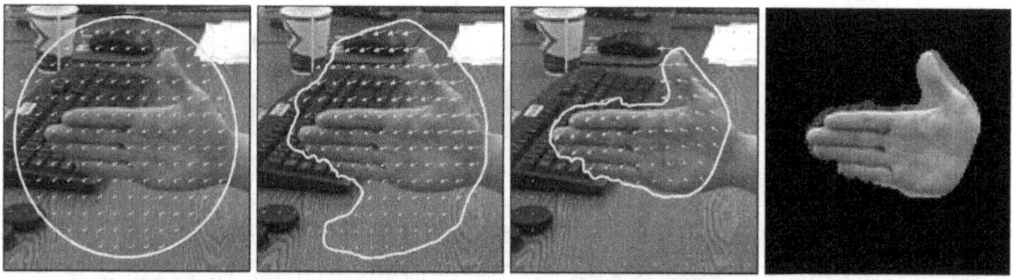

Motion segmentation of a hand rotating around the wrist.

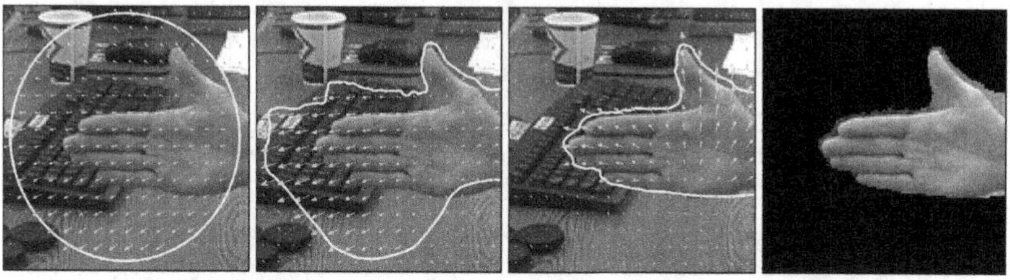

Motion segmentation of a hand moving toward the camera.

Fig. 5. Piecewise affine motion segmentation. Functional (16) allows to segment objects based on the model of affine motion. The above images show contour evolutions obtained for two image pairs showing a hand rotating (top) and moving toward the camera (bottom). Minor discrepancies of the final segmentation (right) are probably due to a lack of gray value variation of the table. Both results were obtained with the same parameter values ($\nu = 8 \cdot 10^{-5}$, $\sigma = 2$). Again certain areas of little intensity variation do not provide sufficient motion information to be reliably associated with one or the other motion model.

contour evolutions obtained for a hand in a cluttered background rotating (in the camera plane) and moving toward the camera. The energy minimization allows to segment the object and estimate its rotational or divergent motion.

The images on the right of Figure 5 demonstrate that the objects of interest can be extracted from a fairly complex background based exclusively on their motion. Applications of such motion-based segmentation schemes to video editing and MPEG compression are conceivable.

8.5 Spatio-temporal Motion Segmentation

While the previous results were obtained using only two consecutive frames from a sequence, we will now present an application of the segmentations in space-time obtained by minimizing a multiphase implementation of the functional (35) for several frames of the flower garden sequence [35], which shows a static scene filmed by a moving camera. Figure 6 shows the evolution of the surfaces separating the motion phases in space-time (top rows). The lower rows depict the corresponding temporal slices of these surfaces associated with the frames 2, 5 and 8. During energy minimization, the surfaces propagate to the final segmentation both in space and in time. The final segmentation clearly separates foreground, midplane and background. The simultaneously evolving piecewise constant motion field is depicted in Figure 7.

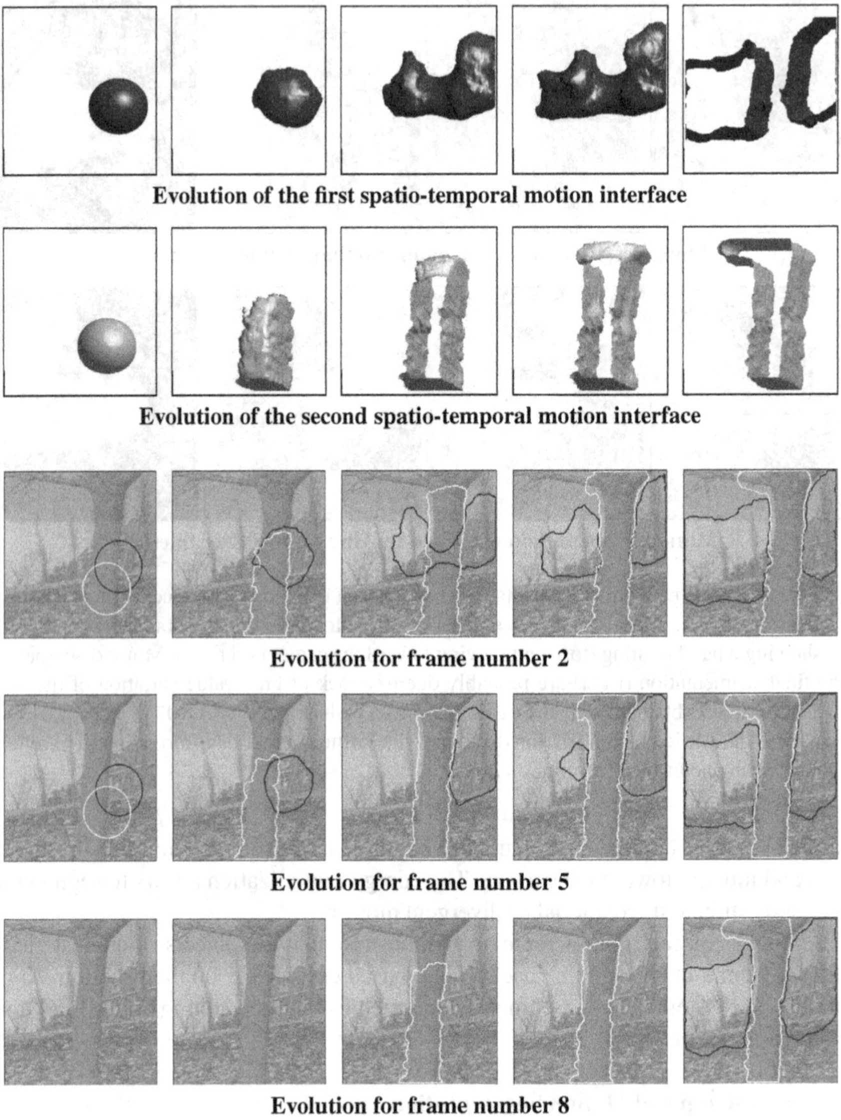

Fig. 6. Spatio-temporal sequence segmentation with the multiphase model. The top rows show the evolution of the spatio-temporal surfaces given by the zero level sets of two embedding functions ϕ_1 and ϕ_2. The lower rows show various temporal slices of these surfaces, corresponding to the 2nd, 5th and 8th frame of the sequence. The evolving surfaces propagate both in space and time during minimization of the energy (35). In the final segmentation the phases clearly separate foreground, midplane and background. For better visibility, the simultaneously estimated piecewise constant motion field is shown separately in Figure 7.

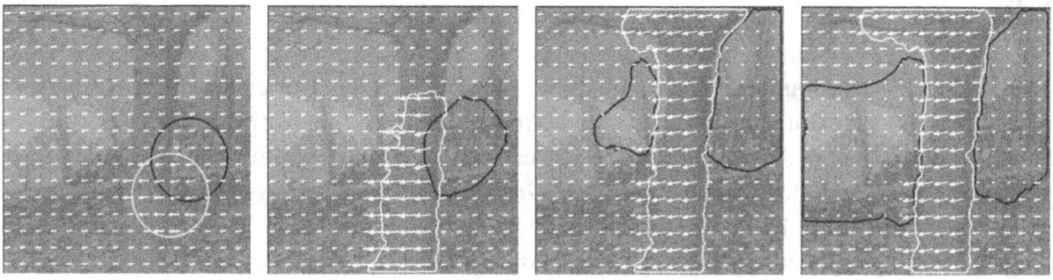

Fig. 7. Temporal slice through the evolving surfaces shown in Figure 6. The final segmentation separates the tree in the foreground, the grass in the midplane and the houses and smaller trees in the background. Boundary and the motion estimates are obtained by simultaneously minimizing an appropriate cost functional defined on the spatio-temporal image derivatives. Unlike most alternative approaches to layer extraction, no preprocessing (such as local disparity estimation, camera calibration and prior rectification of individual frames [33]) is applied to the image data.

9 Conclusion

We derived a variational framework for segmenting the image plane (or the space-time volume of an image sequence) into a set of phases of parametric motion. The proposed functional depends on parametric velocity models for a set of phases and the boundary separating them. The only free parameter in the functional is the fundamental scale parameter intrinsic to all segmentation schemes.

The motion discontinuity set is implemented by a multiphase level set formulation (for contours in 2D or surfaces in 3D). The resulting model has the following properties:

- The minimization of a *single* functional jointly solves the problems of segmentation and motion estimation. It generates a segmentation of the image plane (or the space-time volume) in terms of piecewise parametric motion.
- An extension to surfaces in space-time allows to segment moving regions over time, providing an additional temporal regularity of the segmentation.
- *Implicit multiphase representations* allow for topological changes of the evolving boundaries. They permit a segmentation of the image plane (or the space-time volume) into several (possibly multiply-connected) motion phases.
- Local minimization of the proposed functional results in an eigenvalue problem for the motion vectors, and an evolution equation of the level set functions embedding the motion boundary.
- Due to the region-based homogeneity criterion rather than an edge-based formulation, motion boundaries converge over fairly large spatial distances.
- Segmentation and motion estimates can be generated from two consecutive frames of an image sequence. Therefore the approach is in principle amenable to real-time implementations and tracking.

Acknowledgments

The author thanks C. Schnörr, S. Soatto and A. Yuille for fruitful discussions.

References

1. J. Bigün, G. H. Granlund, and J. Wiklund. Multidimensional orientation estimation with applications to texture analysis and optical flow. *IEEE PAMI*, 13(8):775–790, 1991.
2. M. J. Black and P. Anandan. The robust estimation of multiple motions: Parametric and piecewise–smooth flow fields. *Comp. Vis. Graph. Image Proc.: IU*, 63(1):75–104, 1996.
3. P. Bouthemy and E. Francois. Motion segmentation and qualitative dynamic scene analysis from an image sequence. *Int. J. of Comp. Vis.*, 10(2):157–182, 1993.
4. T. Brox, A. Bruhn, N. Papenberg, and J. Weickert. High accuracy optical flow estimation based on a theory for warping. In T. Pajdla and V. Hlavac, editors, *European Conf. on Computer Vision*, volume 3024 of *LNCS*, pages 25–36, Prague, 2004. Springer.
5. V. Caselles and B. Coll. Snakes in movement. *SIAM J. Numer. Anal.*, 33:2445–2456, 1996.
6. V. Caselles, R. Kimmel, and G. Sapiro. Geodesic active contours. In *Proc. IEEE Intl. Conf. on Comp. Vis.*, pages 694–699, Boston, USA, 1995.
7. T. Chan and L. Vese. Active contours without edges. *IEEE Trans. Image Processing*, 10(2):266–277, 2001.
8. D. Cremers. A multiphase level set framework for variational motion segmentation. In L. Griffith, editor, *Int. Conf. on Scale Space Theories in Computer Vision*, volume 2695 of *LNCS*, pages 599–614, Isle of Skye, 2003. Springer.
9. D. Cremers. A variational framework for image segmentation combining motion estimation and shape regularization. In C. Dyer and P. Perona, editors, *IEEE Conf. on Comp. Vis. and Patt. Recog.*, volume 1, pages 53–58, June 2003.
10. D. Cremers and C. Schnörr. Motion Competition: Variational integration of motion segmentation and shape regularization. In L. van Gool, editor, *Pattern Recognition*, volume 2449 of *LNCS*, pages 472–480, Zürich, Sept. 2002. Springer.
11. D. Cremers and S. Soatto. Variational space-time motion segmentation. In B. Triggs and A. Zisserman, editors, *IEEE Int. Conf. on Computer Vision*, volume 2, pages 886–892, Nice, Oct. 2003.
12. D. Cremers and S. Soatto. Motion Competition: A variational framework for piecewise parametric motion segmentation. *Int. J. of Comp. Vis.*, 2004. To appear.
13. D. Cremers and A. L. Yuille. A generative model based approach to motion segmentation. In B. Michaelis and G. Krell, editors, *Pattern Recognition*, volume 2781 of *LNCS*, pages 313–320, Magdeburg, Sept. 2003. Springer.
14. G. Farnebäck. Very high accuracy velocity estimation using orientation tensors, parametric motion, and segmentation of the motion field. In *ICCV*, volume 1, pages 171–177, 2001.
15. F. Heitz and P. Bouthemy. Multimodal estimation of discontinuous optical flow using markov random fields. *IEEE PAMI*, 15(12):1217–1232, 1993.
16. B.K.P. Horn and B.G. Schunck. Determining optical flow. *A.I.*, 17:185–203, 1981.
17. S. Jehan-Besson, M. Barlaud, and G. Aubert. DREAM2S: Deformable regions driven by an eulerian accurate minimization method for image and video segmentation. *Int. J. of Comp. Vis.*, 53(1):45–70, 2003.
18. A. Jepson and M.J. Black. Mixture models for optic flow computation. In *Proc. IEEE Conf. on Comp. Vision Patt. Recog.*, pages 760–761, New York, 1993.
19. S. Kichenassamy, A. Kumar, P. J. Olver, A. Tannenbaum, and A. J. Yezzi. Gradient flows and geometric active contour models. In *Proc. IEEE Intl. Conf. on Comp. Vis.*, pages 810–815, Boston, USA, 1995.
20. J. Konrad and E. Dubois. Bayesian estimation of motion vector fields. *IEEE PAMI*, 14(9):910–927, 1992.
21. P. Kornprobst, R. Deriche, and G. Aubert. Image sequence analysis via partial differential equations. *J. Math. Im. Vis.*, 11(1):5–26, 1999.

22. E. Memin and P. Perez. Dense estimation and object-based segmentation of the optical flow with robust techniques. *IEEE Trans. on Im. Proc.*, 7(5):703–719, 1998.
23. J.-M. Morel and S. Solimini. *Variational Methods in Image Segmentation*. Birkhäuser, Boston, 1995.
24. D. Mumford and J. Shah. Optimal approximations by piecewise smooth functions and associated variational problems. *Comm. Pure Appl. Math.*, 42:577–685, 1989.
25. H.H. Nagel and W. Enkelmann. An investigation of smoothness constraints for the estimation of displacement vector fields from image sequences. *IEEE PAMI*, 8(5):565–593, 1986.
26. O. Nestares, D.J. Fleet, and D.J. Heeger. Likelihood functions and confidence bounds for total-least-squares problems. In *Proc. Conf. Computer Vis. and Pattern Recog.*, volume 1, pages 760–767, Hilton Head Island, SC, June, 2000.
27. J.-M. Odobez and P. Bouthemy. Direct incremental model-based image motion segmentation for video analysis. *Signal Proc.*, 66:143–155, 1998.
28. S. J. Osher and J. A. Sethian. Fronts propagation with curvature dependent speed: Algorithms based on Hamilton–Jacobi formulations. *J. of Comp. Phys.*, 79:12–49, 1988.
29. N. Paragios and R. Deriche. Geodesic active contours and level sets for the detection and tracking of moving objects. *IEEE PAMI*, 22(3):266–280, 2000.
30. C. Schnörr. Computation of discontinuous optical flow by domain decomposition and shape optimization. *Int. J. of Comp. Vis.*, 8(2):153–165, 1992.
31. J. Shi and J. Malik. Motion segmentation and tracking using normalized cuts. In *Intl. Conf. on Comp. Vision*, Bombay, India, 1998.
32. M. Sussman, Smereka P., and S. J. Osher. A level set approach for computing solutions to incompressible twophase flow. *J. of Comp. Phys.*, 94:146–159, 1994.
33. P. H. S. Torr, R. Szeliski, and P. Anandan. An integrated bayesian approach to layer extraction from image sequences. *IEEE PAMI*, 23(3):297–303, 2002.
34. R. Vidal, Y. Ma, and S. Sastry. Generalized principal component analysis (gpca): an analytic solution to segmentation of mixtures of subspaces. In *Proc. IEEE Conf. on Comp. Vision Patt. Recog.* , volume 1, pages 621–628, Madison, 2003.
35. J.Y.A. Wang and E.H. Adelson. Representating moving images with layers. *IEEE Trans. on Image Processing*, 3(5):625–638, 1994.
36. J. Weickert and C. Schnörr. A theoretical framework for convex regularizers in PDE–based computation of image motion. *Int. J. of Comp. Vis.*, 45(3):245–264, 2001.
37. Y. Weiss. Smoothness in layers: Motion segmentation using nonparametric mixture estimation. In *Proc. IEEE Conf. on Comp. Vision Patt. Recog.*, pages 520–527, Puerto Rico, 1997.
38. Y. Weiss and D.J. Fleet. Velocity likelihoods in biological and machine vision. In M.S. Lewicki R.P.N. Rao, B.A. Olshausen, editor, *Probabilistic Models of the Brain: Perception and Neural Function*, pages 81–100. MIT Press, 2001.
39. S. C. Zhu and A. Yuille. Region competition: Unifying snakes, region growing, and Bayes/MDL for multiband image segmentation. *IEEE PAMI*, 18(9):884–900, 1996.

On Variational Methods for Fluid Flow Estimation

Paul Ruhnau, Jing Yuan, and Christoph Schnörr

Department of Mathematics and Computer Science
Computer Vision, Graphics, and Pattern Recognition Group
University of Mannheim, 68131 Mannheim, Germany
{ruhnau,yuanjing,schnoerr}@uni-mannheim.de
www.cvgpr.uni-mannheim.de

Abstract. We present global variational approaches that are capable of extracting high-resolution velocity vector fields from image sequences of fluids. Starting points are existing variational approaches from image processing that we adapt to the requiremements of particle image sequences, paying particular attention to a multiscale representation of the image data.

Additionally, we combine a discrete non-differentiable particle matching term with a continuous regularization term and thus achieve a variational particle tracking approach.

As higher-order regularization can be used to preserve important flow structures, we finally sketch a motion estimation scheme based on the decomposition of motion vector fields into components of orthogonal subspaces.

1 Introduction

Many fields of application require the accurate determination of flows in fluids. In many of these scenarios, DNS computations (direct simulation of the Navier-Stokes equations) are error-prone, caused by high Reynolds numbers or unknown boundary conditions, or not sufficient if, for instance, one is interested in time-resolved velocity data. Imaging measuring methods are used more and more frequently as the technology is progressing with respect to required components such as lasers, CCD cameras, computers and control logics.

In order to be able to extract the motion field, the scene has to be modeled and filmed: First the flow medium is seeded with particles. Then whole velocity fields are to be measured by taking two or more images of the flow, one shortly after the other, and calculating the distance the individual particles have travelled within this time period. Figure 1 shows a typical experimental setup in a wind tunnel. The velocity is calculated from the known time difference and the measured displacement. To avoid blurred images when the flow is fast, laser pulses are used. As they are only 6-10 ns long, they are capable of freezing any motion.

The terms *particle image velocimetry* (PIV) and *particle tracking velocimetry* (PTV) denote established classes of image processing methods for extracting the underlying velocity fields in these kinds of images. PIV methods operate on gray-level images, while PTV approaches determine the flow field by tracking individual tracers [1].

B. Jähne et al. (Eds.): IWCM 2004, LNCS 3417, pp. 124–145, 2007.

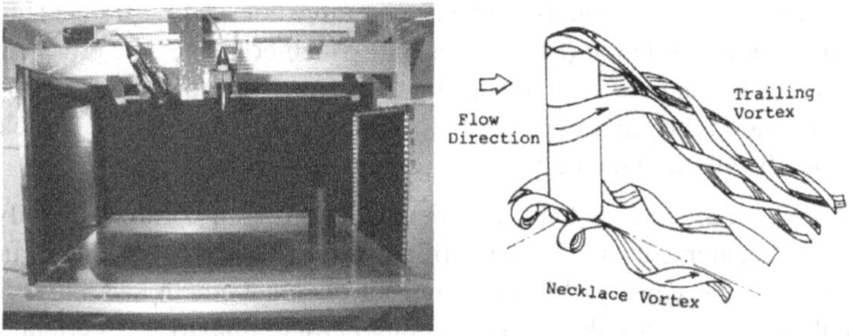

Fig. 1. Left: Experimental setting to study the flow perpendicular to a short cylinder with one endplate and one open end. This setting results in an unsteady, threedimensional flow structure which can only be investigated using advanced imaging measuring techniques. **Right:** Schematic illustration of the observed flow [2].

1.1 Cross-Correlation PIV

Cross-correlation PIV has become the best-known and most widely used experimental method for flow estimation: First, the images are split into multiple windows - so-called interrogation windows. For each pair of corresponding windows, a discrete cross-correlation is computed.

However, despite the success of this technique and numerous investigations into improvements (which are summarized in [3]), it suffers from some fundamental limitations:

- **Limits in spatial resolution:** The partitioning of the image by interrogation areas must not be too fine if you want to detect correlation peaks reliably. This unavoidably limits the spatial resolution of the estimated motion vector field. The advanced hierarchical schemes described in [3] offer the possibility of ending with very small interrogation areas. However, even in these high-performance techniques, post-processing is neccessary to detect erroneous motion vectors.
- **Limits in accuracy:** The size of the interrogation areas determines a spatial scale at which the variation of motion vector fields is (tacitly) assumed to be negligible. This assumption is erroneous and proves inaccurate in many relevant situations. Many authors have concentrated on iterative window deformation methods of 1st or 2nd order that deal with this problem [3].
- **Outliers:** Motion estimation is carried out regardless of spatial context. As a consequence, prior knowledge about spatial flow structures cannot be exploited during estimation, and missing motion estimates in image regions where a correlation analysis yields no reliable estimates, have to be heuristically inferred in a post-processing step.

1.2 PTV

While nearly all PIV algorithms base on the sketched cross-correlation method, PTV methods are more manifold. They are traditionally either based on nearest-neighbour search with geometrical constraints (using four or more consecutive frames) [4,5], or on binary-image cross correlation (two frames) [6] which computes the cross-correlation between regions around particles in the first and in the second frame. More recent approaches include relaxation methods that analyse the probability of particle matching [7]. Basically, all these methods have two assumptions in common:

- **Small displacements:** while nearest-neighbour search algorithms directly rely on small displacements from one frame of an image sequence to the next (in proportion to the particle density), binary-image correlation methods and relaxation methods both search for possibly corresponding particle images in a certain "tracking range".
- **Smoothness of motion:** nearest-neighbour search algorithms assume that a particle changes its motion during an image sequence only smoothly. A similar assumption that tacitly underlies binary-image correlation methods is that the particles within a correlation window move with the same speed (if not, the correlation coefficient would not peak). Finally, using relaxation methods, a matching is considered probable if the movement of particles in a certain region can be reduced to a simple translation.

Due to the "small displacement" assumption, PTV is traditionally applied in situations of low seeding density (compared to the velocity). As it is, however, able to generate a higher resolution than PIV, it can be eventually used to increase the resolution of the PIV output [8, 9]. Furthermore, in 3D, PTV can be supported and combined with stereoscopic analysis and 3D reconstruction.

1.3 Variational PIV/PTV

The term *Optical Flow* $u(x,t) = (u(x,y,t), v(x,y,t))^\top$ denotes the estimation of the induced velocity vector field caused by a relative motion between camera and scene. Global variational approaches for estimating of the optical flow were introduced by Horn & Schunck in 1981 [10]:

$$J(u) = \int_\Omega \{\underbrace{(\nabla f^\top u + \frac{\partial f}{\partial t})^2}_{\text{data term}} + \lambda \underbrace{(|\nabla u|^2 + |\nabla v|^2)}_{\text{smoothness term}}\} dx, \; 0 < \lambda \in \mathbb{R} \tag{1}$$

The basic idea is not to estimate displacement vectors locally and individually, but to estimate vector fields as a whole by minimizing (1). The data term is based on the assumption of gray value conservation of $f(x(t), t)$. The smoothness term causes spatial coherence of the vector field, making corresponding post-processing steps in connection with traditional local PIV approaches obsolete. The basic approach (1) has been generalized over the years: data-driven control of the smoothness term [11, 12, 13], specification of conditions under which the approach is well-posed [12], detection of motion boundaries by minimizing convex non-quadratic smoothness terms [14, 15] and use of spatio-temporal smoothness terms [16]. [17] gives an overview.

Organisation. Section 2 summarizes a PIV approached based on variational optical flow estimation and its adaption to the specific grayvalue-functions induced by particles in PIV image pairs [18, 19].

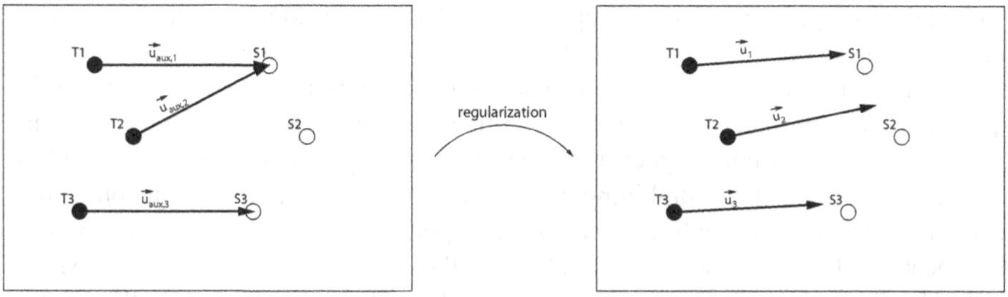

Fig. 2. Black circles denote particle positions in the first frame, white circles denote positions in the second frame. **Left:** Simple nearest-neighbour search yields mismatches. **Right:** Nearest-neighbour search followed by regularization with smoothness constraint. In the next iteration, T2 will find the correct match.

Section 3 generalizes the class of variational approaches to Particle *Tracking* Velocimetry. To this end, we have to replace the *continuous* data term of variational approaches to PIV with a *discrete* non-differentiable particle matching term for PTV. This raises the problem of minimizing such data terms together with a *continuous* regularization term. We accomplish this with an advanced mathematical method which guarantees convergence to a local minimum of such a non-convex variational approach to PTV. Figure 2 illustrates the basic behaviour of this new type of variational approaches to PTV. On the left, figure 2 depicts a common situation where particle matching by nearest-beighbor search fails. The variational PTV-approach presented in this paper is able to avoid, and even to revise, such erroneous local decisions through the smoothness term (figure 2, right). A key advantage in our opinion is that all "rules" guiding the matching of particles are encoded by the choice of a smoothness term which, in turn, can be related to physical properties of the underlying fluid, like low divergence for example.

From numerical fluid dynamics, in turn, it is well known that standard discretizations, like piecewise linear finite elements, are not appropriate. Imposing the constraint of vanishing divergence, for example, may result in a constant flow. In section 4, we will therefore sketch how the mimetic finite difference method can be used to discretize higher order regularizers and physically plausible constraints, like vanishing divergence of the flow.

2 Variational Optical Flow Estimation

2.1 Adaption to PIV Data

The accuracy of motion estimation critically depends on the magnitude of image motion. In fact, depending on the spatial image frequency, very large motions even may cause aliasing along the time frequency axis. Due to the Nyquist-condition $|\omega_t| < \pi$ (with $\omega_t := \omega_x u$), only motions up to $|u| < \pi/\omega_x$ are correctly represented by samples of the signal.[1] Faster motions lead to aliasing. In other words, for a fixed global velocity, spatial frequencies moving more than half of their period per frame cause

[1] Without loss of generality we assume sampling rates $\Delta x = \Delta t = 1$.

temporal aliasing. In practice, this upper bound has to be lowered because derivatives of the signal can only be robustly estimated in connection with low-pass filtering.

As a remedy, we first compute a coarse motion field by using only low spatial frequency components and "undo" the motion, thus roughly stabilizing the position of the image over time. Then the higher frequency subbands are used to estimate optical flow on the warped sequence. Combining this "optical flow correction" with the previously computed optical flow yields a refined overall optical flow estimate. This process may be repeated at finer and finer spatial scales until the original image resolution is reached [20,21]. A standard technique for generating multi-scale representations in this context is to construct an image pyramid (fig. 3) by recursively applying lowpass filtering and subsampling operations. Note that the images at different scales are represented by different sampling rates. Thus, the same derivative filters may be used at each scale and we do not have to design multiple derivative filters, one for each different scale. Let us define the pyramid representation of a generic image f of size $n_x \times n_y$. Let $f^0 = f$ be the "$zero^{th}$" level image. This image is essentially the highest resolution image (the raw image). The image width and height at that level are defined as $n_x^0 = n_x$ and $n_y^0 = n_y$. The pyramid representation is then built in a recursive fashion: Compute f^1 from f^0, then compute f^2 from f^1, and so on ... . Let $k = 0, 1, 2, ..., L-1$ be a generic pyramidal level, and let f^k be the image at level k. n_x^k and n_y^k denote the width and the height of f^k. First the lowpass filter $[1/4\ 1/2\ 1/4] \times [1/4\ 1/2\ 1/4]^\top$ is used for image anti-aliasing before image subsampling. Then a bilinear interpolation performs the adaption to the new coarser grid, as every new vertex is located exactly in the middle of four finer vertices (if the respective image size is even-numbered, cmp. fig. 4). This procedure results in a convolution mask of $[1/8\ 3/8\ 3/8\ 1/8] \times [1/8\ 3/8\ 3/8\ 1/8]^\top$. In the first step the optical flow between the top level images f_1^{L-1} and f_2^{L-1} (lowest frequency images) is computed,using the variational approach (1). The computed coarse-level flow field must then be projected onto the next finer pyramid level. This flow field estimate is used to warp the second image towards the first image:

$$\mathcal{W}\{f_2^{L-1}, d^{L-1}\}(x, y, t+\Delta t) = f_2^{L-1}(x-u\Delta t, y-v\Delta t, t+\Delta t), \;\; d^{L-1} = \begin{pmatrix} u \\ v \end{pmatrix} \quad (2)$$

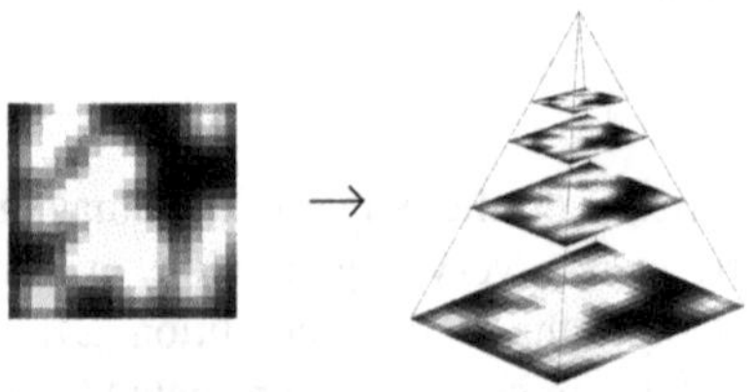

Fig. 3. Image Pyramid: Each level in the pyramid is a subsampled version of the level below convoved with a Gaussian filter

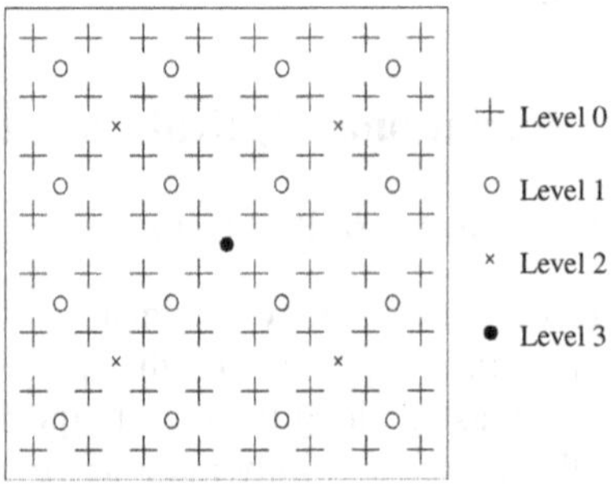

Fig. 4. Image Pyramid: Location of the vertices in the respective levels

At pyramid level $L-2$, we compute a new and finer flow field between the images f_1^{L-2} and $\mathcal{W}\{f_2^{L-2}, d^{L-1}\}$. While the expression to be minimized is analogous to (1), the first-order Taylor series expansion is performed around $(x + d^{L-1}(x), t+1)$. This results in the cost functional:

$$J(u,v) = \int_{\Omega} \Big\{ \Big[\nabla f \cdot \begin{pmatrix} u \\ v \end{pmatrix} + \partial_t f\Big]^2 + \lambda\big(|\nabla(u+d_u^{L-1})|^2 + |\nabla(v+d_v^{L-1})|^2\big) \Big\} dx dy \quad (3)$$

with $0 < \lambda \in \mathbb{R}$. The unique flow field minimizing (3) is the correction-field Δd^{L-2} of the coarser flow d^{L-1}. To obtain the overall flow field d^{L-2} at level $L-2$ we have to add the coarse motion d^{L-1} and the correction field Δd^{L-2}:

$$d^{L-2}(x,y) = d^{L-1}(x,y) + \Delta d^{L-2}(x,y) \quad (4)$$

This correction process is repeated for each level of the pyramid until the finest pyramid level d^0 has been reached. Details about the discretization can be found in [18]. In the experimental evaluation section below, we will refer to this approach as Horn & Schunck Multi-Resolution (**H&S R**). So far, we have introduced a *dyadic* pyramid structure which is equivalent to using lowpass filters with bandwidths $\frac{\Omega}{2^{L-1}}$, $\frac{\Omega}{2^{L-2}}$, ..., $\frac{\Omega}{2^1}$, $\frac{\Omega}{2^0}$ combined with subsampling. Now we introduce additional filters that slice the bandwidth into even smaller pieces, e.g. $\Omega/4$, $3/8\Omega$, $\Omega/2$, $3/4\Omega$, Ω. In order to implement these extra steps which do not fit into the dyadic pyramid structure, we apply at each pyramid level pre-filters when estimating derivatives: The lower the cut-off frequency of the pre-filter, the more the particles seem to melt down and form a smooth gray value structure. A coarse motion estimate can reliably be computed using this structure. Then, we update and refine the motion field (in the same way as described in detail for the multi-resoluion case) using the less low-pass filtered image derivatives. For the experiments in this paper, we use nine scale-space levels and thus nine different filters with cut-off frequencies of $\frac{\pi}{2}$, $\frac{9}{16}\pi$, $\frac{5}{8}\pi$, $\frac{11}{16}\pi$, $\frac{3}{4}\pi$, $\frac{13}{16}\pi$, $\frac{7}{8}\pi$, $\frac{15}{16}\pi$, π. An inverse Fourier Transform yields the filter coefficients. Low pass filtering with cut-off frequencies below $\pi/2$ is not neccessary since this is what the anti-aliasing filter of the preceding lower resolution level has already done. Below, we will refer to this combined approach as Horn&Schunck Multi-Resolution + Multi-Scale (**H&S R+S**).

2.2 Experimental Evaluation

In this section, we report comparisons of the variational approach with two other approaches for various data sets.

Data. The experimental evaluation was carried out on the basis of the following data sets:

- **Synthetic Data:** The "Quénot image pair" was introduced in [22] and is available on the internet. The analyzed velocity field (av. velocity = 7.58 px./frame) is taken from a numerical solution obtained for two-dimensional flow around a pair of cylinders. We examined different test cases:

- **Perfect:** "Perfect" case means that the second image was computer-generated from the first image and the target flow field.
- **Mixed N%:** The specified percentage of noise was superimposed. Additionally, the specified percentage of particles was randomly removed and the same amount of particles was randomly added.

- **Real world image:** We will also analyze an image from a time-resolved PIV measurement of periodically vortices in the transitional cylinder wake [23, 24]. The mean displacement is about 9 px./frame and the maximum displacement about 16 px./frame.

Approaches and Parameter Settings. The data sets described above were evaluated using the following approaches and parameter settings:

- **Variational approach:** The spatial (∇f) and temporal ($\partial_t f$) derivatives were estimated using derivative of Gaussian filters of size five at every point in the image domain. In a first series of experiments (**H&S R**) five resolution levels were used, in a second series of experiments (**H&S R+S**) a setup of five resolution levels and nine scale space levels on every resolution level was chosen. For the Quénot image pair computations, the smoothness parameter λ was set to $7 * 10^{-4}$ in the H&S R case and to $7 * 10^{-3}$ in the H&S R+S case. For the real world image pair only H&S R+S computations were performed. The smoothness parameter λ was also set to $7 * 10^{-3}$ in these rows of experiments. The gray values were scaled in each case to the interval $[0, 1]$.
- **DIPV approach:** For comparison we took the error measures of the classical 2D FFT based digital particle image velocimetry (DPIV) method from [22] in the synthetic test cases. Two different interrogation window sizes were applied: 32×32 pixel (**DPIV 32**) and 48×48 pixel (**DPIV 48**). We analyzed the "cylinder wake" real world image pair using a hierarchical DPIV approach with an interrogation window size beginning with 512×512 pixels and ending up with 64×64 pixels with window-shifting and peak-height validation.
- **ODP2 approach [25]:** We considered also the results of a dynamic programming based optical flow technique. This approach transforms the two-dimensional correspondence problem to a sequence of one-dimensional search problems. It has been successfully applied to PIV in [22, 26].

Error Measures. As quantitative error measures we computed the angular error (between correct and computed motion vectors) as defined in [27] along with its standard deviation as well as the mean velocity error (L_1 norm of the difference between the correct and computed velocities in px./frame). The error measure was computed for the whole image except for the inner circular regions corresponding to the cylinders.

Numerical Results and Discussion. Table 1 summarizes the error measures for Quénot's image pair and their standard deviation ($\pm$) [2]. Furthermore, typical execution times of the respective algorithms are indicated. Note that DPIV yields a sparse vector

---

[2] Error measures for the three algorithms not implemented by the authors were taken from [22], the execution times from [28].

Table 1. Angular error and absolute displacement error. Best performance for every setting is marked in bold.

		DPIV32	DPIV48	ODP2	H&S R	H&S R+S
Perfect	angle	5.95 ± 13.9	9.35 ± 18.3	$\mathbf{1.23 \pm 2.24}$	2.32 ± 3.69	1.42 ± 2.16
	disp	0.55 ± 0.94	0.87 ± 1.46	$\mathbf{0.13 \pm 0.10}$	0.39 ± 0.66	0.19 ± 0.18
Mixed 5%	angle	6.40 ± 14.4	9.59 ± 19.0	1.77 ± 2.87	3.04 ± 4.38	$\mathbf{1.54 \pm 2.34}$
	disp	0.60 ± 1.12	0.86 ± 1.51	$\mathbf{0.20 \pm 0.13}$	0.52 ± 0.80	0.21 ± 0.30
Mixed 10%	angle	10.2 ± 19.6	11.3 ± 20.8	4.30 ± 11.7	4.39 ± 5.89	$\mathbf{1.81 \pm 2.74}$
	disp	0.91 ± 1.89	0.93 ± 1.66	0.57 ± 1.71	0.78 ± 1.07	$\mathbf{0.26 \pm 0.46}$
Mixed 20%	angle	40.8 ± 34.5	38.3 ± 29.7	6.15 ± 9.01	9.33 ± 9.93	$\mathbf{2.96 \pm 4.23}$
	disp	3.73 ± 4.39	2.49 ± 3.19	0.74 ± 0.52	2.03 ± 2.13	$\mathbf{0.39 \pm 0.53}$
Time		10 min	10 min	20 min	16 sec / 2 sec	2 min / 15 sec

field whereas both ODP2 and H&S compute dense vector fields. All of the tested algorithms are (in varying degrees) sensitive to superimposed noise. In the case of DPIV, extending the interrogation window size increases the robustness to noise while decreasing the accuracy at the same time. However, irrespective of the window size the performance of DPIV is much worse than the performance of the other approaches.

We realize that H&S R+S provides much better results than H&S R in all test cases. This had to be expected because temporal aliasing as well as linearization errors of the optical flow approach are suppressed by additional scale space computations. Fig. 5

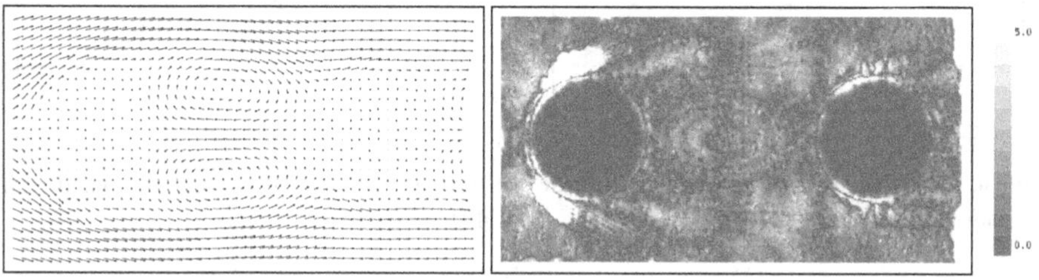

Fig. 5. Results for the Quénot image pair "Mixed 20%". Estimated flow field with H&S R+S (left), absolute displacement error (right).

shows the results for the "Mixed 20%" case. One can see that the highest estimation errors are reached at the borders of the cylinders. The smoothness term penalizes the discontinuities at these locations and smoothes over the discontinuities. The error at regions close to the left cylinder is the highest because of the high velocity of the fluid. Possible solutions to this problem include the insertion of border conditions and higher order regularization (cmp. sec. 4).

ODP2 provides the best result for the "perfect" test case. However, it is much less robust to noise than H&S: While the error measures of the variational coarse-to-fine approach are slightly higher in the perfect case (cf. table 1), this changes with the presence of noise. The error for the ODP2 approach then rises much faster so that, for noise rates of 5 % and above, the H&S R+S approach provides better results. This gap rises even more for higher amounts of noise. Since noise is always present in real world images pairs, we expect the H&S algorithm to perform better than both the DPIV and the ODP2 approaches.

When we use a preconditioned conjugate gradient method to solve the H&S system matrices, the execution time of our algorithm is about 16 sec for H&S R and 2 min for H&S R+S (when choosing a residual error of 10^{-4} as a stopping criterion). Using a multi-grid approach [29, 30] to solve the linear systems, the computation time of H&S R is approx. 2 sec, while the H&S R+S computation takes about 15 sec on an up-to-date computer. Information about the different multi-grid cycles and stopping criterions can be taken from [31]. Even real time operation can be achieved through parallelization using domain decomposition [32].

Figures 6 and 7 show the results for the real world image pair ("cylinder wake") computed with H&S R+S and DPIV, respectively. One can clearly see that the variational approach resembles the true motion field much better than the cross-correlation approach. At regions with abruptly changing motion (i.e. the turbulence emerging behind the cylinder in the middle of the image), the DPIV method is not able to accurately determine the velocity field. This is mainly due to the limited spatial resolution which leads to a violation of the assumption of a constant velocity inside interrogation windows at these locations. The statistical character of correlation-based processing, however, prohibits the use of smaller interrogation windows. Furthermore, in regions dominated by out-of-plane velocities (i.e. at the left border of the image), the cross correlation approach fails as well: Since no global velocity information is used, the probability of outliers is markedly increased at these locations, hence a valid flow field cannot be computed.

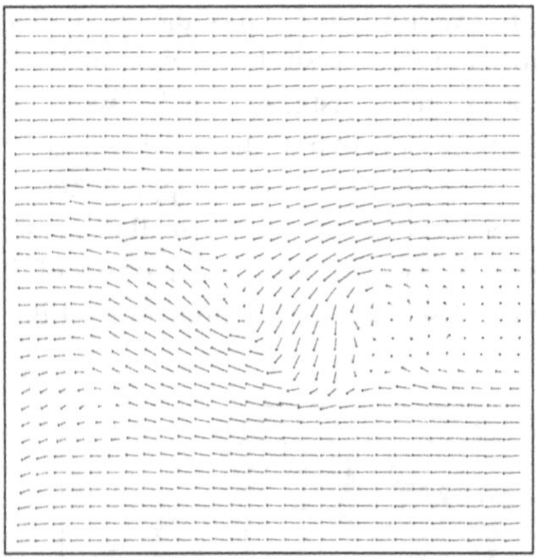

Fig. 6. Dense vector field computed with the variational approach

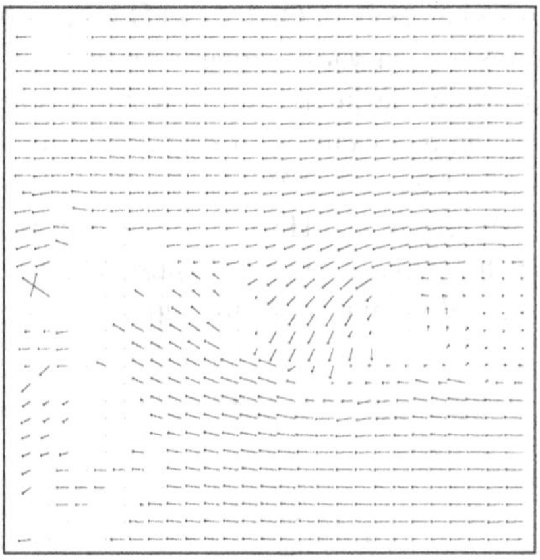

Fig. 7. None-dense vector field computed with DPIV

3 Variational PTV

3.1 General Problem Formulation

Let S denote the coordinates of the extracted particles in the first image of an image pair, and T denote the coordinates of the extracted particles in the second image. Then, we define the distance of a specific particle with coordinates S_i to T by

$$d_T(S_i) := d(S_i, T) = \inf_{T_i \in T} d(S_i, T_i),$$

where $d(S_i, T_i)$ is just the Euclidean distance. Therefore, the target velocity field $\boldsymbol{u}$ (where $\boldsymbol{u}_i$ denotes the displacement of particle S_i from frame 1 to frame 2) minimizes the accumulated distance function

$$D(\boldsymbol{u}) = \sum_{i=1}^{M} d_T(S_i + \boldsymbol{u}_i) \tag{5}$$

where $\boldsymbol{u} = \boldsymbol{u}_1, \boldsymbol{u}_2, ..., \boldsymbol{u}_M$, and where M is the number of extracted particles in image 1.

Unfortunately, minimization of (5) is a highly non-convex problem, as *every* other possible matching minimizes the equation as well. The *local* minimum is just the "nearest-neighbour" solution. Therefore, we define a convex attraction potential as an increasing continuous function that attracts every particle to its closest neighbour:

$$E_{local}(\boldsymbol{u}) = \sum_{i=1}^{M} \frac{\alpha}{2} \big(d_T(S_i + \boldsymbol{u}_i)\big)^2 \tag{6}$$

Until now, the particles are only attracted to their nearest neighbours and the minimization of (6) is trivial. This is why we have to make an additional assumption about $\boldsymbol{u}$. The prototypical assumption that we want to make use of in this paper is the assumption of *smoothness*. We will show in section 4 that other assumptions (that include e.g. physical knowledge) can also be exploited.

However, rather than considering vector fields that are close to constant in a small region (the predominant assumption in PTV) we want to rule out too irregular vector fields by minimizing the magnitudes of the spatial (and, in case of image sequences, spatio-temporal) gradients of $\boldsymbol{u}$:

$$E_{global}(\boldsymbol{u}) = \int_{\Omega} \sum_{j=1}^{N} |\nabla \boldsymbol{u}^j(s)|^2 ds. \tag{7}$$

Please note that $\boldsymbol{u} = (\boldsymbol{u}^1, \boldsymbol{u}^2, ..., \boldsymbol{u}^N)^\top$, where N indicates the dimensionality of the problem (N is usually 2 or 3). The integration variable s is for image pairs in 2D $s = \big(x, y\big)^\top$, and in 3D $s = \big(x, y, z\big)^\top$, where x, y and z denote the spatial coordinates within the domain Ω. For image sequences follows $s = (x, y, t)^\top$ in 2D, and $s = (x, y, z, t)$ in 3D, where x,y and z denote the spatial coordinates, and t the temporal coordinate ($t = [1, 2, ..., T]$).

Equations (6) and (7) can be combined into the variational framework

$$E(\boldsymbol{u}) = E_{loc.}(\boldsymbol{u}) + \lambda E_{glob.}(\boldsymbol{u}) = \underbrace{\sum_{i=1}^{M} \frac{\alpha}{2} \big(d_T(S_i + \boldsymbol{u}_i)\big)^2}_{\text{data}} + \underbrace{\lambda \int_{\Omega} \sum_{j=1}^{N} |\nabla \boldsymbol{u}^j(s)|^2 ds}_{\text{regularization}}, \tag{8}$$

where E_{local} is called "data term" which incorporates *local* information, and E_{global} is the *global* regularization term. In this work, the so-called smoothness parameter $\lambda \geq 0$ is considered a user parameter that controls the smoothness of the resulting velocity field. If we choose $\lambda = 0$, no regularization is performed. The reconstructed velocity field is therefore just the "nearest neighbour" solution, as the *locally* optimal solution for every particle in image 1 is the matching with its nearest neighbour in image 2.

3.2 Outlier Treatment

An important problem in the PTV analysis is raised by the fact, that usually not all the particles are detected correctly. In 2D it may happen that a particle is visible in the first frame, but moves out of the illuminated plane and is therefore not visible (or beneath the threshold) in the second frame. In 3D, additional problems occur when the 3D reconstruction fails, e.g. due to a very high particle density. Further problems arise from particle images tending to coalesce.

We can distinguish between two likely error scenarios:

- A particle is extracted from the second image, but not from the first image: in this case the proposed algorithm can still estimate a reliable velocity field, as it searches matches for all particles in the first frame.
- A particle is visible only in the first frame but not in the second frame: in this error case, the nearest-neighbour search (10) of the proposed algorithm will necessarily find the wrong match in *every* iteration (cf. figure 8). Through the smoothness term of (11) this error is propagated to the neighbourhood of the erroneous vector.

The strategy that we want to take is to eliminate vectors that contribute a high energy to (11). This is achieved through a threshold: we replace the attraction potential of the data term of (10) by a robust potential - a cut-off potential that cuts off points located beyond an adjustable threshold. These outliers are not considered in the regularization step of the current iteration.

However, the *result* of the regularization step is propagated to the outliers: linear interpolation yields the velocity field also at the location of the outliers, the positions of which are updated, as are the positions of the inliers. The idea is that they may be torn below the threshold in case they were wrongly detected outliers.

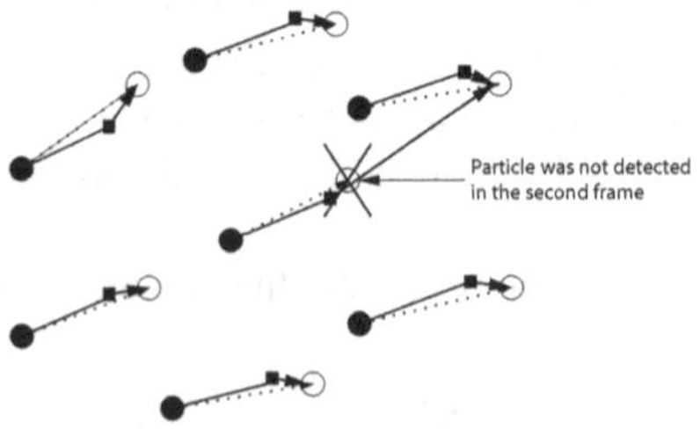

Fig. 8. Black circles denote particle position in the first frame, white circles denote positions in second frame. Filled rectangles denote the current estimate. One particle has not been detected in second frame. Minimization of (10) necessarily leads to the wrong match.

In order to improve the performance in image regions with high velocity, we start with a very high outlier threshold and then slowly increase this threshold: Thus, in the first iterations, particles in fast moving regions will tend to be considered outliers, while particles in slowly moving regions will tend to be considered inliers. The idea is that, in the course of several iterations with an attenuating threshold, more and more particles are considered inliers and the estimated velocity field in the high-velcotiy regions can converge to the correct flow field.

3.3 Optimization

Note that the implicit data constraint defined by equation (5) is a non-convex function. Thus, retrieving a local minimum of (8) does not imply having found the global optimum.

We use an auxiliary variable approach that represents a sound mathematical framework and guarantees convergence [33]: In a two-stage iterative algorithm, each iteration is composed of a local deformation followed by a global regularization. To justify this approach we modify the energy $E(\boldsymbol{u})$ of (8) by introducing an auxiliary variable $\boldsymbol{u}_{aux}$. The two above steps can then be interpreted as alternate minimizations with respect to each of the two variables, the variable of the initial energy $\boldsymbol{u}$ and the auxiliary variable $\boldsymbol{u}_{aux}$.

A general formulation of the energy E_{aux} following [33] based on formula (8), with the extra auxiliary variable $\boldsymbol{u}_{aux} = \boldsymbol{u}_{aux,1}, \boldsymbol{u}_{aux,2}, ..., \boldsymbol{u}_{aux,M}$, has the form:

$$
\begin{aligned}
E_{aux}(\boldsymbol{u}, \boldsymbol{u}_{aux}) = &\sum_{i=1}^{M} \Big(\frac{1-\alpha}{2} \big(d_{S+\boldsymbol{u}}(S + \boldsymbol{u}_{aux,i})\big)^2 + \frac{\alpha}{2} \big(d_T(S + \boldsymbol{u}_{aux,i})\big)^2 \Big) \\
&+ \lambda \int_{\Omega} \sum_{j=1}^{N} |\nabla \boldsymbol{u}^j(s)|^2 ds
\end{aligned}
\tag{9}
$$

The first two terms of equation (9) indicate the auxiliary variable's function as an intermediary between $S + \boldsymbol{u}$ and T. As a geometric interpretation, we can imagine the iterative minimization of E_{aux} as a deformation of the current vector field followed by a regularization. The successive minimization of E_{aux} is equal to subsequent minimization of the following two energies E_I and E_{II}, each with respect to a different variable - E_I with respect to $\boldsymbol{u}_{aux}$, and E_{II} with respect to $\boldsymbol{u}$:

Local deformation:

$$
E_I(\boldsymbol{u}, \boldsymbol{u}_{aux}) = \sum_{i=1}^{M} \Big(\frac{1-\alpha}{2} \big(d_{S+\boldsymbol{u}}(S + \boldsymbol{u}_{aux,i})\big)^2 + \frac{\alpha}{2} \big(d_T(S + \boldsymbol{u}_{aux,i})\big)^2 \Big) \tag{10}
$$

Global regularization:

$$
E_{II}(\boldsymbol{u}, \boldsymbol{u}_{aux}) = \sum_{i=1}^{M} \Big(\frac{1}{2} \big(d_{S+\boldsymbol{u}}(S + \boldsymbol{u}_{aux,i})\big)^2 \Big) + \lambda \int_{\Omega} \sum_{j=1}^{N} |\nabla \boldsymbol{u}^j(s)|^2 ds \tag{11}
$$

The two equations can be subsequently iterated in the given order until a stable condition is reached. Equations (10) and (11) demonstrate how both minimizations are linked

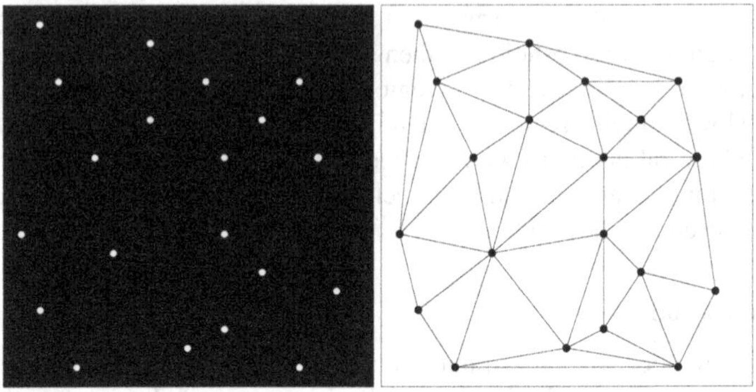

Fig. 9. Delauney trianguation of the area covered by particles from an image plane; the line intersections denote the extracted particle positions

by the term $\sum_{i=1}^{M} \left(d_{S+\boldsymbol{u}}(S+\boldsymbol{u}_{aux,i})\right)^2$. The minimizing $\boldsymbol{u}_{aux}$ of E_I can be interpreted as a trade-off between the closeness to $S+\boldsymbol{u}$ and the closeness to T. This gives a good direction of displacement and avoids too large deformations of the auxiliary flow field $\boldsymbol{u}_{aux}$. The grid generation is performed using a Delaunay triangulation [34] (cf. Fig. 9). For details about grid generation and discretization of eqn. (11), for 2D and 3D image pairs and image sequences, we refer to [35].

3.4 Experimental Evaluation

Data. The Visual Society of Japan (VSJ) has published standard images for particle image velocimetry that are freely available on the internet [36, 37]. For 2D data, we will refer to the test image classified as 301 in the VSJ library. It consists of 10 frames taken in intervals of 0.005 sec; each frame consists of about 4,150 particles. It shows the vertical portion of the impinging jet, with a maximum velocity of 10 pixels/ frame.

We will analyze our 3D approach using the test images classified as 331 in the VSJ library (jet shear flow). The advantage of the VSJ images is that the underlying motion fields, as well as the particle coordinates, are available so that the evaluation of different approaches, as well as that of different parameter settings, is possible. By basing our computations on this particle position data, we have to deal with very high particle concentrations (approx. 4,150 particles to be tracked in the 2D case and 3,500 particles in the 3D case). We want to evaluate the performance of our algorithm in cases of high particle concentrations, as up-to-date CCD cameras yield increasingly high resolutions, and thus an up-to-date tracking system must be capable of managing high particle concentrations.

Parameter Settings. The particle coordinates are normalized so that all particles lie between 0 and 1 in all spatial dimensions; the temporal dimension is numbered in integer steps ($t = 1, 2, ..., T$).

For all the test cases we use a smoothness parameter of $\lambda = 0.1$. The parameter α is set to 0.8. In the first iteration, 75% of the particles are considered outliers and in every iteration 0.1% particles in addition are considered inliers. No additional particles are considered inliers if the outlier threshold reaches 0.01.

The iteration is stopped if no further decrease in energy is perceived.

Error Measures. In this work, we want to concentrate on two error measures: *yield* and *reliability*.

- Yield (E_Y) is the measure of the number of correct vectors produced between two images (n) divided by the total number of vectors known to exist between the two images (v):

$$E_Y = \frac{n}{v} \tag{12}$$

- Reliability (E_R) is the measure of the number of correct vectors that were reconstructed by the tracking method (n), divided by the total number of vectors determined by the tracking method (d):

$$E_R = \frac{n}{d} \tag{13}$$

Numerical Results and Discussion. The first test case is the computation of the velocity field between the frames 0 and 1 of the VSJ 301 image sequence. After 700 iterations the solution presented in figure 10 (outlier ratio: 3%) is generated. The next step is the additional exploitation of temporal smoothness information. Therefore we have to analyze the whole VSJ 301 image sequence consisting of 10 frames. Figure 11 shows the computed trajectories. Table 2 shows the parameters we use and the results that we achieve. Furthermore, the results of the analysis of image pairs only are indicated. In every frame, the computation based on the whole sequence is at least as good as the image pair result. This had to be expected, as additional information is available in the sequence case. The reason why only slight improvements are achieved has already been addressed: We analyse a 2D projection of a 3D velocity field, therefore the smoothness assumption does not necessarily hold at every point in the image.

This is why we will now turn to three-dimensional problems: First we want to compute the 3D velocity field between the frames 0 and 1 of the VSJ 331 image sequence. The solution that was generated after 750 iterations is presented in figure 12. In this test

Table 2. Error measures for VSJ Standard Image 301

	$\alpha = 0.8, \lambda_{sp} = 0.1, \lambda_{tmp} = 10$		$\alpha = 0.8, \lambda = 0.1$	
Frames	Image Sequence		Image Pairs	
	Yield	Reliability	Yield	Reliability
00→01	97.72	96.41	96.34%	95.93%
01→02	97.62	96.61	96.83%	95.83%
02→03	97.69	96.45	97.05%	95.81%
03→04	97.64	96.64	96.90%	95.90%
04→05	97.32	96.63	97.05%	96.35%
05→06	97.64	96.70	97.11%	96.18%
06→07	97.28	96.10	92.99%	91.86%
07→08	97.28	96.30	93.11%	92.10%
08→09	96.33	95.24	93.94%	92.87%

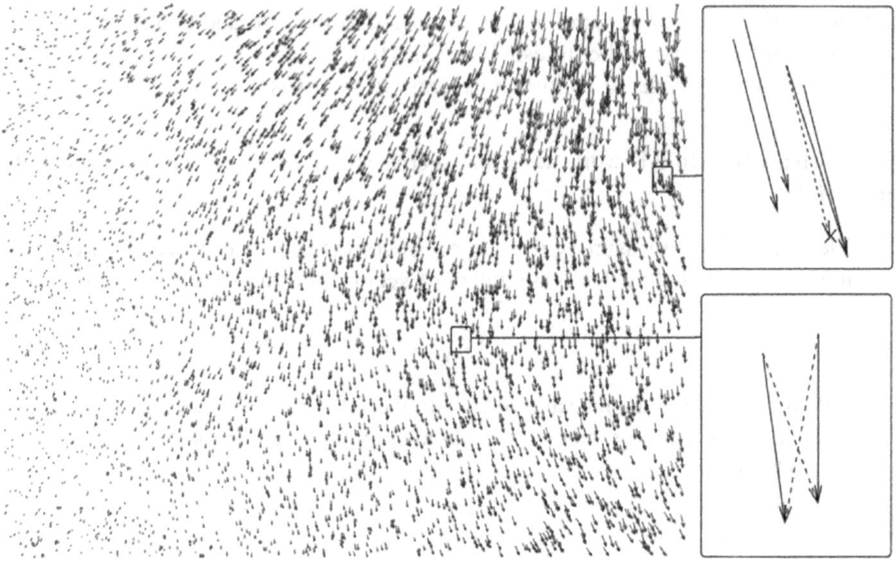

Fig. 10. Left: Estimated velocity field VSJ Image 301. **Right:** Two likely error constellations: One particle has not been extracted in frame 2, the matching is performed with a close neighbour of this vanished particle **(top)**. Due to three-dimensionality of the velocity field, two particles "cross" in the two-dimensional projection. The two-dimensional variational approach presumes smoothness of the projection and chooses the wrong match **(bottom)**.

Fig. 11. Computed trajectories from sequence VSJ 301

case, $3,364$ particles are visible in both images and $3,372$ matchings are computed. These matches include all exact matches, and 8 particles that do not have a counterpart in the second image but are erroneously matched to another particle. As expected, the 3D results are much better than the 2D results. Computations with volume coordinates of the VSJ 301 sequence show that we achieve matching rates very close to 100% in these test cases, too.

Table 3 shows that even an increase in outlier probability does not deteriorate the results significantly: In these test cases, the indicated percentage of particles (first column) has been randomly removed from *both* images to simulate problems in particle extraction and 3D reconstruction. The second column indicates the number of particles that are visible in both frames, columns three and four show the two performance measures.

In order to assess the limits of our approach we want to consider only every second image. The results indicated in table 3 show that the error measures are still very good. When considering only every third image, however, the approach is no longer able to determine a valid velocity field. In fact, both yield and reliability drop to 0% (i.e. not a single velocity vector is recovered correctly). The algorithm does not find a starting point as the offsets at *every* position in the image are so high that *no* particle is able to find its counterpart in the first iteration and thus the algorithm converges to the wrong minimum. This drawback had to be expected as we are minimizing a highly non-convex functional (cf. eqn. (10)).

4 Higher Order Regularization and Natural Discretization

The experimental evaluation of sec. 2.2 suggests the use of higher-order regularization. This type of regularization is necessary to accurately recover important flow structures like vortices, for example, and to incorporate physically plausible constraints, like vanishing divergence of the flow.

Table 3. Error measures for VSJ Standard Image 331

	00 → 01			00 → 02		
Removed Particles	Possible Matches	Yield	Reliability	Possible Matches	Yield	Reliability
0%	3,364	100.00%	99.76%	3,192	99.97%	99.47%
5%	3,037	100.00%	99.84%	2,881	99.86%	99.45%
10%	2,731	100.00%	99.60%	2,586	99.38%	99.34%
15%	2,440	100.00%	99.59%	2,307	98.22%	99.60%
20%	2,170	100.00%	99.40%	2,053	98.30%	99.56%
25%	1,885	100.00%	99.74%	1,809	44.83%	44.81%
30%	1,649	100.00%	99.40%	1,557	38.79%	39.35%
35%	1,403	99.93%	99.64%	1,339	31.14%	31.17%
40%	1,211	100.00%	99.26%	1,131	32.98%	33.01%

4.1 Orthogonal Decomposition

We represent vector fields directly in terms of their irrotational and solenoidal components. These components are defined by the first-order variations of velocity potentials ψ and stream functions ϕ, respectively [38]. The representation of the 2D vector field $u \in H^1(\Omega)^2$ in terms of ψ, ϕ reads:

$$\begin{aligned} u &= \nabla\psi + \nabla^{\perp}\phi \,, \\ u_{\partial\Omega} &= \partial_n \psi \,, \end{aligned} \tag{14}$$

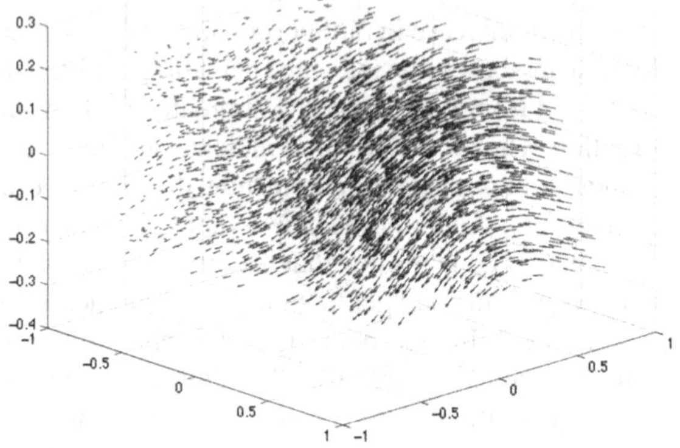

Fig. 12. Estimated 3D velocity field for sequence VSJ 331

where $\phi_{\partial\Omega} = 0$ is unique up to a constant of ψ. Here, Ω denotes the image section (grid) and n the corresponding outer normal vector. Let

$$u = v + w, \qquad v = \nabla\psi, \qquad w = \nabla^{\perp}\phi, \qquad \phi|_{\partial\Omega} = 0 \tag{15}$$

according to (14). Because of

$$\operatorname{curl} v = 0, \qquad \operatorname{div} w = 0, \tag{16}$$

we have:

$$\langle v, w\rangle = \int_{\Omega} \nabla\psi \cdot \nabla^{\perp}\phi dx = -\int_{\Omega} (\operatorname{curl} \nabla\psi)\phi dx + \int_{\partial\Omega} \partial_n\psi\phi dl = 0, \tag{17}$$

which shows that the decomposition (14) is orthogonal. Discretizing such vector fields with standard finite differences or finite elements yields *approximate* decompositions only, and may lead to numerical instabilities in applications. This is why we use a *mimetic* finite differencing scheme that provides an *exact* orthogonal decomposition of the *finite*-dimensional space of vector fields [39, 40]. Furthermore, the decomposition allows to estimate ϕ, ψ directly, using variational approaches and subspace correction methods. Alternatively, we may first estimate u and then compute ϕ, ψ in a subsequent step by solving the Neumann and Dirichlet problems:

$$\begin{aligned} \Delta\psi &= \operatorname{div} u, & \partial_n\psi &= u_{\partial\Omega} \\ -\Delta\phi &= \operatorname{curl} u, & \phi_{\partial\Omega} &= 0 \end{aligned} \tag{18}$$

For a more detailed exposition, we refer to [41].

4.2 Regularization and Optimization Problems

We use the conventional data term for optical flow estimation, along with regularizers $L(u)$ to be specified below

$$\min_{u\in H^1(\Omega)^2} F(u), \qquad F(u) := (\nabla f^{\top} u + \frac{\partial f}{\partial t})^2 + L(u) \tag{19}$$

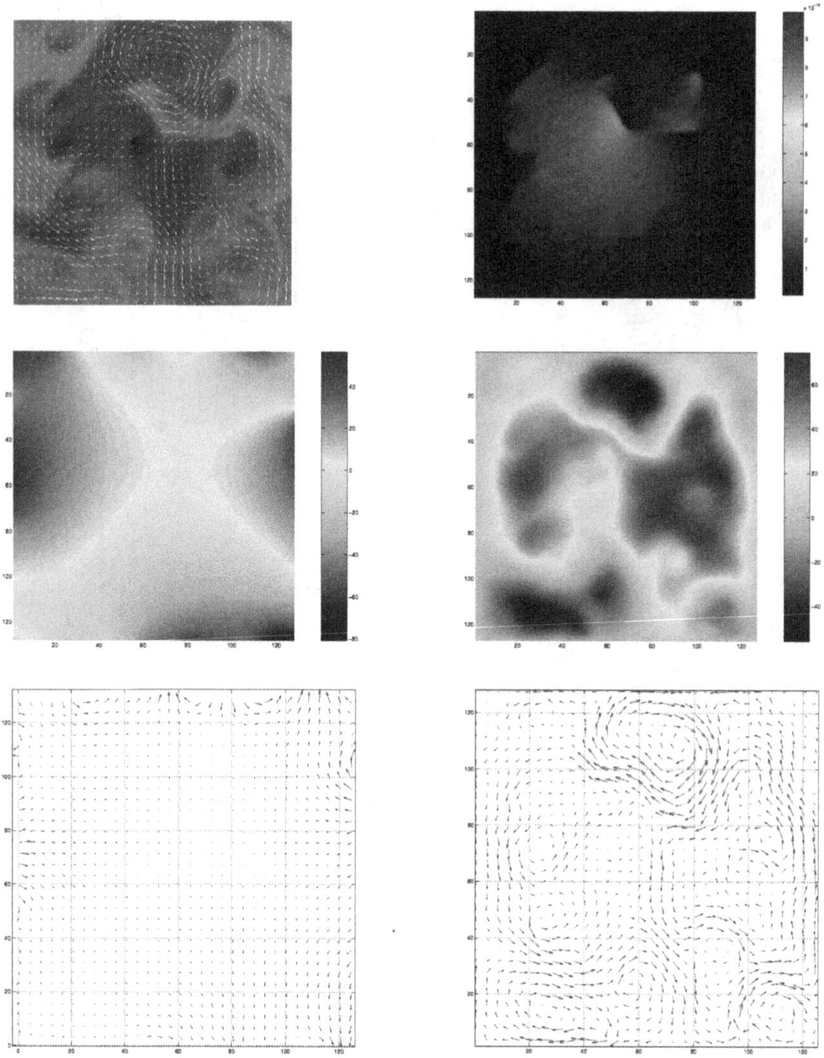

Fig. 13. Top Left: The first image I_1 with the restored solenoidal flow. **Top Right:** The divergence field of the flow which is less than $3e - 12$. **Middle Left:** The potential field $\psi_l(\Omega)$ related to the laminar flow. **Middle Right:** The potential field $\phi(\Omega)$. **Bottom Left:** The first component of flow: the laminar flow u_{lam}. **Bottom Right:** The second component of flow related to potential $\phi(\Omega)$. The comparison with standard regularization is depicted in figure 14.

We wish to apply the following second-order regularizer

$$L(u) = \int_{\Omega} \lambda_1 |\nabla \operatorname{div} u|^2 + \lambda_2 |\nabla \operatorname{curl} u|^2 dx \tag{20}$$

where λ_1 and λ_2 are two positive constants. This term measures the variation of the basic flow components divergence and curl, but *does not penalize* the components itself.

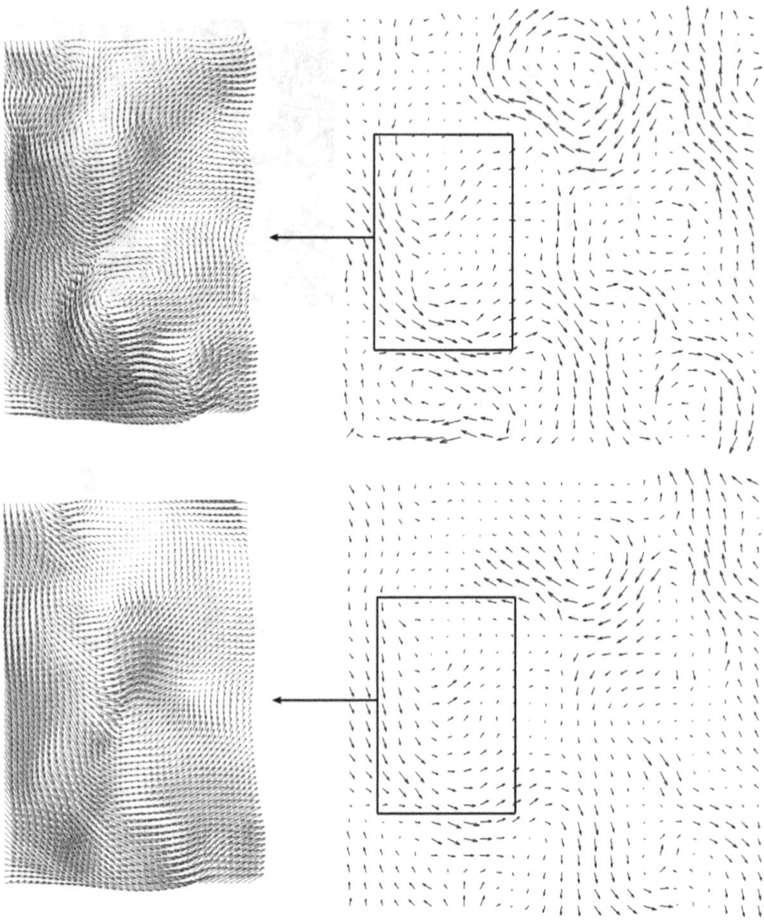

Fig. 14. Top: The restored solenoidal flow $u(\Omega)$. **Bottom:** The restored flow $u_{hs}(\Omega)$ using the Horn-Schunck regularization (sec. 2). This results clearly show that vortex structures are better recovered by our approach. Furthermore, the magnitude of the divergence is below 10^{-11} throughout the image plane.

However, both standard finite differences or finite elements discretization lead to finite-dimensional representations which do not satisfy (14), (18). As a result, penalizing one component may affect the other component too. Therefore, we adopt the framework described in [41].

4.3 Estimation of Solenoidal Flows

An important special case, particularly in applications of experimental fluid mechanics, concerns the estimation of solenoidal (divergence-free) flows. In this case the decomposition (14) reduces to

$$u = \nabla \psi_l + \nabla^{\perp} \phi := u_l + \nabla^{\perp} \phi \tag{21}$$

where the *laminar flow* u_l can be computed through the full flow u by solving:

$$\triangle\phi_l = 0, \qquad \partial_n\psi_l = u_{\partial\Omega} \tag{22}$$

and $u_l = \nabla\psi_l$. The laminar flow u_l is both divergence- and curl-free. In order for (22) to be solvable, we require the compatibility condition $\int_{\partial\Omega} u_{\partial\Omega} dl = 0$ (cf., e.g., [42]). Using the mimetic finite difference method [41], this condition is satisfied naturally. If we fix $\triangle\phi_l = 0$, then $\int_{\partial\Omega} u_{\partial\Omega} dl = 0$.

4.4 Numerical Example

Figure 13 shows the result of estimating the solenoidal flow for a real image sequence. The comparison with first-order regularization (Horn-Schunck approach, sec. 2) in figure 14 cleary reveals the superiority of our approach regarding the reconstruction of vortex structures. Furthermore, the (in this case) physically plausible constraint of vanishing divergence is satisfied quite accurately.

For further experimental evaluations we refer to [41].

5 Conclusion and Future Works

We presented a range of variational approaches to the fluid flow estimation problem. Traditional variational approaches to optical flow estimation apply to PIV scenarios, whereas a novel variational framework has been introduced to solve the PTV problem. All these approaches favourably compare with established PIV and PTV image processing techniques based on cross-correlation and sophisticated post-processing.

Finally, we sketched a variational framework exploiting higher-order regularization, as well as motion representation and estimation in terms of velocity potentials and stream functions. The integration of these variational schemes in our future work will provide the basis for qualitative motion and time series analysis of complex motion patterns in fluids.

Acknowledgement. Support by the Deutsche Forschungsgemeinschaft (DFG) within the priority programme "Bildgebende Messverfahren in der Strömungsmechanik"(SPP-1147) is gratefully acknowledged. The images depicted in figure 1 were kindly provided by Dr. Brede (Chair of Fluid Mechanics, University of Rostock) and O. Frederich (Chair of Fluid Mechanics, Technical University of Berlin).

References

1. Raffel, M., Willert, C., Kompenhans, J.: Particle Image Velocimetry. A Practical Guide. Springer (1999)
2. Kawamura, T., Hiwada, M., Hibino, T., Mabuchi, I., Kumada, M.: Flow around a finite circular cylinder on a flat plate. Bulletin of the JSME **27** (1984) 2142–2151
3. Scarano, F.: Iterative image deformation methods in piv. Meas. Sci. Technol. **13** (2002) R1–R19

4. Kobayashi, T., Saga, T., Segawa, S.: Multipoint velocity measurement for unsteady flow field by digital image processing. Journal of Visualization **5** (1989) 197–202
5. Hassan, Y., Canaan, R.: Full-field bubbly flow velocity measurements using a multiframe particle trackingg technique. Exp. Fluids **12** (1991) 49–60
6. Uemura, T., Yamamoto, F., Ohmi, K.: A high speed algorithm of image analysis for real time measurement of two-dimensional velocity distribution. Flow Visualization (1989) 129–133
7. Ohmi, K., Li, H.Y.: Particle-tracking velocimetry with new algorithms. Meas. Sci. Technol. **11** (2000) 603–616
8. Keane, R., Adrian, R., Zhang, Y.: Super-resolution particle image velocimetry. Meas. Sci. Technol. **6** (1995) 754–768
9. Cowen, E., Monismith, S.: A hybrid digital particle tracking velocimetry technique. Exp. Fluids **22** (1997) 199–211
10. Horn, B., Schunck, B.: Determining optical flow. Artificial Intelligence **17** (1981) 185–203
11. Nagel, H.H.: On the estimation of optical flow(): Relations between different approaches and some new results. Artificial Intelligence **33** (1987) 299–324
12. Schnörr, C.: Determining optical flow for irregular domains by minimizing quadratic functionals of a certain class. International Journal of Computer Vision **6** (1991) 25–38
13. Schnörr, C.: On functionals with greyvalue-controlled smoothness terms for determining optical flow. IEEE Transactions on Pattern Analysis and Machine Intelligence **15** (1993) 1074–1079
14. Schnörr, C.: Segmentation of visual motion by minimizing convex non-quadratic functionals. In: 12th Int. Conf. on Pattern Recognition, Jerusalem, Israel. Volume A., IEEE Computer Society Press (1994) 661–663
15. Schnörr, C.: Convex variational segmentation of multi-channel images. In: 12th Int. Conf. on Analysis and Optimization of Systems: Images, Wavelets and PDE's. Volume 219 of Lect. Notes in Control and Information Sciences. (1996) 201–207
16. Weickert, J., Schnörr, C.: Variational optic flow computation with a spatio-temporal smoothness constraint. Journal of Mathematical Imaging and Vision **14** (2001) 245–255
17. Weickert, J., Schnörr, C.: A theoretical framework for convex regularizers in pde-based computation of image motion. Int. J. Computer Vision **45** (2001) 245–264
18. Ruhnau, P., Kohlberger, T., Nobach, H., Schnörr, C.: Variational optical flow estimation for particle image velocimetry. Exp. Fluids (2004) in press.
19. Kohlberger, T., Mémin, E., Schnörr, C.: Variational dense motion estimation using the helmholtz decomposition. In Griffin, L., Lillholm, M., eds.: Scale Space Methods in Computer Vision. Volume 2695 of LNCS., Springer (2003) 432–448
20. Krishnamurthy, R., Moulin, P., Woods, J.: Multiscale motion models for scalable video coding. In: Proc. IEEE Int. Conf. Image Processing, Lausanne, Switzerland. (1996) 965–968
21. Simoncelli, E.P.: Distributed representation and analysis of visual motion. PhD thesis, Massachusetts Institute of Technology (1993)
22. Quénot, G.M., Pakleza, J.: Particle image velocimetry with optical flow (1998)
23. Brede, M., Leder, A., Westergaard, C.H.: Time-resolved piv investigation of the separated shear layer in the transitional cylinder wake. In: Proc. 5th Int. Symp. on Particle Image Velocimetry (PIV'03),Busan, Korea. (2003)
24. Westergaard, C.H., Brede, M., Leder, A.: Time-space analysis of time resolved piv data. In: Proc. 5th Int. Symp. on Particle Image Velocimetry (PIV'03),Busan, Korea. (2003)
25. Quénot, G.M.: The orthogonal algorithm for optical flow detection using dynamic programming. In: Proc. Intl.. Conf. on Acoustics, Speech and Signal Proc. (1992) 249–252
26. Quénot, G.M.: Performance evaluation of an optical flow technique applied to piv using the vsj standard images. In: Third International Workshop on PIV. (1999) 579–584
27. Barron, J., Fleet, D., Beauchemin, S.: Performance of optical flow techniques. International Journal of Computer Vision **39** (1994) 43–77

28. Chetverikov, D.: Applying feature tracking to piv. International Journal of Pattern Recognition and Artificial Intelligence **17** (2003) 477–504
29. Brandt, A.: Multi-level adaptive solutions to boundary-value problems. Mathematics of Computation **31** (1977) 333–390
30. Hackbusch, W.: Iterative Solution of Large Sparse Systems of Equations. Volume 95 of Applied Mathematical Sciences. Springer (1993)
31. Bruhn, A., Weickert, J., Feddern, C., Kohlberger, T., , Schnörr, C.: Variational optic flow computation in real-time. In: IEEE Trans. Image Proc., in press. (2004)
32. Kohlberger, T., Schnörr, C., Bruhn, A., Weickert, J.: Parallel variational motion estimation by domain decomposition and cluster computing. In Pajdla, T., Matas, J., eds.: Proc. ECCV 2004. Volume 3024., Springer (2004) 205–216
33. Cohen, L.D.: Auxiliary variables and two-step iterative algorithms in computer vision problems. J. Math. Imaging Vis. **6** (1996) 59–83
34. Aurenhammer, F.: Voronoi diagrams – a survey of a fundamental geometric data structure. ACM Computing Surveys **23** (1991) 345–405 Habilitationsschrift. [Report B 90-09, FU Berlin, Germany, 1990].
35. Ruhnau, P., Gütter, C., Schnörr, C.: A variational approach for particle tracking velocimetry. Comp. science series, technical report, Dept. Math. and Comp. Science, University of Mannheim, Germany (2004)
36. Okamoto, K., Nishio, S., Kobayashi, T.: Standard images for particle-image velocimetry. Meas. Sci. Technol. **11** (2000) 685–691
37. Okamoto, K., Nishio, S., Kobayashi, T., Saga, T., Takehara, K.: Evaluation of the 3d-piv standard images (piv-std project). Journal of Visualization **3** (2000) 115–124
38. Hyman, J.M., Shashkov, M.J.: The orthogonal decomposition theorems for mimetic finite difference methods. SIAM J. Numer. Anal. **36** (1999) 788–818 (electronic)
39. Hyman, J.M., Shashkov, M.J.: Natural discretizations for the divergence, gradient, and curl on logically rectangular grids. Comput. Math. Appl. **33** (1997) 81–104
40. Hyman, J.M., Shashkov, M.J.: Adjoint operators for the natural discretizations of the divergence, gradient and curl on logically rectangular grids. Appl. Numer. Math. **25** (1997) 413–442
41. Yuan, J., Ruhnau, P., Mémin, E., Schnörr, C.: Discrete orthogonal decomposition and variational fluid flow estimation. In: 5th International Conference on Scale Space and PDE Methods in Computer Vision. (2005) in preparation.
42. Evans, L.C.: Partial differential equations. Volume 19 of Graduate Studies in Mathematics. American Mathematical Society, Providence, RI (1998)

Motion Based Estimation and Representation of 3D Surfaces and Boundaries

Klas Nordberg and Fredrik Vikstén

Computer Vision Laboratory
Department of Electrical Engineering
Linköping University
SE-581 83 Linköping

Abstract. This paper presents a novel representation for 3D shapes in terms of planar surface patches and their boundaries. The representation is based on a tensor formalism similar to the usual orientation tensor but extends this concept by using projective spaces and a fourth order tensor, even though the practical computations can be made in normal matrix algebra. This paper also discusses the possibility of estimating the proposed representation from motion field which are generated by a calibrated camera moving in the scene. One method based on 3D spatio-temporal orientation tensors is presented and results from this method are included.

1 Introduction

Motion analysis can be divided into two relatively separate problem areas, each area having its own set of models and methods. The first one is that of estimating a motion vector at a particular point in an image which represents a certain time point of an image sequence. The standard approach is based on the brightness constancy constraint equation (BCCE) (or optic flow equation),

$$v_1 \frac{\partial g}{\partial y_1} + v_2 \frac{\partial g}{\partial y_2} + \Delta t \frac{\partial g}{\partial t} = 0 \tag{1}$$

where g is the image intensity as a function of the two image coordinates

$$\overline{\mathbf{y}} = \begin{pmatrix} y_1 \\ y_2 \end{pmatrix} \tag{2}$$

and time t, Δt is the temporal distance between two frames in the image sequence, and

$$\overline{\mathbf{v}} = \begin{pmatrix} v_1 \\ v_2 \end{pmatrix} \tag{3}$$

is the motion vector which we want to estimate. The problem of estimating $\overline{\mathbf{v}}$ from image data can be solved in a variety of ways by using a number of different approaches, see for example [2]. These methods typically produce an image which at each point contains an estimate of the motion vector $\overline{\mathbf{v}}$, in some cases complemented by a measure certainty or confidence in the estimate.

B. Jähne et al. (Eds.): IWCM 2004, LNCS 3417, pp. 146–164, 2007.

We can also rewrite Equation (1) as

$$(\nabla g)^T \overline{\mathbf{v}} = 0 \tag{4}$$

where

$$\nabla g = \begin{pmatrix} \frac{\partial g}{\partial y_1} \\ \frac{\partial g}{\partial y_2} \\ \frac{\partial g}{\partial t} \end{pmatrix} \qquad \mathbf{v} = \begin{pmatrix} v_1 \\ v_2 \\ \Delta t \end{pmatrix} \tag{5}$$

and instead see the projective element $\mathbf{v}$ as the interesting variable which should be estimated. One way to estimate this is done by forming the 3×3 symmetric matrix (the so-called structure tensor) $\mathbf{T}$ according to

$$\mathbf{T}(\overline{\mathbf{y}}, t) = W * (\nabla g \, \nabla^T g) \tag{6}$$

where the convolution is over the entire spatio-temporal data of the image sequence and W is a localized weighting function of both space and time. If the support of W is sufficiently small to allow the assumption that $\overline{\mathbf{v}}$ is constant within the region, it follows from Equation (4) that

$$\mathbf{T}\,\mathbf{v} = \mathbf{0} \tag{7}$$

i.e., $\mathbf{v}$ is a null vector of $\mathbf{T}$. Another interpretation of this relation is that $\mathbf{T}$ represents the local 3D orientation of the spatio-temporal image data at point $(\overline{\mathbf{y}}, t)$, and from this follows that the estimation of $\mathbf{T}$ can be computed in other ways than is described above, see [2] and [3].

Regardless of whether an explicit or implicit representation of the local motion has been estimated, the result can normally be regarded as a motion descriptor, e.g. $\overline{\mathbf{v}}$ or $\mathbf{T}$, which is a function of the image position $\overline{\mathbf{y}}$. In the following, this function is referred to as the *motion field*, which of course also is a function of the time t.

The second area of motion analysis uses the motion field defined above and tries to analyze the field, e.g., determine how the motion field varies with $\overline{\mathbf{y}}$ and possibly also with t. Again, this analysis can be done in different ways and the methods used are normally based on both the goal of the analysis and the underlying assumption about what has caused the image data to vary over time, e.g., is it the objects in the scene which are moving, is it the camera that moves, or perhaps both.

In this paper we will consider the problem of estimating the features and shapes of objects in a static scene based on the motion field caused by moving a calibrated camera according to a known motion model. To simplify the presentation this model contains only translation of the scene relative to the camera with a known motion vector

$$\mathbf{w} = \begin{pmatrix} w_1 \\ w_2 \\ w_3 \end{pmatrix} \tag{8}$$

In the following, we will assume that all 3D coordinates are defined relative to a camera-centric reference system with the third dimension pointing in the view direction of the camera. The resulting motion field can then be analyzed to obtain various forms of information about the 3D structure of the scene. Assuming a standard pin-hole camera model, which maps the coordinates of a point

$$\mathbf{x} = \begin{pmatrix} x_1 \\ x_2 \\ x_3 \end{pmatrix} \tag{9}$$

in the scene, to a point $\overline{\mathbf{y}}$ in the image according to

$$\overline{\mathbf{y}} = \begin{pmatrix} y_1 \\ y_2 \end{pmatrix} = \frac{f}{x_3} \begin{pmatrix} x_1 \\ x_2 \end{pmatrix} \tag{10}$$

where f is the focal distance of the camera. The motion of the camera causes the projection of $\mathbf{x}$ to $\overline{\mathbf{y}}$ to change over time in accordance to

$$\begin{pmatrix} \frac{dy_1}{dt} \\ \frac{dy_2}{dt} \end{pmatrix} = \frac{f}{x_3^2} \begin{pmatrix} \frac{dx_1}{dt} x_3 - x_1 \frac{dx_3}{dt} \\ \frac{dx_2}{dt} x_3 - x_2 \frac{dx_3}{dt} \end{pmatrix} \tag{11}$$

We can now make the following identifications

$$\begin{pmatrix} v_1 \\ v_2 \end{pmatrix} = \begin{pmatrix} \frac{dy_1}{dt} \\ \frac{dy_2}{dt} \end{pmatrix} \qquad \begin{pmatrix} w_1 \\ w_2 \\ w_3 \end{pmatrix} = \begin{pmatrix} \frac{dx_1}{dt} \\ \frac{dx_2}{dt} \\ \frac{dx_3}{dt} \end{pmatrix} \tag{12}$$

The insertion of these two expressions together with Equation (10) into Equation (11) gives us

$$\overline{\mathbf{v}} = \begin{pmatrix} v_1 \\ v_2 \end{pmatrix} = \frac{1}{x_3} \begin{pmatrix} f\, w_1 - y_1\, w_3 \\ f\, w_2 - y_2\, w_3 \end{pmatrix} = \frac{1}{x_3} \overline{\mathbf{u}} \tag{13}$$

Notice that both $\overline{\mathbf{v}}$ and $\overline{\mathbf{u}}$ are functions of the image position $\overline{\mathbf{y}}$.

One of the most common approaches of motion analysis for shape description is to simply estimate the corresponding depth x_3 at each image point $\overline{\mathbf{y}}$. Given the above relations between the point in the scene $\mathbf{x}$, the image coordinate $\overline{\mathbf{y}}$ and the local image velocity $\overline{\mathbf{v}}$, x_3 can be determined in different ways. For example, from Equation (13) it follows directly that

$$x_3 = \frac{\overline{\mathbf{u}}(\overline{\mathbf{y}})^T \overline{\mathbf{u}}(\overline{\mathbf{y}})}{\overline{\mathbf{u}}(\overline{\mathbf{y}})^T \overline{\mathbf{v}}(\overline{\mathbf{y}})} \tag{14}$$

which, however, does not take into account that $\overline{\mathbf{v}}$ may not be the correct velocity due to the aperture problem, nor does it manage the situation which occurs when the denominator of Equation (14) comes close to zero. Whatever approach is used, the result is a function $x_3(\overline{\mathbf{y}})$ which we may refer to as the *depth field* corresponding to the motion field. By rewriting Equation (10) as

$$\mathbf{x} = \begin{pmatrix} x_1 \\ x_2 \\ x_3 \end{pmatrix} = \frac{x_3}{f} \begin{pmatrix} y_1 \\ y_2 \\ f \end{pmatrix} = \frac{x_3}{f} \mathbf{y} \tag{15}$$

the depth field can be transformed into a field of points $\mathbf{x}$ given as a function of the image position $\mathbf{y}$ according to

$$\mathbf{x} = \frac{x_3(\overline{\mathbf{y}})}{f} \mathbf{y} \tag{16}$$

This type of field can be visualized as a "cloud" of points in the 3D space which, however, does not contain any relations or interpretations of what shape the points represent.

One way to introduce a shape interpretation which also has consequences for how we analyze the underlying motion field is to assume that the points in the scene all lie on planar surfaces and that a set of such surfaces are observed by the translating camera. This means that to each planar surface there is a corresponding segment in the motion field in which the field varies according to the parameters of the plane. Each planar surface[1] can be described by a vector

$$\mathbf{l} = \begin{pmatrix} l_1 \\ l_2 \\ l_3 \end{pmatrix} \tag{17}$$

such that a point $\mathbf{x}$, Equation (9), lies on the surface if and only if

$$l_1\, x_1 + l_2\, x_2 + l_3\, x_3 = \|\mathbf{l}\|^2 \tag{18}$$

Notice that $\mathbf{l}$ is a normal vector to the plane and that $\|\mathbf{l}\|$ is the normal distance from the origin to the plane. If we insert Equation (10) to produce

$$f\, \|\mathbf{l}\|^2 = x_3\, (y_1\, l_1 + y_2\, l_2 + f\, l_3) = x_3\, \mathbf{y}^T \mathbf{l} \tag{19}$$

we can solve for x_3 and insert into Equation (13) to get the following relation

$$\overline{\mathbf{v}} = \frac{\mathbf{y}^T \mathbf{l}}{f\, \|\mathbf{l}\|^2}\, \overline{\mathbf{u}} \tag{20}$$

Notice that together with Equation (13) this relation implies that the motion field is a second order function of the image coordinates (y_1, y_2).

Given a segment S of the motion field which corresponds to a particular planar surface, the vector $\mathbf{l}$ can be estimated by substituting $\mathbf{m}$ for $\mathbf{l}$, where

$$\mathbf{m} = \frac{\mathbf{l}}{f\|\mathbf{l}\|^2} \tag{21}$$

[1] This representation does not include planes which pass through the origin since they would all be represented by the zero vector and Equation (18) is true for any $\mathbf{x}$ if $\mathbf{l} = \mathbf{0}$. In practice such planes will be of little interest for this application, and in Section 2 1 will be replaced by a homogeneous representation $\mathbf{l}^H$ which solves this ambiguity.

and minimize

$$\begin{aligned}\epsilon &= \sum_{\overline{\mathbf{y}} \in S} \left\| \overline{\mathbf{v}}(\overline{\mathbf{y}}) - \frac{\overline{\mathbf{u}}(\overline{\mathbf{y}})\, \mathbf{y}^T \mathbf{l}}{f \|\mathbf{l}\|^2} \right\|^2 = \\ &= \sum_{\overline{\mathbf{y}} \in S} \left\| \overline{\mathbf{v}}(\overline{\mathbf{y}}) - \overline{\mathbf{u}}(\overline{\mathbf{y}})\, \mathbf{y}^T \mathbf{m} \right\|^2\end{aligned} \tag{22}$$

over $\mathbf{m}$. This $\mathbf{m}$ is found by solving a system of linear equations:

$$\left(\sum_{\overline{\mathbf{y}} \in S} \mathbf{y}\, \overline{\mathbf{u}}^T \overline{\mathbf{u}}\, \mathbf{y}^T \right) \mathbf{m} = \sum_{\overline{\mathbf{y}} \in S} \mathbf{y}\, \overline{\mathbf{u}}^T \overline{\mathbf{u}} \tag{23}$$

and by inserting it into the inverse of Equation (21):

$$\mathbf{l} = \frac{\mathbf{m}}{f \|\mathbf{m}\|^2} \tag{24}$$

the corresponding $\mathbf{l}$ is produced. A similar method is described in [3] which assumes that the motion field of each segment is a second order function of $\overline{\mathbf{y}}$, but instead of estimating $\mathbf{l}$ given a known camera motion it estimates the parameters of the second order mapping from $\overline{\mathbf{y}}$ to $\overline{\mathbf{v}}$ which can be done without any assumption about the cause of the motion.

A major difficulty with this approach is of course that normally we do not know the segments of the motion field. There are different approaches for finding a set of segments, each having a motion field according to Equation (20) for some $\mathbf{l}$, see [4]. The most common methods are region based, using either the split-and-merge approach or the region growing approach. Both make use of a computation of the residual error ϵ, Equation (22), corresponding to the estimated parameter $\mathbf{l}$. In the first case, the entire motion field constitutes one single initial segment. Each segment is split into smaller segments if its residual error is not small enough and this process is repeated until no more segments split. Then, neighboring segments are merged if their parameters $\mathbf{l}$ are sufficiently close, a process which also continues until no more merging occurs. In the second case, a segment is growing from a seed point by adding new points, normally at its boundary, to the segments if they decrease the residual error. There exist also combinations of the two approaches.

Region based segmentation is normally computationally demanding, which can be explained with the fact that the computations often have to be iterated a large number of times and that they typically include processing of the segments which cannot be implemented as regular operations on image data. Another problem is the fact that the resulting segments are sensitive to noise and to small changes in the image data. In particular, a motion field which has a slow variation in $\mathbf{l}$ will be segmented into a set of homogenous segments, but the boundaries of these segments will to a significant extent depend on the implementation of the chosen method and may change dramatically even for small changes in the image data.

An alternative approach to region based segmentation is finding the boundary points of each segment rather than all the points which constitute the segment. For segmentation of gray valued or color images, this may be a feasible approach with the additional assumption that the gray-value or color is relatively constant within each segment and that it changes relatively abrupt between each segment. However, in the case of motion fields, neither of the two assumptions may be true. The field itself may vary within a segment, even if the parameters, e.g. $\mathbf{l}$, is constant, and the rate of change can be small or large depending on the parameters. The same is true for the transition between two neighboring segments, it is large if the change in $\mathbf{l}$ is large and vice versa. Consequently, boundary based approaches to segmentation of motion fields normally have to be restricted to the cases when we know that the motion field is relatively constant within the field and that the field itself changes relatively much between neighboring segments.

1.1 Thesis of the Paper

In this paper, we will discuss the possibility of describing the motion field without making an explicit segmentation of the field. However, this description is still based on the assumption that the motion field constitutes a set of segments, each having a homogenous field according to Equation (20). The description to be presented has the following characteristic properties:

- It is a local feature, i.e., it describes the motion field in a local region around the point in the image.
- It uses an explicit representation of the motion field $\overline{\mathbf{v}}$ in terms of the geometric shape of planar surfaces in the scene.
- It can both represent the case of a single homogenous field, according to Equation (20), and the boundary between two such field. Also junction points of three different field can be detected.
- Assuming planar surfaces, the boundary points normally correspond to edges between planes, and the junction points correspond to corners.
- At the boundary and junction points, the descriptor represents where in the local region each field has its center of gravity and the corresponding vector $\mathbf{l}$ of the field.
- It uses tensors as the primary tool for constructing the representation.

2 Points and Planes

In this section we will formalize some of the results presented in the previous section. Let $\mathbf{x}$ represent a 3D point and let $\mathbf{l}$ represent a 3D plane such that $\mathbf{x}$ lies in the plane if and only if Equation (18) is satisfied. This relation can be rewritten in a more compact form if we introduce a homogenous representation of $\mathbf{x}$ and $\mathbf{l}$ according to

$$\mathbf{x}_H = \begin{pmatrix} 1 \\ \mathbf{x} \end{pmatrix} \qquad \mathbf{l}^H = \begin{pmatrix} -\|\mathbf{l}\| \\ \hat{\mathbf{l}} \end{pmatrix} \tag{25}$$

where $\hat{\mathbf{l}}$ is the normal vector corresponding to $\mathbf{l} = \|\mathbf{l}\|\,\hat{\mathbf{l}}$. The condition for $\mathbf{x}$ lying in the plane represented by $\mathbf{l}$ can then be written

$$0 = \mathbf{x}^T\hat{\mathbf{l}}\,\|\mathbf{l}\| - \|\mathbf{l}\|^2 = \|\mathbf{l}\|(\mathbf{x}^T\hat{\mathbf{l}} - \|\mathbf{l}\|) = \|\mathbf{l}\|\,\mathbf{x}_H^T\mathbf{l}^H \tag{26}$$

This relation assumes that $\|\mathbf{l}\| \neq 0$, i.e., that the plane does not pass through the origin, which means that we can replace Equation (18) with

$$\mathbf{x}_H^T \mathbf{l}^H = 0 \tag{27}$$

which then is true if and only if $\mathbf{x}$ lies in the plane. However, if the plane passes through the origin, i.e., $\|\mathbf{l}\| = 0$, $\mathbf{l}^H$ is still a well-defined entity except for its sign, given that we chose $\hat{\mathbf{l}}$ as a normal of the plane. Furthermore, in this case and regardless of which sign we choose for $\mathbf{l}^H$, Equation (27) is true if and only if $\mathbf{x}$ lies in the plane. It should be noticed, though, that the possibility of representing also planes which pass through the origin will not be of any practical use to us, and we will in the following assume that $\|\mathbf{l}\| \neq 0$.

A natural consequence of the last result is that we will use $\mathbf{x}_H$ and $\mathbf{l}^H$ for the representation of a point and a line, respectively. Furthermore, if we replace either of $\mathbf{x}_H$ or $\mathbf{l}^H$ in Equation (27) by the same vector multiplied by an arbitrary non-zero scalar, it is still the case that the relation is true if and only if $\mathbf{x}$ lies in the plane. Consequently, $\mathbf{x}_H$ and $\mathbf{l}^H$ can be considered as elements of a projective space. In the following, we will use this fact to derive some useful results. A more thorough treatment of the mathematical foundations for points and other geometrical entities is found in [5] and [6].

3 A Representation of Points

In this section we will develop a representation of the points in the scene. The resulting representation follows the results presented in [7], but here we also show that the representation can be estimated directly from image data.

Let us consider a specific image point $\bar{\mathbf{y}}$ for which we have estimated a corresponding motion vector $\bar{\mathbf{v}}$ corresponding to the motion $\mathbf{w}$ of the camera. To $\bar{\mathbf{y}}$ there is a corresponding 3D point $\mathbf{x}$ in the scene which we assume to lie in a planar surface. The point is represented by $\mathbf{x}_H$ and the surface is represented by $\mathbf{l}^H$, both being elements of a projective space. Since $\mathbf{x}$ is observed through a pin-hole camera and is defined in a coordinate system centered at the camera's focal point, we can assume that $\mathbf{x} \neq \mathbf{0}$. As was mentioned above, we also assume that the plane does not pass trough the origin, i.e., $\mathbf{l} \neq \mathbf{0}$.

Related to the point $\bar{\mathbf{y}}$ we can define a 4×3 matrix $\mathbf{K}$ as

$$\mathbf{K} = \begin{pmatrix} 0 & \bar{\mathbf{u}}\,\mathbf{y}^T \\ -f\,\Delta t & \mathbf{0} \end{pmatrix} \tag{28}$$

where $\bar{\mathbf{u}}$ is a 2D vector defined in Equation (13) which carries information about $\mathbf{w}$ and $\bar{\mathbf{y}}$, $\mathbf{y}$ is the 3D vector defined in Equation (15) which represents the image coordinate $\bar{\mathbf{y}}$, f is the focal distance of the camera, and Δt is the temporal distance between two images in the sequence from which the motion field is estimated. Notice that $\mathbf{K}$ can be fully determined from local measurements on image data and parameters which are known.

We will now define the symmetric 4×4 matrix

$$\mathbf{S}_{20} = \mathbf{K}\,\mathbf{T}\,\mathbf{K}^T \tag{29}$$

Notice that since both $\mathbf{T}$ and $\mathbf{K}$ depend on $\overline{\mathbf{y}}$ and t, so does $\mathbf{S}_{20}$. It then follows from the previous results that $\mathbf{S}_{20}$ can have at most rank one, and that $\mathbf{x}_H$ is an eigenvector of $\mathbf{S}_{20}$ with non-zero eigenvalue or, more precisely,

$$\mathbf{S}_{20} = \xi\, \mathbf{x}_H\, \mathbf{x}_H^T \tag{30}$$

for $\xi \geq 0$.

To prove this property of $\mathbf{S}_{20}$, we need first to construct the 4D vector $\mathbf{x}^H$ as

$$\mathbf{x}^H = \begin{pmatrix} -\|\mathbf{x}\|^2 \\ \mathbf{x} \end{pmatrix} \tag{31}$$

i.e., $\mathbf{x}^H$ is the homogenous representation of the plane which passes through $\mathbf{x}$ with $\mathbf{x}$ as normal vector. We also need two 4D vectors

$$\mathbf{p}_0 = \begin{pmatrix} 0 \\ \mathbf{p} \end{pmatrix} \qquad\qquad \mathbf{q}_0 = \begin{pmatrix} 0 \\ \mathbf{q} \end{pmatrix} \tag{32}$$

where $\mathbf{p}$, $\mathbf{q}$ and $\mathbf{x}$ form an orthogonal set of $3D$ vectors, i.e., neither of $\mathbf{p}$ or $\mathbf{q}$ is the zero vector. Notice that $\mathbf{x}_H$, $\mathbf{x}^H$, $\mathbf{p}_0$ and $\mathbf{q}_0$ form an orthogonal set of 4D vectors.

Given these four vectors, we get

$$\begin{aligned} \mathbf{K}^T\,\mathbf{x}^H &= \begin{pmatrix} \mathbf{0} & \overline{\mathbf{u}}\,\mathbf{y}^T \\ -f\,\Delta t & \mathbf{0} \end{pmatrix} \begin{pmatrix} -\|\mathbf{x}\|^2 \\ \mathbf{x} \end{pmatrix} = \\ &= \begin{pmatrix} \overline{\mathbf{u}}\,\mathbf{y}^T\mathbf{x} \\ f\,\|\mathbf{x}\|^2\,\Delta t \end{pmatrix} = f\,\|\mathbf{x}\|^2 \begin{pmatrix} \overline{\mathbf{v}} \\ \Delta t \end{pmatrix} \end{aligned} \tag{33}$$

where the last identity follows from Equations (13) and (15). From Equation (5) follows then

$$\mathbf{K}^T\,\mathbf{x}^H = f\,\|\mathbf{x}\|^2\,\mathbf{v} \tag{34}$$

and, using Equation (7), we get

$$\mathbf{S}_{20}\,\mathbf{x}^H = \mathbf{K}\,\mathbf{T}\,\mathbf{K}^T\,\mathbf{x}^H = f\,\|\mathbf{x}\|^2\,\mathbf{K}\,\mathbf{T}\,\mathbf{v} = \mathbf{0} \tag{35}$$

i.e., $\mathbf{x}^H$ is an eigenvector of zero eigenvalue relative to $\mathbf{S}_{20}$. This is also the case for $\mathbf{p}_0$, since

$$\begin{aligned} \mathbf{K}^T\mathbf{p}_0 &= \begin{pmatrix} \mathbf{0} & \overline{\mathbf{u}}\,\mathbf{y}^T \\ -f\,\Delta t & \mathbf{0} \end{pmatrix} \begin{pmatrix} 0 \\ \mathbf{p} \end{pmatrix} = \begin{pmatrix} \overline{\mathbf{u}}\,\mathbf{y}^T\mathbf{p} \\ 0 \end{pmatrix} = \\ &= \frac{f}{x_3} \begin{pmatrix} \overline{\mathbf{u}}\,\mathbf{x}^T\mathbf{p} \\ 0 \end{pmatrix} = \frac{f}{x_3} \begin{pmatrix} 0 \\ 0 \end{pmatrix} = \mathbf{0}, \end{aligned} \tag{36}$$

and for $\mathbf{q}_0$ using a similar derivation. We have thus proven that $\mathbf{x}^H$, $\mathbf{p}_0$ and $\mathbf{q}_0$ are all eigenvectors of zero eigenvalue relative to $\mathbf{S}_{20}$, i.e., $\mathbf{S}_{20}$ can have at most rank one.

Since the four vectors form an orthogonal set, it then follows that also $\mathbf{x}_H$ is an eigenvector of $\mathbf{S}_{20}$ with an eigenvalue ξ still to be determined. Hence, we have proven that Equation (30) is true but $\xi \geq 0$ has still to be established.

To find this eigenvalue, consider the expression

$$\mathbf{x}_H^T \mathbf{S}_{20}\, \mathbf{x}_H = \xi\, \|\mathbf{x}_H\|^4 \tag{37}$$

Assuming that $\mathbf{T}$ is estimated according to Equation (6), this can be rewritten

$$\begin{aligned} \xi\, \|\mathbf{x}_H\|^4 &= \mathbf{x}_H^T \mathbf{K}\, \mathbf{T}\, \mathbf{K}^T \mathbf{x}_H = \\ &= \mathbf{x}_H^T \mathbf{K} \,[\sum_{\overline{\mathbf{y}}} W(\overline{\mathbf{y}}) \nabla g\, \nabla^T g]\, \mathbf{K}^T \mathbf{x}_H = \\ &= \sum_{\overline{\mathbf{y}}} W\, |\nabla^T g\, \mathbf{K}^T \mathbf{x}_H|^2 \end{aligned} \tag{38}$$

Under the assumption that W is not negative, this means that ξ cannot be zero unless $\nabla^T g\, \mathbf{K}^T \mathbf{x}_H$ vanishes for all $\overline{\mathbf{y}}$ within the region which we use to compute $\mathbf{T}$ for a certain image point. Consequently, we have to look at

$$\begin{aligned} \nabla^T g\, \mathbf{K}^T \mathbf{x}_H &= \nabla^T g \begin{pmatrix} \mathbf{0} & \overline{\mathbf{u}}\, \mathbf{y}^T \\ -f\, \Delta t & \mathbf{0} \end{pmatrix} \begin{pmatrix} 1 \\ \mathbf{x} \end{pmatrix} = \\ &= \nabla^T g \begin{pmatrix} \overline{\mathbf{u}}\, \mathbf{y}^T \mathbf{x} \\ -f\, \Delta t \end{pmatrix} = \nabla^T g \begin{pmatrix} f\, \overline{\mathbf{v}}\, \|\mathbf{x}\|^2 \\ -f\, \Delta t \end{pmatrix} \end{aligned} \tag{39}$$

where again we have made use of Equations (13) and (15) to obtain the last identity. Now, we can insert the definition of ∇g, Equation (5):

$$\begin{aligned} \nabla^T g\, \mathbf{K}^T \mathbf{x}_H &= f \begin{pmatrix} \frac{\partial g}{\partial y_1} & \frac{\partial g}{\partial y_2} & \frac{\partial g}{\partial t} \end{pmatrix} \begin{pmatrix} v_1\, \|\mathbf{x}\|^2 \\ v_2\, \|\mathbf{x}\|^2 \\ -\Delta t \end{pmatrix} = \\ &= f \left(v_1 \frac{\partial g}{\partial y_1}\, \|\mathbf{x}\|^2 + v_2 \frac{\partial g}{\partial y_2}\, \|\mathbf{x}\|^2 - \Delta t\, \frac{\partial g}{\partial t} \right) = \\ &= -f\, \Delta t\, \frac{\partial g}{\partial t} (1 + \|\mathbf{x}\|^2) \end{aligned} \tag{40}$$

where the last identity follows from Equation (1). We can write this in a more compact form as

$$\nabla^T g\, \mathbf{K}^T \mathbf{x}_H = -f\, \Delta t\, \frac{\partial g}{\partial t} \|\mathbf{x}_H\|^2 \tag{41}$$

By combining this with Equation (38), we get

$$\xi = (f\, \Delta t)^2 \sum_{\overline{\mathbf{y}}} W \left| \frac{\partial g}{\partial t} \right|^2 \tag{42}$$

The conclusion that we can draw from this derivation is that ξ does not vanish by default. It is always non-negative and furthermore positive if the temporal derivatives of the image data is not zero for all points in the region used to compute $\mathbf{T}$. Clearly, this situation occurs if and only if the local region is constant or if the true image velocity $\overline{\mathbf{v}}$ is parallel to all local structures. In these cases, no motion can be estimated at the local level, and the result is also that $\mathbf{S}_{20}$ vanishes.

Before continuing, let us summarize the results of this section. We assume that at image point $\overline{\mathbf{y}}$, a local representation of the image velocity has been estimated in terms of $\mathbf{T}$, Equation (6). Given the focal distance f of the camera and the motion $\mathbf{w}$ of the camera, we can also compute the matrix $\mathbf{K}$, Equation (28), associated with point $\overline{\mathbf{y}}$. Given $\mathbf{T}$ and $\mathbf{K}$, a 4×4 symmetric matrix $\mathbf{S}_{20}$ can then be computed according to Equation (29). It then follows that $\mathbf{S}_{20}$ can be written as Equation (30) where ξ is non-zero unless no local motion can be estimated.

4 A Representation of Planes

The matrix $\mathbf{S}_{20}$ described in the previous section can be described as a "point descriptor" even though it is computed from descriptors which are estimated from neighborhood operations, i.e., $\mathbf{T}$. Next, we will estimate a corresponding descriptor for the representation of the planar surfaces which the points are assumed to lie in. Clearly, this information cannot be derived from a single point and in order to obtain it we need to integrate information from several points in a region.

Let us begin by revisiting Equation (18). This relation can be interpreted as: given a point $\mathbf{x}$ which we represent by $\mathbf{x}_H$, any vector which is perpendicular to $\mathbf{x}_H$ can be seen as a representation of a plane which passes through $\mathbf{x}$. A consequence of this observation is that the null space of $\mathbf{S}_{20}$, Equation (30), consists of the homogeneous representations of all planes which passes through the point $\mathbf{x}_H$.

Next, we compute a weighted average of $\mathbf{S}_{20}$ in a local region around a point $\overline{\mathbf{y}}$:

$$\mathbf{S}'_{20} = \sum_{\overline{\mathbf{y}}} W(\overline{\mathbf{y}})\, \mathbf{S}_{20}(\overline{\mathbf{y}}) \tag{43}$$

where $W \geq 0$. The main result of the last section is that we can rewrite this as

$$\mathbf{S}'_{20} = \sum_{\overline{\mathbf{y}}} W(\overline{\mathbf{y}})\, \xi(\mathbf{y})\, \mathbf{x}_H(\mathbf{y})\, \mathbf{x}_H(\mathbf{y})^T \tag{44}$$

which implies that the null space of $\mathbf{S}'_{20}$ contains the homogeneous representations $\mathbf{l}^H$ of planes that pass trough *all* of the points $\mathbf{x}_H$ in the region.

Depending on the features of the local image data around the point $\overline{\mathbf{y}}$, the resulting matrix $\mathbf{S}'_{20}$ can therefore have the following characteristics:

- If the region only contains one single point, then $\mathbf{S}'_{20}$ has rank one, according to Equation (30).
- If the region contains points on a single line, then $\mathbf{S}'_{20}$ has rank two. The null space of $\mathbf{S}_{20}$ contains all planes $\mathbf{l}^H$ which contain the line.

- If the region contains points which all lie on a single plane, then $\mathbf{S}'_{20}$ has rank three. The null space is one-dimensional and is spanned by $\mathbf{l}^H$, the projective element which represents the plane.
- If the region contains points which do not all lie on a plane, then $\mathbf{S}'_{20}$ has rank four (full rank). The null space is trivial and no information about the local 3D structure in terms of planes can be inferred.

In the following, we will focus on the third case. By analyzing the rank of $\mathbf{S}'_{20}$ by computing its eigenvalues or characteristic polynomial, the image points $\overline{\mathbf{y}}$ which have a corresponding $\mathbf{S}'_{20}$ of rank three can be filtered out, or a measure of confidence on $\mathbf{S}'_{20}$ having rank three can be estimated. In points of high confidence for rank three, we want to estimate the corresponding plane, i.e., the corresponding vector $\mathbf{l}^H$. This can be done by finding an eigenvector $\mathbf{S}'_{20}$ of zero eigenvalue given that the eigensystem of $\mathbf{S}'_{20}$ has been computed. Here we will instead use an indirect method based on an operation called rank complement. The basic idea is to form a new symmetric matrix where the range and null space are interchanged relative to $\mathbf{S}'_{20}$. For the case of symmetric matrices, the two matrices have a common set of eigenvectors but non-zero eigenvalues are mapped to zero and zero eigenvalues are mapped to non-zero values.

In [8], it is shown that for each size of the matrix and for each rank of that matrix, there is a specific polynomial function which maps the matrix to another matrix such that they are each others rank complement. For all $\mathbf{S}'_{20}$ labelled as "rank three", the corresponding rank complement polynomial is applied to produce

$$\mathbf{S}_{02} = R_{3,1}(\mathbf{S}'_{20}) = \gamma\, \mathbf{l}^H (\mathbf{l}^H)^T, \tag{45}$$

where $R_{m,n}$ is the rank complement from rank m to rank n. The symmetric 4×4 matrix $\mathbf{S}_{02}$ then carries a representation of the planar surface which all points in the region lie in.

5 A Representation of Points and Planes

At each point in the image we can now estimate the matrix $\mathbf{S}_{20}$, which describes the position of the corresponding point in the scene, and the matrix $\mathbf{S}_{02}$ which represents the plane that the point lies in. What we will do next is to combine these two representations into a single representation of both position and plane parameters.

Furthermore, both descriptors can be seen as elements of projective spaces since multiplication by non-zero scalars do not change their information content, at least in relation to other descriptors scaled in the same way.

Let $\mathbf{S}_{20}(\overline{\mathbf{y}})$ and $\mathbf{S}_{02}(\overline{\mathbf{y}})$ be the descriptors of scene position $\mathbf{x}$ and plane parameters $\mathbf{l}$ which are estimated at image position $\overline{\mathbf{y}}$. To begin with, both descriptors are symmetric 4×4 matrices and, consequently, we can see them as elements of a 10-dimensional vector space.

As such, we can take the outer product between them to construct a 10×10 matrix:

$$\mathbf{S}_{22} = \mathbf{S}_{20}\, \mathbf{S}_{02}^T \tag{46}$$

At this point it is not obvious why this construction is of any use. If $\mathbf{S}_{20}$ and $\mathbf{S}_{02}$ previously where available as separate entities, their combination into $\mathbf{S}_{22}$ is such that we can still extract them by means of operations which perhaps are straightforward but still unnecessary.

To see the potential of $\mathbf{S}_{22}$, let us integrate it over a local region around a point $\bar{\mathbf{y}}$ in the image together with a weighting function A:

$$\begin{aligned} \mathbf{S}'_{22} &= \sum_{\bar{\mathbf{y}}} A(\bar{\mathbf{y}})\, \mathbf{S}_{22}(\bar{\mathbf{y}}) = \\ &= \sum_{\bar{\mathbf{y}}} A(\bar{\mathbf{y}})\, \mathbf{S}_{20}(\bar{\mathbf{y}})\, \mathbf{S}_{02}^T(\bar{\mathbf{y}}) \end{aligned} \tag{47}$$

We will then make the following assumption:

- The local region contains N planar surfaces, each being represented by the homogenous vector $\mathbf{l}_k^H$ where $k = 1, \ldots, N$.

A consequence of this assumption is that all points $\bar{\mathbf{y}}$ which belong to the same segment of the region, i.e., belong to the same planar surface, will have the same value for $\mathbf{S}_{02}$, with the exception that its norm may change. Consequently, the summation over $\bar{\mathbf{y}}$ in Equation (47) can be replaced with a summation over the N segments, according to

$$\mathbf{S}'_{22} = \sum_{k=1}^{N} \mathbf{S}'_{20,k}\, \mathbf{S}_{02,k}^T \tag{48}$$

In this expression

$$\mathbf{S}'_{20,k} = \sum_{\bar{\mathbf{y}} \in \Gamma_k} A'(\bar{\mathbf{y}})\, \mathbf{S}_{20}(\bar{\mathbf{y}}) \tag{49}$$

where Γ_k is the set of image points belonging to segment k and A' is the weighting function modified with the variation in the norm of $\mathbf{S}_{02}$, and $\mathbf{S}_{02,k}$ is the 10-dimensional vector version of the 4×4 matrix

$$\mathbf{l}_k^H\, (\mathbf{l}_k^H)^T \tag{50}$$

The expression for $\mathbf{S}'_{22}$ in Equation (48) is interesting since it implies that each planar segment found in the region contributes with a term $\mathbf{S}'_{20,k}\, \mathbf{S}_{02,k}^T$ which, in turn, suggests that the rank of $\mathbf{S}'_{22}$ is related to the number of segments. In [9] this is shown to indeed be the case, at least if the number of segments is three or less. It is also shown that for the case of one, two and three segments, it is possible to analyze $\mathbf{S}'_{22}$ in order to obtain the corresponding values for $\mathbf{S}'_{20,k}$ and $\mathbf{S}_{02,k}$. The method is based on making a Singular Value Decomposition (SVD) of the 10×10 matrix $\mathbf{S}'_{22}$, but since $\mathbf{S}_{02,k}$ are not orthogonal for different segments we need to apply specific operations in order to extract corresponding pairs of $\mathbf{S}'_{20,k}$ and $\mathbf{S}_{02,k}$. For each such pair, $\mathbf{S}_{02,k}$ is given as in Equation (50) and from Equations (30) and (49) it follows that $\mathbf{S}'_{20,k}$ can be written

$$\mathbf{S}'_{20,k} = a \begin{pmatrix} 1 & \mathbf{x}_{c,k}^T \\ \mathbf{x}_{c,k} & \mathbf{C}_k + \mathbf{x}_{c,k}\mathbf{x}_{c,k}^T \end{pmatrix} \tag{51}$$

where $\mathbf{x}_{c,k}$ is the weighted mean of all 3D points corresponding to the image points of segment k. The weighting is made with a combination of the function A and the norm of $\mathbf{S}_{02}$. The 3×3 matrix $\mathbf{C}$ is the corresponding weighted covariance, which describes how the 3D points are distributed in space around the mean.

Let us summarize the discussion to this point before looking at some experiments. At each point $\bar{\mathbf{y}}$ in the image, we can compute a 10×10 matrix $\mathbf{S}'_{22}$ according to Equation (47), a weighted mean of the outer product between $\mathbf{S}_{20}$ and $\mathbf{S}_{02}$. Both of these are 10-dimensional vectors which are formed by reshaping the two symmetric 4×4 matrices $\mathbf{S}_{20}$ and $\mathbf{S}_{02}$ given by Equations (29) and (45), respectively. This implies that the matrix $\mathbf{S}_{20}$ is formed by just multiplying the spatio-temporal orientation tensor $\mathbf{T}$ at point $\bar{\mathbf{y}}$ with a 4×3 matrix $\mathbf{K}$ which both contains information about the position in the image and the camera motion. Furthermore, the matrix $\mathbf{S}_{02}$ is formed by taking the proper rank complement of a local average of $\mathbf{S}_{20}$.

Once $\mathbf{S}'_{22}$ has been computed, it can be analyzed in terms of rank. If the number of planar segments in the region which has been used for computing $\mathbf{S}'_{22}$ is three or less, the rank of this matrix is the same as the number of segments, and there is a procedure for extracting, for each segment, both the corresponding vector $\mathbf{l}^H$ and the local statistics of the 3D positions of all points on the planar segment up to second order.

It should be noted that the descriptor $\mathbf{S}'_{22}$ holds $10 \cdot 10 = 100$ elements, which may seem a bit unmanageable. However, each such matrix has to be computed from a relatively large region in the image, since it uses three region based operations in succession, the computation of $\mathbf{T}$, local average of $\mathbf{S}_{20}$, and local average of $\mathbf{S}_{22}$. Consequently, it will contain information which can be subsampled in both image coordinates with a factor which is in the order of 10 in each direction, and the resulting field of matrices $\mathbf{S}'_{22}$ therefore corresponds to a reasonable data volume.

6 Estimation and Results

In this section we will describe a practical implementation for estimation of the tensor $\mathbf{S}'_{22}$, based on the previous presentation, and illustrate some of results obtained by applying the method on synthetic data. A synthetic image sequence has been chosen in order to be able to demonstrate the performance of the method.

Starting from a sequence of images, illustrated in Figure 1, where a camera of known focal length is moving with a known velocity $\mathbf{w}$ relative to a known object, we estimate a structure tensor $\mathbf{T}$ using the method described in [3]. The choice of estimation method for $\mathbf{T}$ does not seem to be important, in particular if the structure tensor field also is averaged in small spatio-temporal neighborhoods before being used. A certainty measure that regards structure tensors of small norm as noise is then computed. This certainty measure is then used throughout the procedure and is the reason for all the missing data in the following figures.

At each image point $\bar{\mathbf{y}}$ we can then compute the corresponding matrices $\mathbf{K}$ and $\mathbf{S}_{20}$ according to Equations (28) and (29). Since $\mathbf{S}_{20}$ is a matrix of at most rank one, Equation (30), it can easily be analyzed to find the corresponding 3D point $\mathbf{x}$. However, the result of this operation is to a significant degree dependent on the accuracy related to the camera motion $\mathbf{w}$ and the correctness of the pin-hole model of the camera. If any of these assumptions are wrong the geometrical distribution of points in the scene will become distorted. Figure 2 shows the 3D points estimated from $\mathbf{S}_{20}$ which all seem to lie on the correct surfaces.

Before further processing, the matrix $\mathbf{S}_{20}$ will be modified by the process of *channel smoothing*. This operation, which is applied to the vector $\mathbf{x}$ extracted from $\mathbf{S}_{20}$, both performs a local averaging of the position to reduce any noise introduced by the measurements, and removes outliers. The channel smoothing operation is presented in more detail in [1, 10].

Given the value of $\mathbf{x}$ regularized by channel smoothing, we construct the tensor $\mathbf{S}'_{20}$ as

$$\mathbf{S}'_{20} = \sum_{\overline{\mathbf{y}}} W(\overline{\mathbf{y}})\, \mathbf{x}_H(\overline{\mathbf{y}})\, \mathbf{x}_H^T(\overline{\mathbf{y}}) \tag{52}$$

where $W(\overline{\mathbf{y}})$ is the weighting function described in Equation (43) and $\mathbf{x}_H(\overline{\mathbf{y}})$ is the homogenous representation of $\mathbf{x}$ at image point $\overline{\mathbf{y}}$. The tensor $\mathbf{S}'_{20}$ will then have the structure described in Equation (51) from which a center of gravity $\mathbf{x}_c$ and covariance $\mathbf{C}$ around $\mathbf{x}_c$ can be extracted. Notice that the rank of $\mathbf{C}$ is always one less than that of $\mathbf{S}'_{20}$.

The underlying assumption is that the 3D points in the local region used to construct $\mathbf{S}'_{20}$ are lying on a plane, which implies that the corresponding $\mathbf{C}$ has rank two (or $\mathbf{S}'_{20}$ has rank three). In order to analyze the rank of $\mathbf{C}$, we can compute its SVD, which gives the singular values $\sigma_1 \geq \sigma_2 \geq \sigma_3$. From these, we then compute the following three parameters

$$c_1 = \frac{9\,d - 4\,q\,t + t^3}{3\,d - 3\,q\,t + t^3} \qquad c_2 = \frac{-9\,d + q\,t}{3\,d - 3\,q\,t + t^3}$$

$$c_3 = \frac{3\,d}{3\,d - 3\,q\,t + t^3}$$

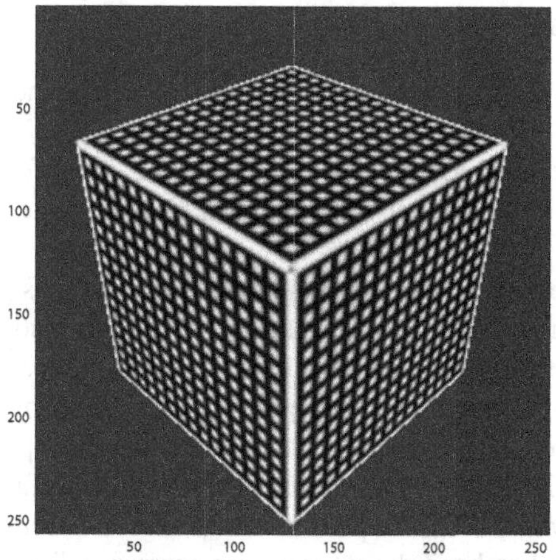

Fig. 1. Mid-image of generated sequence

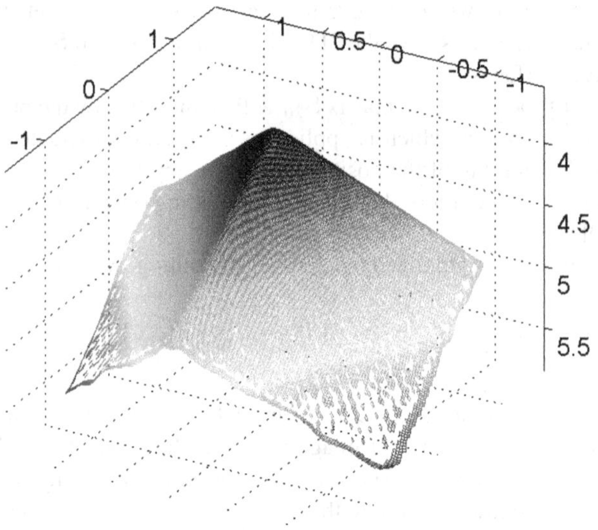

Fig. 2. Depth from point estimate of S_{20}

where

$$t = \sigma_1 + \sigma_2 + \sigma_3 \qquad d = \sigma_1\,\sigma_2\,\sigma_3$$
$$q = \sigma_1\,\sigma_2 + \sigma_2\,\sigma_3 + \sigma_3\,\sigma_1$$

Notice that $c_1 + c_2 + c_3 = 1$ and that

- $c_1 = 1, c_2 = 0, c_3 = 0$ if $\sigma_2 = \sigma_3 = 0$.
- $c_1 = 0, c_2 = 1, c_3 = 0$ if $\sigma_1 = \sigma_2$ and $\sigma_3 = 0$.
- $c_1 = 0, c_2 = 0, c_3 = 1$ if $\sigma_1 = \sigma_2 = \sigma_3$.

which means that c_k can be used as a measure of confidence of rank k. Figure 3 illustrates the rank of $\mathbf{S}'_{20}$, where green points indicate that c_2 is the largest, i.e., rank three, and blue points indicate that c_3 is the largest, i.e., rank four. The latter case happens in regions close to edges between different planar segments, as indicated in the figure.

A further test of the correctness of the estimated data in $\mathbf{S}'_{20}$ is to consider the position and orientation information which it contains relative to the estimated depth map or to the ground truth. In image points for which $\mathbf{S}'_{20}$ has rank three, i.e., which corresponds to a single planar segment, the null space of $\mathbf{S}'_{20}$ is spanned by $\mathbf{l}^H$ which describes a 3D plane both in terms of position and orientation. For image points where the rank of $\mathbf{S}'_{20}$ is three we can thus obtain both a position $\mathbf{x}_c$ and a surface normal. Figure 4(a) illustrates this information for some points in the image, i.e., for each such image point, a normal given by $\mathbf{l}^H$ has been drawn from the corresponding center of gravity. This

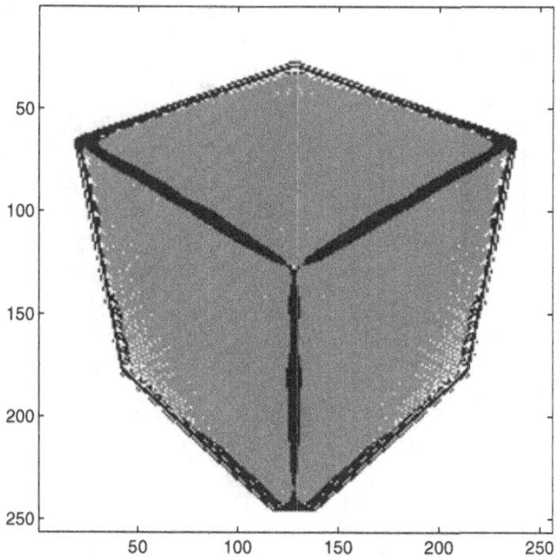

Fig. 3. Rank of the $\mathbf{S}'_{20}$ tensor. Green is rank three and blue is rank four.

image also shows the set of points $\mathbf{x}$ which are plotted in Figure 2. The normals can also be drawn in the synthetic 3D model which is used for generating the image sequence, as seen in Figure 4(b).

The next step is then to compute the rank complement, going from rank three to rank one, which gives us $\mathbf{S}_{02}$ for this point in the image. This means that we have both a $\mathbf{S}_{20}$ and $\mathbf{S}_{02}$ for each image point, from which the tensor $\mathbf{S}'_{22}$ can be computed according to Equation (47), but with the additional weighting of certainty for rank three of $\mathbf{S}'_{20}$:

$$\mathbf{S}'_{22} = \sum_{\overline{\mathbf{y}}} A(\overline{\mathbf{y}})\, c_2(\overline{\mathbf{y}})\, \mathbf{S}_{20}(\overline{\mathbf{y}})\, \mathbf{S}^T_{02}(\overline{\mathbf{y}}) \tag{53}$$

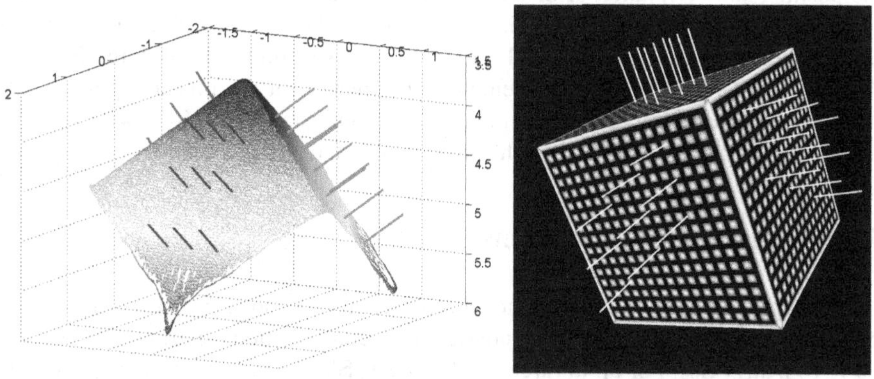

(a) Estimated depth data *(b)* Synthetic data

Fig. 4. Selected normals to x_H set

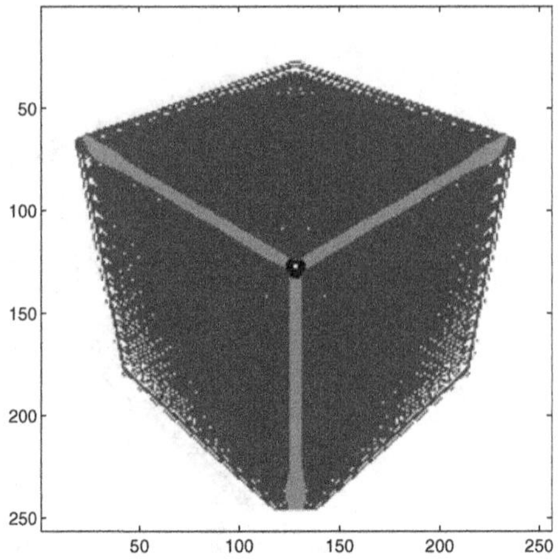

Fig. 5. Rank of S_{22} tensor

The $\mathbf{S}'_{22}$ tensor, which can be estimated at an arbitrary image point according to the above procedure, can now be analyzed in terms of how many planar surfaces it contains and also to extract their positions and orientations. For up to three surfaces, the rank of the matrix $\mathbf{S}'_{22}$ is the same as the number of surfaces, which implies that we want some measure of confidence for each of the three cases of rank. This can of course be done by first computing an SVD of $\mathbf{S}'_{22}$, giving the three largest singular values $\sigma_1 \geq \sigma_2 \geq \sigma_3$, which then are plugged into the same computations as above for the three measures of rank confidence c_k. Figure 5 illustrates the result of this operation, where red indicates rank one, green indicates rank two, and blue indicates rank three. As seen, local regions which only contain a single planar surface are red, close to edges between two surfaces we get green points, and at the corner where three surfaces meet we get blue points.

Finally, at points close to edges or corners we can decompose $\mathbf{S}'_{22}$ in order to obtain the position and orientation of the two or three planar surfaces which are represented in the descriptor. This is illustrated in Figures 6(a) and 6(b), where a few image points corresponding to rank two $\mathbf{S}'_{22}$ and one point corresponding to rank three $\mathbf{S}'_{22}$ have been analyzed for position and orientation information of the planar segments. The position and orientation of each segment is indicated using a red circle with a normal line overlayed on the depth data or the ground truth data.

7 Summary and Conclusions

In this paper we have presented a novel representation of local 3D shape in terms of planar surface patches and their boundaries. The representation can be constructed as a 10×10 matrix $\mathbf{S}'_{22}$. For up to three local patches, $\mathbf{S}'_{22}$ contains information about the number of patches and their relative position and orientation. This information can be extracted by making an SVD of $\mathbf{S}'_{22}$ and analyzing the resulting factors. In particular, the rank of $\mathbf{S}'_{22}$ is the same as the number of patches.

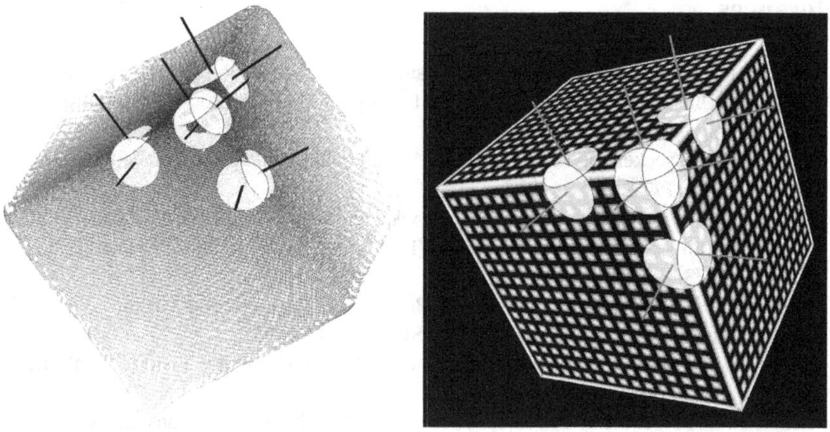

(a) Estimated depth data *(b)* Synthetic data

Fig. 6. Normals extracted from S_{22}

Given a calibrated camera which translates with a known linear motion, the proposed representation can be estimated from the corresponding motion field. In this paper one method is presented which is based on first computing spatio-temporal orientation tensors $\mathbf{T}$ from the image sequence and mapping these into $\mathbf{S}'_{22}$ by means of the following computation steps at each point in the image:

1. Form $\mathbf{S}_{20} = \mathbf{K}\,\mathbf{T}\,\mathbf{K}^T$
2. Form $\mathbf{S}'_{20}$ = local average of $\mathbf{S}_{20}$
3. Form $\mathbf{S}_{02}$ as the rank complement of $\mathbf{S}'_{20}$
4. Form $\mathbf{S}_{22} = \mathbf{S}_{20}\,\mathbf{S}_{02}^T$
5. Form $\mathbf{S}'_{22}$ = local average of $\mathbf{S}_{22}$

Here, $\mathbf{K}$ is a 4×3 matrix which contains formation about the camera parameters, the camera motion, and the position in the image where we want to estimate $\mathbf{S}_{22}$, Equation (28).

It should be emphasized that the method for estimating $\mathbf{S}'_{22}$ presented here requires that the local spatio-temporal orientation represented by $\mathbf{T}$ can provide an accurate measure of the local image velocity by means of Equation (7). In general, this may not be the case if the scene depicted by the camera contains surface patches of which some are relatively close and others are distant. By choosing the estimation of $\mathbf{T}$ appropriately, we can estimate $\mathbf{v}$ with high accuracy either for small or high velocities, but it is difficult to get good accuracy in both cases.

Since $\mathbf{S}_{22}$ is the outer product of $\mathbf{S}_{20}$ and $\mathbf{S}_{02}$ and these two elements are second order tensors, it follows that formally we can regard $\mathbf{S}_{22}$, and therefore also $\mathbf{S}'_{22}$ as fourth order tensors defined on a projective space. Furthermore, $\mathbf{S}_{22}$ is constructed out of two factors, where $\mathbf{S}_{20}$ describes *where* in the scene a particular surface patch is located, and $\mathbf{S}_{02}$ describes *what* surface it is in terms of orientation.

References

1. Forssén, P.E.: Low and Medium Level Vision using Channel Representations. PhD thesis, Linköping University, Sweden, SE-581 83 Linköping, Sweden (2004) Dissertation No. 858, ISBN 91-7373-876-X.
2. Jähne, B., Haussecker, H., eds.: Computer Vision and Applications. Academic Press (2000) ISBN 0-12-379777-2.
3. Farnebäck, G.: Polynomial Expansion for Orientation and Motion Estimation. PhD thesis, Linköping University, Sweden, SE-581 83 Linköping, Sweden (2002) Dissertation No 790, ISBN 91-7373-475-6.
4. Sonka, M., Hlavac, V., Boyle, R.: Image Processing, Analysis, and Machine Vision. International Thomson Publishing Inc. (1999) ISBN 0-534-95393-X.
5. Hartley, R., Zisserman, A.: Multiple View Geometry in Computer Vision. Cambridge University Press (2000)
6. Triggs, B.: The geometry of projective reconstruction I: Matching constraints and the joint image. In: Proc. International Conference on Computer Vision. (1995) 338–343
7. Seitz, S.M., Anandan, P.: Implicit representation and scene reconstruction from probability density functions. In: Proc. Computer Vision and Pattern Recognition Conf. (1999) 28–34
8. Nordberg, K., Farnebäck, G.: Rank complement of diagonalizable matrices using polynomial functions. Report LiTH-ISY-R-2369, Dept. EE, Linköping University, SE-581 83 Linköping, Sweden (2001)
9. Nordberg, K.: A fourth order tensor for representation of orientation and position of oriented segments. Technical Report LiTH-ISY-R-2587, Dept. EE, Linköping University, SE-581 83 Linköping, Sweden (2004)
10. Michael Felsberg, Per-Erik Forssén, and Hanno Scharr, "Efficient robust smoothing of low-level signal features," Tech. Rep. LiTH-ISY-R-2619, Dept. EE, Linköping University, SE-581 83 Linköping, Sweden, August 2004.

A Probabilistic Formulation of Image Registration

Christoph Strecha, Rik Fransens, and Luc Van Gool

Katholieke Universiteit Leuven, Belgium
firstname.surname@esat.kuleuven.ac.be
http://www.esat.kuleuven.ac.be/psi/visics

Abstract. This paper deals with the computation of dense image correspondences and the detection of occlusion. We propose a Bayesian approach to the image registration problem. The images are regarded as noisy measurements of an underlying 'true' image-function. Additionally, the image data is considered incomplete, in the sense that we do not know which pixels from a particular image are occluded in the other images. We describe an EM-algorithm, which iterates between estimating values for all hidden quantities, and optimizing the optical flow by differential techniques. The Bayesian way of describing the problem leads to more insight in existing differential approaches, and offers some natural extensions to them. The resulting system involves less parameters and gives an interpretation to the remaining ones. An important feature is the photometric detection of occluded pixels.

1 Introduction

A fundamental problem in the processing of image sequences is the computation of optical flow. Optical flow is caused by the time-varying projection of objects onto a possibly moving image plane. It is therefore the most general transformation, assigning a two dimensional displacement vector to every pixel. The number of unknown parameters is twice the number of pixels in the image. In the case when one knows more about the specific registration problem, the degrees of freedom can be reduced. Knowing the cameras and assuming rigid scenes lead to the constrained stereo or multi-view stereo situation. In specific application one could decrease the number of parameters that describe the optical flow at each pixel and use spline, homography, affine models or models obtained from a principal component analysis.

In this paper we want to give a probabilistic recipe for general image matching which can be used in case the flow fields can be described parametrically, as well as in the most general case of optical flow. We formulate the correspondence problem in a probabilistic framework. This results in an EM algorithm, whose maximization step involves diffusion equations similar to existing differential optical flow approaches [3,4,5,6,7].

However, the probabilistic description now gives an interpretation to the most important parameter (λ) which controls the balancing between image matching and flow field smoothness. The formulation leads naturally to the detection of occlusions based on the image values themself, which prevents the computation of the two (forward-backward) optical flow fields. A similar strategy for the occlusion detection was used by Aach *et al.* [8] for the stereo case. Our algorithm needs no additional parameters for detecting

B. Jähne et al. (Eds.): IWCM 2004, LNCS 3417, pp. 165–176, 2007.

occlusions, and the relative contribution of the spectral components to the matching term is handled automatically. With respect to our previous work [9] in this paper we continue the discussion about optical flow priors and use a more sophisticated color model. This allows to a certain extend to deal with differences in camera responses.

This paper is organized as follows. We proceed in section 2 with the explanation of the image formation model and the associated probabilistic formalism. Both parametric and non-parametric optical flow are dealt with and described in a single framework. Section 3 describes an EM-based solution to the resulting energy. We discuss the implications of the probabilistic view and compare our algorithm with other approaches. Experiments on ground truth and real data are discussed in section 4.

2 Image Formation Model

Suppose we are given two $n \times m$ images $\mathcal{I}_1$ and $\mathcal{I}_2$ which associate a 2D-coordinate $\mathbf{x}$ with an image value $\mathcal{I}_i(\mathbf{x})$. If we are dealing with color images, this value is a 3-vector and for intensity images it is a scalar. [1] Our goal is to estimate a displacement field $\mathcal{F}$, parametrised by a parameter vector ϕ, which maps positions $\mathbf{x}_1$ in $\mathcal{I}_1$ onto corresponding positions $\mathbf{x}_2$ in $\mathcal{I}_2$:

$$\mathcal{F} : \mathcal{R}^2 \rightarrow \mathcal{R}^2 : \mathbf{x}_1 \rightarrow \mathbf{x}_2 = \mathcal{F}(\mathbf{x}_1; \phi) \tag{1}$$

The most general expression of this displacement field is a two component optical flow field, which allows unconstrained correspondences between both images:

$$\mathcal{F} : \mathcal{R}^2 \rightarrow \mathcal{R}^2 : \begin{bmatrix} x_1 \\ y_1 \end{bmatrix} \rightarrow \begin{bmatrix} x_2 \\ y_2 \end{bmatrix} = \begin{bmatrix} x_1 + u(x_1, y_1) \\ y_1 + v(x_1, y_1) \end{bmatrix}, \tag{2}$$

where $u()$ and $v()$ are the X and Y-components of the flow field, respectively. In the remainder of this paper, we will call this type of flow field *non-parametric optical flow*. The nr. of DOF of the flow field is $2nm$ (twice the number of pixels in the images) and the parameter vector ϕ contains all X and Y-components of the flow field:$\phi = [u(1,1), v(1,1), u(1,2), v(1,2), ...u(n,m), v(n,m)]^T$.

Sometimes, both images display objects of the same object class (e.g. faces, cars,...) and the optical flow field can be constrained to be a linear combination of prototypical flow fields which are derived as the principal components of example flows. The displacement field is defined as:

$$\mathcal{F} : \mathcal{R}^2 \rightarrow \mathcal{R}^2 : \begin{bmatrix} x_1 \\ y_1 \end{bmatrix} \rightarrow \begin{bmatrix} x_2 \\ y_2 \end{bmatrix} = \begin{bmatrix} x_1 + \langle u(x_1, y_1) \rangle + \sum_i \phi_i u_i(x_1, y_1) \\ y_1 + \langle v(x_1, y_1) \rangle + \sum_i \phi_i v_i(x_1, y_1) \end{bmatrix}, \tag{3}$$

where $\langle u(x_1, y_1) \rangle$ and $\langle v(x_1, y_1) \rangle$ are the average flow field components and $u_i(x_1, y_1)$ and $v_i(x_1, y_1)$ are the ith principal component of the flow field. The parameter vector ϕ now consists of the linear coefficients ϕ_i of the motion model, and the number of parameters is much less than $2nm$. Alternatively, sometimes one would also like to use

[1] In fact one could add other features such as filter responses to the image [7]. We continue the discussion for general n-band images.

simpler parametrical models for displacement such as translational, affine, homographic, etc... motion. In this case, the displacement field is defined as:

$$\mathcal{F} : \mathcal{R}^2 \rightarrow \mathcal{R}^2 : \begin{bmatrix} x_1 \\ y_1 \end{bmatrix} \rightarrow \begin{bmatrix} x_2 \\ y_2 \end{bmatrix} = \begin{bmatrix} u(x_1, y_1, \phi) \\ v(x_1, y_1, \phi) \end{bmatrix}, \tag{4}$$

where ϕ contains the particular set of coefficients that parametrise the motion model. We will refer to both the linear principal component motion model and the parametric motion models as *parametric optical flow*. Note that both parametric and non-parametric flow are denoted by $\mathcal{F}(\mathbf{x}; \phi)$, where the content of the parameter vector depends on the type of model employed. With this joint notation, we wish to emphasise that both types of optical flow are essentially the same. Furtheron, it will be shown that this joint treatment can be maintained at the procedural level.

Faithful to the Bayesian philosophy, we regard the input images as noisy measurements of an unknown ideal image $\mathcal{I}_1^*$. This allows us to write:

$$\begin{aligned} \mathcal{I}_1(\mathbf{x}) &= \mathcal{I}_1^*(\mathbf{x}) + \epsilon \\ \mathcal{C}\big(\mathcal{I}_2(\mathcal{F}(\mathbf{x}; \phi))\big) &= \mathcal{I}_1^*(\mathbf{x}) + \epsilon \,; \epsilon \sim \mathcal{N}(\mathbf{0}, \mathbf{\Sigma}). \end{aligned} \tag{5}$$

where $\mathcal{N}$ is a zero-mean normal noise distribution with covariance matrix $\mathbf{\Sigma}$. The model includes a color transformation $\mathcal{C}$, which takes into account different camera responses for image $\mathcal{I}_1$ and $\mathcal{I}_2$. We use an affine color transformation defined by:

$$\mathcal{C} : \mathcal{R}^d \rightarrow \mathcal{R}^d : \mathcal{I}(\mathbf{x}) \rightarrow S\, \mathcal{I}(\mathbf{x}) + \mathbf{o}, \tag{6}$$

where S is a $d \times d$ scaling matrix and $\mathbf{o}$ is a d-dimensional offset vector. The image formation model assumes that (*i*) all objects in the scene are perfect diffuse reflectors, (*ii*) the difference in camera response can be modeled by an affine color transformation, and (*iii*) the absense of pixel discretisation effects. The noise component captures all deviations from these assumptions. The ideal image $\mathcal{I}_1^*$, the noise covariance matrix $\mathbf{\Sigma}$ and color transformation parameters S and $\mathbf{o}$ are unknown, and their estimation becomes part of the optimization procedure.

A major complication, especially when dealing with large displacements, is the occlusion problem. This arises from the fact that not all parts of the scene, which are visible in the first image, are also visible in the second image due to geometrical occlusion. When computing image correspondences, such occluded regions should be identified and excluded from the matching procedure. This will be modeled by introducing a visibility map $\mathcal{V}(\mathbf{x})$, which signal whether a scene point X that projects onto $\mathbf{x}$ in $\mathcal{I}_1$ is also visible in image $\mathcal{I}_2$ or not. Every element of $\mathcal{V}(\mathbf{x})$ is a binary random variable which is either 1 or 0, corresponding to visibility or occlusion, respectively. $\mathcal{V}(\mathbf{x})$ is a hidden variable, and its value must be inferred from the input images.

Estimating the optical flow field $\mathcal{F}(\mathbf{x}; \phi)$ can now be formally stated as finding those parameters ϕ which make the image correspondences $\mathcal{I}_1^*(\mathbf{x}) \Leftrightarrow \mathcal{C}\big(\mathcal{I}_2(\mathcal{F}(\mathbf{x}; \phi))\big)$, restricted to those pixels for which $\mathcal{V}(\mathbf{x}) = 1$, most probable. We have restricted ourselves to an image registration scenario involving two images. The case of N images has been discussed in previous work on multi-view stereo and superresolution [10, 11].

2.1 MAP Estimation

We are now facing the hard problem of estimating the quantities $\boldsymbol{\theta} = \{\phi, \mathcal{I}_1^*, \boldsymbol{\Sigma}, S, \mathbf{o}\}$ given input images $\mathcal{I}_1$ and $\mathcal{I}_2$. Furthermore, we have introduced the unobservable or hidden variables $\mathcal{V}$, which must also be inferred over the course of the optimization. In a Bayesian framework, the optimal value for $\boldsymbol{\theta}$ is the one that maximizes the posterior probability $p(\boldsymbol{\theta}|\mathcal{I}_1, \mathcal{I}_2)$. According to Bayes' rule, this posterior can be written as:

$$p(\boldsymbol{\theta}\,|\,\mathcal{I}_1, \mathcal{I}_2) = \frac{\int p(\mathcal{I}_1, \mathcal{I}_2\,|\,\boldsymbol{\theta}, \mathcal{V}) p(\boldsymbol{\theta}\,|\,\mathcal{V}) p(\mathcal{V}) d\mathcal{V}}{p(\mathcal{I}_1, \mathcal{I}_2)}, \tag{7}$$

where we have conditioned the data likelihood and the prior on the hidden variables $\mathcal{V}$. The denominator or 'evidence' is merely the integral of the numerator over all possible values of $\boldsymbol{\theta}$ and can be ignored in the maximization problem. Hence, we will try to optimize the numerator only. In order to find the most probable value for $\boldsymbol{\theta}$, we need to integrate over all possible values of $\mathcal{V}$ which is computationally intractable. Instead, we assume that the probability density function (PDF) of $\mathcal{V}$ is peaked about a single value, i.e. $p(\mathcal{V})$ is a Dirac-function centered at this value. This leads to an Estimation-Maximization (EM) based solution, which iterates between (*i*) estimating values for $\mathcal{V}$, given the current estimate of $\boldsymbol{\theta}$, and (*ii*) maximizing the posterior probability of $\boldsymbol{\theta}$, given the current estimate of $\mathcal{V}$. A more detailed description of this procedure will be given later. So, given a current estimate $\hat{\mathcal{V}}$ for the hidden variables, we want to optimize:

$$q(\boldsymbol{\theta}\,|\,\mathcal{I}_1, \mathcal{I}_2) = p(\mathcal{I}_1, \mathcal{I}_2\,|\,\boldsymbol{\theta}, \hat{\mathcal{V}}) p(\boldsymbol{\theta}\,|\,\hat{\mathcal{V}}) \tag{8}$$

The a-posteriori probability of $\boldsymbol{\theta}$ is proportional to the product of two terms: the data-likelihood $p(\mathcal{I}_1, \mathcal{I}_2|\boldsymbol{\theta}, \hat{\mathcal{V}})$ and a prior $p(\boldsymbol{\theta}|\hat{\mathcal{V}})$, which we call L and P, respectively. We now discuss both terms in turn.

2.2 Likelihood

Under the assumption that the image noise is i.i.d. for all pixels in both views, the data likelihood L can be written as the product of all individual pixel probabilities.

$$L = \prod_{\mathbf{x}} p(\mathcal{I}_1(\mathbf{x}))\,|\,\boldsymbol{\theta}) \prod_{\mathbf{x}} p\Big(\mathcal{C}(\mathcal{I}_2(\mathcal{F}(\mathbf{x};\phi)))\,|\,\boldsymbol{\theta}\Big), \tag{9}$$

where the last product is restricted to those $\mathbf{x}$ for which $\mathcal{V}(\mathbf{x}) = 1$. Note that, by definition, all pixels in $\mathcal{I}_1^*$ are visible in $\mathcal{I}_1$. The assumption that neighbouring pixels are uncorrelated is commonly made in dense image registration procedures. In practice, however, correlations are present by non-lambertian reflectance or other local systematic intensity deviations.

Given the current estimate of the ideal image $\mathcal{I}_1^*(\mathbf{x})$, the noise distribution $\boldsymbol{\Sigma}$ and the color transformation parameters S and $\mathbf{o}$, we can further specify the likelihood by the normal distribution $\mathcal{N}$:

$$L = \prod_{i=1}^{2} \prod_{\mathbf{x}} \frac{1}{(2\pi)^{d/2}|\boldsymbol{\Sigma}|^{1/2}} \exp\big(-\frac{1}{2}\mathbf{m}_i(\mathbf{x})^T \boldsymbol{\Sigma}^{-1} \mathbf{m}_i(\mathbf{x})\big), \tag{10}$$

where $\mathbf{m}_2(\mathbf{x}) = \mathcal{I}_1^*(\mathbf{x}) - S\,\mathcal{I}_2(\mathcal{F}(\mathbf{x};\boldsymbol{\phi})) - \mathbf{o}$ and $\mathbf{m}_1(\mathbf{x}) = \mathcal{I}_1^*(\mathbf{x}) - \mathcal{I}_1(\mathbf{x})$ are the differences between the ideal image function and the input images $\mathcal{I}_i$, the former one estimated at the current values of the color and motion model parameters. The variable d in the normalization constant denotes the dimensionality of the color space.

2.3 Prior

Assuming we have no specific preference for the image related parameters $\mathcal{I}_1^*, \Sigma, S$ and $\mathbf{o}$, for the current estimate $\hat{\mathcal{V}}$ the prior reduces to $P \propto p(\boldsymbol{\phi})$. Depending on the type of flow field, several choices for $p(\boldsymbol{\phi})$ can be made. In this section we show that most common choices can be casted as a Gaussian prior on the parameter vector $\boldsymbol{\phi}$. The prior P then takes the following general form:

$$P \propto \frac{1}{|\boldsymbol{\Sigma}_f|^{1/2}} \exp\left(-\frac{1}{2}\left(\boldsymbol{\phi} - \boldsymbol{\phi}_0\right)^T \boldsymbol{\Sigma}_f^{-1}\left(\boldsymbol{\phi} - \boldsymbol{\phi}_0\right)\right), \tag{11}$$

where $\boldsymbol{\phi}_0$ is the a-priori average parameter vector and $\boldsymbol{\Sigma}_f$ is a covariance matrix.

For *parametrical optical flow* we need to distinguish between two cases. In the case of simple parametric motion models (affine, homography,...), a prior on $\boldsymbol{\phi}$ is usually ommited (i.e. $p(\boldsymbol{\phi})$ is assumed to be constant), and the MAP-estimate turns into a maximum likelihood estimate. Alternatively, this can be casted in the general form of equation 11 by assuming a distribution characterised by $\boldsymbol{\phi}_0 = \mathbf{0}$ and $\boldsymbol{\Sigma}_f = \lambda\mathbf{1}$, where λ is very large. For PCA derived linear optical flow field models, on the other hand, $\boldsymbol{\phi}_0$ is the average flow field of the example flows and $\boldsymbol{\Sigma}_f = \lambda\Lambda$, where Λ is a diagonal matrix consisting of the eigenvalues of the principal components of the flow field. The parameter λ can be tuned to adjust the relative importance of P w.r.t. L.

For *non-parametrical optical flow*, it is well known that that the problem is ill-posed, i.e. multiple equally likely solutions exist, and an additional smoothness constraint needs to be imposed on the solution. Often the connection between the smoothness or regularisation terms and the associated prior distribution is not made. Establishing this connection, however, leads to an interpretation of the most critical parameter in the optical flow energy equations, which is the relative weight between the matching and smoothness term. The smoothness constraint on the solution can be written as:

$$P \propto \frac{1}{|\boldsymbol{\Sigma}_d|^{1/2}} \exp\left(-\frac{1}{2}\left(\mathbf{D}(\boldsymbol{\phi} - \boldsymbol{\phi}_0)\right)^T \boldsymbol{\Sigma}_d^{-1}\left(\mathbf{D}(\boldsymbol{\phi} - \boldsymbol{\phi}_0)\right)\right) \tag{12}$$

where $\mathbf{D}$ is a $2nm \times 2nm$ derivative operator and $\boldsymbol{\Sigma}_d$ is a covariance matrix for the derivative distribution. The operator $\mathbf{D}$ is given by:

$$\mathbf{D}\boldsymbol{\phi} = \begin{pmatrix} \partial/\partial x & 0 & \dots & 0 \\ \partial/\partial y & 0 & \dots & 0 \\ 0 & \partial/\partial x & 0 & \dots \\ 0 & \partial/\partial y & 0 & \dots \\ . & . & . & . \\ 0 & \dots & 0 & \partial/\partial x \\ 0 & \dots & 0 & \partial/\partial y \end{pmatrix} \begin{pmatrix} u(0,0) \\ v(0,0) \\ u(0,1) \\ v(0,1) \\ . \\ u(n,m) \\ v(n,m) \end{pmatrix} \tag{13}$$

and takes at each pixel location the partial derivatives of the two flow field components with respect to x and y.

Isotropic prior. The simplest form to introduce prior knowledge on the optical flow field has been introduced by Horn and Schunk. It is the classical smoothness assumption, which penalizes all deviations from a constant flow field [3]. This model can be explained by making the following substitution in equation 12: $\phi_0 = 0$ and $\mathbf{\Sigma}_d = \lambda\mathbf{1}$. Equation 12 now simplifies to:

$$P \propto \frac{1}{|\lambda(D^T D)^{-1}|^{-1/2}} \exp\left(-\frac{1}{2\lambda}\phi^T D^T D\phi\right) \tag{14}$$

where $D^T D$ is the Laplacian operator and λ controls the width of the distribution of $D\phi$. Note that this equation can be casted in the general form of equation 11, by setting $\mathbf{\Sigma}_f$ equal to $\lambda(D^T D)^{-1}$. This covariance matrix corresponds to a decay of the correlation between the flow field vectors in function of the distance between their locations in the image plane: nearby flow vectors are highly correlated, whereas flow vectors which are far apart are uncorrelated. Smaller values of λ realize a stronger spatial correlation of the nearby optical flow vectors. Note that a value for λ can be estimated as the expected range of correlation between the optical flow vectors. Discontinuities in the flow field cannot be modeled.

Anisotropic prior. Anisotropic versions of the Horn and Schunck constraint are used by Alvarez *et al.* [6], Proesmans *et al.* [5], Nagel [4] or Brox *et al.* [7]. All assume a zero mean flow distribution, i.e. $\phi_0 = \mathbf{0}$. In the work of Alvarez *et al.*, anisotropy is dependent on the local direction of the image gradient. The regularisation is data-driven: if the image $\mathcal{I}_1^*$ suggests a discontinuity by the presence of a high image gradient at a particular location $\mathbf{x}$, a flow field discontinuity at $\mathbf{x}$ is allowed. In [12], a diffusion tensor at pixel location $\mathbf{x}$ is defined as follows:

$$T(\nabla\mathcal{I}_1(\mathbf{x})) = \frac{1}{|\nabla\mathcal{I}_1(\mathbf{x})|^2 + 2\nu^2}\left(\nabla\mathcal{I}_1^{\perp}(\mathbf{x})\nabla\mathcal{I}_1^{\perp T}(\mathbf{x}) + \nu^2\mathbf{1}\right), \tag{15}$$

where $\mathbf{1}$ is the identity matrix, ν is a parameter controlling the degree of anisotropy and $\nabla\mathcal{I}_1^{\perp}(\mathbf{x})$ is the vector perpendicular to $\nabla\mathcal{I}_1(\mathbf{x})$. For color images, the tensor is defined as the sum of the three individual color channel tensors. The associated diffusion process can be formulated as a Gaussian prior on the flow field vector ϕ, by defining $\mathbf{\Sigma}_d^{-1}$ in eq.12 to be a block diagonal matrix with entries $T(\nabla\mathcal{I}_1(\mathbf{x}))$. This guarantees the realization of the prior belief that discontinuities have their origin at hight gradient directions. Equation 12 now becomes:

$$P \propto \frac{1}{|\lambda(D^T\mathbf{\Sigma}_d^{-1}D)^{-1}|^{-1/2}} \exp\left(-\frac{1}{2\lambda}\phi^T D^T\mathbf{\Sigma}_d^{-1}D\phi\right). \tag{16}$$

This equation can be casted in the general form of equation 11, by setting $\mathbf{\Sigma}_f$ equal to $\lambda(D^T\mathbf{\Sigma}_d^{-1}D)^{-1}$. Like in the isotropic case, this covariance matrix correlates flowfield vectors which are nearby in the image plane, but this correlation is broken if large image gradients exist between the image locations from which these flowfield vectors emanate. In principle, the values of ν and λ could be estimated by evaluating $P(\lambda, \nu|\mathbf{p}, \mathcal{I}_0^*)$ on ground truth data.

We can now turn back to the optimization of $\boldsymbol{\theta}$. Instead of maximizing the posterior in (8), we minimize its negative logarithm. This leads (upto a constant) to the following energy:

$$E[\boldsymbol{\theta}] = \sum_{i=1}^{2} \sum_{\mathbf{x}} \mathcal{V}_i(\mathbf{x}) \left[\frac{1}{2} \mathbf{m}_i(\mathbf{x})^T \boldsymbol{\Sigma}^{-1} \mathbf{m}_i(\mathbf{x}) + \log((2\pi)^{\frac{d}{2}} |\boldsymbol{\Sigma}|) \right]$$
$$+ \log(|\boldsymbol{\Sigma}_f|) + \boldsymbol{\phi}^T \boldsymbol{\Sigma}_f^{-1} \boldsymbol{\phi}. \quad (17)$$

The first line of equation 17 represents the likelihood (eq. 10) and is usually called the matching or data term. The second line is the prior or smoothness term.

By comparing this result with other important optical flow approaches, described for instance in [5,6,7] or [2] for an overview, we want to discuss now the implications of the Bayesian approach to the energy 17. First of all, the data term in eq.(17) now contains $\boldsymbol{\Sigma}^{-1}$, which performs a global, relative weighting of the different spectral components. By adding also the derivative of the image to the matching term as for instance in Brox *et al.* $\boldsymbol{\Sigma}$ would also take care of the different magnitude of signal and derivative signal such that both contributions to the data term are weighted correctly. By doing so the additional parameter introduced in [7] would disappear.

Furthermore, $\boldsymbol{\Sigma}^{-1}$ also globally weights the importance of the matching term w.r.t. the smoothness term. More image noise decreases the norm of $\boldsymbol{\Sigma}^{-1}$. This automatically results in a more smooth solution, which is a desirable mechanism. A further modification of the data term is the local weighting of the image value differences by the visibilities $\mathcal{V}(\mathbf{x})$. When a pixel receives a low visibility score, the smoothness term locally gets more important. This avoids that wrongly matched occluded pixels pull, by the action of the smoothness term, neighboring unoccluded pixels in the wrong direction. Another difference is related to the model image $\mathcal{I}_1^*$. Instead of comparing $\mathcal{I}_1(\mathbf{x})$ with $\mathcal{C}(\mathcal{I}_2(\mathcal{F}(\mathbf{x};\boldsymbol{\phi})))$, which is the usual practice in OF computation, the Bayesian framework tells us to use $\mathcal{I}_1^*(\mathbf{x})$ instead. This results again in a visibility dependent weighting.

3 EM Solution

In the previous paragraph, an energy equation, w.r.t. the unknown quantities $\boldsymbol{\theta}$, was derived. This energy corresponds to the negative logarithm of the posterior distribution of $\boldsymbol{\theta}$, given the current estimate of the hidden variable $\mathcal{V}$. Now we will derive the EM-equations, which iterate between the estimation of $\mathcal{V}$ and the minimization of $E(\boldsymbol{\theta})$.

3.1 E-Step

On the $(k+1)^{th}$ iteration, the hidden variable $\mathcal{V}(\mathbf{x})$, is replaced by their conditional expectation given the data, where we use the current estimates $\boldsymbol{\theta}^{(k)}$ for $\boldsymbol{\theta}$. The expected value for the visibility is given by:

$$E[\mathcal{V}|\mathcal{I}_1^*, \boldsymbol{\Sigma}, \boldsymbol{\phi}, S, \mathbf{o}] \equiv \Pr(\mathcal{V}=1|\mathcal{I}_1^*, \boldsymbol{\Sigma}, \boldsymbol{\phi}, S, \mathbf{o}). \quad (18)$$

According to Bayes' rule, the latter probability can be expressed as:

$$\Pr(\mathcal{V}=1|\mathcal{I}_1^*, \boldsymbol{\Sigma}, \phi, S, \mathbf{o}) = \frac{p(\phi|\mathcal{V}=1, \mathcal{I}_1^*, \boldsymbol{\Sigma}, S, \mathbf{o})}{p(\phi|\mathcal{V}=1, \mathcal{I}_1^*, \boldsymbol{\Sigma}, S, \mathbf{o}) + p(\phi|\mathcal{V}=0, \mathcal{I}_1^*, \boldsymbol{\Sigma}, S, \mathbf{o})}, \quad (19)$$

where we have assumed equal priors on the probability of a pixel being visible or not. Given the current estimate of $\boldsymbol{\theta}$, the PDF $p(\phi|\mathcal{V} = 1, \mathcal{I}_1^*, \boldsymbol{\Sigma}, S, \mathbf{o})$ is given by the value of the noise distribution evaluated over the color-difference between $\mathcal{I}_1^*(\mathbf{x})$ and $\mathcal{C}(\mathcal{I}_2(\mathcal{F}(\mathbf{x};\phi)))$: $p(\phi|\mathcal{V} = 1, \mathcal{I}_1^*, \boldsymbol{\Sigma}, S, \mathbf{o}) = \mathcal{N}(\mathbf{m}_2; \mathbf{0}, \boldsymbol{\Sigma})$. The second PDF is more difficult to estimate, because it is hard to say what the color distribution of a pixel, which has no real counter-part in $\mathcal{I}_2$, looks like. We provide a *global* estimate for the PDF of occluded pixels by building a histogram of the color-values in $\mathcal{I}_1^*$ which are currently invisible. This is merely the histogram of $\mathcal{I}_1^*$ where the contribution of each pixel is weighted by $(1 - \mathcal{V}(\mathbf{x}))$. Note that, if a particular pixel in $\mathcal{I}_1^*$ is marked as not-visible, in the next iterations this will automatically decrease the visibility estimates of all similarly colored pixels. This makes sense from a perceptual point of view, and has a regularizing effect on the visibility maps. The update equations for $\mathcal{V}(\mathbf{x})$ are now:

$$\mathcal{V} \leftarrow \frac{\mathcal{N}(\mathbf{m}_2; \mathbf{0}, \boldsymbol{\Sigma})}{\mathcal{N} + \text{HIST}_{\mathcal{I}_1^*,(1-\mathcal{V})}(\mathcal{I}_1^*)}. \quad (20)$$

3.2 M-Step

At the M-step, the intent is to compute values for $\boldsymbol{\theta}$ that maximizes (17), given the current estimates of $\mathcal{V}$. This is achieved by setting the parameters $\boldsymbol{\theta}$ to the appropriate root of the derivative equation, $\partial E(\boldsymbol{\theta})/\partial\theta = 0$.

For the image related parameters $\mathcal{I}_1^*$, S, $\mathbf{o}$ and $\boldsymbol{\Sigma}$, a closed form expressions for the roots can be derived and the update equations are:

$$\begin{aligned}
\mathcal{I}_1^*(\mathbf{x}) &\leftarrow \frac{\mathcal{I}_1(\mathbf{x}) + \mathcal{V}(\mathbf{x})\mathcal{C}(\mathcal{I}_2(\mathcal{F}(\mathbf{x};\phi))}{1 + \mathcal{V}(\mathbf{x})} \\
\boldsymbol{\Sigma} &\leftarrow \frac{\sum_x \left(\mathbf{m}_1(\mathbf{x})\mathbf{m}_1(\mathbf{x})^T + \mathcal{V}(\mathbf{x})\mathbf{m}_2(\mathbf{x})\mathbf{m}_2(\mathbf{x})^T\right)}{\sum_x (1 + \mathcal{V}(\mathbf{x}))} \\
S &\leftarrow \left(\sum_x \mathcal{V}(\mathbf{x})(\mathcal{I}_1^*(\mathbf{x}) - \mathbf{o})\mathcal{I}_2(\mathbf{x})^T\right)\left(\sum_x \mathcal{V}(\mathbf{x})\mathcal{I}_2(\mathbf{x})\mathcal{I}_2(\mathbf{x})^T\right)^{-1} \\
\mathbf{o} &\leftarrow \frac{\sum_x \mathcal{V}(\mathbf{x})(\mathcal{I}_1^*(\mathbf{x}) - S\mathcal{I}_2(\mathbf{x}))}{\sum_x \mathcal{V}(\mathbf{x})}
\end{aligned} \quad (21)$$

The ideal image $\mathcal{I}_1^*$ is, conform to intuition, a weighted sum of the input images. The value of Σ is similarly weighted and composed of the mean color covariances.

To derive the update equation for the transformation $\mathcal{F}(\mathbf{x};\phi)$, we use here a matrix-vector notation in order to bring parametric and non-parametric optical flow into a single framework. The result is a single equation for which we will later show its interpretation in the more common PDE notation. Consider the main result of the first section - the

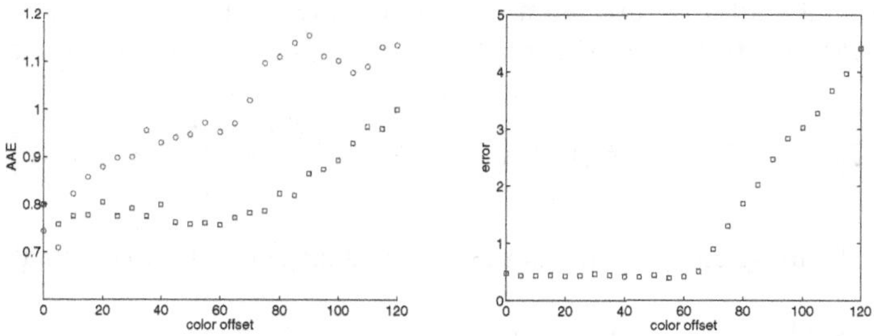

Fig. 1. Synthetic optical flow experiments. left:the average angular error of the optical flow field for different values of color offset between the images (circles and boxes indicate the experiment with and without the update of $\mathbf{o}$. right: error in estimating the color offset.

energy in eq. 17 - where we only retain the terms depending on the transformation parameters ϕ:

$$E[\phi] = \sum_{\mathbf{x}} \mathcal{V}(\mathbf{x}) \frac{1}{2} \mathbf{m}_2(\mathbf{x})^T \mathbf{\Sigma}^{-1} \mathbf{m}_2(\mathbf{x}) + \phi^T \mathbf{\Sigma}_f^{-1} \phi \,, \tag{22}$$

The visibilities $\mathcal{V}(\mathbf{x})$ are fixed for a particular instance of the M-step. For a given maximization step the four unknowns are estimated in turn while keeping the others fixed. In that case the minimum of the energy is again given by a vanishing first derivative $\partial E[\phi)]/\partial\phi$. This derivative is given by:

$$\frac{\partial E[\phi)]}{\partial \phi} = \sum_{\mathbf{x}} \mathcal{V}(\mathbf{x}) \left(\frac{\partial \mathbf{m}_2(\mathbf{x})}{\partial \phi} \right)^T \mathbf{\Sigma}^{-1} \mathbf{m}_2(\mathbf{x}) + \mathbf{\Sigma}_f^{-1} \phi \,, \tag{23}$$

with:

$$\begin{aligned} \frac{\partial \mathbf{m}_2(\mathbf{x})}{\partial \phi} &= - \left[\frac{\partial S\mathcal{I}_2(\mathcal{F}(\mathbf{x};\phi))}{\partial x}, \frac{\partial S\mathcal{I}_2(\mathcal{F}(\mathbf{x};\phi))}{\partial y} \right] \begin{bmatrix} \frac{\partial \mathcal{F}_x(\mathbf{x};\phi)}{\partial \phi_0}, \cdots, \frac{\partial \mathcal{F}_x(\mathbf{x};\phi)}{\partial \phi_n} \\ \frac{\partial \mathcal{F}_y(\mathbf{x};\phi)}{\partial \phi_0}, \cdots, \frac{\partial \mathcal{F}_y(\mathbf{x};\phi)}{\partial \phi_n} \end{bmatrix} \\ &= -\nabla S\mathcal{I}_2(\mathcal{F}(\mathbf{x};\phi)) \frac{\partial \mathcal{F}(\mathbf{x};\phi)}{\partial \phi} \,. \end{aligned} \tag{24}$$

Equation 23 can be written in matrix-vector form as follows:

$$\frac{\partial \mathbf{M}_2}{\partial \phi}^T \mathbf{V} \mathbf{\Sigma}_l^{-1} \mathbf{M}_2 + \frac{1}{\lambda} \mathbf{\Sigma}_f^{-1} \phi = 0 \,. \tag{25}$$

$\mathbf{M}_2$ is a vector of dimension nmd (number of pixels times number of image bands) containing the values of $\mathbf{m}_2(\mathbf{x})$ for every pixel. $\mathbf{V}$ is a diagonal matrix with elements $\mathcal{V}(\mathbf{x})$ and $\mathbf{\Sigma}_l^{-1}$ a block diagonal matrix, with block diagonal elements $\mathbf{\Sigma}^{-1}$.

Equation 25 is a nonlinear matrix equation of the form $\mathbf{A}\phi = \mathbf{b}$, in which $\mathbf{b}$ is still dependent on the unknown solution ϕ. In order to solve this system a linearization similar to Proesmans *et al.* [5, 6] leads to an approximation of $\mathcal{I}_2(\mathcal{F}(\mathbf{x};\phi))$ in eq. 25.

We split the value of $\mathcal{F}(\mathbf{x};\phi)$ into a current and a residual estimate, i.e. $\mathcal{F}(\mathbf{x};\phi) = \mathcal{F}(\mathbf{x};\phi_o+\phi_r)$. Cutting of terms $\geq O(\phi_r^2)$ from the Taylor expansion we get for $\mathbf{m}_2$:

$$\mathbf{m}_2 = \mathcal{I}_1^* - S\left(\mathcal{I}_2(\mathcal{F}(\mathbf{x};\phi_0)) + \nabla\mathcal{I}_2(\mathcal{F}(\mathbf{x};\phi_0))\frac{\partial\mathcal{F}(\mathbf{x};\phi_0)}{\partial\phi}(\phi-\phi_0)\right) - \mathbf{o} \quad (26)$$

which leads by using eq. 23 with this $\mathbf{m}_2$-term and his derivative to the final equation:

$$\left(\mathbf{\Sigma}_p^{-1}+\mathbf{A}\right)\phi = \mathbf{A}\phi_0 + \mathbf{b}$$
$$\mathbf{A} = \frac{\partial\mathbf{M}_2}{\partial\phi}^T \mathbf{V}\mathbf{\Sigma}_l^{-1}\frac{\partial\mathbf{M}_2}{\partial\phi}^T ;\mathbf{b} = \frac{\partial\mathbf{M}_2}{\partial\phi}^T \mathbf{V}\mathbf{\Sigma}_l^{-1}\mathbf{M}_2 \quad (27)$$

For non-parametric optical flow eq. 27 is a huge, but sparse matrix equation and the solution can be obtained by Gauss-Seidel or SOR iterations. It is for this case similar to our previous formulation of optical flow [9], but now containing also terms that allow affine color transformations.

Parametric optical flow is described by only a few parameters, so the size of the matrix $\mathbf{\Sigma}_p^{-1}$ is small and the system can be solve by standard matrix solvers.

4 Experiments

The synthetic experiment shows the advantage of using a transformation model for the image intensities compared to the case where one would not allow the intensities to change. The results of a non-parametric optical flow experiment with isotropic prior, where we have added different magnitudes of color offsets $\mathbf{o}$ to one images, is shown in fig. 1.

The experiment on a real image pair shows the solution of different parameterizations an a nearly planar wall. Under the assumption that the camera is not disturbed by radial distortion and the wall is perfectly planar a homography would explane this transformation. In fig. 2 the two input images are shown next to the checker board image of the two images without applying the geometric and color transformation. One can see a small change in the color values between the images. Fig.3 shows the resulting checker board image with the applied transformation and with the compensation of the color changes on the left side. On the right side one can see the visibility maps $\mathcal{V}(\mathbf{x})$. We have used here different paramterisations for the transformation.

1) pure global translation $\mathcal{T}:(x',y') = (x+tx, y+ty)$ (2 parameters).
2) non-parametric optical flow $\mathcal{T}:(x',y') = (x+u(x,y), y+v(x,y)$ $(n_x n_y * 2$ parameters).

One can see nicely that the translation transformation cannot explane the real transformation and so the visibility maps show black areas, indicating outliers from the transformations model. Non-parametric optical flow can explane this transformation and the outliers in this case are caused by deviations from the noise model.

Fig. 2. Two input images for the parametric optical flow experiment (left). Right: Checker board image by zero transformation.

Fig. 3. Left: Checker board image of the registrations with taking into account the intensity offset (left). Right: visibility maps $\mathcal{V}(\mathbf{x})$. from top to button the results of a translation and non-parametric optical flow are shown.

5 Conclusions

We have presented an optical flow algorithm that simultaneously estimates image displacements and occlusions, as well as the noise distribution and denoised image, as part of an EM algorithm. Starting from relatively straightforward probabilistic considerations, we arrive at an energy formulation with a strong intuitive appeal. The energy often taken as a point of departure in other differential optical flow approaches, turns out to be a special case of this result. More specifically, it can be derived from our formulation by assuming unit strength noise, full visibility and by setting the unknown 'true' irradiance equal to the first image. Our formulation is general enough to combine parametric and non-parametric optical flow approaches into a single scheme. The estimation of visibilities (occlusions) is naturally incorporated into the algorithm, similar in flavor to outlier detection in iteratively reweighted least squares estimation. Noticeably, our algorithm does not introduce additional parameters to realize anisotropic diffusion and to detect occluded pixels.

We have further shown the relation of the smoothness term in many optical flow algorithms with Bayesian priors leading to the interpretation of the λ parameter that controls the relative importance of smoothness and matching. In our opinion this is an important aspect and hopefully opens the focus on specific priors as a way to develop nearly parameter free optical flow algorithms.

Acknowledgment. The investigations reported in this contribution have been partially supported by the European Union IST ERMIS and K.U. Leuven Research fund GOA-VHS.

References

1. Weickert, J., Brox, T.: Diffusion and regularization of vector- and matrix-valued images. Inverse Problems, Image Analysis, and Medical Imaging. Contemporary Mathematics, AMS, Providence **313** (2002) 251–268
2. Barron, J., Fleet, D., Beauchemin, S.: Performance of optical flow techniques. IJCV **12** (1994) 43–77
3. Horn, B., Schunck, G.: Determining optical flow. Artificial Intelligence **17** (1981) 185–203
4. Nagel, H.: Constraints for the estimation of displacement vector fields from image sequences. Proc. Int. Joint Conf. Artificial Intell. (1983) 914–951
5. Proesmans, M., Van Gool, L., Pauwels, E., Oosterlinck, A.: Determination of optical flow and its discontinuities using non-linear diffusion. Proc. ECCV **2** (1994) 295–304
6. Alvarez, L., Weickert, J., Sánchez, J.: Reliable estimation of dense optical flow fields with large displacements. IJCV (2000) 41–56
7. Brox, T., Bruhn, A., Papenberg, N., Weickert, J.: High accuracy optical flow estimation based on a theory for warping. ECCV **4** (2004) 25–36
8. Aach, T., Kaup, A., Mester, R.: Combined displacement estimation and segmentation of stereo image pairs based on gibbs random fields. International Conference on Acoustics, Speech and Signal Processing ICASSP (1990) 2301–2304
9. Strecha, C. Fransens, R., Van Gool, L.: A probabilistic approach to large displacement optical flow and occlusion detection. Workshop SMVP2004 in conjunction with ECCV 2004 (2004)
10. Strecha, C. Fransens, R., Van Gool, L.: Wide-baseline stereo from multiple views: a probabilistic account. Proc. CVPR **1** (2004) 552–559
11. Fransens, R., Strecha, C., Van Gool, L.: A probabilistic approach to optical flow based super-resolution. Workshop GMBV in conjunction with CVPR 2004 (2004)
12. Alvarez, L., Deriche, R., Sánchez, J., Weickert, J.: Dense disparity map estimation respecting image derivatives: a pde and scale-space based approach. Journal of Visual Communication and Image Representation **13** (2002) 3–21
13. Mandelbaum, R., Salgian, G., Sawhney, H.: Correlationbased estimation of ego-motion and structure from motion and stereo. Proc. ICCV (1999) 544–550

Myocardial Motion and Strain Rate Analysis from Ultrasound Sequences

Michael Sühling[1], Muthuvel Arigovindan[1], Christian Jansen[2], Patrick Hunziker[2], and Michael Unser[1]

[1] Ecole Polytechnique Fédérale de Lausanne (EPFL)
Biomedical Imaging Group
CH-1015 Lausanne, Switzerland
{michael.suehling, muthuvel.arigovindan, michael.unser}@epfl.ch
http://bigwww.epfl.ch/
[2] University Hospital Basel
Medical Intensive Care Unit
CH-4031 Basel, Switzerland
{christian.jansen, patrick.hunziker}@unibas.ch

Abstract. We present an optical flow-based algorithm to estimate heart wall motion from ultrasound sequences. The method exploits two ultrasound modalities, i.e., B-mode (grayscale data) and tissue Doppler (partial velocity measurements). We use a local affine velocity model to account for typical heart motions such as contraction/expansion and shear. The affine model parameters give also access to so-called strain rate parameters that describe local myocardial deformation such as wall thickening. The estimation of large motions is made possible through the use of a coarse-to-fine multi-scale strategy, which also adds robustness to the method.

1 Introduction

Echocardiography is a widely used imaging technique to examine myocardial function in patients with known or suspected heart disease. The analysis of ventricular wall motion and deformation, in particular, allows to assess the extent of myocardial ischemia and infarction. In clinical practice, the analysis mainly relies on visual inspection or manual measurements by experienced cardiologists. Manual methods are tedious and time-consuming, and visual assessment leads to qualitative and subjective diagnoses that suffer from considerable inter- and intraobserver variability. Automating the analysis of echocardiographic images is therefore highly desirable but also challenging because of the low image quality and the high amount of speckle noise.

Modern ultrasound systems provide different imaging modalities among which *B(rightness)-mode* and *tissue Doppler* play a crucial role; B-mode sequences provide dynamic grayscale information of the cardiac structures, while tissue Doppler yields one-dimensional velocity estimates of the moving tissue along the scan lines.

Different methods have been proposed to estimate two-dimensional ventricular motion from the grayscale information of the B-mode loops. Among others, so-called active contour or snake techniques [1] were proposed to track cardiac borders [2]. This

B. Jähne et al. (Eds.): IWCM 2004, LNCS 3417, pp. 177–189, 2007.

approach was extended to active shape models, which were applied to echocardiograms with partial success [3].

To obtain a dense motion field that covers the whole myocardium and is not restricted to its borders, some researchers proposed to compute cardiac displacement fields using non-rigid registration techniques; however, their application to ultrasound is still limited [4,5].

Another approach to obtain dense motion data is based on the so-called *optical flow* principle [6]. Application examples of this approach to echocardiograms yielded promising results [7, 8]. An evaluation of different optical flow methods applied to echocardiograms can be found in [9].

In this paper, we propose a new motion analysis approach that is based on both modalities, B-mode and tissue Doppler. Based on the optical flow principle, we estimate a velocity field from the B-mode echocardiograms; in addition, we constrain the motion field such that its projections along the scan lines are in good agreement with the tissue Doppler measurements.

Besides rigid displacement, systolic myocardial function is characterized by a significant wall thickening and circumferential/longitudinal shortening. Quantification of myocardial deformation allows to differentiate actively contracting tissue from infarcted one that merely moves along with neighboring healthy segments. To account for this, we use a local affine model for the velocity in space that inherently yields regional deformation information in terms of so-called *strain rate*. The affine motion model also covers basic motion patterns such as rotation and shear that typically appear during cardiac contraction and expansion.

The paper is organized as follows. We first describe the optical flow principle to analyze motion from B-mode echocardiograms in Section 2. After reviewing the principles of tissue Doppler imaging in Section 3, we present the proposed bimodal algorithm in Section 4. Our coarse-to-fine multi-scale strategy that allows to estimate large motions is sketched in Section 5. The extraction of myocardial strain rate information from the affine model parameters is described in Section 6. Finally, numerical results from synthetic data and clinical echocardiograms are presented in Section 7. Further details and experimental results can be found in the monograph [10].

2 Motion Analysis from B-Mode Echocardiograms

Gradient-based optical flow estimation relies on the assumption that the intensity of a particular point in a moving pattern does not change with time. Let $I(x, y, t)$ denote the intensity of pixels at location $\mathbf{r} = (x, y)$ and time t in a B-mode image sequence. Then the constant intensity assumption can be expressed as [6]

$$I_x(\mathbf{r}, t)\, u(\mathbf{r}, t) + I_y(\mathbf{r}, t)\, v(\mathbf{r}, t) + I_t(\mathbf{r}, t) = 0, \tag{1}$$

where I_x, I_y and I_t denote the spatial and temporal derivatives of the image intensity. The velocities u and v are, respectively, the x- and y-components of the optical flow that we wish to estimate. Since (1) is a single equation in two unknowns u and v, it cannot be solved uniquely without introducing additional constraints. The Lucas-Kanade method [9], for instance, assumes the velocity to be constant within small spatial neighborhoods. It has been applied to echocardiograms by Chunke *et al.* [11].

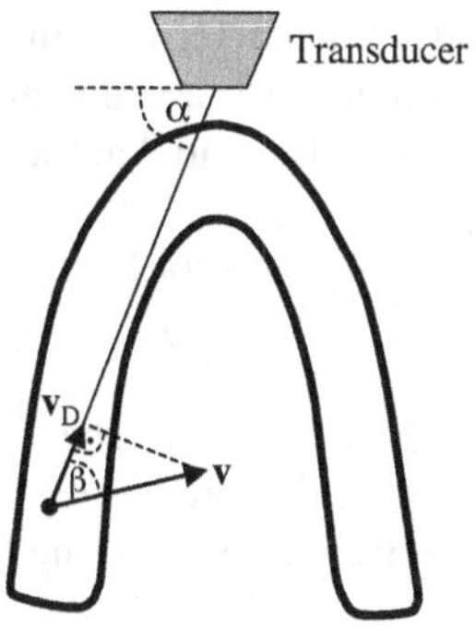

Fig. 1. The tissue Doppler velocity v_D corresponds to the projection of the true velocity $\mathbf{v}$ along the beam direction α

3 Principles of Tissue Doppler Imaging

Velocity measurements using pulsed-wave ultrasound have become an important diagnostic tool in echocardiography [12]. In two-dimensional tissue Doppler imaging (TDI), the beam is scanned radially over the region to be imaged. As illustrated in Fig. 1, the system measures the tissue velocity component

$$v_D = \|\mathbf{v}\|_2 \cos(\beta)$$

at positions along each beam, where β denotes the angle between the true velocity vector $\mathbf{v}$ and the beam direction α. Thus, the measured motion depends highly on β. In particular, the modality is totally blind to displacements orthogonal to the scan line.

Conventional Doppler ultrasonography is based on the principle that v_D is proportional to the small frequency shift f_D in the ultrasound carrier frequency f_0 between transmitted and received echoes, i.e.,

$$v_D = \frac{c}{2f_0} f_D,$$

where c denotes the speed of sound.

Current ultrasound systems allow the simultaneous acquisition of B-mode and tissue Doppler signals in real-time. The Doppler velocities are usually color-coded and superimposed onto the B-mode echocardiogram as shown in Fig. 8(b) in Section 7.2. However, the interpretation of these radial projections of complex motion patterns, such as translation, rotation and shear, is difficult and requires a sufficient level of experience [12].

4 Bimodal Motion Analysis from B-Mode and Tissue Doppler Echocardiograms

Since both modalities, B-mode and tissue Doppler, provide valuable motion information, we integrate these two kinds of information to estimate a true two-dimensional velocity field. Inspired by the Lucas-Kanade method, we propose a sliding-window algorithm. Since typical heart motions are given by rotation, expansion, contraction, and shear, we use a local affine model for the velocity in space. Let $\mathbf{r}_0 = (x_0, y_0)^T$ denote the center of a small image region for a frame at time t. Omitting the temporal parameter for notational convenience, the spatial affine model is defined as

$$\mathbf{v}(\mathbf{r}) = \mathbf{v}_0 + \begin{pmatrix} u_x & u_y \\ v_x & v_y \end{pmatrix} \cdot (\mathbf{r} - \mathbf{r}_0), \tag{2}$$

where $\mathbf{r} = (x, y)^T$ and $\mathbf{v}(\mathbf{r}) = (u(\mathbf{r}), v(\mathbf{r}))^T$. The vector $\mathbf{v}_0$ corresponds to the velocity at the center point $\mathbf{r}_0$; u_x, u_y, v_x, and v_y are the first order spatial derivatives of u and v, respectively. These derivatives are assumed to be constant within the local neighborhood.

We estimate the local model parameters by minimizing the weighted least-squares criterion

$$\sum_n w(\mathbf{r}_n - \mathbf{r}_0)\Big(\big(I_x(\mathbf{r}_n)\, u(\mathbf{r}_n) + I_y(\mathbf{r}_n)\, v(\mathbf{r}_n) + I_t(\mathbf{r}_n)\big)^2 \\ + \lambda\big(\cos(\alpha_n)\, u(\mathbf{r}_n) + \sin(\alpha_n)\, v(\mathbf{r}_n) - v_D(\mathbf{r}_n)\big)^2\Big), \tag{3}$$

where the sum is taken over all pixels $\mathbf{r}_n$ inside an observation window w centered at position $\mathbf{r}_0$. The first term of the cost function is equal to the optical flow constraint applied to the B-mode data. The second term corresponds to the difference between the measured tissue Doppler velocities and the velocity field projection along the scan line. The scan line direction at position $\mathbf{r}_n$ is given by the unit vector $(\cos(\alpha_n), \sin(\alpha_n))$. The relative influence of the B-mode data versus the tissue Doppler measurements to the resulting velocity estimate is controlled by the non-negative weighting parameter λ. The symmetric window function w gives more weight to constraints at the center of the local spatial region than to those at the periphery. A well suited window function is $w(x, y) = \beta^n(x)\beta^n(y)$, where β^n is the symmetrical B-spline of degree $n \in \mathbb{N}$ [13]. B-splines rapidly converge to Gaussians when their degree increases which ensures isotropy of the window in multiple dimensions.

By inserting (2) into (3) and differentiating the latter one with respect to each of the six unknown model parameters $\mathbf{x} = (u_0, v_0, u_x, u_y, v_x, v_y)^T$, we obtain a symmetric linear system $\mathbf{A}\mathbf{x} = \mathbf{b}$ of size (6×6) that has to be solved at each window position.

Besides the proposed least-squares approach, the model parameters may also be determined using other local techniques, such as the total-least-squares method [14]. Global methods based on Horn-Schunk-like regularization schemes [15, 16] may also be applied. However, these options are not considered here.

4.1 Choice of Window Size

The optimal size of the window function w depends on the underlying motion field and is thus not known *a priori*. In regions where the displacement field is essentially homogeneous in space, the motion can be well fitted by the affine model within a large observation window. On the other hand, smaller windows will be better suited for processing areas where the motion pattern varies rapidly, which is for example the case at myocardial boundaries.

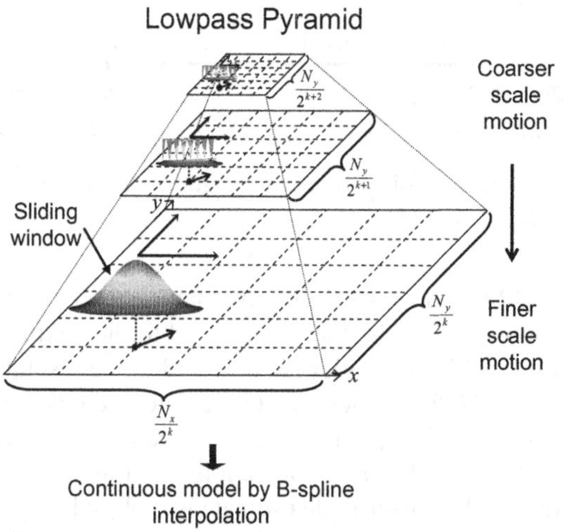

Fig. 2. Coarse-to-fine multi-scale strategy in space. N_x and N_y are the $x-$ and y-dimensions of the images at level $k = 0$, respectively. Larger motions are estimated at coarser scales while smaller motions are refined at finer scales.

To be locally adaptive, we compute and solve the local linear systems for different window sizes and choose the most promising fit based on a figure of merit; in particular, we use windows at dyadic scales. Our strategy is to use windows as large as possible to increase noise robustness, while not violating the motion model assumptions. To increase computational efficiency, we developed a multi-channel, wavelet-like algorithm to compute the system coefficients recursively for successively larger window sizes [17].

5 Coarse-to-Fine Multi-scale Strategy

Estimating large motions of moving patterns that contain high frequencies may lead to aliasing artifacts. To be able to estimate larger motions, we apply a coarse-to-fine strategy in space. As sketched in Fig. 2, we compute an image pyramid for each frame in the image sequence. In particular, we use a spline-based least-squares pyramid [18] with dyadic scale progression. At each pyramid level $0 \leq k \leq K$, the original image $I^{(0)}(x,y) = I(x,y)$, at level $k = 0$, is approximated by the spline model

$$I^{(k)}(x,y) = \sum_{m,n} c^{(k)}(m,n)\beta^n\left(\frac{x}{2^k} - m, \frac{y}{2^k} - n\right). \tag{4}$$

At each level, the number of spline coefficients $c^{(k)}$ is reduced by the factor 2 in each dimension, resulting in a successively coarser image approximation. The corresponding Doppler signal is decomposed analogously using the same pyramid structure.

Our coarse-to-fine multiresolution strategy for motion estimation works as follows. Starting at the coarsest pyramid level $k = K$, the motion vectors at each grid

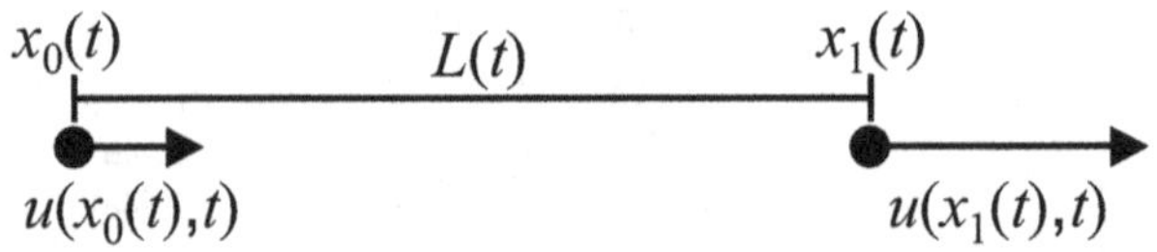

Fig. 3. Deformation of a one-dimensional object of length L at time t. The end points x_0 and x_1 move with velocities $u(x_0, t)$ and $u(x_1, t)$, respectively.

position are determined by choosing locally the optimal window size as described in Section 4.1. The motion vectors are then transferred to the next finer resolution level $k-1$ as initial estimates. The velocities are upscaled to the resolution level $k = 0$ by multiplying the vectors with 2^k. Values on intermediate grid positions are computed by using linear interpolation. If the upscaled coarser-scale motion vector does not exceed the level-dependent length 2^{k-1} (*a priori* test), it is re-estimated in the same fashion as described above. An initial, coarser-scale estimate is replaced only, if the length of the re-estimated vector does not exceed the level-dependent limit 2^{k-1} (*a posteriori* test). Having completed the finest pyramid level, we fit a spatio-temporal B-spline model to the discrete output to obtain a global, continuous representation of the velocity field.

6 Strain Rate Analysis

Local myocardial velocity is an important feature to asses myocardial function. However, it does not allow to differentiate actively contracting tissue from infarcted one that merely moves along with neighboring healthy segments. During normal physiological contraction, the pumping capacity of the ventricle is usually raised by an additional wall-thickening and a longitudinal contraction of the basal segments towards the apex. Due to the wall thickening, the velocity of the endocardium (inner border) is higher than that of the epicardium (outer border), but the difference is not necessarily related to the underlying wall displacement. Thus, the spatial velocity gradient—also known as *strain rate* [19]—can be of great diagnostic value to differentiate active form passive tissue.

6.1 Definition of Strain and Strain Rate

Strain defines the amount of deformation of an object caused by an applied force. As sketched for the one-dimensional case in Fig. 3, the so-called *natural* or *Eulerian* strain ϵ_N is defined as

$$\epsilon_N(t_1) = \int_{t_0}^{t_1} d\epsilon_N(t), \tag{5}$$

where

$$d\epsilon_N(t) = \frac{L(t+dt) - L(t)}{L(t)} \tag{6}$$

is an infinitesimally amount of deformation occurring during the infinitesimally time interval dt.

The instantaneous rate of deformation—the so-called natural *strain rate*—is defined as

$$\frac{d\epsilon_N(t)}{dt} = \frac{\dot{L}(t)}{L(t)}. \tag{7}$$

Using the definition $L(t) = x_1(t) - x_0(t)$ and the fact that $\dot{L}(t) = \dot{x}_1(t) - \dot{x}_0(t) = u(x_1(t),t) - u(x_0(t),t)$, it follows that

$$\frac{d\epsilon_N(t)}{dt} = \frac{u(x_1(t),t) - u(x_0(t),t)}{x_1(t) - x_0(t)}. \tag{8}$$

For $\lim_{x_1 \to x_0}$, this converges to the spatial derivative $\frac{\partial u}{\partial x}\big|_{x_0(t)} = u_x\big|_{x_0(t)}$ of the instantaneous velocity $u(x,t)$. Thus, strain rate can be interpreted as the speed at which tissue deformation (i.e., strain) occurs; it is measured in (cm/s)/cm = 1/s units. Strain and strain rate relate to each other as displacement does to velocity.

Current approaches to calculate myocardial strain rate are based on tissue Doppler imaging [20, 21], where the axial strain rate component is computed as the spatial derivative of the Doppler velocities along the scan lines. Since this method critically depends on the insonification direction, it is highly desirable to extend the strain rate analysis to two dimensions.

6.2 Two-Dimensional Strain Rate Analysis

In the case of our motion analysis method, two-dimensional strain rate is inherently contained in the underlying local motion model (2). The Jacobian matrix of spatial velocity derivatives,

$$\mathbf{J} = \begin{pmatrix} u_x & u_y \\ v_x & v_y \end{pmatrix}, \tag{9}$$

is also known from mechanical engineering as *strain rate tensor*. It can be decomposed into two terms which are symmetric and antisymmetric, respectively [22]:

$$\mathbf{J} = \mathbf{R} + \mathbf{D}, \tag{10}$$

where

$$\mathbf{R} = \frac{1}{2}(\mathbf{J} - \mathbf{J}^T) = \begin{pmatrix} 0 & -\frac{v_x - u_y}{2} \\ \frac{v_x - u_y}{2} & 0 \end{pmatrix} \tag{11}$$

and

$$\mathbf{D} = \frac{1}{2}(\mathbf{J} + \mathbf{J}^T) = \begin{pmatrix} u_x & \frac{v_x + u_y}{2} \\ \frac{v_x + u_y}{2} & v_y \end{pmatrix}. \tag{12}$$

The matrix $\mathbf{R}$ corresponds to a rigid, rotational velocity field that leaves the local tissue area unchanged. The angular velocity is given by $\omega = (v_x - u_y)/2$ which corresponds to one-half of the curl of the velocity field. The second term, $\mathbf{D}$, accounts for the deformation of the heart tissue, both contraction/expansion and shear. The components

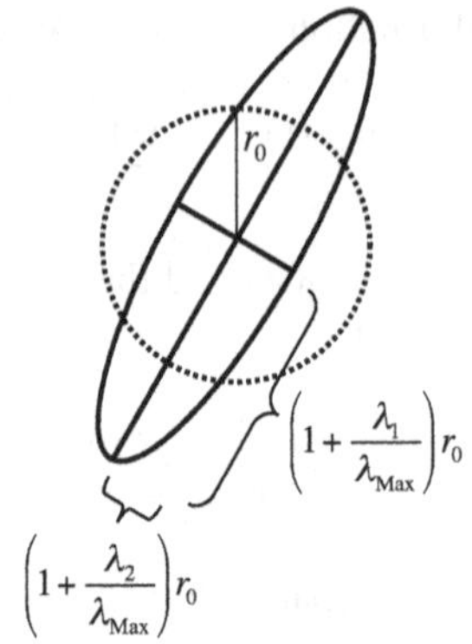

Fig. 4. Strain rate visualization by means of ellipses. The semi-axes of a circle with radius r_0 are scaled according to the corresponding eigenvalues of the deformation matrix $\mathbf{D}$.

on the principal diagonal describe a dilation along the coordinate axes, whereas the off-diagonal components correspond to a shearing. Since $\mathbf{D}$ is symmetric, it has real eigenvalues λ_1, λ_2 and orthonormal eigenvectors $\mathbf{u}_1$ and $\mathbf{u}_2$; it can be decomposed as

$$\mathbf{D} = \mathbf{U} \begin{pmatrix} \lambda_1 & 0 \\ 0 & \lambda_2 \end{pmatrix} \mathbf{U}^T, \tag{13}$$

where

$$\mathbf{U} = (\mathbf{u}_1, \mathbf{u}_2) = \begin{pmatrix} \cos\phi & -\sin\phi \\ \sin\phi & \cos\phi \end{pmatrix} \tag{14}$$

is the rotation matrix specified by the eigenvectors, and where ϕ denotes the rotation angle of the coordinate system. Thus, the deformation matrix $\mathbf{D}$ can be interpreted as a pure contraction/expansion along the directions of the eigenvectors. Negative eigenvalues λ_i describe contraction, while positive eigenvalues correspond to dilation of the heart tissue. The divergence, given by the trace of $\mathbf{D}$ (or equivalently by the sum of its eigenvalues), describes the local area change of the tissue.

6.3 Strain Rate Visualization

For visualization, the principal deformation directions and magnitudes are superimposed in the form of small ellipses onto the echocardiograms inside the time varying ROI as shown in Fig. 4. The semi-axes directions correspond to the eigenvectors of $\mathbf{D}$ and their lengths are given by

$$\left(1 + \frac{\lambda_i}{\lambda_{\text{Max}}}\right) r_0, \quad i = 1, 2,$$

respectively. The normalization parameter λ_{Max} is the maximum absolute value of all eigenvalues computed within the ROI. The parameter r_0 corresponds to the radius of the non-deformed circle and controls the overall size of the ellipses. Negative eigenvalues (tissue contraction) lead to an axis-shortening, whereas positive eigenvalues (tissue dilation) correspond to an elongation of the corresponding semi-axis.

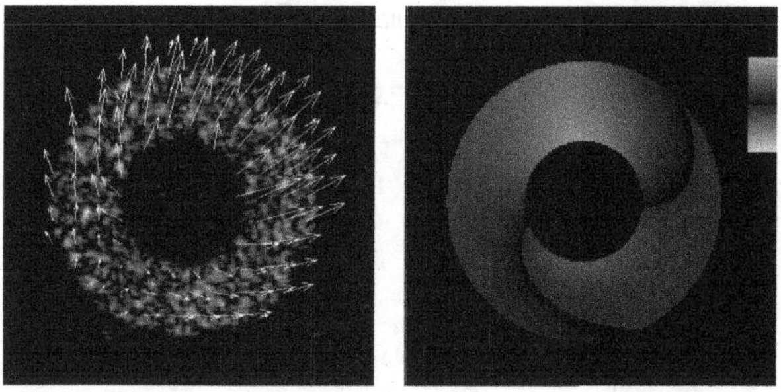

(a) (b)

Fig. 5. (a) Frame of synthetic B-mode echocardiogram with superimposed estimated velocity field during diastole. (b) Color-coded simulated tissue Doppler velocities.

7 Numerical Results

For validation purposes, the algorithm was tested on synthetic data and on clinical echocardiograms. The echocardiograms were acquired with a HP Sonos 5500 ultrasound system.

7.1 Application to Synthetic Data

The algorithm was first tested on synthetic ultrasound sequences for which the exact motion field and corresponding tissue Doppler velocities are known. The data was generated by warping a single reference frame of point scatterers. To simulate noise, we added scatterers of random echogenicity to each frame. The final B-mode images were obtained by applying a simple, linear ultrasound imaging model to the perturbed point scatterer images [23]. The example sequence used here simulates a full cardiac cycle of a left ventricular short axis view (SAX) with an underlying translation to the upper right. The applied wall thickening and thinning was chosen such that it satisfies the incompressibility constraint. Fig. 5(a) shows one diastolic frame of the sequence together with the superimposed estimated velocity field. The color-coded simulated tissue Doppler velocities are shown in Fig. 5(b).

To assess the performance of the algorithm, we use an angular error measure between the estimated velocity $\hat{\mathbf{v}}$ and the exact velocity $\mathbf{v}$ which is given by $\theta = \arccos(< \mathbf{v}, \hat{\mathbf{v}} > / (\|\mathbf{v}\|_2 \|\hat{\mathbf{v}}\|_2))$. The mean angular error $\overline{\theta}$ is computed by averaging θ over the whole image sequence.

Fig. 6 illustrates the average error for different values of the parameter λ that controls the relative influence of B-mode versus tissue Doppler data in (3). First, the mean error decreases significantly with increasing weight of the tissue Doppler term. The relative error improvement between $\lambda = 0$ (only B-mode data is used) and $\lambda = 500$ is 19.82%. For larger values of λ, the error increases again and the local linear systems become more and more ill-conditioned.

Since the motion field captures the superposition of translational motion, radial outward/inward motion and deformation, its interpretation remains difficult; in contrast, the estimated strain rate (Fig. 7) is independent from the underlying rigid translation and

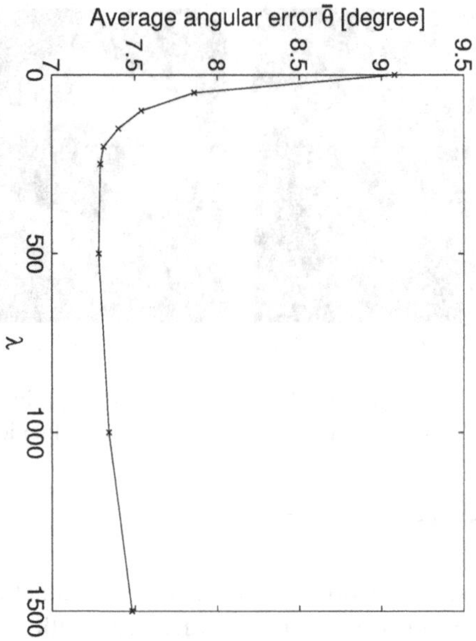

Fig. 6. Average angular error $\overline{\theta}$ of synthetic ultrasound data for different values of λ

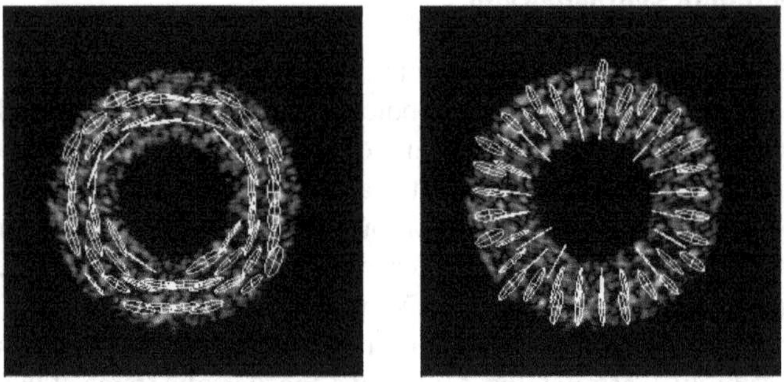

(a) Diastole *(b)* Systole

Fig. 7. Estimated strain rates from synthetic ultrasound data during diastole (a) and systole (b). Strain rate is independent from underlying rigid translation.

represents well the uniform deformation of the model. The myocardial thinning during expansion is clearly indicated by the circumferentially elongated ellipses in Fig. 7(a); likewise, the myocardial thickening during contraction is represented by the radially dilated ellipses in Fig. 7(b). The fact that the applied deformation close to the inner boundary is larger than at the outer boundary is also indicated by the different ratios of long to short semi-axis lengths.

7.2 Application to Clinical Data

For a first in vivo validation, we applied the method to a set of clinical echocardiograms. Fig. 8(a) shows one frame of a B-mode sequence during systole. The

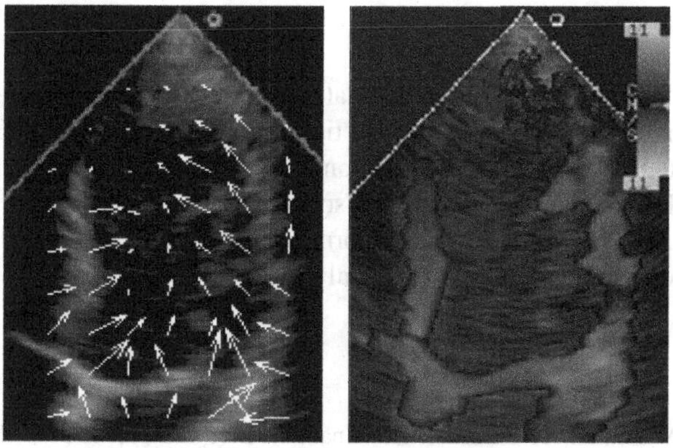

(a) *(b)*

Fig. 8. Results from clinical echocardiogram during systole. (a) Estimated velocity field. (b) Input data: B-mode echocardiogram with superimposed color-coded Doppler velocities. Colors code measured motion towards the transducer (Range: −11 to 11 cm/s).

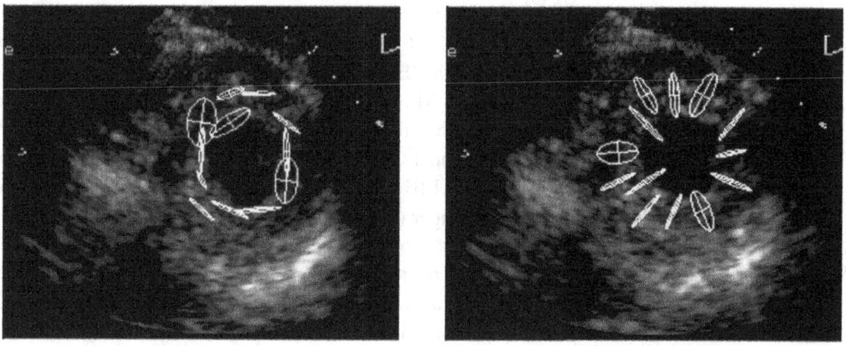

(a) Diastole *(b)* Systole

Fig. 9. Estimated strain rates from apical short axis view. Myocardial radial wall thinning and circumferential lengthening during diastole is indicated by the deformation map (a). The reversed deformation during systole is shown in (b).

corresponding estimated velocity field is superimposed. In contrast to TDI, that measures mainly the motion towards the apex (Fig. 8(b)), the estimated motion field also captures the significant inward motion of the cardiac walls. This corresponds well to the expert echocardiographic reading.

The ability to estimate myocardial deformation in clinical echocardiograms acquired during routine clinical examinations is demonstrated in the short axis view shown in Figure 9. Since tissue Doppler was not acquired in this case, the motion field was estimated from the B-mode data only ($\lambda = 0$). The circumferential alignment of the ellipses in Fig. 9(a) documents the typical wall thinning and circumferential lengthening during diastole. In contrast, the ellipses are elongated and aligned radially in Fig. 9(b), indicating myocardial wall thickening and circumferential shortening during systole.

8 Conclusion

We have proposed a new method to estimate heart motion from echocardiograms that combines information from B-mode and tissue Doppler modalities. Experiments on synthetic data demonstrate that the inclusion of tissue Doppler measurements improves the motion field accuracy. The method also yields two-dimensional strain rate information that characterizes myocardial deformation. First applications of the method to clinical echocardiograms give realistic results.

References

1. Kass, M., Witkin, A., Terzopoulos, D.: Snakes: active contour models. Intl. J. Computer Vision **1** (1988) 321–332
2. Chalana, V., Linker, D., Haynor, D., Kim, Y.: A multiple active contour model for cardiac boundary detection on echocardiographic sequences. IEEE Trans. Med. Imag. **15** (1996) 290–298
3. Jacob, G., Noble, J., Behrenbruch, C., Kelion, A., Banning, A.: A shape-space-based approach to tracking myocardial borders and quantifying regional left-ventricular function applied in echocardiography. IEEE Trans. Med. Imag. **21** (2002) 226–238
4. Yeung, F., Levinson, S., Fu, D., Parker, K.: Feature-adaptive motion tracking of ultrasound image sequences using a deformable mesh. IEEE Trans. Med. Imag. **17** (1998) 945–956
5. Ledesma-Carbayo, M., Kybic, J., Desco, M., Santos, A., Unser, M.: Cardiac motion analysis from ultrasound sequences using non-rigid registration. In Niessen, W., Viergever, M., eds.: Proceedings of the Fourth International Conference on Medical Image Computing and Computer-Assisted Intervention (MICCAI'01). Volume 2208 of Lecture Notes in Computer Science., Utrecht, The Netherlands, Springer (2001) 889–896
6. Horn, B., Schunk, B.: Determining optical flow. Artificial Intelligence **17** (1981) 185–203
7. Mailloux, G., Langlois, F., Simard, P., Bertrand, M.: Restoration of the velocity field of the heart from two-dimensional echocardiograms. IEEE Trans. Med. Imag. **8** (1989) 143–153
8. Zini, G., Sarti, A., Lamberti, C.: Application of continuum theory and multi-grid methods to motion evaluation from 3D echocardiography. IEEE Trans. Ultrason., Ferroelect., Freq. Contr. **44** (1997) 297–308
9. Baraldi, P., Sarti, A., Lamberti, C., Prandini, A., Sgallari, F.: Evaluation of differential optical flow techniques on synthesized echo images. IEEE Trans. Biomed. Eng. **43** (1996) 259–272
10. Sühling, M.: Myocardial Motion and Deformation Analysis from Echocardiograms. EPFL thesis no. 3049 (2004), 181 p., Swiss Federal Institute of Technology Lausanne (EPFL) (2004)
11. Chunke, Y., Terada, K., Oe, S.: Motion analysis of echocardiograph using optical flow method. IEEE International Conference on Systems, Man and Cybernetics **1** (1996) 672–677
12. Hunziker, P., Picard, M., Jander, N., Scherrer-Crosbie, M., Pfisterer, M., Buser, P.: Regional wall motion assessment in stress echocardiography by tissue Doppler bull's-eyes. J. Am. Soc. Echocardiography **12** (1999) 196–202
13. Unser, M.: Splines: A perfect fit for signal and image processing. IEEE Signal Processing Mag. **16** (1999) 22–38
14. Mühlich, M., Mester, R.: The role of total least squares in motion analysis. In Burkhardt, H., Neumann, B., eds.: Proceedings of the 5th European Conference on Computer Vision (ECCV). Volume 1407 of Lecture Notes in Computer Science., Freiburg, Germany, Springer (1998) 305–321

15. Mota, C., Stuke, I., Aach, T., Barth, E.: Divide-and-conquer strategies for estimating multiple transparent motions. In: Proceedings of the First Workshop on Complex Motion (IWCM'04). Lecture Notes in Computer Science, Springer (2004)
16. Schnörr, C.: Variational methods for fluid flow estimation. In: Proceedings of the First Workshop on Complex Motion (IWCM'04). Lecture Notes in Computer Science, Springer (2004)
17. Sühling, M., Arigovindan, M., Hunziker, P., Unser, M.: Multiresolution moment filters: Theory and applications. IEEE Trans. Image Processing **13** (2004) 484–495
18. Unser, M., Aldroubi, A., Eden, M.: The L_2-polynomial spline pyramid. IEEE Trans. Pattern Anal. Machine Intell. **15** (1993) 364–379
19. D'hooge, J., Heimdal, A., Jamal, F., Kukulski, T., Bijnens, B., Rademakers, F., Hatle, L., Suetens, P., Sutherland, G.R.: Regional strain and strain rate measurements by cardiac ultrasound: Principles, implementation and limitations. European Journal of Echocardiography **1** (2000) 154–170
20. Fleming, A., Xia, X., McDicken, W., Sutherland, G., Fenn, L.: Myocardial velocity gradients detected by doppler imaging system. British J. Radiology **67** (1994) 679–688
21. Uematsu, M., Miyatake, K., Tanaka, N., Matsuda, H., Sano, A., Yamazaki, N., Hirama, M., Yamagishi, M.: Myocardial velocity gradient as a new indicator of regional left ventricular contraction: detection by a two-dimensional tissue doppler imaging technique. J. Am. Coll. Cardiology **26** (1995) 217–223
22. Feistauer, M.: Mathematical Methods in Fluid Dynamics. Volume 67 of Pitman Monographs and Surveys in Pure and Applied Mathematics. Longman Scientific & Technical, Harlow (1993)
23. Bertrand, M., Meunier, J.: Ultrasonic texture motion analysis: theory and simulation. IEEE Trans. Med. Imag. **14** (1995) 293–300

Determining the Translational Speed of a Camera from Time-Varying Optical Flow

Anton van den Hengel, Wojciech Chojnacki, and Michael J. Brooks

School of Computer Science, Adelaide University, SA 5005, Australia
{anton,wojtek,mjb}@cs.adelaide.edu.au

Abstract. Under certain assumptions, a moving camera can be self-calibrated solely on the basis of instantaneous optical flow. However, due to a fundamental indeterminacy of scale, instantaneous optical flow is insufficient to determine the magnitude of the camera's translational velocity. This is equivalent to the baseline length indeterminacy encountered in conventional stereo self-calibration. In this paper we show that if the camera is calibrated in a certain weak sense, then, by using time-varying optical flow, the velocity of the camera may be uniquely determined relative to its initial velocity. This result enables the calculation of the camera's trajectory through the scene over time. A closed-form solution is presented in the continuous realm, and its discrete analogue is experimentally validated.

1 Introduction

It is well known that, under certain assumptions, a camera moving smoothly through a stationary environment can be self-calibrated based on instantaneous optical flow. However, because of a fundamental indeterminacy of scale, instantaneous optical flow is insufficient to determine the magnitude of the camera's instantaneous translational velocity.

The aim of this paper is to show that if a point in the static scene is tracked over a period of time as part of time-varying optical flow and if the camera is calibrated in a certain weak sense, then successive translational speeds of the camera evolve in a way that is uniquely determined by the camera's initial translational speed. A closed-form solution is presented in the continuous realm, and its discrete analogue is experimentally validated.

2 Camera and Image Settings

Consider a full-perspective, pinhole camera undergoing smooth motion in a stationary world. Associate with the camera a 3D coordinate frame such that:

- the frame's origin coincides with the camera's optical centre C,
- two basis vectors span the focal plane,
- the other basis vector coincides with the optical axis.

Let $\boldsymbol{v} = [v_1, v_2, v_3]^T$ and $\boldsymbol{\omega} = [\omega_1, \omega_2, \omega_3]^T$ specify the camera's instantaneous *translational velocity* and instantaneous *angular velocity* with respect to the camera frame.

B. Jähne et al. (Eds.): IWCM 2004, LNCS 3417, pp. 190–197, 2007.

Let P be a static point in space. Suppose that the vector connecting C with P has the coordinates $\boldsymbol{x} = [x_1, x_2, x_3]^T$ with respect to the camera frame. As the camera moves, the position of P relative to the camera frame will change and will be recorded in the function $t \mapsto \boldsymbol{x}(t)$. The evolution of the relative position is governed by the equation

$$\dot{\boldsymbol{x}} + \widehat{\boldsymbol{\omega}}\boldsymbol{x} + \boldsymbol{v} = \boldsymbol{0}, \tag{1}$$

where $\widehat{\boldsymbol{\omega}}$ is defined as

$$\widehat{\boldsymbol{\omega}} = \begin{bmatrix} 0 & -\omega_3 & \omega_2 \\ \omega_3 & 0 & -\omega_1 \\ -\omega_2 & \omega_1 & 0 \end{bmatrix}$$

(cf. [1]). Let f be the focal length of the camera. Let $\boldsymbol{p} = [p_1, p_2, p_3]^T$ be the vector of the coordinates of the perspective projection of P, through C, onto the image plane $\{\boldsymbol{x} \in \mathbb{R}^3 \colon x_3 = -f\}$, relative to the camera frame. Then

$$\boldsymbol{p} = -f\frac{\boldsymbol{x}}{x_3}. \tag{2}$$

To account for the geometry of the image, we introduce a separate, 2D coordinate frame in the image plane, with two basis vectors aligned with rows and columns of pixels, and with the origin located in one of the four corners of the rectangular image boundary. In the case of rectangular image pixels, it is natural to assume that each of the image frame basis vectors is proportional to one of the two vectors of the camera frame spanning the focal plane. The corresponding proportionality coefficients s_1 and s_2 characterise the pixel sizes in the basis directions, expressed in length units of the camera frame. If an image point has coordinates $\boldsymbol{p} = [p_1, p_2, -f]^T$ and $[m_1, m_2]^T$ relative to the camera and image frames, respectively, and if $\boldsymbol{m} = [m_1, m_2, 1]^T$, then

$$\boldsymbol{p} = \boldsymbol{A}\boldsymbol{m}, \tag{3}$$

where $\boldsymbol{A}$ is a 3×3 invertible matrix called the *intrinsic-parameter matrix*. With $[i_1, i_2]^T$ the coordinates of the principal point (at which the optical axis intersects the image plane) in the image frame, $\boldsymbol{A}$ takes the form

$$\boldsymbol{A} = \begin{bmatrix} s_1 & 0 & -s_1 i_1 \\ 0 & s_2 & -s_1 i_2 \\ 0 & 0 & -f \end{bmatrix}.$$

In particular, if pixels are square with unit length, then $\boldsymbol{A}$ is given by

$$\boldsymbol{A} = \begin{bmatrix} 1 & 0 & -i_1 \\ 0 & 1 & -i_2 \\ 0 & 0 & -f \end{bmatrix}. \tag{4}$$

When pixels are non-rectangular, eq. (3) still applies but $\boldsymbol{A}$ takes a more complicated form accommodating an extra parameter that encodes shear in the camera axes (see [2, Section 3]).

With time t varying, the function $t \mapsto \boldsymbol{p}(t)$ describes the changing position of the image of P in the camera frame, and the function $t \mapsto \dot{\boldsymbol{p}}(t)$ records the rate of change.

Likewise, the function $t \mapsto \boldsymbol{m}(t)$ describes the changing position of the image of P in the image frame, and the function $t \mapsto \dot{\boldsymbol{m}}(t)$ records the corresponding rate of change.

For a given time instant t, any set of length 6 *flow vectors* $[\boldsymbol{m}(t)^T, \dot{\boldsymbol{m}}(t)^T]^T$—each vector corresponding to a point P from a set $\mathcal{P}$ of stationary points in the scene—is termed an *instantaneous true image velocity field*. Similarly, for a given time interval $[a, b]$, any set of trajectories of the form $t \mapsto [\boldsymbol{m}(t)^T, \dot{\boldsymbol{m}}(t)^T]^T$ with $t \in [a, b]$—each trajectory corresponding to a point P from a set $\mathcal{P}$ of stationary points in the scene—is called a *time-varying true image velocity field*. As is customary, we shall identify an image velocity field with an appropriate *observed image velocity field* or *optical flow field* (see [3, Chapter 12]).

The terms "instantaneous optical flow field" and "time-varying flow field" are employed even if the underlying set $\mathcal{P}$ contains a small number of elements. In particular, $\mathcal{P}$ can be reduced to a single point.

The velocities $\boldsymbol{v}$ and $\boldsymbol{\omega}$ are examples of so-called *extrinsic* parameters of the camera. Another example of an extrinsic parameter is the *projective form* $\boldsymbol{\pi}(\boldsymbol{v})$ of $\boldsymbol{v}$, defined as the composite ratio

$$\boldsymbol{\pi}(\boldsymbol{v}) = (v_1 : v_2 : v_3)$$

provided $\boldsymbol{v} \neq \mathbf{0}$. As is clear, $\boldsymbol{\pi}(\boldsymbol{v})$ captures the direction of $\boldsymbol{v}$.

A camera for which the intrinsic parameters (encoded in $\boldsymbol{A}$) and the extrinsic parameters $\boldsymbol{v}$ and $\boldsymbol{\omega}$ are known will be referred to as *strongly calibrated*. A camera for which the intrinsic parameters and the extrinsic parameters $\boldsymbol{\pi}(\boldsymbol{v})$ and $\boldsymbol{\omega}$ are known will be termed *weakly calibrated*. Strong calibration is typically performed using equipment external to the camera. In contrast, the process of *self-calibration* is carried out using purely image-based information and results in weak calibration (cf. [1,4,5]).

Assuming that $\boldsymbol{v} \neq \mathbf{0}$, the *focus of expansion* (FOE), or instantaneous epipole, of the image is the image point whose coordinate representation $\boldsymbol{p}$ in the camera frame is a multiple of $\boldsymbol{v}$—see [6, Subsection 12.3.1 C] for a discussion of certain subtleties involved in this definition. A moment's reflection reveals that an image point $\boldsymbol{p}$ is *not* the FOE if and only if

$$\widehat{\boldsymbol{v}}\boldsymbol{p} \neq \mathbf{0}. \tag{5}$$

3 Determining Relative Translational Speed

3.1 Theoretical Result

In reconstructing a scene from instantaneous optical flow seen by a weakly calibrated camera, the magnitude $\|\boldsymbol{v}\|$ of the translational velocity determines the scale of the reconstruction; here, of course, $\|\cdot\|$ denotes the Euclidean length of 3-vectors. It is not possible, however, to recover this velocity magnitude, or *translational speed*, from image-based information and a symbolic value must be chosen to set the reconstruction scale. The fact that any positive value may be selected reflects the inherent scale indeterminacy of the projective interpretation of optical flow [1].

Suppose that a time-varying optical flow field is given over a period of time $[a, b]$. It is *a priori* conceivable that the corresponding scale factor may change in an uncontrollable way from one time instant to another—see comments in [7, Section 9]. However, as we show below, this indeterminacy can be significantly reduced if a single point in the static scene is tracked over the entire period $[a, b]$. A single trajectory in a time-varying optical flow field suffices to determine the *relative translational speed* $\|\boldsymbol{v}(t)\|/\|\boldsymbol{v}(a)\|$ for all $t \in [a, b]$, with the consequence that the speed $\|\boldsymbol{v}(t)\|$ is uniquely determined for each $t \in [a, b]$ once the initial speed $\|\boldsymbol{v}(a)\|$ is fixed.

The precise formulation of our result is as follows:

Theorem. *Assume that a weakly calibrated camera moves smoothly so that $\boldsymbol{v}(t) \neq 0$ for each $t \in [a, b]$. Suppose that, for each $t \in [a, b]$, a trajectory $t \mapsto [\boldsymbol{m}(t)^T, \dot{\boldsymbol{m}}(t)^T]^T$ represents a moving image of a point in the static scene. Suppose, moreover, that, for each $t \in [a, b]$, $\boldsymbol{m}(t)$ is not the FOE. Then the relative translational speed $\|\boldsymbol{v}(t)\|/\|\boldsymbol{v}(a)\|$ is uniquely determined for all $t \in [a, b]$. More specifically, there exists a function $g\colon [a, b] \to \mathbb{R}$ such that, for each $t \in [a, b]$, $g(t)$ is explicitly expressible in terms of $\boldsymbol{A}(t)$, $\dot{\mathbf{A}}(t)$, $\boldsymbol{\pi}(\boldsymbol{v}(t))$, $\boldsymbol{\omega}(t)$, $\boldsymbol{m}(t)$ and $\dot{\boldsymbol{m}}(t)$, and such that*

$$\frac{\|\boldsymbol{v}(t)\|}{\|\boldsymbol{v}(a)\|} = \exp\left(\int_a^t g(u)\, du\right). \tag{6}$$

Note. The exact form of g will be given in the course of the proof.

Proof. Given $t \in [a, b]$, we first find the value of $\boldsymbol{p}(t)$ by applying (3) to $\boldsymbol{m}(t)$. We next use the equation

$$\dot{\boldsymbol{p}} = \dot{\mathbf{A}}\boldsymbol{m} + \boldsymbol{A}\dot{\boldsymbol{m}},$$

obtained by differentiating both sides of (3), to determine $\dot{\boldsymbol{p}}(t)$ from $\boldsymbol{m}(t)$ and $\dot{\boldsymbol{m}}(t)$.

Note that (2) can be equivalently rewritten as

$$\boldsymbol{x} = -\frac{x_3 \boldsymbol{p}}{f}. \tag{7}$$

Differentiating both sides of the latter equation, we obtain

$$\dot{\boldsymbol{x}} = \frac{x_3 \dot{f} - \dot{x}_3 f}{f^2}\boldsymbol{p} - \frac{x_3}{f}\dot{\boldsymbol{p}}. \tag{8}$$

Substituting (7) and (8) into (1), we find that

$$x_3\big(\dot{f}\boldsymbol{p} - f(\dot{\boldsymbol{p}} + \widehat{\boldsymbol{\omega}}\boldsymbol{p})\big) - \dot{x}_3 f \boldsymbol{p} + f^2 \boldsymbol{v} = \mathbf{0}. \tag{9}$$

Omitting in notation the dependence upon t, define

$$\begin{aligned} \boldsymbol{k} &= \widehat{\boldsymbol{v}}(\dot{f}\boldsymbol{p} - f(\dot{\boldsymbol{p}} + \widehat{\boldsymbol{\omega}}\boldsymbol{p})), \\ \boldsymbol{l} &= f\widehat{\boldsymbol{v}}\boldsymbol{p}. \end{aligned}$$

Applying $\widehat{\boldsymbol{v}}$ to both sides of (9) and taking into account that $\widehat{\boldsymbol{v}}\boldsymbol{v} = 0$, we see that

$$x_3 \boldsymbol{k} - \dot{x}_3 \boldsymbol{l} = 0.$$

Hence

$$\frac{\dot{x}_3}{x_3} = \frac{\boldsymbol{l}^T \boldsymbol{k}}{\|\boldsymbol{l}\|^2}. \tag{10}$$

For the last formula to be meaningful the denominators on both sides of (10) have to be non-zero. Without loss of generality we may always assume that $x_3 > 0$, as this assumption reflects the fact that the scene is in front of the camera. On the other hand, since $\boldsymbol{p}$ is not the FOE, it follows from (5) that $\boldsymbol{l} \neq 0$.

If $\boldsymbol{v}$ is multiplied by a non-zero scalar factor, then both $\boldsymbol{k}$ and $\boldsymbol{l}$ are multiplied by the same factor, and consequently $\boldsymbol{l}^T\boldsymbol{k}/\|\boldsymbol{l}\|^2$ does not change. As a result, $\boldsymbol{l}^T\boldsymbol{k}/\|\boldsymbol{l}\|^2$ can be regarded as a function of $\boldsymbol{\pi}(\boldsymbol{v})$—not just $\boldsymbol{v}$—and $\boldsymbol{\omega}$, f, $\dot{f}$, $\boldsymbol{p}$, $\dot{\boldsymbol{p}}$, and treated as known. Define

$$\boldsymbol{q} = \frac{1}{f^2}\left(\frac{\boldsymbol{l}^T\boldsymbol{k}}{\|\boldsymbol{l}\|^2} f\boldsymbol{p} - \dot{f}\boldsymbol{p} + f(\dot{\boldsymbol{p}} + \widehat{\boldsymbol{\omega}}\boldsymbol{p})\right).$$

Clearly, being a composite of known entities, $\boldsymbol{q}$ can be regarded as known. In view of (9) and (10), we have

$$\boldsymbol{v} = x_3\boldsymbol{q}$$

and further

$$\|\boldsymbol{v}\| = |x_3|\,\|\boldsymbol{q}\|. \tag{11}$$

To simplify the notation, let $v = \|\boldsymbol{v}\|$ and $q = \|\boldsymbol{q}\|$. Taking the logarithmic derivative of both sides of (11) and next using (10), we deduce that

$$\frac{\dot{v}}{v} = \frac{\dot{x}_3}{x_3} + \frac{\dot{q}}{q} = \frac{\boldsymbol{l}^T\boldsymbol{k}}{\|\boldsymbol{l}\|^2} + \frac{\dot{q}}{q}. \tag{12}$$

Let

$$g = \frac{\boldsymbol{l}^T\boldsymbol{k}}{\|\boldsymbol{l}\|^2} + \frac{\dot{q}}{q}.$$

Since $\boldsymbol{l}^T\boldsymbol{k}/\|\boldsymbol{l}\|^2$ is known and since q and $\dot{q}$ are known too (both functions being derivable from the known function $\boldsymbol{q}$), one can regard g as known. In view of (12), we finally find that

$$\frac{v(t)}{v(a)} = \exp\left(\int_a^t g(u)\,du\right),$$

which, of course, is the desired formula (6) for the relative translational speed. □

3.2 Computational Aspects

The result given above is applicable only in the case where the camera is weakly calibrated. There are many means by which this information may be recovered, and the method presented here will only be of interest in situations when this form of calibration information is available.

One method by which the required weak calibration of a moving camera may be achieved is as follows. If we assume that $\boldsymbol{A}$ takes the form given in (4) (so that pixels are square and have unit length) with the known principal point $[i_1, i_2]^T$, then the only unknown intrinsic parameters are the focal length and its derivative. These parameters, along with the required instantaneous velocities, can be estimated on the basis of an instantaneous optical flow field comprising at least eight elements $[\boldsymbol{m}_i^T, \dot{\boldsymbol{m}}_i^T]^T$ $(i \geq 8)$. A first step is the estimation, up to a common scalar factor, of two matrices, a symmetric matrix $\boldsymbol{C}$ and an antisymmetric matrix $\boldsymbol{W}$, entering the *differential epipolar equation for uncalibrated optical flow*

$$\boldsymbol{m}^T \boldsymbol{W} \dot{\boldsymbol{m}} + \boldsymbol{m}^T \boldsymbol{C} \boldsymbol{m} = 0$$

and the *cubic constraint*[1]

$$\boldsymbol{w}^T \boldsymbol{C} \boldsymbol{w} = 0,$$

with $\boldsymbol{w}$ such that $\boldsymbol{W} = \widehat{\boldsymbol{w}}$. Once the composite ratio

$$\boldsymbol{\pi}(\boldsymbol{C}, \boldsymbol{W}) = (c_{11} : c_{12} : c_{13} : c_{22} : c_{23} : c_{33} : w_1 : w_2 : w_3)$$

is estimated, recovering f and $\dot{f}$ proceeds by exploiting explicit formulae that involve $\boldsymbol{\pi}(\boldsymbol{C}, \boldsymbol{W})$ [1]. Estimation of $\boldsymbol{\pi}(\boldsymbol{C}, \boldsymbol{W})$ can be done by applying one of a host of methods available [8].

To show how this approach works in practice, suppose that a set of at least eight points is tracked simultaneously over time. For each $i = 1, \ldots, I$ with $I \geq 8$, let $\{\boldsymbol{m}_i(t_j)\}_{j=1}^n$ be a sequence of images of the ith point in the scene, and let $\{\dot{\boldsymbol{m}}_i(t_j)\}_{j=1}^{n-1}$, $\dot{\boldsymbol{m}}_i(t_j) = (t_{j+1} - t_j)^{-1}(m_i(t_{j+1}) - m_i(t_j))$, be the sequence of corresponding image velocities. At each time instant t_j with $j < n$, the camera is first weakly calibrated based on the set $\{[\boldsymbol{m}_i(t_j)^T, \dot{\boldsymbol{m}}_i(t_j)^T]^T\}_{i=1}^N$ of all current flow vectors. Then, for each i, a value $g_i(t_j)$ is evolved based on the ith flow vector $[\boldsymbol{m}_i(t_j)^T, \dot{\boldsymbol{m}}_i(t_j)^T]^T$. In absence of information on the reliability of the $g_i(t_j)$, a simple average $\bar{g}(t_j) = I^{-1} \sum_{i=1}^I g_i(t_j)$ is next formed. Finally, the current relative translational velocity $\|\boldsymbol{v}(t_j)\| / \|\boldsymbol{v}(t_1)\|$ is updated to

$$\frac{\|\boldsymbol{v}(t_{j+1})\|}{\|\boldsymbol{v}(t_1)\|} = \frac{\|\boldsymbol{v}(t_j)\|}{\|\boldsymbol{v}(t_1)\|} \exp[(\bar{g}(t_j))(t_{j+1} - t_j)].$$

4 Experimental Evaluation

In order to assess the accuracy of the method presented above synthetic testing was carried out. The tests involved generating the equivalent of 5 seconds of video from a moving camera and comparing the estimated and true magnitudes of the instantaneous translational velocity. The 5 second duration was selected as a reasonable period over which it might be expected that all tracked points would remain visible within the boundaries of the image. The video has been generated at the equivalent of 25 frames per second, and the simulated motion of the camera is of the type that might be expected of a real camera.

An optical flow field of 100 elements was generated, and Gaussian noise (mean 0, standard deviation 0.5 pixels) added to both the location and velocity components of each flow vector. Given that optical flow is usually calculated across the majority of the image plane, it seems reasonable to assume that at least 100 flow vectors are available for velocity magnitude estimation. It is important to note also that in testing the method noise has not been added to the calibration information. The weak calibration used is

[1] Note that $\boldsymbol{w}^T \boldsymbol{C} \boldsymbol{w}$ is a cubic polynomial in the entries of $\boldsymbol{C}$ and $\boldsymbol{W}$.

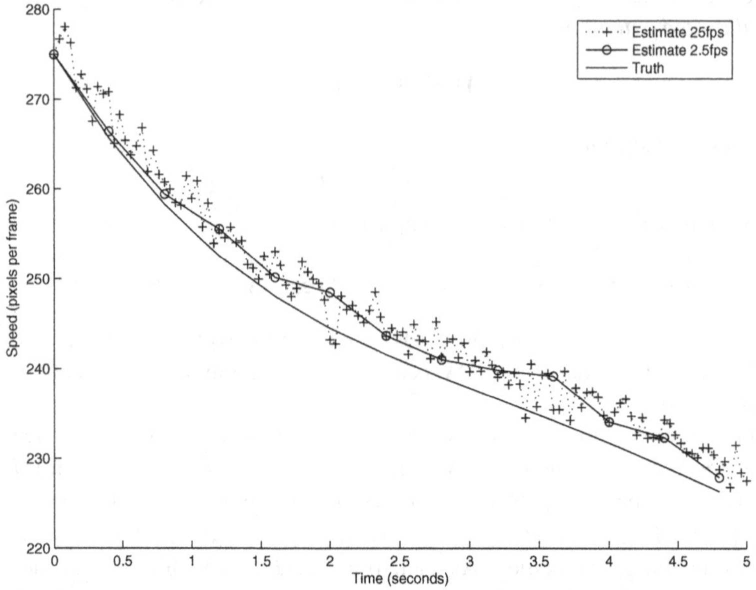

Fig. 1. Speed estimates for 5 seconds of video

thus "true". This reflects the fact that we present here a method of estimating the velocity magnitude, not a method of weak calibration. Figure 1 shows the velocity magnitude estimated using all of the available 25 frames per second, and the magnitude estimated using only 2.5 frames per second. The result based on the lower frame rate is intended to show the degradation in performance in the case where a full weak calibration is not available for each frame of the video. The velocity magnitudes are represented in units of pixels per frame of video (at 25 frames per second).

The graph shows that, despite small variations in the estimated magnitude, on average the method performs very well. The maximum speed error in the 25 frames per second estimate is 0.93%. The decreased frame rate of the 2.5 frames per second test causes a decrease in accuracy as would be expected. The maximum error in the 2.5 frames per second estimate is 1.5%.

5 Conclusion

A novel method was presented for incremental recovery of the magnitude of a camera's translational velocity from time-varying optical flow, relative to an arbitrarily fixed starting value. Results of preliminary synthetic testing confirmed the validity of the approach. Future work will explore how the method may be improved via techniques such as Kalman-like smoothing, use of multiple optical-flow trajectories, and reduction of error accumulation effects.

Acknowledgement

This research was partially supported by the Australian Research Council.

References

1. Brooks, M.J., Chojnacki, W., Baumela, L.: Determining the egomotion of an uncalibrated camera from instantaneous optical flow. Journal of the Optical Society of America A **14** (1997) 2670–2677
2. Faugeras, O.D.: Three-Dimensional Computer Vision: A Geometric Viewpoint. MIT Press, Cambridge, Mass. (1993)
3. Horn, B.K.P.: Robot Vision. MIT Press, Cambridge, Mass. (1986)
4. Faugeras, O.D., Luong, Q.T., Maybank, S.J.: Camera self-calibration: Theory and experiments. In Sandini, G., ed.: Computer Vision—ECCV '92, Second European Conference on Computer Vision. Volume 588 of Lecture Notes in Computer Science., Santa Margherita Ligure, Italy, May 19–22, 1992, Springer-Verlag, Berlin (1992) 321–334
5. Maybank, S.J., Faugeras, O.D.: A theory of self-calibration of a moving camera. International Journal of Computer Vision **8** (1992) 123–151
6. Kanatani, K.: Statistical Optimization for Geometric Computation: Theory and Practice. Elsevier, Amsterdam (1996)
7. Åström, K., Heyden, A.: Multilinear forms in the infinitesimal-time case. In: Proceedings, CVPR '96, IEEE Computer Society Conference on Computer Vision and Pattern Recognition, San Francisco, CA, June 18–20, 1996, IEEE Computer Society Press, Los Alamitos, CA (1996) 833–838
8. Armangué, X., Araújo, H., Salvi, J.: A review on egomotion by means of differential epipolar geometry applied to the movement of a mobile robot. Pattern Recognition **36** (2003) 2927–2944

A Robust Approach for Ego-Motion Estimation Using a Mobile Stereo Platform

Hernán Badino

DaimlerChrysler AG, Research and Technology
D-70546 Stuttgart, Germany
Hernan.Badino@DaimlerChrysler.com

Abstract. We propose a robust approach to the problem of ego-motion estimation using a mobile stereo platform. Stereo is computed for every frame obtaining 3D points of the environment. In addition optical flow establishes correspondences between points in successive frames. A smoothness motion constraint is applied in order to detect flow vectors which are inconsistent with the current ego-motion. The optimal rotation and translation between the resulting clouds of static points is then computed using a closed form solution based on unit quaternions, providing the motion between the current and previous frame. Stabilization and a better estimation are achieved computing the observed motion between the current frame and many frames in the past in a multi-frame fashion. The integration of successive movements allows the reconstruction of the travelled path. Experimental results with sequences covering more than 1.5 kilometers of travelled distance are presented and compared with GPS and odometry.

1 Introduction

The extraction of the observed motion of a camera has been an active area of research over the last decades. Ego-motion computation is motivated by applications like autonomous navigation, self-localization, obstacle-detection and scene reconstruction. Ego-motion is also needed by other applications which require the relative orientation of the cameras with respect to a reference frame. Our interest lies in the computation of the six degrees of freedom of the movement of a vehicle in typical traffic situations. For that purpose, a binocular platform has been mounted in the vehicle, which provides the main input to the ego-motion algorithm. Our method is a passive one, in the sense that no additional information is required, i.e. ego-motion is computed only analyzing the images provided by the cameras and the required calibration parameters.

Many approaches have been proposed with monocular and multi-ocular platforms. When using more than one camera ([1] [2] [3] [4] [5] [6] [7] [8]) the scene structure can be directly recovered through triangulation providing 3D points of the environment. Monocular approaches, instead, do not compute the scene structure ([9] [10] [11]) or they do it at the cost of integrating measurements of the image points (and possible also of other sensors) over a long time, until a reliable structure is obtained ([5] [12] [13]). Therefore multi-ocular approaches perform better in most of the cases.

Computing ego-motion from an image sequence means obtaining the camera movement with respect to a static scene, i.e. the motion is relative to something which can be

B. Jähne et al. (Eds.): IWCM 2004, LNCS 3417, pp. 198–208, 2007.

considered static. The scenarios we are interested in are typical traffic situations. Such an environment presents many participants with self-motion which can make our estimation fail if they are considered static. Also the incorrect computation of a 3D position or the incorrect tracking of features can introduce errors in the computation. Therefore an effective rejection rule must be applied in order to identify which image points are not showing a coherent movement. We propose a very effective constraint which we call smoothness motion constraint (SMC).

Mallet et al [4] present an approach very similar to the one presented here, where they focus on the reduction of errors produced by the stereo and tracking algorithms. The reduction of errors is of course important to improve accuracy, but a robust method should still be able to work well with noisy measurements, since errors are unavoidable. The computation of ego-motion is also normally computed considering only the current and previous state, which provides the current relative motion. The complete motion is then obtained concatenating the individual estimations. This may lead to poor results because of destabilization. A more stable estimation can be achieved if considering not only the last two frames, but also many frames back in the time (multi-frame estimation).

In the following section we propose a robust method for the computation of ego-motion and present the first experimental results with two sequences, summing both sequences together a travelled distance of more than 1.5 kilometers.

1.1 Organization of the Paper

In section two we present a block diagram of the method and describe shortly the stereo and tracking algorithm. Section three summarizes the least-square approach used to compute the 6 degrees of freedom of motion. Section four introduces the smoothness motion constraint. In section five we describe the multi-frame motion estimation procedure. Experimental results are shown in section six. Conclusions comprise the last section.

2 A General Description of the Approach

Figure 1 shows a block diagram of the method. The inputs are given by the left and right images from a stereo imaging system. We assume that the calibration parameters are known and that the provided images are rectified. Optical flow is computed using the current and previous left image. Disparities between the left and right image are only computed for those image positions where the flow algorithm was successful. Triangulation is performed and a list with the tracked points for the current frame is generated. The list is added to a table where the last m lists of tracked 3D points are stored. This will allow the integration of a multi-frame motion estimation, i.e. motion is not only obtained based on the last observed movement, but also between m frames in the past and the current frame.

The six motion parameters (three components for translation and three for rotation) are then computed as the optimal translation and rotation found between the current and previous list of 3D points using a least squares closed-form solution based on rotation quaternions as shown in the next section. In order to avoid the introduction of erroneous data in the least square computation, a smoothness motion constraint is applied,

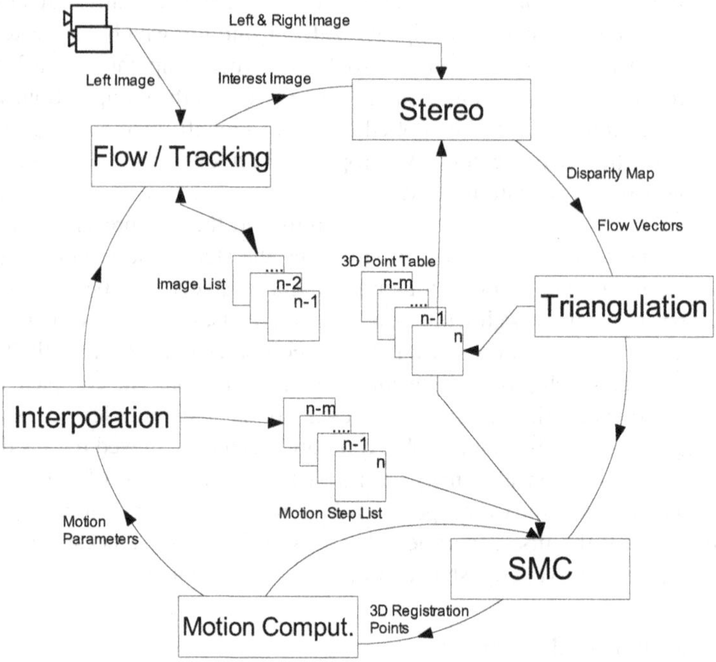

Fig. 1. Block Diagram of the Approach

rejecting all pairs of points which represent an incoherent movement with respect to the current ego-motion (section 4). These two steps are repeated but using the list of tracked points between the current frame and m frames in the past. The two motion hypotheses are then interpolated obtaining our final ego-motion estimation, and updating the list of motion steps (section 5). The whole process is then repeated for every new input data stream.

The flow and stereo algorithms to be used are not constraint to a specific implementation. In fact, our approach was tested with different algorithms obtaining almost identical results. Nevertheless, we describe shortly the stereo and optical flow algorithms used in the experimental results of section 6. The stereo algorithm works based on a coarse-to-fine scheme in which a gaussian pyramid for left and right images is constructed with a sampling factor of two. The search for the best disparity is only performed at the top level of the pyramid and then a translation of the disparity map is made to the next level, where a correction is done within an interval ± 1 of the calculated disparity. We use the sum of squared differences as the default correlation function. Different filters and constraints are applied between pyramid translations. The zero-mean normalized cross-correlation (ZNCC) is used in order to check the confidence of the match. A match is considered reliable if the ZNCC coefficient is larger than a predefined threshold. Dynamic programming can also be applied between pyramid translations in order to eliminate matches which invalidate the ordering constraint. Finally a sub-pixel disparity map is computed as the last step in the pyramid. This is achieved by fitting a second degree curve to the best match and its neighbors and finding the sub-pixel disparity where the slope is zero in the quadratic function.

The tracking algorithm we use for the computation of optical flow is the Kanade / Lucas / Tomasi (KLT) tracker. An extended description of the algorithm can be found in [12] and therefore we skip the description of this method here. Our experience with different tracker algorithms has shown that the KLT tracker can track feature points with a small error over tens of frames.

3 Obtaining the Relative Orientation

Let $P = \vec{p}_i$ be the set of static points of the previous time and $X = \vec{x}_i$ the sets of static points observed at the current time, where $\vec{p}_i \leftrightarrow \vec{x}_i$, i.e. $\vec{x}_i$ is the transformed version at time t_n of the point $\vec{p}_i$ at time t_{n-1}. If the measurement of point positions were free of noise, only three non-collinear points of each set would be enough to obtain the exact translation and rotation between both sets, which at the same time corresponds to the inverse movement of the camera. Therefore the optimal rotation and translation between two noisy sets must be found minimizing some error function. We use the closed form solution based on quaternions presented by Horn [14]. The main steps of the closed form are presented here. For more details see the above reference.

The error function to be minimized can be expressed as the sum of the weighted residual errors between the rotated and translated data set P with data set X, i.e.:

$$e = \sum_{i=1}^{n} w_i \|e_i\|^2 = \sum_{i=1}^{n} w_i \|\vec{p}_i - R(\vec{q})\vec{x}_i - \vec{t}\|^2 \tag{1}$$

where n is the amount of points in the sets, R is a rotation matrix obtained as a function of the unit rotation quaternion $\vec{q}$, $\vec{t}$ is a translation vector and w_i are individual weights representing the expected error in the measurement of the points.

We compute first the cross-covariance matrix of both sets:

$$\Sigma_{XP} = \frac{\sum_{i=1}^{n} [w_i(\vec{x}_i - \vec{u}_X)(\vec{p}_i - \vec{u}_P)^t]}{\sum_{i=1}^{n} w_i} = \frac{\sum_{i=1}^{n} [w_i \vec{x}_i \vec{p}_i^t]}{\sum_{i=1}^{n} w_i} - \vec{u}_X \vec{u}_P^t$$

where

$$\vec{u}_X = \frac{\sum_{i=1}^{n} w_i \vec{x}_i}{\sum_{i=1}^{n} w_i} \qquad \vec{u}_P = \frac{\sum_{i=1}^{n} w_i \vec{p}_i}{\sum_{i=1}^{n} w_i}$$

correspond to the weighted centroids of each set. Through the definition of the anti-symmetric matrix:

$$A = (\Sigma_{XP} - \Sigma_{XP}^t)$$

and a vector consisting of the elements of A:

$$\Delta = [\, A_{2,3} \; A_{3,1} \; A_{1,2} \,]$$

the optimal rotation quaternion $\vec{q}$ is found as the unit eigenvector corresponding to the maximum eigenvalue of the matrix:

$$Q(\Sigma_{XP}) = \begin{bmatrix} tr(\Sigma_{XP}) & \Delta^t \\ \Delta & \Sigma_{XP} + \Sigma_{XP}^t - tr(\Sigma_{XP}) I_3 \end{bmatrix}$$

where I_3 is the 3×3 identity matrix and $tr(M)$ expresses the trace of a matrix M. The rotation matrix $R(\vec{q})$ of equation 1 is obtained from the lower right hand 3×3 sub-matrix of:

$$\overline{Q}^T Q = \begin{bmatrix} \vec{q} \cdot \vec{q} & 0 & 0 & 0 \\ 0 & (q_0^2 + q_x^2 - q_y^2 - q_z^2) & 2(q_x q_y - q_0 q_z) & 2(q_x q_z + q_0 q_y) \\ 0 & 2(q_y q_x + q_0 q_z) & (q_0^2 - q_x^2 + q_y^2 - q_z^2) & 2(q_y q_z - q_0 q_x) \\ 0 & 2(q_z q_x + q_0 q_y) & 2(q_z q_y - q_0 q_x) & (q_0^2 - q_x^2 - q_y^2 + q_z^2) \end{bmatrix}$$

where $\overline{Q}^T$ and Q are the 4×4 orthogonal matrices corresponding to the quaternion $\vec{q}$ (see [14]). The translation can now be obtained as the difference of the rotated and translated centroid of the current set with the centroid of the previous set:

$$\vec{t} = \vec{u}_P - R(\vec{q})\vec{u}_X.$$

3.1 Motion Representation with Matrices

The computed motion of the camera at time t_n (i.e. the motion observed from frame $n-1$ to frame n, which we call single step estimation) is represented by the matrix M_n' where:

$$M_n' = \begin{bmatrix} R(\vec{q}_n) & \vec{t}_n \\ 0 & 1 \end{bmatrix}$$

The complete motion of the camera since initialization can be obtained as the products of individual motion matrices:

$$M_n = \prod_{i=1}^{n} M_i'$$

Being the initial position of the camera $\vec{p}_0 = \begin{bmatrix} x_0 \; y_0 \; z_0 \; 1 \end{bmatrix}$ the current ego-position $\vec{p}_n = \begin{bmatrix} x_n \; y_n \; z_n \; 1 \end{bmatrix}$ can be obtained by multiplying the complete motion matrix with

p_0, i.e. $\vec{p}_n = M_n \vec{p}_0$. A sub-chain of movement from time t_j to time t_k can also be obtained as:

$$M_{j,k} = M_j^{-1} M_k = \prod_{i=j+1}^{k} M_i' \tag{2}$$

Figure 2 shows an example of motion integration with matrices. As it will be seen in section 5, equation 2 will help in the integration of the motion produced between two non-consecutive frames (multi-frame estimation) in order to stabilize the computed ego-motion parameters.

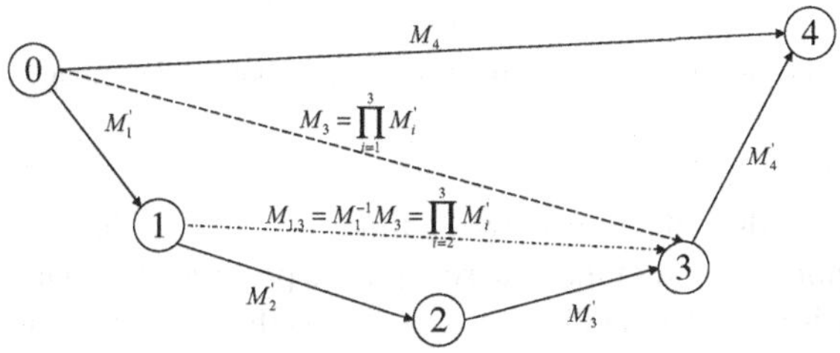

Fig. 2. The integration of single-step estimations can be obtained by just multiplying the individual motion matrices. Every circle denotes the state (position and orientation) of the camera between time t_0 and time t_4. Lines indicate motion in 3D-space.

4 Smoothness Motion Constraint

Optical flow and/or stereo can deliver false information about 3D position or image point correspondence between image frames, or some of the points can correspond to a self-moving object. Typical traffic situations present many actors with self-motion such as other vehicles and pedestrians. The situation where more than 50% of the image area is composed of moving objects is not very unusual. A robust method should still be able to give accurate results in front of such situations. If the frame rate is high enough to obtain a smooth motion between consecutive frames, then the current motion to be estimated should be similar to the immediate previous motion. Therefore, before including the pair of points $\vec{p}_i$ and $\vec{x}_i$ into their corresponding data sets P and X we evaluate if the vector $\vec{v}_i = \overrightarrow{x_i p_i}$ indicates a coherent movement. Let us define $\vec{d} = \begin{bmatrix} \dot{x}_{max} & \dot{y}_{max} & \dot{z}_{max} & 1 \end{bmatrix}$ as the maximal accepted error of the position of 3D point with respect to a predicted position. Based on our previous estimation of motion at time t_{n-1} we evaluate the movement coherence of the vector $\vec{v}_i$ as:

$$\vec{c}_i = M_{n-1}' \vec{x}_i - \vec{p}_i \tag{3}$$

i.e., the error of the point position with respect to our prediction. If the absolute value of any component of c_i is larger than

$$\vec{d'} = \frac{\Delta t_n}{\Delta t_{n-1}} \vec{d} \tag{4}$$

Fig. 3. Example of SMC. The images show the flow vectors before (left image) and after (right image) the SMC.

where a Δt_k corresponds to the time between time t_{k-1} and t_k, then the pair of points are discarded and not included in the data sets for the posterior computation of relative orientation. Otherwise, we weight the pair of points as the ratio of change with respect to the last motion:

$$w_i = 1 - \frac{||\vec{c}_i||^2}{||\vec{d}'||^2} \tag{5}$$

which later is used as indicated in section 3. Equations (3) to (5) define the smoothness motion constraint. In figure 3 an example of the effectiveness of the SMC is shown. The left image shows all the flow vectors computed with the KLT tracker. The right image shows only those vectors which were selected by the SMC. Comparing both images it can be seen how the SMC has eliminated most of the incorrect vectors and has left only those which provide the most reliable information.

5 Multi-frame Estimation

Single step estimation, i.e. the estimation of the motion parameters from the current and previous frame is the standard case in most approaches. If we were able to compute the motion also between non-consecutive frames, the estimation would be improved thanks to the integration of more measurements. Also robustness is increased, since when one of the estimations fail, the motion will be still provided by some of the others. Another problem is the propagation of errors. An error produced in one step will propagate superlinearly in the future ego-position estimations [7]. For example, if the yaw rate is incorrectly estimated in one step, it is implausible that this will be corrected later. A stabilization process is then also required.

We propose a simple approach in order to provide stabilization to the estimation process. If we are able to track points in m frames, then we can also compute the motion produced between the current and the m previous frames. The estimation of motion between frame m and current frame n ($m < n - 1$) follows exactly the same procedure as explained above. Only when applying the SMC, a small change takes place, since the

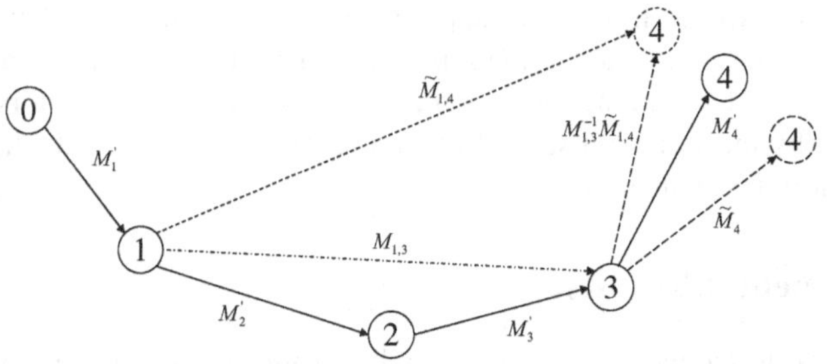

Fig. 4. Multi-frame approach for ego-motion estimation. The motion between times t_3 and t_4 is obtained as the interpolation of two motion matrices.

Fig. 5. Aerial images of the tested routes for the sequence *Curves* (left image) and sequence *Ring* (right image). The arrows indicates the start and end of the tested routes.

prediction of the position for m frames is not the same as for a single step. In other words, the matrix M'_{n-1} of equation (3) is not valid any more. If the single step estimation matrix $\tilde{M}_n$ for the current frame was already computed, then equation (3) becomes:

$$\vec{c}_i = M_{n-m}^{-1} M_{n-1} \tilde{M}_n \vec{x}_i - \vec{p}_i$$

i.e. the estimated motion between times t_{n-m} and t_{n-1}, updated with the current simple step estimation of time t_n. This allows the SMC to be even more precise, since the uncertainty in the movement is now centered around an updated prediction, while for the single step estimation, the uncertainty is centered around a position defined by the last motion.

Once the camera motion matrix $\tilde{M}_{m,n}$ between times t_{n-m} and t_n is obtained, it must be integrated with the single step estimation. This is performed by interpolation. The interpolation of matrices makes sense if they are estimations of the same motion. This is not the case since the single step motion matrix is referred as the motion between the last two frames and the multi-frame motion matrix as the motion between m frames in the past to the current one. Therefore, the matrices to be interpolated are $\tilde{M}_n$ and $M_{m,n-1}^{-1} \tilde{M}_{m,n}$ (see figure 4). The corresponding rotation matrices are converted to quaternions in order to apply a spherical linear interpolation. The interpolated quaternion is converted to the final rotation matrix R_n. Translation vectors are linearly interpolated, obtaining the new translation vector $\vec{t}_n$. The factors of interpolation are given by the weighted sum of quadratic deviations obtained when computing the relative motion of equation 1.

6 Experimental Results

The method was tested with two sequences taken from a vehicle while driving in typical traffic situations. Aerial views[1] of the tested route of each sequence can be seen in figure 5 where the arrows indicate the start and the end of the sequence. The frame rate was selected to 10 frames per second. The baseline of the stereo camera is 0.35 meters and the images have a standard VGA resolution (640×480 pixels). The velocity of the vehicle varies between 18 and 55 km/h. The first sequence, which we call *Curves*,

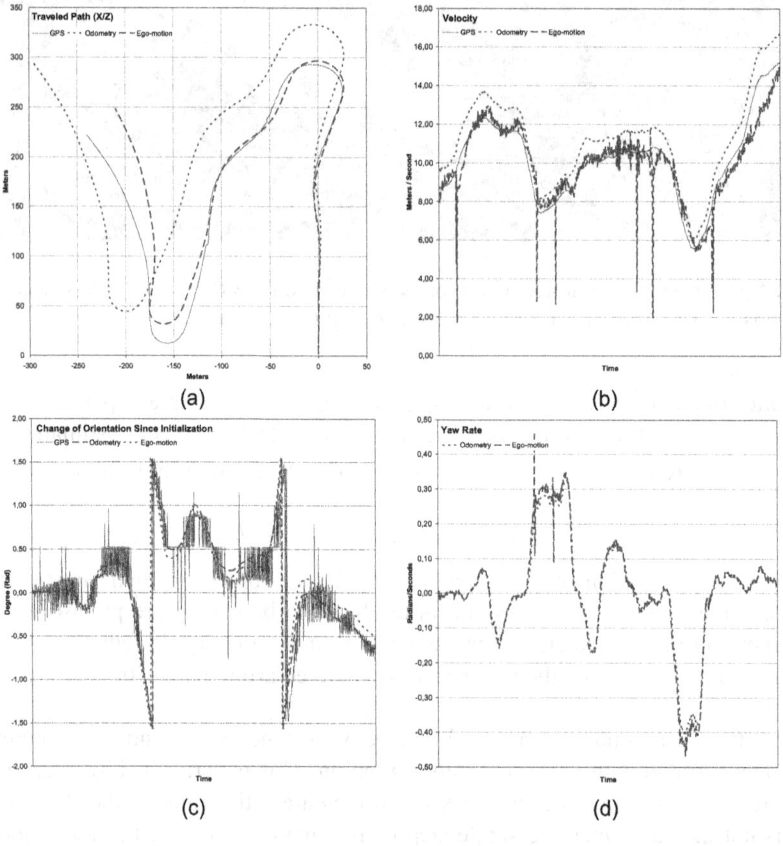

Fig. 6. Results for the sequence *Curves*

[1] Courtesy of the Municipality of Esslingen am Neckar. Source: www.esslingen.de.

covers a travelled distance of around 900 meters, while the second sequence, called *Ring* covers a distance of 650 meters.

The computed ego-position for the *Curves* sequence is shown in figure 6 (a). Comparing the curve with GPS information, one observes that the error in the ego-position is relatively small. In fact, the estimation is better than using odometry, which overestimates the travelled distance. This can be seen more clearly when comparing the velocity estimations of figure 6 (b), which shows the computed velocity curves in time. Observe how the curve of our approach fits very good to the one obtained with GPS while odometry estimates the velocity too high. The estimation of the travelled distance for GPS was 696.30 meters, for our approach 664.55 meters, and using odometry 715.99 meters. The GPS distance was expected to be larger than the distance computed with our approach, since the GPS position oscillates around the true position. In figures 6(c) is shown the change in the vehicle orientation since initialization, where the curves corresponding to odometry and ego-motion are smooth in comparison to the GPS estimation. Finally, the yaw-rate estimation for odometry and ego-motion is shown in 6(d) where almost a complete overlap of both curves is observed.

The ego-position estimations for the sequence *Ring* can be seen in figure 7 (a). Our purpose here was to observe the behavior of each method when driving 360°. The ego-motion estimation could close the ring, while odometry failed to do so. The distance between start position and end position for odometry at the point where the ring should have been closed is about 37.63 meters, for GPS is 1.73 meters and using our method 16.97 meters. The yaw rate estimation for odometry and ego-motion is shown in figure 7 (b), where once again both curves overlap most of the time.

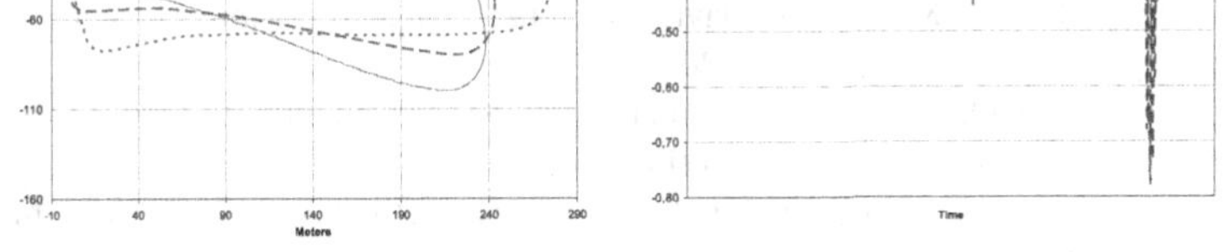

(a) (b)

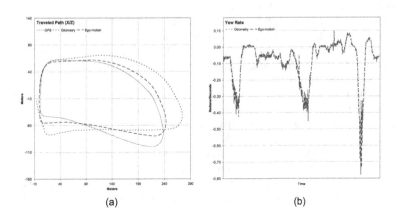

Fig. 7. Results for the sequence *Ring*

7 Conclusion

We have presented an approach for the computation of ego-motion which is very robust against moving objects and stereo/flow failures. The 6 degrees of freedom of motion can be accurately extracted with our method by computing the optimal rotation and translation between the clouds of 3D points of multiple frames. Robustness is given by an effective constraint which eliminates all flow vectors which are inconsistent with the current ego-motion. Motion can also be better estimated if the motion is computed not only based on the current and last frame, but also between the current frame and many frames in the past, providing motion stability.

The method has demonstrated to be better than odometry and yields more accurate results than GPS for short travelled distances since the position obtained with GPS are rough estimations around the true position.

References

1. Morency, L.P., Darrell, T.: Stereo tracking using icp and normal flow constraint. In: Proceedings of International Conference on Pattern Recognition, Quebec, Canada (2002)
2. Demirdjian, D., Horaud, R.: Motion-egomotion discrimination and motion segmentation from image pair streams. In: Computer Vision and Image Understanding. Volume 78(1). (2000) 53–68
3. Demirdjian, D., Darrel, T.: Motion estimation from disparity images. In: Technical Report AI Memo 2001-009, MIT Artificial Intelligence Laboratory. (2001)
4. Mallet, A., Lacroix, S., Gallo, L.: Position estimation in outdoor environments using pixel tracking and stereovision. In: Proceedings of the 2000 IEEE International Conference on Robotics and Automation, ICRA 2000, San Francisco (2000) 3519–3524
5. Mandelbaum, R., Slagian, G., Sawhney, H.: Correlation-based estimation of ego-motion and structure from motion and stereo. In: Proceedings of the Internation Conference on Computer Vision (ICCV'98), Kerkyra, Greece (1999) 544–550
6. Matthies, L., Shafer, S.A.: Error modeling in stereo navigation. In: IEEE Journal of Robotics and Automation. Volume RA-3(3). (1987) 239–248
7. Olson, C.F., Matthies, L.H., Schoppers, M., Maimone, M.W.: Rover navigation using stereo ego-motion. In: Robotics and Autonomous Systems. Volume 43(4). (2003) 215–229
8. van der Mark, W., Fontijne, D., Dorst, L., Groen, F.C.: Vehicle ego-motion estimation with geometric algebra. In: Proceedings IEEE Intelligent Vehicle Symposium, Versialles, France, May 18-20 2002. (2002)
9. Suzuki, T., Kanade, T.: Measurements of vehicle motion using optical flow. In: IEEE Conference on Intelligent Transportation Systems, Tokyo, Japan. (1999)
10. Bruss, A.R., Horn, B.K.: Passive navigation. In: Computer Vision, Graphics, and Image Processing. Volume 21(1). (1983) 3–20
11. Stein, G.P., Mano, O., Shashua, A.: A robust method for computing vehicle ego-motion. In: IEEE Intelligent Vehicles Symposium (IV2000), Dearborn, MI. (2000)
12. Tomasi, C., Kanade, T.: Shape and motion from image streams: a factorization method – 3. detection and tracking of point features. Technical Report CMU-CS-91-132, School of CS – CMU (1991)
13. Carlsson, S.: Recursive estimation of ego-motion and scene structure from a moving platform. In: Proc. 7:th Scand. Conf. on Image Analysis, Aalborg (1991) 958–965
14. Horn, B.K.P.: Closed-form solution of absolute orientation using unit quaternions. In: Journal of the Optical Society of America A. Volume 4(4). (1987) 629–642

Robust Monocular Detection of Independent Motion by a Moving Observer

Felix Woelk and Reinhard Koch

Christian-Albrechts-Universität zu Kiel,
Institute für Informatik und Praktische Mathematik,
Ohlshausenstr. 40, 24098 Kiel, Germany
{woelk, rk}@mip.informatik.uni-kiel.de

Abstract. A fast and robust algorithm for the detection of independently moving objects by a moving observer by means of investigating optical flow fields is presented. The detection method for independent motion relies on knowledge about the camera motion. Even though inertial sensors provide information about the camera motion, the sensor data does not always satisfy the requirements of the proposed detection method. The first part of this paper therefore deals with the enhancement of earlier work [29] by ego-motion refinement. A linearization of the ego-motion estimation problem is presented. Further on a robust enhancement to this approach is given.

Since the measurement of optical flow is a computationally expensive operation, it is necessary to restrict the number of flow measurements. The proposed algorithm uses two different ways to determine the positions, where optical flow is calculated. A fraction of the positions is determined by using a sequential Monte Carlo sampling resampling algorithm, while the remaining fraction of the positions is determined by using a random variable, which is distributed according to an initialization distribution. This approach results in a fixed number of optical flow calculations leading to a robust real time detection of independently moving objects on standard consumer PCs.[1]

1 Introduction

The detection of independently moving objects by an also moving observer is a vital ability for any animal. The early detection of an enemy while moving through visual clutter can be a matter of life and death. Also for modern humans it is useful, e.g. for collision prevention in traffic. Using the human head as an inspiration, a lightweight monocular camera mounted on a pan-tilt-unit (PTU) is chosen to investigate the environment in this application. The analysis of optical flow fields gathered from this camera system is a cheap and straight forward approach avoiding heavy and sensitive stereo rigs.

The method for the detection of independent motion used in this work relies on the knowledge of the camera motion. Even though inertial sensors provide information about this motion, the accuracy of these sensors does not satisfy the requirements of the used detection methods. To overcome this handicap, a novel algorithm for the refinement of the essential matrix is developed and compared against other approaches.

[1] This work was supported by BMBF Grant No. 1959156C.

B. Jähne et al. (Eds.): IWCM 2004, LNCS 3417, pp. 209–222, 2007.

Extensive studies about essential matrix estimation [7, 9, 18] and the closely related problem of fundamental matrix computation [8, 9, 15, 16, 26, 27, 32] exist. Further on there is a vast variety of literature about ego-motion estimation [4, 23, 24]. Two other papers from this workshop also deal with ego-motion refinement: Badino [1] fuses data from optical flow algorithm with depth data gathered from a mobile stereo platform for ego-motion estimation and Hengel [10] estimates the relative translational speed from dense optical flow fields.

Since determining highly accurate optical flow with subpixel precision is a computationally expensive operation, restrictions on the maximum number of optical flow computations have to be made in real time environments. The approach chosen in this work is inspired by [12] and determines the sample positions (i.e. points where optical flow will be calculated) partly by using a vector of random variables, which are distributed according to an initialization distribution function (IDF), and partly by propagating samples from the last time step using a sequential Monte Carle sampling resampling approach.

While a wide range of literature on the application of particle filters to tracking tasks [12,13,20] and lately on improvements on the particle filter to overcome the degeneracy problem [11, 14, 17, 30] exist, only little work has been done in the field of using such probabilistic techniques for the investigation and interpretation of optical flow fields: In [3] motion discontinuities are tracked using optical flow and the CONDENSATION algorithm and in 2002 Zelek [31] used a particle filter to predict and therefore speedup a correlation based optical flow algorithm.

In the following sections, the basic concept used for the detection of independent motion is explained first. Afterwards an algorithm for the estimation of the necessary camera motion parameters is presented. A sequential Monte Carle sampling resampling approach to speedup and stabilize the detection of independent motion is described next. Finally experiments on synthetic data are shown.

2 Detection of Independently Moving Objects

The basic concepts used for the detection of independently moving objects by a moving observer through investigation of the optical flow are introduced in this section.

Computation of the Optical Flow: A large number of algorithms for the computation of optical flow exist [2]. Any of these algorithms calculating the full 2D optical flow can be used for the proposed algorithm. Algorithms calculating the normal flow only (i.e. the flow component parallel to the image gradient) are, however, inappropriate. The optical flow in this work is calculated using an iterative gradient descend algorithm [19], applied to subsequent levels of an image pyramid.

Detection of Independent Motion: Each optical flow field resulting from a relative motion between the camera and a static object consists of a rotational part and a translational part (Fig. 1). The rotational part is independent of the scene geometry and can be computed from the camera rotation. Subtraction of the rotational flow field from the overall flow field results in the translational flow field, where all flow vectors point away from the focus of expansion (FOE), which can be calculated from the camera

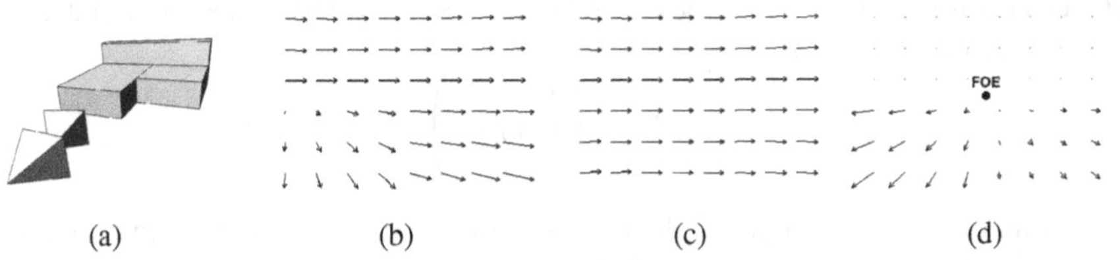

Fig. 1. Theoretical flow fields for a simple scene. The 3D scene is shown at (a). The scene consists of 3 blocks. The camera, displayed as small pyramids, translates towards the blocks while rotating around the y axis. The flow field F as induced by this movement is shown in (b). Its rotational component F_R (c) and translational component F_T (d) with the Focus of Expansion (FOE) are shown on the right.

motion. With known camera motion, only the direction of the translational part of the optical flow field can be predicted. The angle between the predicted direction and the (also rotation corrected) flow calculated from the two images serves as a measure for independent motion [28] (Fig. 5). In this context, independent motion means motion inconsistent with the camera motion. This detection method requires the exact knowledge of the camera motion. In our approach, the camera motion (relative to the static scene) can be derived from rotation sensor and speed sensor data of the car, or it can alternatively be measured directly from the static scene [21]. A robust approach for the estimation of the necessary camera motion parameters is presented in the next section.

3 Essential Matrix Refinement from Image Point Correspondences

In this section a new iterative linearized method for the estimation of the essential matrix is proposed. First the basic concepts for the description of image relations, the fundamental matrix and the essential matrix, are introduced. After a brief review of 8-point and the Levenberg-Marquard (LM) algorithm, the new iterative linearized approach is derived in detail and compared against the two previous mentioned approaches. In the last part, an enhancement to the new approach is suggested to make it robust against gross errors in the image point correspondences. Large errors in image point correspondences may result from either measurement errors or from the presence of independent motion in the images.

The fundamental matrix. F describes the relationship between two views of a static scene. Any point p in the first view is constrained to lie on the epipolar line l in the second view. The fundamental matrix F relates x to l via $l = Fx$. The well known fundamental constraint relates two corresponding image points $\overline{p}'$ and $\overline{p}$ through:

$$\overline{p}'^T F \overline{p} = 0 \tag{1}$$

Although the matrix F has 9 entries it has only 7 degrees of freedom (dof) [9] [2].

[2] F is scale independent and has rank 2.

The essential matrix. E describes the relationship between two views of a static scene if the calibration matrix K

$$K = \begin{pmatrix} f & s & c_x \\ 0 & af & c_y \\ 0 & 0 & 1 \end{pmatrix} \tag{2}$$

consisting of the focal length f, the aspect ratio a, the skew s and the principal point $(c_x, c_y)^T$ is known. The fundamental constraint (eq. 1) then holds on normalized image coordinates $\overline{p} = K^{-1}p$:

$$p'^T E p = 0 \tag{3}$$

In contrast to F, the essential matrix E has only 5 dof (3 for the rotation and 2 for the translation direction between the two views). If the epipole and the rotation are known, the essential matrix can be computed as follows:

$$E = [e]_\times \cdot R = \begin{pmatrix} 0 & -1 & e_y \\ 1 & 0 & -e_x \\ -e_y & e_x & 0 \end{pmatrix} \cdot R \tag{4}$$

where $(e_x, e_y, 1)^T$ is the epipole in homogenous coordinates, [3] $[e]_\times$ denotes the 3 by 3 skew symmetric matrix with entries from the vector e and R is the rotation matrix. For a thorough discussion on multiple view geometry and projective geometry see [9].

3.1 Comparison of Different Approaches

8 Point: In this approach (which is described in detail in [9]), the 8 point algorithm is used to estimate a first approximation of the essential matrix E. A linear system A in the 9 unknown entries of the essential matrix $f = (E_{1,1}, E_{1,2}, \ldots, E_{3,3})^T$ is constructed using homogenized, normalized image point correspondences $p_n = (x_n, y_n, 1)^T$ and $p'_n = (x'_n, y'_n, 1)^T$ in the fundamental constraint (eq. 1):

$$A \cdot f = 0 \tag{5}$$

where each row A_n of A has the form

$$A_n = (x'_n x_n, x'_n y_n, x'_n, y'_n x_n, y'_n y_n, y'_n, x_n, y_n, 1) \tag{6}$$

After retrieving the least squares solution (subject to $||f||_2 = 1$) of the system (eq. 5), the SVD of the resulting matrix $E' = UDV^T$ is used to enforce the 5 dof constraint by setting the smallest singular value to zero and the remaining two singular values to their mean [4]. Updating the diagonal matrix D with the new singular values leads to D'. Recomputation of the essential matrix with the updated D' leads to the closest essential matrix $E'' = UD'V^T$ to E in Frobenius norm. The epipole e and rotation matrix R can be extracted from E'' by using the SVD of $E'' = UD'V^T$:

$$[e]_\times = UZU^T \qquad \text{and} \qquad R = UWV^T \text{ or } UW^TV^T \tag{7}$$

[3] Homogenous coordinates are members of a projective space $\mathbb{P}$ (in this case $\mathbb{P}^2$). The projective space $\mathbb{P}^2$ is an extension of the Euclidean space $\mathbb{R}^2$.

[4] From the three singular values of an essential matrix, two are equal and the remaining is zero.

with the matrices

$$W = \begin{pmatrix} 0 & -1 & 0 \\ 1 & 0 & 0 \\ 0 & 0 & 1 \end{pmatrix} \qquad \text{and} \qquad Z = \begin{pmatrix} 0 & 1 & 0 \\ -1 & 0 & 0 \\ 0 & 0 & 0 \end{pmatrix} \tag{8}$$

Levenberg-Marquard: In this approach the essential matrix is parameterized using the direction of translation (the angles of the spherical representation of the vector between the two camera centers) and an axis and angle representation of the rotation matrix R. In order to restrict the number of parameters to 5 (the dof of the essential matrix), the angle is encoded using the length of the axis. Two different error functions are investigated here:

- A: The geometric error function uses the sums of the distances between the image point and the corresponding epipolar line as error function.
- B: The algebraic error function uses the residuum resulting from the fundamental constraint (eq. 3) directly.

A starting approximation to the essential matrix needs to be known in both versions A and B of this approach.

Iterative Linearized: The true epipole e and the true rotation R are assumed to be known up to small errors Δe and ΔR:

$$e = e_c + \Delta e \qquad\qquad R = \Delta R \cdot R_c \tag{9}$$

The starting approximations e_c and R_c are calculated using the inertial sensors of the car (speed, yawrate, steering angle, pan angle and tilt angle) [28]. If only an approximate essential matrix is known, eq. 7 can be used to extract e_c and R_c from the essential matrix. In order to solve the problem with low computational cost, ΔR is approximated by a Taylor series expansion up to the linear term:

$$\Delta R \approx (I + [r]_\times) = \begin{pmatrix} 1 & 0 & 0 \\ 0 & 1 & 0 \\ 0 & 0 & 1 \end{pmatrix} + \begin{pmatrix} 0 & -r_z & r_y \\ r_z & 0 & -r_x \\ -r_y & r_x & 0 \end{pmatrix} = \begin{pmatrix} 1 & -r_z & r_y \\ r_z & 1 & -r_x \\ -r_y & r_x & 1 \end{pmatrix} \tag{10}$$

where $r = (r_x, r_y, r_z)^T$ is a vector of the Euler rotation angles around the x, y and z axis resp., I is the identity matrix and $[r]_\times$ again describes a skew symmetric 3×3 matrix with entries from r. The linearization is only valid for small angles r_ν and small epipole error $\Delta e = (\Delta e_x, \Delta e_y, 0)^T$:

$$r_x, r_y, r_z \ll 1 \qquad \Delta e_x, \Delta e_y \ll 1 \tag{11}$$

Using eq. 9 and eq. 10 in fundamental constraint (eq. 3) results in:

$$\begin{aligned} e_y p'_{x,r} - e_x p'_{y,r} + e_x p_y - e_y p_x - e_x r_x - p'_{x,r} p_y + p'_{y,r} p_x + p'_{x,r} r_x + \\ p_x \Delta e_x r_z + p_y \Delta e_y r_z - e_x p'_{y,r} p_y r_x + e_y p'_{x,r} p_y r_x + p'_{y,r} p_x \Delta e_x r_y + \\ \Delta e_y (p'_{x,r} - p_x + p'_{x,r} p_y r_x) + \Delta e_y r_y (-p'_{x,r} p_x - 1) + \\ r_y (p'_{y,r} - e_y + e_x p'_{y,r} p_x - e_y p'_{x,r} p_x) + r_z (e_x p_x + e_y p_y - p'_{x,r} p_x - p'_{y,r} p_y) + \\ \Delta e_x (p_y - p'_{y,r} - r_x - p'_{y,r} p_y r_x) = 0 \end{aligned} \tag{12}$$

with the point correspondence between $p = (p_x, p_y, 1)^T$ and the rotated point $p'_r = R_c * p' = (p'_{x,r}, p'_{y,r}, 1)^T$.

Neglecting the terms with quadratic small values (e.g. $r_z \Delta e_x$) and using at least 5 point correspondences leads to a somehow simpler linear equation system in Δe and r:

$$A \cdot \begin{pmatrix} \Delta e_x \\ \Delta e_y \\ r_x \\ r_y \\ r_z \end{pmatrix} = B \tag{13}$$

with $A = (A_1, A_2, \ldots)^T$ consisting of the rows A_i:

$$A_i^T = \begin{pmatrix} p_y - p'_{y,r} \\ p'_{x,r} - p_x \\ p'_{x,r} - e_x - e_x p'_{y,r} p_y + e_y p'_{x,r} p_y \\ p'_{y,r} - e_y + e_x p'_{y,r} p_x - e_y p'_{x,r} p_x \\ e_x p_x + e_y p_y - p'_{x,r} p_x - p'_{y,r} p_y \end{pmatrix} \tag{14}$$

and

$$B = \begin{pmatrix} e_x p'_{y,r} - e_y p'_{x,r} - e_x p_y + e_y p_x + p'_{x,r} p_y - p'_{y,r} p_x \\ \vdots \end{pmatrix} \tag{15}$$

Solving this linear system iteratively and updating the epipole and the rotation matrix

$$e_{c,k+1} = (\Delta e_{x,k}, \Delta e_{y,k}, 0) + e_{c,k} \qquad \text{with } e_{c,0} = e_c \tag{16}$$

$$R_{c,k+1} = R(r_k) \cdot R_{c,k} \qquad \text{with } R_{c,0} = R_c \tag{17}$$

from iteration k to $k + 1$ quickly converges against the true solution. Hereby $R(r_k)$ denotes the rotation matrix as composed from the Euler angles contained in the vector r_k. In order to demonstrate the convergence of the algorithm empirically, the mean absolute rotation error Δr_{abs} and the mean absolute epipole error δe_{abs} are used:

$$\Delta r_{\text{abs}} = \frac{1}{N} \sum_{n=1}^{N} ||r(R_c, k, n) - r_{t,n}||_2 \qquad \delta e_{\text{abs}} = \frac{1}{N} \sum_{n=1}^{N} ||e_{c,k,n} - e_{t,n}||_2 \tag{18}$$

where $r_{t,n}$ is the vector consisting of the Euler angles describing the true rotation of the nth run and $r(R_c, k, n)$ is the vector consisting of the Euler angles extracted from the rotation matrix $R_{c,k}$ of the nth run.

Figure 2 shows the mean absolute rotation error Δr_{abs} and the mean absolute epipole error δe_{abs} over 100 runs on simulated point correspondences. The experiment has been carried out several times varying the variances of normal distributed noise added to the image point positions. Fig. 2 shows that a final result is reached in the first 4 iteration steps, even though the quality of the result, especially of the epipole position, is not very high. Further investigations in the next section compare this result to the results from other estimation methods.

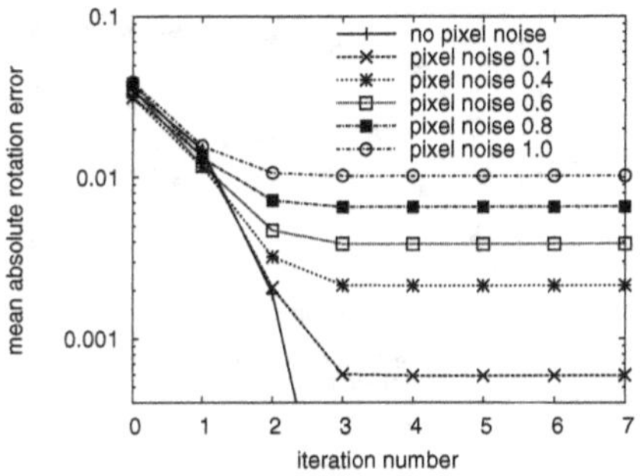

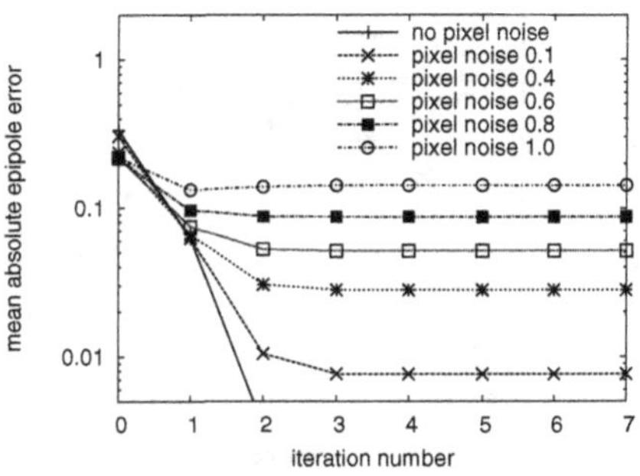

Fig. 2. Convergence of the iterative linearized essential matrix estimation approach on simulated point correspondences. The mean absolute rotation error Δr_{abs} is plotted against the iteration (left). In the right image, the mean absolute epipole error δe_{abs} is plotted against the iteration. Normal distributed noise with different variances has been added to each of the image point positions.

Comparison: The error after the final iteration of the proposed linearized iterative approach was compared to the other 3 algorithms (fig. 3) with varying additional noise on the image point positions. For this investigation the absolute mean rotational error Δr and the absolute mean epipole error δe are used:

$$\Delta r = ||\frac{1}{N}\sum_{n=1}^{N} r(R_c, k, n) - r_{t,n}||_2 \qquad \delta e = ||\frac{1}{N}\sum_{n=1}^{N} e_{c,k,n} - e_{t,n}||_2 \tag{19}$$

Fig. 3 shows the superiority of the LM algorithm with the geometric error function. The accuracy for the epipole position and the rotation error which is achieved by the three algorithms using the algebraic error is within the same magnitude range.

3.2 Robust Essential Matrix Refinement

The algorithms for robust parameter estimation can be sorted into 4 different categories [22, 26, 33], namely:

1. Algorithms that use clustering techniques.
2. M-Estimators use an iterative re-weighting technique to achieve robustness, while using all available data.
3. Case deletion diagnostic algorithms try to identify outliers and reject them from the computation.
4. Algorithms that use random sampling techniques to achieve a solution with a minimal data set.

In [26] a comparison between some of the above mentioned robust estimation methods has been carried out for the case of estimating the fundamental matrix. In this study the best random sampling algorithm (LMedS) shows superior results in comparison to the best member of the M-Estimator class, while the best method in case deletion diagnostics is only slightly worse than the LMedS algorithm. The RANSAC method performs only slightly worse than the LMedS method. In this system the MSAC algorithm,

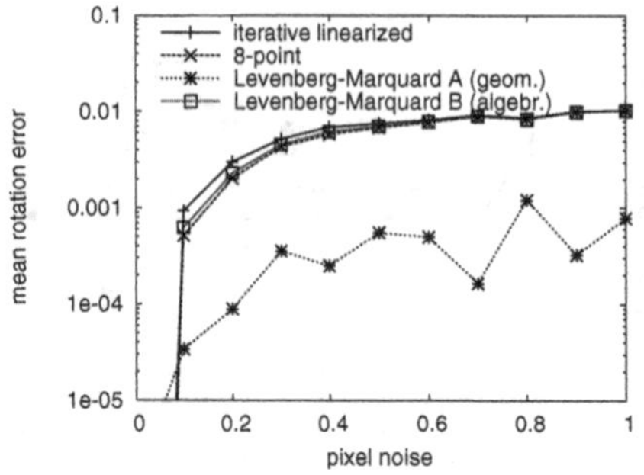

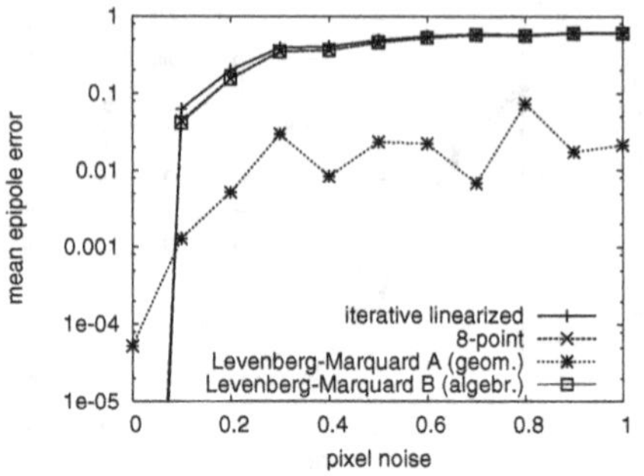

Fig. 3. Comparison of the accuracy of the 4 different approaches described in section 3.1. The mean rotational error Δr (left figure) and the mean epipole error δe (right figure) is plotted against the variance of the normal distributed noise added to the image point positions. The Levenberg-Marquard algorithm with the geometric error function shows superior results to the three other approaches. The error after the final iteration is used in the linearized iterative approach.

a method similar to RANSAC and LMedS, is chosen. Because the MSAC algorithm is an enhancement to the RANSAC algorithm and shares the main ideas, the RANSAC algorithm is described first:

RANSAC: The RANSAC algorithm [6] is robust in the case of data heavily corrupted with outliers. Assume that there are m data and a minimum of n of them is needed to estimate the parameter vector. The approach works as follows:

- Randomly select a minimum set of n data and extract the parameters x from them.
- Calculate the number k of data from the overall set supporting the parameters x with respect to a given threshold t over the residue r_i.
- If k is bigger than a given fraction, calculate the least squares solution from all data supporting x and exit with success.
- Repeat the above steps L times.
- Either use the parameters with the biggest support k, calculate the least squares solution and exit with success or exit with failure.

This is in fact a search for the solution that minimizes the cost function [25]

$$C = \sum_i \rho(r_i) \qquad \text{with} \qquad \rho(r_i) = \begin{cases} 0 & r_i^2 < t^2 \\ \text{const.} & r_i^2 \geq t^2 \end{cases} \tag{20}$$

The number of trials L needed to ensure at least one outlier free set of data with probability z can be calculated by

$$L = \frac{\log(1-z)}{\log(1-p^n)}, \tag{21}$$

where p is the expected outlier fraction in the data [6].

MSAC: In the RANSAC algorithm, the penalty for each datum is either 0 or some constant value. The residuum associated with the datum is only used to make a binary decision about the penalty. This undesirable situation can be resolved with no extra cost by replacing $\rho(r_i)$ by

$$\rho_2(r_i) = \begin{cases} r_i^2 & r_i^2 < t^2 \\ \text{const.} & r_i^2 \geq t^2 \end{cases} \tag{22}$$

in the cost function (eq. 20) of the RANSAC algorithm [25]. The cosine of the angle between the predicted and the measured flow is used as the residual value in this application.

4 Sequential Monte Carle Sampling Resampling

First the general concept of the CONDENSATION algorithm is summarized. The CONDENSATION algorithm is a particle filter and hence a Sequential Monte Carle Sampling Resampling SMCSR algorithm. Then the application of the SMCSR algorithm for detection of independent motion is described.

4.1 CONDENSATION

The CONDENSATION algorithm is designed to propagate any probability density function (pdf) over time. Due to the computational complexity of this task, pdfs are approximated by a set of weighted samples. The weight π_n is given by

$$\pi_n = \frac{p_z(s^{(n)})}{\sum_{j=1}^{N} p_z(s^{(j)})} \tag{23}$$

where $p_z(x) = p(z|x)$ is the conditional observation density representing the probability of a measurement z, given that the system is in the state x. $s^{(n)}$ represents the position of sample n in the state space.

Propagation: From the known a priori pdf, samples are randomly chosen with regard to their weight π_i. In doing so, a sample can be chosen several times. A motion model is applied to the sample positions and diffusion is done by adding Gaussian noise to each sample position. A sample that was chosen multiple times results in several spatial close samples after the diffusion step. Finally, the weight is calculated by measuring the conditional observation $p(z|x)$ and using it in eq. 23. The a posteriori pdf represented by these samples is acting as a priori pdf in the next time step. This iterative evaluation scheme is closely related to Bayes' law

$$p(x|z) = \frac{p(z|x)p(x)}{p(z)} \tag{24}$$

where $p(z)$ can be interpreted as a normalization constant, independent of the system state x [12]. The sample representation of the a posteriori pdf $p(x|z)$ is calculated by implicitly using the a priori pdf $p(x)$ as the sample base from which new samples are chosen and the probability of a measurement $p(z|x)$ given a certain state of the system x (eq. 23). The sample representation of the a posterior pdf converges "almost sure" against the true a posteriori pdf when using an infinite number of samples [5].

Initialization: In order to initialize without human interaction a fraction of the samples are chosen by using a random variable which is distributed according to an initialization distribution in every time step. With a very high initialization fraction, the samples will most probably no longer represent the correct a posteriori pdf, even with a very large number of samples. The disturbance of the a posteriori pdf representation from the initialization samples can be reduced by using importance sampling [5]. Since this is not (yet) done, the algorithm will be called a sequential Monte Carlo sampling resampling algorithm rather than a particle filter. In the first time step, all samples are chosen using the initialization function.

4.2 Amplified Detection of Independent Motion

Since optical flow (OF) is computationally expensive, the number of OF measurements have to be restricted. However, when computing OF at sparse locations, one would like to capture as much flow on independently moving objects as possible. An adapted particle filter is chosen for this task. In this application the probability for a position belonging to an independently moving object is chosen as the pdf for the CONDENSATION algorithm, resulting in a state dimension of 2. A fraction of the samples are chosen by propagating samples from the last time step using the CONDENSATION approach. Hereby samples are chosen randomly with respect to their weight. Samples with a high weight (a high probability for an independently moving object) are chosen with a higher probability. In general these high weight samples are chosen multiple times, resulting in more samples in the vicinity of the old sample after the diffusion in the next time step. The remaining part of the samples are generated by using a random variable with a distribution depending on the image gradient. OF is measured at each sample position.

Measurement: The measurement at each sample position should represent the probability $p(x)$ that this sample is located on an independently moving object. Let α denote the angle between the predicted translational optical flow pointing away from FOE_S and the rotation corrected OF vector pointing away from FOE_M (see Fig. 5). $c_\alpha = \cos(\alpha)$ is used as a basis for the calculation of this probability [28]. The probability for an independently moving object $p_{c_i}(c_\alpha)$ in dependence of c_α is modeled as a rounded step function:

$$p_{c_i}(c_\alpha) = \begin{cases} e^{f(c_i)\cdot c_\alpha + \ln(0.5) - c_i \cdot f(c_i)} & \text{if } c_\alpha > c_i, \\ 1.0 - e^{-f(c_i)\cdot c_\alpha + \ln(0.5) + c_i \cdot f(c_i)} & \text{if } c_\alpha \leq c_i, \end{cases} \tag{25}$$

where $f(c_i) = \frac{ln(0.01) - \ln(0.5)}{1.0 - |c_i|}$ is a function of the inflection point c_i. Since it is not feasible to set probabilities to 1.0 or 0.0, $p_{c_i}(c_\alpha)$ is scaled and shifted to represent a minimum uncertainty. Fig. 4 shows $p_{c_i}(c_\alpha)$.

In the proposed algorithm, the inflection point is chosen automatically to be $c_i = \tilde{c}_\alpha - \sigma_{c_\alpha}$, where $\tilde{c}_\alpha$ is the median of all the cosine angles not detected as "moving" in the last time step, and σ_{c_α} is the variance of the c_α. Choosing c_i automatically has the advantage, that erroneous camera positions do not disturb the measurement. This only holds under the assumption that more than half of the flow vectors are located on the static scene.

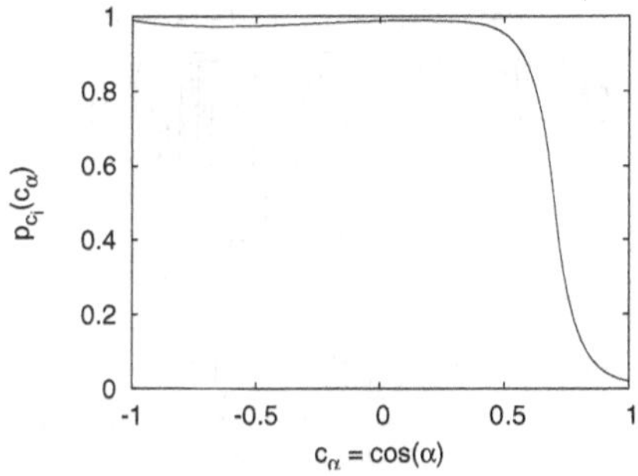

Fig. 4. The probability $p_{c_i}(c_\alpha)$ that a flow measurement is located on an independently moving object in dependence of $c_\alpha = \cos(\alpha)$ at a given inflection point $c_i = 0.7$

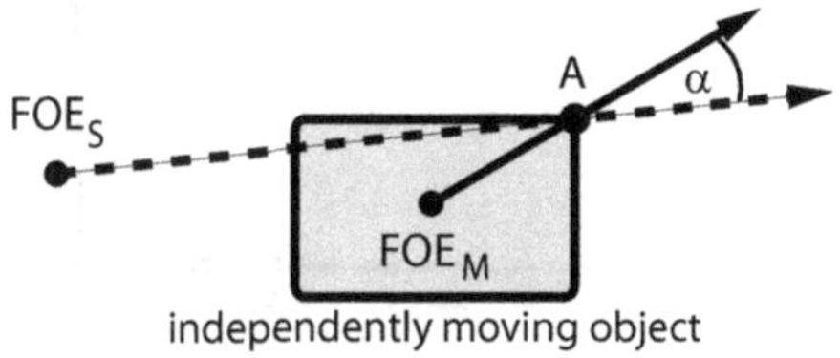

Fig. 5. Detection of moving object by the angle between the predicted flow direction (pointing away from FOE_S) and the measured flow direction (pointing away from FOE_M)

Similar terms ensuring a minimum cornerness p_c (since OF can only be computed with spatial structure), a minimum flow length p_f (standing for the accuracy of the OF computation) and a minimum distance from the focus of expansion p_{FOE} (since errors in the FOE position influence the direction prediction for closer points more than for points further away) are introduced. The overall probability $p(x) = p(z|x)$ is then given by:

$$p(x) = p_{c_i}(c_\alpha) \cdot p_c \cdot p_f \cdot p_{FOE} \qquad (26)$$

In order to further stabilize the result, spatial and temporal filters are applied to the resulting probability images [29].

5 Experiments

To investigate the results of the essential matrix estimation process, the histogram over all angles between the predicted and the measured direction of the translational flow component is used (fig 6). Fig 6 shows that most flow vectors have the expected direction ($\cos(\alpha) \approx 1.0$) after the refinement process, in contrast to before. At the same time, the flow vectors lying on independently moving objects still have a significant angle to the predicted translational flow ($\cos(\alpha) \approx -1.0$). As a simple way to score these histograms, the median of all angles is chosen. The closer the median lies to the expected value of 1.0, the better is the given essential matrix under the assumption that more than half of the flow measurements are located on points belonging to the static scene. To test the algorithm a simulated street intersection was realized in VRML. Simple block models of houses, textured with real image data, are located on the corners of the intersecting street (Fig. 8). A model of a car was used as an independently moving object. Screenshots of a ride through this intersection provided the image data, while the sensor information was calculated from the known camera pose and parameters. The uncertainty of the camera pose was modeled as additional normal distributed noise on the camera position and rotation. In fig. 7 the median of the cosine of all angles between the predicted and the measured translational flow vectors is evaluated over

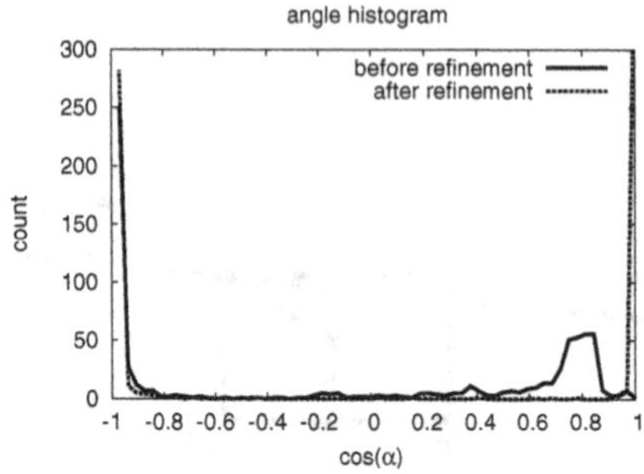

Fig. 6. Histogram over the cosine of the angles between the predicted and the measured flow vectors before and after refinement. The histogram after refinement shows that a lot more flow vectors have the expected value of 1.0, even though the flow vectors located on an independent moving object still have a significant angle to the predicted flow direction.

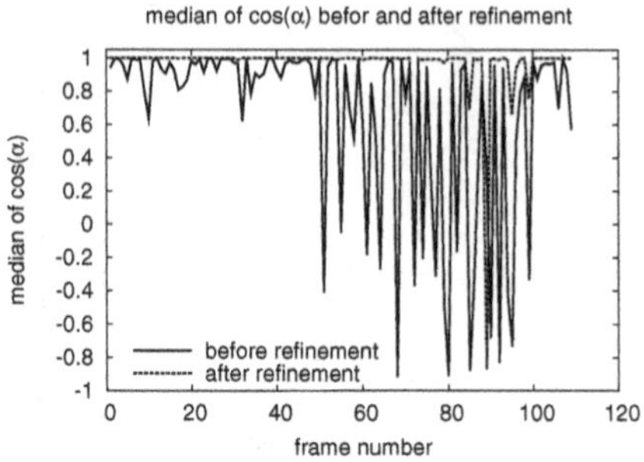

Fig. 7. The median of the cosine of the angles between the predicated and the measured flow vectors is evaluated before and after refinement over a synthetic image sequence

the synthetic image sequence. In most of the images, the correct essential matrix is estimated (median = 1.0) while in some images an incorrect estimate of the essential matrix was estimated. This behavior results from the restricted number of tries in the MSAC algorithm, and vanishes (at the expense of additional computation time) when more tries are conducted. The resulting detector output is shown in fig. 8. Points where the spatio-temporal filter output is above a certain threshold are marked with white blobs.

Fig. 8. Some images from the synthetic intersection sequence. The camera is moving on a straight line, while the car in the image is on a collision course. Points where the filter output is above a threshold of 0.35 are marked white.

6 Conclusions and Further Work

A fast and robust sequential Monte Carlo sampling resampling system for the detection of independently moving objects by a moving observer has been presented. The robustness against single measurement errors in the optical flow mainly results from the sequential Monte Carlo sampling resampling approach, while its robustness against erroneous camera pose data results from the chosen random sampling consensus approach. Experiments with synthetic were accomplished. Further work will include:

- experiments on real data
- run time optimization
- clustering of detected independently moving points
- investigation of the trajectory extraction possibility of moving objects
- enhanced fusion of inertial sensor information (speed, yawrate and steering angle) with image based measurements (optical flow from static scene).

References

1. H. Badino, "A Robust Approach for Ego-Motion Estimation Using a Mobile Stereo Platform." *Proc. IWCM*, 2004.
2. J.L. Barron, D.J. Fleet, S.S. Beauchemin and T.A. Burkitt, "Performance Of Optical Flow Techniques", *Proc. CVPR*, Vol. 92, pp. 236-242, 1994.
3. M.J. Black and D.J. Fleet, "Probabilistic Detection and Tracking of Motion Discontinuities." *ICCV*, 1999.
4. A.R. Bruss and B.K.P. Horn, "Passive Navigation." *CGIP*, 21:3-20, 1983.
5. A. Doucet, N.d. Freitas, N. Gordon, *Sequential Monte Carlo Methods in Practice*, Springer, 2001.
6. M. Fischler and R. Bolles. "RANdom SAmpling Consensus: a paradigm for model fitting with application to image analysis and automated cartography." *Commun. Assoc. Comp. Mach. 24* , 1981.
7. R. Hartley, "Computation of the essential matrix from 6 points." http://rsise.anu.edu.au/ hartley/Papers/6pt/6ptnew.pdf
8. R. Hartley, "In defence of the eight-point algorithm.", *IEEE TPAMI*, 19(6):580-593, 1997.
9. R. Hartley and A. Zisserman, *Multiple View Geometry*, Cambridge University Press, 2000.
10. A.v.d. Hengel, W. Chojnacki, M.J. Brooks, "Determining the Translational Speed of a Camera from Extended Optical Flow." *Proc. IWCM*, 2004.
11. C. Hue, J.-P. Le Cardre and P. Perez, "Tracking Multiple Objects with Particle Filtering." *IEEE Transactions on Aerospace and Electronic Systems*, 38(3):791-812, 2002
12. M. Isard and A. Blake "Condensation – conditional density propagation for visual tracking." *IJCV*, 29(1), pp.5-28, 1998.
13. M. Isard and A. Blake "ICONDENSATION: Unifying low-level and high-level tracking in a stochastic framework." *ECCV*, vol. 1 893-908, 1998.
14. M. Isard, J. McCormick, "BraMBLe: A Bayesian Multiple-Blob Tracker." *ICCV*, 2001.
15. K. Kanatani, "Optimal fundamental matrix computation: Algorithm and reliability analysis." *SSII*, 2000.
16. K. Kanatani et al., "Fundamental matrix from optical flow: Optimal computation and reliability evaluation." *JEI*, 2000.
17. Z.Khan, T. Balch and F. Dellaert, "An MCMC-Based Particle Filter for Tracking Multiple Interacting Targets." *ECCV*, 2004
18. H.C. Longuet-Higgins, "A computer algorithm for reconstructing a scene from two projections." *Nature*, Vol. 293:10, 1981.
19. B. Lucas and T. Kanade, "An iterative image registration technique with an application to stereo vision" *Proc. DARPA IU Workshop*, pp. 121-130, 1981.

20. P. Perez et al., "Color-Based Probabilistic Tracking." *ECCV*, 2002.
21. M. Pollefeys, R. Koch and Luc J. Van Gool, "Self-Calibration and Metric Reconstruction in Spite of Varying and Unknown Internal Camera Parameters", *IJCV*, 32(1):7-25, 1999.
22. P. J. Rousseeuw and A. M. Leroy, *Robust Regression and Outlier Detection.* John Wiley and Sons, 1987.
23. T. Suzuki and T. Kanade, "Measurement of vehicle motion and orientation using optical flow." *IEEE ITS*, Tokyo, 1999.
24. T.Y. Tian, C. Tomasi and D.J. Heeger, "Comparison of robust approaches to ego-motion computation." *CVPR*, 1996.
25. P.H.S. Torr and A. Zisserman, "MLESAC: A new robust estimator with application to estimating image geometry." *CVIU*, 1996.
26. P.H.S. Torr and D.W. Murray, "Development and Comparison of Robust Methods for Estimating the Fundamental Matrix." *IJCV*, 1996.
27. R.Y. Tsai and T.S. Huang, "The perspective view of three points.", *IEEE TPAMI*, 6:13-27, 1984.
28. F. Woelk, S. Gehrig and R. Koch, "A Monocular Image Based Intersection Assistant." *IEEE Intelligent Vehicles*, Parma, Italy, 2004.
29. F. Woelk and R. Koch, "Fast Monocular Bayesian Detection of Independently Moving Objects by a Moving Observer." *DAGM*, pp:27-35, Tübingen, Germany, 2004.
30. J. Vermaak et al., "Maintaining Multi-Modality through Mixture Tracking." *ICCV*, 2003.
31. J.S. Zelek, "Bayesian Real-time Optical Flow." *Proc VI*, 2002.
32. Z. Zhang, "Determining the epipolar geometry and its uncertainty - a review." *IJCV*, 27(2):161-195, 1998.
33. Z. Zhang, "Parameter Estimation Techniques: A Tutorial with Application to Conic Fitting." http://www-sop.inria.fr/robotvis/personnel/zzhang/Publis/Tutorial-Estim/Main.html, 1996.

Tracking Complex Objects Using Graphical Object Models

Leonid Sigal[1], Ying Zhu[3], Dorin Comaniciu[2], and Michael Black[1]

[1] Department of Computer Science, Brown University, Providence, RI 02912
{ls, black}@cs.brown.edu
[2] Integrated Data Systems, Siemens Corporate Research, Princeton, NJ 08540
dorin.comaniciu@scr.siemens.com
[3] Real Time Vision & Modeling, Siemens Corporate Research, Princeton, NJ 08540
ying.zhu@scr.siemens.com

Abstract. We present a probabilistic framework for component-based automatic detection and tracking of objects in video. We represent objects as spatio-temporal two-layer graphical models, where each node corresponds to an object or component of an object at a given time, and the edges correspond to learned spatial and temporal constraints. Object detection and tracking is formulated as inference over a directed loopy graph, and is solved with non-parametric belief propagation. This type of object model allows object-detection to make use of temporal consistency (over an arbitrarily sized temporal window), and facilitates robust tracking of the object. The two layer structure of the graphical model allows inference over the entire object as well as individual components. AdaBoost detectors are used to define the likelihood and form proposal distributions for components. Proposal distributions provide 'bottom-up' information that is incorporated into the inference process, enabling automatic object detection and tracking. We illustrate our method by detecting and tracking two classes of objects, vehicles and pedestrians, in video sequences collected using a single grayscale uncalibrated car-mounted moving camera.

1 Introduction

The detection and tracking of complex objects in natural scenes requires rich models of object appearance that can cope with variability among instances of the object and across changing viewing and lighting conditions. Traditional optical flow methods are often ineffective for tracking objects because they are memoryless; that is, they lack any explicit model of object appearance. Here we seek a model of object appearance that is rich enough for both detection and tracking of objects such as people or vehicles in complex scenes. To that end we develop a probabilistic framework for automatic component-based detection and tracking. By combining object detection with tracking in a unified framework we can achieve a more robust solution for both problems. Tracking can make use of object detection for initialization and re-initialization during transient failures or occlusions, while object detection can be made more reliable by considering the consistency of the detection over time. Modeling objects by an arrangement of image-based (possibly overlapping) components, facilitates detection of

B. Jähne et al. (Eds.): IWCM 2004, LNCS 3417, pp. 223–234, 2007.

complex articulated objects, as well as helps in handling partial object occlusions or local illumination changes.

Object detection and tracking is formulated as inference in a two-layer graphical model in which the coarse layer node represents the whole object and the fine layer nodes represent multiple component "parts" of the object. Directed edges between nodes represent learned spatial and temporal probabilistic constraints. Each node in the graphical model corresponds to a position and scale of the component or the object as a whole in an image at a given time instant. Each node also has an associated AdaBoost detector that is used to define the local image likelihood and a proposal process. In general the likelihoods and dependencies are not Gaussian. To infer the 2D position and scale at each node we exploit a form of non-parametric belief propagation (BP) that uses a variation of particle filtering and can be applied over a loopy graph [8, 15].

The problem of describing and recognizing categories of objects (e.g. faces, people, cars) is central to computer vision. It is common to represent objects as collections of features with distinctive appearance, spatial extent, and position [2, 6, 10, 11, 16, 17]. There is however a large variation in how many features one must use and how these features are detected and represented. Most algorithms rely on semi-supervised learning [11, 16, 17] schemes where examples of the desired class of objects must be manually aligned, and then learning algorithms are used to automatically select the features that best separate the images of the desired class from background image patches. More recent approaches learn the model in an unsupervised fashion from a set of unlabeled and unsegmented images [2, 6]. In particular, Fergus *et al* [6] develop a component based object detection algorithm that learns an explicit spatial relationship between parts of an object, but unlike our framework assumes Gaussian likelihoods and spatial relationships and does not model temporal consistency.

In contrast to part-based representations, simple discriminative classifiers treat an object as a single image region. Boosted classifiers [16], for example, while very successful tend to produce a large set of false positives. While this problem can be reduced by incorporating temporal information [17], discriminative classifiers based on boosting do not explicitly model parts or components of objects. Such part-based models are useful in the presence of partial occlusions, out-of-plane rotation and/or local lighting variations [5, 11, 18]. Part- or component-based detection is also capable of handling highly articulated objects [10], for which a single appearance model classifier may be hard to learn. An illustration of the usefulness of component-based detection for vehicles is shown in Fig. 1. While all vehicles have almost identical parts (tires, bumper, hood, etc.) their placement can vary significantly due to large variability in the height and type of vehicles.

Murphy *et al* [12] also use graphical models in the patch-based detection scheme. Unlike our approach they do not incorporate temporal information or explicitly reason about the object as a whole. Also closely related is the work of [13] which uses AdaBoost for multi-target tracking and detection. However, their Boosted Particle Filter [13] does not integrate component-based object detection and is limited to temporal propagation in only one direction (forward in time). In contrast to these previous approaches we combine techniques from discriminative learning, graphical models, belief

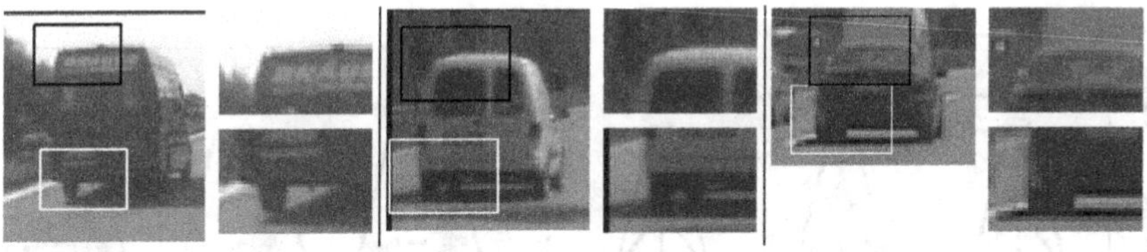

Fig. 1. Variation in the vehicle class of objects is shown. While objects shown here have a drastically different appearance as a whole due to the varying height and type of the vehicle, their components tend to be very homogeneous and are easy to model.

propagation, and particle filtering to achieve reliable multi-component object detection and tracking.

In our framework, object motion is represented via temporal constraints (edges) in the graphical model. These model-based constraints for the object and components are learned explicitly from the labeled data, and make no use of the optical flow information. However the model could be extended to use explicit flow information as part of the likelihood model, or as part of the proposal process. In particular, as part of the proposal process, optical flow information can be useful in focusing the search to the regions with "interesting" motion, that are likely to correspond to an object or part/component of an object.

2 Graphical Object Models

Following the framework of [14] we model an object as a spatio-temporal directed graphical model. Each node in the graph represents either the object or a component of the object at time t. Nodes have an associated state vector $X^T = (x, y, s)$ defining the component's real-valued position and scale within an image. The joint probability distribution for this spatio-temporal graphical object model with N components and over T frames can be written as:

$$P(\mathbf{X}_0^O, \mathbf{X}_0^{C_0}, \mathbf{X}_0^{C_1}, ..., \mathbf{X}_0^{C_N}, ..., \mathbf{X}_T^O, \mathbf{X}_T^{C_0}, \mathbf{X}_T^{C_1}, ..., \mathbf{X}_T^{C_N}, \mathbf{Y}_0, \mathbf{Y}_1, ..., \mathbf{Y}_T) =$$
$$\frac{1}{Z} \prod_{ij} \psi_{ij}(\mathbf{X}_i^O, \mathbf{X}_j^O) \prod_{ik} \psi_{ik}(\mathbf{X}_i^O, \mathbf{X}_i^{C_k}) \prod_{ikl} \psi_{kl}(\mathbf{X}_i^{C_k}, \mathbf{X}_i^{C_l})$$
$$\prod_i \phi_i(\mathbf{Y}_i, \mathbf{X}_i^O) \prod_{ik} \phi_i(\mathbf{Y}_i, \mathbf{X}_i^{C_k})$$

where $\mathbf{X}_t^O$ and $\mathbf{X}_t^{C_n}$ is the state of the object, O, and object's n-th component, C_n, at time t respectively ($n \in (1, N)$ and $t \in (1, T)$); $\psi_{ij}(\mathbf{X}_i^O, \mathbf{X}_j^O)$ is the temporal compatibility of the object state between frames i and j; $\psi_{ik}(\mathbf{X}_i^O, \mathbf{X}_i^{C_k})$ is the spatial compatibility of the object and it's components at frame i; $\psi_{kl}(\mathbf{X}_i^{C_k}, \mathbf{X}_i^{C_l})$ is the spatial compatibility between object components at frame i; and $\phi_i(\mathbf{Y}_i, \mathbf{X}_i^O)$ and $\phi_i(\mathbf{Y}_i, \mathbf{X}_i^{C_k})$ denote the local evidence (likelihood) for the object and component states respectively.

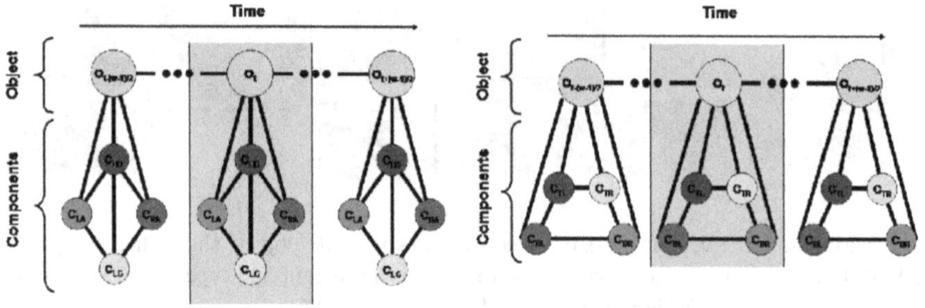

(*a*) (*b*)

Fig. 2. Graphical models for the (*a*) pedestrian and (*b*) vehicle detection and tracking. Spatio-temporal models are obtained by replicating a spatial model (shown by the shaded region) along the temporal domain to a w-length window and then connecting the object layer nodes across time.

Our framework can be viewed as having five distinct components: (i) a graphical model, (ii) an inference algorithm that infers a probability distribution over the state variables at each node in the graph, (iii) a local evidence distribution (or image likelihood), (iv) a proposal process for some or all nodes in a graphical model, and (v) a set of spatial and/or temporal constraints corresponding to the edges in a graph. We will now discuss each one of these in turn.

2.1 Building the Graphical Model

For a single frame we represent objects using a two-layer spatial graphical model. The fine, component, layer contains a set of loosely connected "parts." The coarse, object, layer corresponds to an entire appearance model of the object and is connected to all constituent components. Examples of such models for pedestrian and vehicle detection are shown in a the shaded regions of Fig. 2*a* and 2*b* respectively. In both cases objects are modeled using four overlapping image components. For the vehicle the components are: top-left (TL), top-right (TR), bottom-right (BR) and bottom-left (BL) corners; while for the pedestrian, they are: head (HD), left arm (LA), right arm (RA) and legs (LG) (see Fig. 3*ab*).

To integrate temporal constraints we extend the spatial graphical models over time to an arbitrary-length temporal window. The resulting spatio-temporal graphical models are shown in Fig. 2*a* and 2*b*. Having a two-layer graphical model, unlike the single component layer model of [14], allows the inference process to reason explicitly about the object as a whole, as well as helps reduce the complexity of the graphical model, by allowing the assumption of independence of components over time conditioned on the overall object appearance. Alternatively, one can also imagine building a single object layer model, which would be similar to the Boosted Particle Filter [13] (with bi-directional temporal constraints).

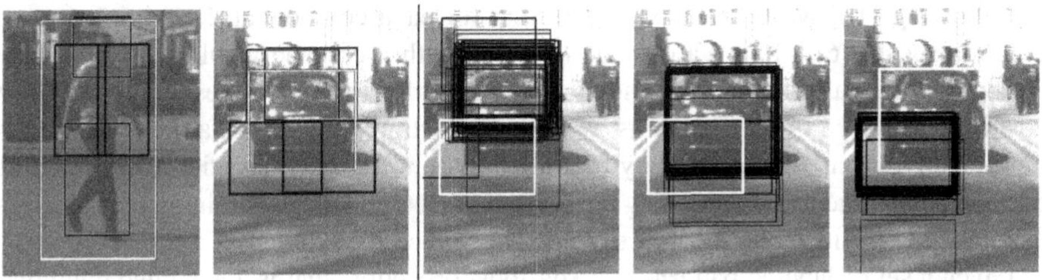

Fig. 3. Components for the (*a*) pedestrian and (*b*) vehicle object models (entire appearance model is in cyan) and learned conditional distributions from (*c*) Bottom-Left (BL) to Top-Left (TL) component, (*d*) Bottom-Left (BL) to the whole appearance model, and (*e*) whole appearance model to the Bottom-Left (BL) component

2.2 Learning Spatial and Temporal Constraints

Each directed edge between components i and j has an associated potential function $\psi_{ij}(\mathbf{X}_i, \mathbf{X}_j)$ that encodes the compatibility between pairs of node states. The potential $\psi_{ij}(\mathbf{X}_i, \mathbf{X}_j)$ is modeled using a mixture of M_{ij} Gaussians (following [14])

$$\psi_{ij}(\mathbf{X}_i, \mathbf{X}_j) = \lambda^0 \mathcal{N}(\mathbf{X}_j; \mu_{ij}, \Lambda_{ij}) + (1 - \lambda^0) \sum_{m=1}^{M_{ij}} \pi_{ijm} \mathcal{N}(\mathbf{X}_j; F_{ijm}(\mathbf{X}_i), G_{ijm}(\mathbf{X}_i))$$

where λ^0 is a fixed outlier probability, μ_{ij} and Λ_{ij} are the mean and covariance of the Gaussian outlier process, and $F_{ijm}(\mathbf{X}_i)$ and $G_{ijm}(\mathbf{X}_i)$ are functions that return the mean and covariance matrix respectively of the m-th Gaussian mixture component. π_{ijm} is the relative weight of an individual component and $\sum_{m=1}^{M_{ij}} \pi_{ijm} = 1$. For experiments in this paper we used $M_{ij} = 2$ mixture components.

Given a set of labeled images, where each component is associated with a single reference point, we use standard iterative Expectation-Maximization (EM) algorithm with K-means initialization to learn $F_{ijm}(\mathbf{X}_i)$ of the form:

$$F_{ijm}(\mathbf{X}_i) = \mathbf{X}_i + \left[\frac{\mu^x_{ijm}}{\mu^s_{ijm}}, \frac{\mu^y_{ijm}}{\mu^s_{ijm}}, \mu^s_{ijm} \right]^T \tag{1}$$

where $\mu^x_{ijm}, \mu^y_{ijm}, \mu^s_{ijm}$ is the mean position and scale of component or object j relative to i. $G_{ijm}(\mathbf{X}_i)$ is assumed to be diagonal matrix, representing the variance in relative position and scale. Examples of the learned conditional distributions can be seen in Fig. 3*cde*.

2.3 AdaBoost Image Likelihoods

The likelihood, $\phi(\mathbf{Y}, \mathbf{X}^i)$ models the probability of observing the image $\mathbf{Y}$ conditioned on the state $\mathbf{X}^i$ of the node i, and ideally should be robust to partial occlusions and the variability of image statistics across many different inputs. To that end we build our likelihood model using a boosted classifier.

Following [16] we train boosted detectors for each component. For simplicity we use AdaBoost [16] without a cascade (training with a cascade would likely improve the computational efficiency of the system). In order to reduce the number of false positives produced by the detectors, we use a bootstrap procedure that iteratively adds false positives that are collected by running the trained strong classifier over the set of background images (not containing the desired object) and then re-training the detectors using the old positive and the new extended negative sets.

Given a set of labeled patterns the AdaBoost procedure learns a weighted combination of base weak classifiers, $h(I) = \sum_{k=1}^{K} \alpha_k h_k(I)$, where I is an image pattern, and $h_k(I)$ is the weak classifier chosen for the round k of boosting, and α_k is the corresponding weight. We use a weak classifier scheme similar to the one discussed in [16]: $h_k(I) = p_k \left(\left[\sqrt[\beta_k]{(f_k(I))^{\beta_k}} < \theta_k \right] \right)$, where $f_k(I)$ is a feature of the pattern I computed by convolving I with the delta function over the extent of a spatial template; θ_k is a threshold, p_k is the polarity indicating the direction of inequality, and $\beta_k \in [1, 2]$ allowing for a symmetric two sided pulse classification.

The output of the AdaBoost classifier is a confidence $h_k(I)$ that the given pattern I is of the desired class. It is customary to consider an object present if $h_k(I) \geq \frac{1}{2} \sum_{k=1}^{K} \alpha_k$. We convert this confidence into a likelihood function by first normalizing the α_k's, so that $h(I) \in [0, 1]$, and then exponentiating

$$\phi(\mathbf{Y}, \mathbf{X}^i) \propto \exp(h(I)/T) \tag{2}$$

where image pattern I is obtained by cropping full image $\mathbf{Y}$ based on the state of the object or component $\mathbf{X}^i$; and T is an artificial temperature parameter that controls the smoothness of the likelihood function, with smaller values of T leading to peakier distribution. Consequently we can also anneal the likelihood by deriving a schedule with which T changes. We found an exponential annealing schedule $T = T_0 \upsilon^{\kappa}$, where T_0 is the initial temperature, υ is a fraction $\in (0, 1)$, and κ is the annealing iteration, to work well in practice. AdaBoost classifiers are learned using a database of 861 vehicles and 662 pedestrians [11]. The number of negative examples after bootstrapping tends to be on the order of 2000 to 3000.

Depending on an object one may or may not have a likelihood or a proposal process for the object layer nodes. For example if the whole appearance of an object is indeed too complicated to model as a whole (e.g. arbitrary size vehicles) and can only be modeled in terms of components, we can simply assume a uniform likelihood over the entire state space. In such cases the object layer nodes simply fuse the component information to produce estimates for the object state that are consistent over time.

It is worth noting that the assumption of local evidence independence implicit in our graphical model is only approximate, and may be violated in the regions where object and components overlap. In such cases the correlation or bias introduced into the inference process will depend on the nature of the filters chosen by the boosting procedure. While this approximation works well in practice, we plan to study it more formally in the future.

2.4 Non-parametric BP

Inferring the state of the object and it's components in our framework is defined as estimating belief in a graphical model. We use a form of non-parametric belief propagation [8] PAMPAS to deal with this task. The approach is a generalization of particle filtering [4] which allows inference over arbitrary graphs rather then a simple chain. In this generalization the 'message' used in standard belief propagation is approximated with a kernel density (formed by propagating a particle set through a mixture of Gaussians density), and the conditional distribution used in standard particle filtering is replaced by product of incoming messages. Most of the computational complexity lies in sampling from a product of kernel densities required for message passing and belief estimation; we use efficient sequential multi-scale Gibbs sampling and epsilon-exact sampling [7] to address this problem.

Individual messages may not constrain a node well, however the product over all incoming messages into the node tends to produce a very tight distribution in the state space. For example, any given component of a vehicle is incapable of estimating the height of the vehicle reliably, however once we integrate information from all components in the object layer node, we can get a very reliable estimate for the overall object size.

More formally a message m_{ij} from node i to node j is written as

$$m_{ij}(\mathbf{X}_j) = \int \psi_{ij}(\mathbf{X}_i, \mathbf{X}_j)\phi_i(\mathbf{Y}_i, \mathbf{X}_i) \prod_{k \in A_i/j} m_{ki}(\mathbf{X}_i) d\mathbf{X}_i, \quad (3)$$

where A_i/j is the set of neighbors of node i excluding node j and $\phi_i(\mathbf{Y}_i, \mathbf{X}_i)$ is the local evidence (or likelihood) associated with the node i, and $\psi_{ij}(\mathbf{X}_i, \mathbf{X}_j)$ is the potential designating the compatibility between the states of node i and j. The details of how the message updates can be carried out by stratified sampling from belief and proposal function see [14].

Fig. 4. Vehicle component-based spatio-temporal object detection for multiple targets. The algorithm was queried for 8 targets. The mean of 30 samples from the belief for each object are shown in red. Targets are found one at the time using an iterative approach that adjusts the likelihood functions to down weight regions where targets have already been found.

While it is possible and perhaps beneficial to perform inference over the spatio-temporal model defined for the entire image sequence, there are many applications for which this is impractical due to the lengthy off-line processing required. Hence, we use a w-frame windowed smoothing algorithm where w is an odd integer ≥ 1 (see Fig. 2). There are two ways one can do windowed smoothing: in an object-detection centric way or a tracking-centric way. In the former we re-initialize all nodes every time we shift a window, hence the temporal integration is only applied in the window of size w. In the tracking centric way we only initialize the nodes associated with a new frame, which tends to enforce temporal consistency from before $t-(w-1)/2$. While the later tends to converge faster and produce more consistent results over time, it is also less sensitive to objects entering and leaving the scene. Note that with $w=1$, the algorithm resembles single-frame component-based fusion [18].

2.5 Proposal Process

To reliably detect and track the object non-parametric BP makes use of the bottom-up proposal process, that constantly looks for and suggests alternative hypothesis for the state of the object and components. We model a proposal distribution using a weighted particle set. To form a proposal particle set for a component, we run the corresponding AdaBoost detector over an image at a number of scales to produce a set of detection results that score above the $\frac{1}{2}\sum_{k=1}^{K}\alpha_k$ threshold. While this set tends to be manageable for the entire appearance model, it is usually large for non-specific component detectors (a few thousand locations can easily be found). To reduce the dimensionality we only keep the top P scoring detections, where P is on the order of a 100 to 200. To achieve breadth of search we generate proposed particles by importance sampling uniformly from the detections. For more details on the use of the proposal process in the PAMPAS framework see [14].

3 Experiments

Tests were performed using a set of images collected with a single car-mounted gray-scale camera. The result of vehicle detection and tracking over a sequence of 55 consecutive frames can be seen in Fig. 5. A 3-frame spatio-temporal object model was used and was shifted in a tracking-centric way over time. We run BP with 30 particles for 10 iterations at every frame. For comparison we implemented a simple fusion scheme that averages the best detection result from each of the four components (Fig. 5(b) 'Best Avg.') to produce an estimate for the vehicle position and scale independently at every frame. The performance of the simple fusion detection is very poor suggesting that the noisy component detectors often do not have the global maximum at the correct position and scale. In contrast, the spatio-temporal object model consistently combines the evidence for accurate estimates throughout the sequence.

The performance of the pedestrian spatio-temporal detector is shown in Fig. 6. A 3-frame spatio-temporal object model is run at a single instance in time for two pedestrians in two different scenes. Similar to the vehicle detection we run BP with 30 particles for 10 iterations. For both experiments the temperature of the likelihood is set to $T_0 = 0.2$.

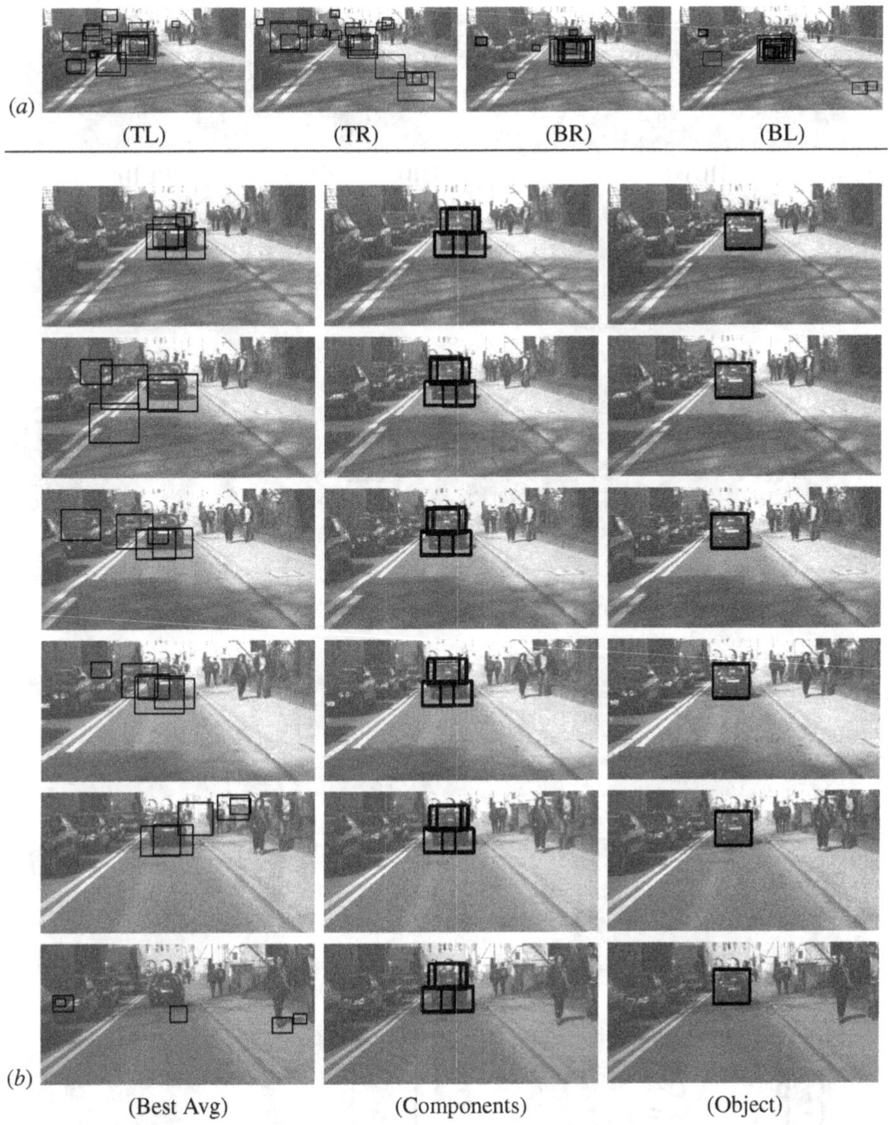

Fig. 5. Vehicle component-based spatio-temporal object detection and tracking. (*a*) shows samples from the initialization/proposal distribution, and (*b*) 30 samples taken from the belief for each of the four component (middle) and an object (right). The detection and tracking was conducted using a 3-frame smoothing window. Frames 2 through 52 are shown (top to bottom respectively) at 10 frame intervals. For comparison (*b*) (left) shows the performance of a very simple fusion algorithm, that fuses the best result from each of the components by averaging.

While in general the algorithm presented here is capable of detecting multiple targets, by converging to multi-modal distributions for components and objects, in practice this tends to be quite difficult and requires many particles. Particle filters in general have

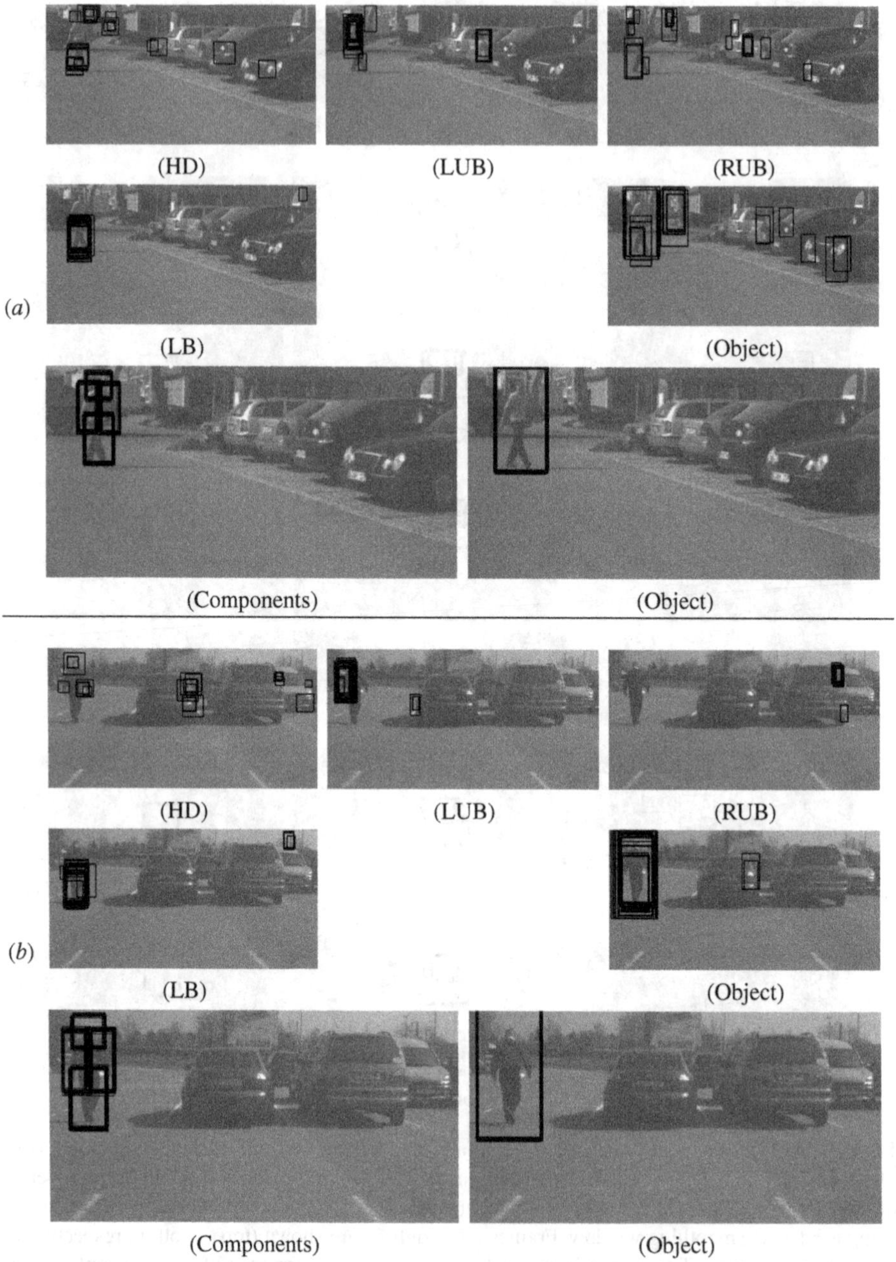

Fig. 6. Pedestrian component-based spatio-temporal object detection for two subjects (*a*) and (*b*). (top) shows the initialization/proposal distribution, and (bottom) 30 samples taken from the belief for each of the four component and an object. The detection was conducted using a 3-frame temporal window.

been shown to have difficulties when tracking multi-modal distributions [13]. The PAMPAS framework used here is an extension of particle filtering, and the message update involves taking a product over particle sets, consequently, PAMPAS suffers from similar problems. Furthermore, belief propagation over a loopy graph such as ours may further hinder the modeling of multi-modal distributions. To enable multi-target tracking then we employ a peak suppression scheme, where modes are detected one at a time, and then the response of the likelihood function is suppressed in the regions where peaks have already been found. An example of this obtained by running a purely spatial graphical model over the image containing 6 vehicles is shown in Fig. 4.

4 Conclusion

In this paper we present a novel object detection and tracking framework exploiting boosted classifiers and non-parametric belief propagation. The approach provides component-based detection and integrates temporal information over an arbitrary size temporal window. We illustrate the performance of the framework with two classes of objects: vehicles and pedestrians. In both cases we can reliably infer position and scale of the objects and their components. Further work needs to be done to evaluate how the method copes with changing lighting and occlusion. Additional work is necessary to develop a mutli-target scheme that incorporates a probabilistic model of the entire image.

The algorithm developed here is quite general and might be applied to other objection tracking and motion estimation problems. For example, we might formulate a parameterized model of facial motion in which the optical flow in different image regions (mouth, eyes, eyebrows) are modeled independently. These motion parameters for these regions could then be coupled via the graphical model and combined with a top-level head tracker. Such an approach might offer improved robustness over previous methods for modeling face motion [1].

References

1. Recognizing facial expressions in image sequences using local parameterized models of image motion, M. J. Black and Y. Yacoob. *International Journal of Computer Vision*, 25(1), pp. 23–48, 1997.
2. M. Burl, M. Weber and P. Perona. A probabilistic approach to object recognition using local photometry and global geometry, *ECCV*, pp. 628–641, 1998.
3. J. Coughlan and S. Ferreira. Finding deformable shapes using loopy belief propagation, *ECCV* Vol. 3, pp. 453–468, 2002.
4. A. Douce, N. de Freitas and N. Gordon. Sequential Monte Carlo methods in practice, *Statistics for Engineering and Information Sciences*, pp. 3–14, Springer Verlag, 2001.
5. P. Felzenszwalb and D. Huttenlocher. Efficient matching of pictorial structures, *CVPR*, Vol. 2, pp. 66–73, 2000.
6. R. Fergus, P. Perona and A. Zisserman. Object class recognition by unsupervised scale-invariant learning, *CVPR*, 2003.
7. A. Ihler, E. Sudderth, W. Freeman and A. Willsky. Efficient multiscale sampling from products of Gaussian mixtures, *Advances in Neural Info. Proc. Sys. 16*, 2003.

8. M. Isard. PAMPAS: Real-valued graphical models for computer vision, *CVPR*, Vol. 1, pp. 613–620, 2003.
9. M. Jordan, T. Sejnowski and T. Poggio. Graphical models: Foundations of neural computation, *MIT Press*, 2001.
10. K. Mikolajczyk, C. Schmid, and A. Zisserman. Human detection based on a probabilistic assembly of robust part detectors, *ECCV*, 2004.
11. A. Mohan, C. Papageorgiou and T. Poggio. Example-based object detection in images by components, *IEEE PAMI*, 23(4):349–361, 2001.
12. K. Murphy, A. Torralba and W. Freeman. Using the forest to see the trees: A graphical model relating features, objects, and scenes, *Advances in Neural Info. Proc. Sys. 16*, 2003.
13. K. Okuma, A. Teleghani, N. de Freitas, J. Little and D. Lowe. A boosted particle filter: Multitarget detection and tracking, *ECCV*, 2004.
14. L. Sigal, S. Bhatia, S. Roth, M. Black and M. Isard. Tracking loose-limbed people, *CVPR*, 2004.
15. E. Sudderth, A. Ihler, W. Freeman and A. Willsky. Nonparametric belief propagation, *CVPR*, Vol. 1, pp. 605–612, 2003; (see also MIT AI Lab Memo 2002-020).
16. P. Viola and M. Jones. Rapid object detection using a boosted cascade of simple features, *CVPR*, 2001.
17. P. Viola, M. Jones and D. Snow. Detecting pedestrians using patterns of motion and appearance, *ICCV*, pp. 734–741, 2003.
18. B. Xie, D. Comaniciu, V. Ramesh, M. Simon and T. Boult. Component fusion for face detection in the presence of heteroscedastic noise, *Annual Conf. of the German Society for Pattern Recognition (DAGM'03)*, pp. 434–441, 2003.

Author Index

Lecture Notes in Computer Science

For information about Vols. 1–4277

please contact your bookseller or Springer

Vol. 4377: M. Abe (Ed.), Topics in Cryptology – CT-RSA 2007. XI, 403 pages. 2006.

Vol. 4371: K. Inoue, K. Satoh, F. Toni (Eds.), Computational Logic in Multi-Agent Systems. X, 315 pages. 2007. (Sublibrary LNAI).

Vol. 4369: M. Umeda, A. Wolf, O. Bartenstein, U. Geske, D. Seipel, O. Takata (Eds.), Declarative Programming for Knowledge Management. X, 229 pages. 2006. (Sublibrary LNAI).

Vol. 4368: T. Erlebach, C. Kaklamanis (Eds.), Approximation and Online Algorithms. X, 345 pages. 2006.

Vol. 4367: K. De Bosschere, D. Kaeli, P. Stenström, D. Whalley, T. Ungerer (Eds.), High Performance Embedded Architectures and Compilers. XI, 307 pages. 2007.

Vol. 4364: T. Kühne (Ed.), Models in Software Engineering. XI, 332 pages. 2007.

Vol. 4362: J. van Leeuwen, G.F. Italiano, W. van der Hoek, C. Meinel, H. Sack, F. Plášil (Eds.), SOFSEM 2007: Theory and Practice of Computer Science. XXI, 937 pages. 2006.

Vol. 4361: H.J. Hoogeboom, G. Păun, G. Rozenberg, A. Salomaa (Eds.), Membrane Computing. IX, 555 pages. 2006.

Vol. 4360: W. Dubitzky, A. Schuster, P.M.A. Sloot, M. Schroeder, M. Romberg (Eds.), Distributed, High-Performance, and Grid Computing in Computational Biology. X, 192 pages. 2007. (Sublibrary LNBI).

Vol. 4357: L. Buttyán, V. Gligor, D. Westhoff (Eds.), Security and Privacy in Ad-Hoc and Sensor Networks. X, 193 pages. 2006.

Vol. 4355: J. Julliand, O. Kouchnarenko (Eds.), B 2007: Formal Specification and Development in B. XIII, 293 pages. 2006.

Vol. 4354: M. Hanus (Ed.), Practical Aspects of Declarative Languages. X, 335 pages. 2006.

Vol. 4353: T. Schwentick, D. Suciu (Eds.), Database Theory – ICDT 2007. XI, 419 pages. 2006.

Vol. 4352: T.-J. Cham, J. Cai, C. Dorai, D. Rajan, T.-S. Chua, L.-T. Chia (Eds.), Advances in Multimedia Modeling, Part II. XVIII, 743 pages. 2006.

Vol. 4351: T.-J. Cham, J. Cai, C. Dorai, D. Rajan, T.-S. Chua, L.-T. Chia (Eds.), Advances in Multimedia Modeling, Part I. XIX, 797 pages. 2006.

Vol. 4349: B. Cook, A. Podelski (Eds.), Verification, Model Checking, and Abstract Interpretation. XI, 395 pages. 2006.

Vol. 4348: S.T. Taft, R.A. Duff, R.L. Brukardt, E. Ploedereder, P. Leroy (Eds.), Ada 2005 Reference Manual. XXII, 765 pages. 2006.

Vol. 4347: J. Lopez (Ed.), Critical Information Infrastructures Security. X, 286 pages. 2006.

Vol. 4345: N. Maglaveras, I. Chouvarda, V. Koutkias, R. Brause (Eds.), Biological and Medical Data Analysis. XIII, 496 pages. 2006. (Sublibrary LNBI).

Vol. 4344: V. Gruhn, F. Oquendo (Eds.), Software Architecture. X, 245 pages. 2006.

Vol. 4342: H. de Swart, E. Orłowska, G. Schmidt, M. Roubens (Eds.), Theory and Applications of Relational Structures as Knowledge Instruments II. X, 373 pages. 2006. (Sublibrary LNAI).

Vol. 4341: P.Q. Nguyen (Ed.), Progress in Cryptology - VIETCRYPT 2006. XI, 385 pages. 2006.

Vol. 4340: R. Prodan, T. Fahringer, Grid Computing. XXIII, 317 pages. 2007.

Vol. 4339: E. Ayguadé, G. Baumgartner, J. Ramanujam, P. Sadayappan (Eds.), Languages and Compilers for Parallel Computing. XI, 476 pages. 2006.

Vol. 4338: P. Kalra, S. Peleg (Eds.), Computer Vision, Graphics and Image Processing. XV, 965 pages. 2006.

Vol. 4337: S. Arun-Kumar, N. Garg (Eds.), FSTTCS 2006: Foundations of Software Technology and Theoretical Computer Science. XIII, 430 pages. 2006.

Vol. 4334: B. Beckert, R. Hähnle, P.H. Schmitt (Eds.), Verification of Object-Oriented Software. XXIX, 658 pages. 2007. (Sublibrary LNAI).

Vol. 4333: U. Reimer, D. Karagiannis (Eds.), Practical Aspects of Knowledge Management. XII, 338 pages. 2006. (Sublibrary LNAI).

Vol. 4332: A. Bagchi, V. Atluri (Eds.), Information Systems Security. XV, 382 pages. 2006.

Vol. 4331: G. Min, B. Di Martino, L.T. Yang, M. Guo, G. Ruenger (Eds.), Frontiers of High Performance Computing and Networking – ISPA 2006 Workshops. XXXVII, 1141 pages. 2006.

Vol. 4330: M. Guo, L.T. Yang, B. Di Martino, H.P. Zima, J. Dongarra, F. Tang (Eds.), Parallel and Distributed Processing and Applications. XVIII, 953 pages. 2006.

Vol. 4329: R. Barua, T. Lange (Eds.), Progress in Cryptology - INDOCRYPT 2006. X, 454 pages. 2006.

Vol. 4328: D. Penkler, M. Reitenspiess, F. Tam (Eds.), Service Availability. X, 289 pages. 2006.

Vol. 4327: M. Baldoni, U. Endriss (Eds.), Declarative Agent Languages and Technologies IV. VIII, 257 pages. 2006. (Sublibrary LNAI).

Vol. 4326: S. Göbel, R. Malkewitz, I. Iurgel (Eds.), Technologies for Interactive Digital Storytelling and Entertainment. X, 384 pages. 2006.

Vol. 4325: J. Cao, I. Stojmenovic, X. Jia, S.K. Das (Eds.), Mobile Ad-hoc and Sensor Networks. XIX, 887 pages. 2006.

Vol. 4323: G. Doherty, A. Blandford (Eds.), Interactive Systems. XI, 269 pages. 2006.

Vol. 4320: R. Gotzhein, R. Reed (Eds.), System Analysis and Modeling: Language Profiles. X, 229 pages. 2006.

Vol. 4319: L.-W. Chang, W.-N. Lie (Eds.), Advances in Image and Video Technology. XXVI, 1347 pages. 2006.

Vol. 4318: H. Lipmaa, M. Yung, D. Lin (Eds.), Information Security and Cryptology. XI, 305 pages. 2006.

Vol. 4317: S.K. Madria, K.T. Claypool, R. Kannan, P. Uppuluri, M.M. Gore (Eds.), Distributed Computing and Internet Technology. XIX, 466 pages. 2006.

Vol. 4316: M.M. Dalkilic, S. Kim, J. Yang (Eds.), Data Mining and Bioinformatics. VIII, 197 pages. 2006. (Sublibrary LNBI).

Vol. 4313: T. Margaria, B. Steffen (Eds.), Leveraging Applications of Formal Methods. IX, 197 pages. 2006.

Vol. 4312: S. Sugimoto, J. Hunter, A. Rauber, A. Morishima (Eds.), Digital Libraries: Achievements, Challenges and Opportunities. XVIII, 571 pages. 2006.

Vol. 4311: K. Cho, P. Jacquet (Eds.), Technologies for Advanced Heterogeneous Networks II. XI, 253 pages. 2006.

Vol. 4309: P. Inverardi, M. Jazayeri (Eds.), Software Engineering Education in the Modern Age. VIII, 207 pages. 2006.

Vol. 4308: S. Chaudhuri, S.R. Das, H.S. Paul, S. Tirthapura (Eds.), Distributed Computing and Networking. XIX, 608 pages. 2006.

Vol. 4307: P. Ning, S. Qing, N. Li (Eds.), Information and Communications Security. XIV, 558 pages. 2006.

Vol. 4306: Y. Avrithis, Y. Kompatsiaris, S. Staab, N.E. O'Connor (Eds.), Semantic Multimedia. XII, 241 pages. 2006.

Vol. 4305: A.A. Shvartsman (Ed.), Principles of Distributed Systems. XIII, 441 pages. 2006.

Vol. 4304: A. Sattar, B.-H. Kang (Eds.), AI 2006: Advances in Artificial Intelligence. XXVII, 1303 pages. 2006. (Sublibrary LNAI).

Vol. 4303: A. Hoffmann, B.-H. Kang, D. Richards, S. Tsumoto (Eds.), Advances in Knowledge Acquisition and Management. XI, 259 pages. 2006. (Sublibrary LNAI).

Vol. 4302: J. Domingo-Ferrer, L. Franconi (Eds.), Privacy in Statistical Databases. XI, 383 pages. 2006.

Vol. 4301: D. Pointcheval, Y. Mu, K. Chen (Eds.), Cryptology and Network Security. XIII, 381 pages. 2006.

Vol. 4300: Y.Q. Shi (Ed.), Transactions on Data Hiding and Multimedia Security I. IX, 139 pages. 2006.

Vol. 4299: S. Renals, S. Bengio, J.G. Fiscus (Eds.), Machine Learning for Multimodal Interaction. XII, 470 pages. 2006.

Vol. 4297: Y. Robert, M. Parashar, R. Badrinath, V.K. Prasanna (Eds.), High Performance Computing - HiPC 2006. XXIV, 642 pages. 2006.

Vol. 4296: M.S. Rhee, B. Lee (Eds.), Information Security and Cryptology – ICISC 2006. XIII, 358 pages. 2006.

Vol. 4295: J.D. Carswell, T. Tezuka (Eds.), Web and Wireless Geographical Information Systems. XI, 269 pages. 2006.

Vol. 4294: A. Dan, W. Lamersdorf (Eds.), Service-Oriented Computing – ICSOC 2006. XIX, 653 pages. 2006.

Vol. 4293: A. Gelbukh, C.A. Reyes-Garcia (Eds.), MICAI 2006: Advances in Artificial Intelligence. XXVIII, 1232 pages. 2006. (Sublibrary LNAI).

Vol. 4292: G. Bebis, R. Boyle, B. Parvin, D. Koracin, P. Remagnino, A. Nefian, G. Meenakshisundaram, V. Pascucci, J. Zara, J. Molineros, H. Theisel, T. Malzbender (Eds.), Advances in Visual Computing, Part II. XXXII, 906 pages. 2006.

Vol. 4291: G. Bebis, R. Boyle, B. Parvin, D. Koracin, P. Remagnino, A. Nefian, G. Meenakshisundaram, V. Pascucci, J. Zara, J. Molineros, H. Theisel, T. Malzbender (Eds.), Advances in Visual Computing, Part I. XXXI, 916 pages. 2006.

Vol. 4290: M. van Steen, M. Henning (Eds.), Middleware 2006. XIII, 425 pages. 2006.

Vol. 4289: M. Ackermann, B. Berendt, M. Grobelnik, A. Hotho, D. Mladenič, G. Semeraro, M. Spiliopoulou, G. Stumme, V. Svátek, M. van Someren (Eds.), Semantics, Web and Mining. X, 197 pages. 2006. (Sublibrary LNAI).

Vol. 4288: T. Asano (Ed.), Algorithms and Computation. XX, 766 pages. 2006.

Vol. 4287: C. Mao, T. Yokomori (Eds.), DNA Computing. XII, 440 pages. 2006.

Vol. 4286: P.G. Spirakis, M. Mavronicolas, S.C. Kontogiannis (Eds.), Internet and Network Economics. XI, 401 pages. 2006.

Vol. 4285: Y. Matsumoto, R.W. Sproat, K.-F. Wong, M. Zhang (Eds.), Computer Processing of Oriental Languages. XVII, 544 pages. 2006. (Sublibrary LNAI).

Vol. 4284: X. Lai, K. Chen (Eds.), Advances in Cryptology – ASIACRYPT 2006. XIV, 468 pages. 2006.

Vol. 4283: Y.Q. Shi, B. Jeon (Eds.), Digital Watermarking. XII, 474 pages. 2006.

Vol. 4282: Z. Pan, A. Cheok, M. Haller, R.W.H. Lau, H. Saito, R. Liang (Eds.), Advances in Artificial Reality and Tele-Existence. XXIII, 1347 pages. 2006.

Vol. 4281: K. Barkaoui, A. Cavalcanti, A. Cerone (Eds.), Theoretical Aspects of Computing - ICTAC 2006. XV, 371 pages. 2006.

Vol. 4280: A.K. Datta, M. Gradinariu (Eds.), Stabilization, Safety, and Security of Distributed Systems. XVII, 590 pages. 2006.

Vol. 4279: N. Kobayashi (Ed.), Programming Languages and Systems. XI, 423 pages. 2006.

Vol. 4278: R. Meersman, Z. Tari, P. Herrero (Eds.), On the Move to Meaningful Internet Systems 2006: OTM 2006 Workshops, Part II. XLV, 1004 pages. 2006.